SAM HOUSTON

Portrait of Sam Houston seated. It is probably the best likeness of him in existence.

— Courtesy Texas State Capitol, Austin, Texas

SAM HOUSTON

Man of Destiny

A Biography

By Clifford Hopewell

EAKIN PRESS ★ Austin, Texas

FIRST EDITION

Library of Congress Cataloging-in-Publication Data

Hopewell, Clifford, 1914–
     Sam Houston: man of destiny.

     Bibliography: p.
     Includes index.
     1. Houston, Sam, 1793–1863. 2. Texas — Governors — Biography. 3. Legislators —
United States — Biography. 4. United States. Congress. Senate — Biography.
I. Title
F390.H84H67   1987   976.4'04'0924 [B]   87-16495
ISBN 0-89015-572-0

This book is dedicated to
Ruth, Alan, Bruce, and Don

Houston

ARMS: Or, a chevron chequey sable and argent between 3 martlets of the second.

CREST: A sandglass winged proper.

SUPPORTERS: Two greyhounds proper, collared and chained or.

MOTTO: In Time

AUTHORITY: Burke's General Armory — 1884 Edition.

TINCTURES: The shield is gold. The chevron is black and silver. The martlets are black. The hour glass (sand glass) and wings are natural color. The mantle is black. The greyhounds are grey with gold collars and chains.

NOTES: Houston is a Scotch name, meaning "One who came from Hough's town, in Scotland."

These arms were registered to the Houston family in County Down, Ireland, but the ancient family place was in County Renfrew, Scotland, where the arms were also registered.

Gold stands for excellence of valor, character, and soul. Black denotes constancy. Silver represents nobility, peace, and serenity.

The Chevron signifies military fortitude. The martlet represents the 4th son. The hourglass stands for time and eternity. The greyhounds stand for swiftness; the wings for fleetness.

Contents

Preface

The writing of this biography of Sam Houston was a distinct pleasure for me. As a native-born Texan, I first became acquainted with the general when studying Texas history in elementary school, and he immediately became my number-one Texas hero. I well remember the thrill I had when, as a lad in my early teens, my father introduced me to a good friend of his with these words: "Son, let me introduce you to Mr. Temple Houston Morrow, who is a grandson of Sam Houston."

Houston was a complex man and like us all had his faults and his frailties, but they were far, far outweighed by his many good qualities. I have tried to present him in a fair and objective light, and hope I have succeeded. It is not uncommon for a biographer to research a person's life history and then, when through, have completely changed the original opinion about that person. I am happy to state that while I admired Houston when I started researching him, I admired him more when I had finished my task.

Many sources have been consulted in the preparation of this volume. Contemporary manuscripts were used extensively, and there were many fascinating ones about the events of Houston's day. Many volumes on the Cherokee Indians furnished much delightful and interesting information. There is an abundance of biographies about Houston, as biographers have had a field day writing about General Sam. The first of these was entitled *Sam Houston and His Republic,* authored by Charles Edwards Lester and published in 1846. The book was written under the direction of and with the complete cooperation of Houston. Consequently, it is laudatory and shows no depth of substance of the man. In 1855, when Houston was a serious contender for the presidency of the United States, the book was revised by Lester with the title *The Life of Sam Houston (The Only Authentic Memoir of Him Ever Published).* With a few minor exceptions it was virtually a rewrite of his original book.

In 1954 the *Autobiography of Sam Houston* appeared. This so-called autobiography was edited by Donald Day and H. H. Ullom and was in reality text from the Lester books, changed from third to first person, and various excerpts from the eight-volume *Writings of Sam Houston,* edited by Amelia W. Williams and Eugene C. Barker. Although Lester's books and the Day and Ullom autobiography contain much pertinent information that should not be ignored by the Houston scholar, in no way should they be considered an authentic memoir or autobiography.

In compiling Houston's letters, Williams and Barker did invaluable work in aiding students of the subject and cannot be complimented too highly. Houston was a prolific writer of letters, and there are still innumerable letters, unpublished, in private hands. The Sam Houston Museum in Huntsville, Texas, is currently microfilming over 400 previously unpublished letters of Houston. Unfortunately, a provision of the donor is that the letters cannot be released to anyone until 1988. Oh, what a treasure trove of information they may contain!

Many biographers have preceded me. One of the major works was the superb *The Raven* by Marquis James, which won the Pulitzer Prize when it was published in 1929. In 1954 Llerena B. Friend wrote *Sam Houston, the Great Designer.* An excellent book, it focuses mostly on Houston's political career. In 1962 M. K. Wisehart's first-rate biography, *Sam Houston, American Giant,* was published. Wisehart titled his book correctly, for Houston *was* an American giant. In 1967 the duo of Jack Gregory and Rennard Strickland chronicled Houston's career in the Indian nation with their remarkable *Sam Houston with the Cherokees 1829–1833.* This volume provided the reader with much hitherto untold valuable information regarding Houston's life and activities with his Cherokee friends, as well as his marriage to the beautiful one-sixteenth Cherokee Diana (or Tiana).

Much information about the formative days of Texas was gleaned from the two-volume *History of Texas, From Its First Settlement in 1685 to Its Annexation to the United States in 1846,* written by Houston's friend Henderson Yoakum. As Yoakum was a participant in many of the activities of Texas during its struggle for independence, and the period afterward, the volumes furnish much accurate information of that exciting time.

A trip to the Tidewater area and Timber Ridge in Rockbridge County, Virginia, provided me with courthouse records of Maj. Samuel Houston's will and the appraisement of his estate. Grace Cummings, librarian at Rockbridge Library in Lexington, found for me the scarce *Brief Biographical Accounts of Many Members of the Houston Family* by the Reverend Sam'l Rutherford Houston. This book provided much pertinent information about the early Houstons. The Timber Ridge Presbyterian Church that the Houston family attended is still in existence and is used to this day, although due to the increase in membership, the church the Houstons attended is only about one-third the size of the present building.

Eugene C. Barker's *The Life of Stephen F. Austin* and *Mexico and Texas, 1821–1835* provided much insight into the career of the selfless Austin and the relations of Mexico and Texas beginning with the independence of Mexico from Spain until the outbreak of the Texas revolution.

Numerous books by Grant Foreman and Emmett Starr about the Indians of the Southwest, and the Cherokees in particular, provided much valuable information concerning those unhappy people.

Newspapers, magazines, and pamphlets were used extensively, and I have tried to be as accurate as possible with facts. Unfortunately, in the early 1800s records were not kept as accurately as they are now, and many primary sources of the day included errors. As I depended upon some of them for general information, the reader should keep this in mind. However, as the author, I accept responsibility for any errors that may have crept into this book and sincerely hope they are of a minor nature.

Nacogdoches Texas
11th August 1838

The Hon.
To Jno Birdsall
          Sir
                    I have the honor of
appointing You Chief Justice of the Republic
of Texas, (pro tem) to fill the vacancy which
has resulted in Consequence of the decease of
the Hon. James Collinsworth.
                    Should You accept the same You
will be pleased to enter upon the duties of the
Office, and notify the fact to President, as early
as Convenient.
                              I have the honor to remain
                              With high Consideration
                              Your Obt Servant

                              Sam Houston

Chief Justice
of Texas

*Houston's appointment of John Birdsall as Chief Justice of Texas. Note typical
Houston signature underscored by rubric.*
— Courtesy Sam Houston State University Library

Acknowledgments

Martha Anne Turner, noted Texas historian and author of *Sam Houston and His Twelve Women*, advised me to "haunt the libraries, haunt the libraries." I took her advice, and among the libraries I haunted were the Rockbridge Library in Lexington, Virginia, and the library of the University of Oklahoma at Norman. The Texas State Library at Austin provided much material, as did the Sam Houston State University Library at Huntsville, Texas. The Fondren and DeGolyer libraries of Southern Methodist University literally amazed me with their depth of material on Texas and the Southwest. Last, but far from least, were the extensive facilities of the Dallas Public Library.

No one could write a book of this scope without the assistance of many other people, and there have been many who have very kindly given much of their time in personal interviews and/or correspondence with this author. I can never thank them enough.

Much appreciation goes to Mr. Charles Thompson of Timber Ridge, Virginia, and to Dr. Homer T. Cornish, pastor of Timber Ridge Presbyterian Church. These two gentlemen furnished me with valuable information about the Houston dwelling in Timber Ridge and the church that the Houston family attended.

Many thanks to my Tennessee "bird dogs," who more than went out of their way to help an author searching for material. I am indebted to Louis Steinberg, secretary of Houston's Cumberland Lodge No. 8 in Nashville, which is still in existence, and John B. Arp, Jr., grand master of the Masonic Lodge of Tennessee, for furnishing me with much valuable information pertaining to Houston's Masonic career in Tennessee and the trial for his duel with General White. Further information about Houston's Masonic career in Texas was kindly furnished by the Texas Masonic Grand Lodge Library in Waco, Texas, and by one of Houston's great-grandsons, who modestly refused me permission to use his name. This kind gentleman also reviewed some of my writing on the Masonic fraternity and corrected some errors I had made through haste.

Among my other Tennessee friends, Elizabeth Allen, Eliza's grandniece of Gallatin, and Louise Davis of Nashville presented me with Eliza Allen's version of why she left General Houston. Adele McKenzie of Maryville escorted my wife and me, along with Inez Burns, to the log cabin school where Houston taught in his youth. She also provided me with various clippings concerning some of the general's visits to Maryville after his retirement as president of the Republic of Texas. To all those women, I am very grateful.

To Mrs. Cornelius (Dorothy) Apffel, great-great-niece of Gen. William White, Houston's opponent in his famous duel, I owe not only a delightful correspondence, but gratitude for providing me with the White family version of the duel.

Special thanks goes to Frank Burns of Tennessee Technological University, Cookeville, Tennessee, and Harry Slater of Murfreesboro, Tennessee. Both of these gentlemen dug deeply in searching for material I could use, and were of more assistance to me than I can ever repay. It was Burns who provided me with the obscure clipping stating that Houston, when leaving Nashville for Indian Territory, gave his little dog "Hero" to a friend and sent his horse to Andrew Jackson. To both Burns and Slater, I owe much.

To Dr. Duane H. King, executive director of the Cherokee National Historical Society at Tahlequah, Oklahoma, and to Wilma Mankiller, principal chief of the Cherokee Nation West at Tahlequah, I express my gratitude for answering many questions about the Cherokees. Dr. King and my friend Lewis Greenway of Dallas solved a problem for me when they correctly answered a question I had about given up hope of having answered.

Special thanks to my editors, Anders Saustrup and Melissa Locke Roberts. Saustrup, a Texas historian of first rank, not only corrected my grammar and punctuation but amazed me with his knowledge of Texas history and rightly kept me on a straight path.

It is encouraging in an enterprise of this sort to have a family that helps. My wife Ruth constantly read my various chapters to screen them for interest and to correct spelling and punctuation. My youngest son Bruce read the chapters with enthusiasm and urged me to hurry up and finish the manuscript so he could read the complete book.

BOOK ONE

The Dreamer

Painting of Sam Houston at a young age, by Thomas Sully.
— Courtesy Library of Congress, Washington, D.C.

CHAPTER 1

An Active Lineage

Timber Ridge, Virginia, is a small Rockbridge County community nestling in the beautiful rolling hills on the western side of the Blue Ridge Mountains — so small that it is not shown on many maps. It was here that Sam Houston, governor of two states and first president of the Republic of Texas, was born. The date was March 2, 1793 — a date which would bear much significance more than forty years later, for on March 2, 1836, while Houston was commanding general of the Texas army, Texas issued its declaration of independence from Mexico.

He was named Samuel, after his father. The name runs through the genealogy of the Houston family, inasmuch as the lad also had a grandfather named Samuel and a son named Samuel. There were many cousins of this name in the family history, and the Bible also furnished its quota of Johns, Jameses, and Matthews.

The first Houston to set foot in America was John Houston, a stocky man in his forties and great-grandfather of young Sam. With his wife, mother, and six children (named, in order, Robert, Isabella, Esther, John, Samuel, and Matthew) he landed in Pennsylvania, near Philadelphia, in the year 1735.[1] David, the eldest son, had been left behind in Ireland to study for the ministry.

The Houstons descended from an ancient lineage of Celtic origin. Their forebears dwelt in the lowlands of Scotland. Adhering to

3

the tenets of John Calvin and John Knox in their Presbyterian faith, they fled to the north of Ireland to escape the religious and political struggles of the day. Eventually, John and his wife, like so many other Protestant families before them, decided they had had enough turmoil and determined to try their luck in the New World.

It is said that many of the passengers on the ship boarded by the Houstons carried a considerable amount of money. Believing that the captain of the vessel and his crew had plans to rob and perhaps murder them, a number of the passengers seized them and put them in irons. Some of the emigrants, skilled in navigation, took command of the ship and landed it safely in Pennsylvania. As John Houston was a man of means and no doubt had his entire wealth with him, he might very well have been one of the ringleaders who took over command of the ship to protect his fortune.

John prospered in the New World and lived in Pennsylvania for twenty-four years, during which time his son John and his two daughters married. He then joined the tide of Scotch-Irish immigrants and headed south for the fertile Upper Valley of Virginia where he settled on what was then known as the "Burden Tract," so named after a large grant of land given a man named Burden. The governor of Virginia, wanting to encourage settlers in that area, had offered two large land grants to two gentlemen named Beverly and Burden on the condition that, within a limited time, a certain number of settlers should be located on them. The terms were generous, as an inducement to bring in settlers: twenty-five dollars per hundred acres. Soon a swarm of Scotch-Irish came in from Pennsylvania and other colonies to settle permanently in the valley. Among them were the Paxtons, Davidsons, Montgomerys, Stuarts, McCorkles, McCormicks, and McClungs — all Presbyterians, and all names found in the valley today. There would be considerable intermarriage later between the Houstons and some of these families.

Squire John was an important figure in this new community. The owner of many acres, he had fought in the French and Indian Wars and later served as a magistrate for the king. He had built roads that still exist and, together with his son-in-law, was one of the principal founders of the Congregation of New Providence. While one day walking under a tree that was on fire, John was killed when a limb fell and its foremost point penetrated his skull. John, his wife and mother, and several descendants lie today in the cemetery of the Timber Ridge Presbyterian Church.

The Houstons, having money, married money. The squire's

son Robert had married a daughter of the well-to-do Davidson family and settled on Timber Ridge Plantation, building a two-story house with a wood-shingle roof and a balcony. At each end of the house was a huge fireplace. This building stood until it burned not long after the Civil War, and on the site of the original home another two-story home was built which is today owned and occupied by Mr. and Mrs. Charles Thompson. It has been in the possession of the family since the days of Thompson's great-grandfather. Some doorknobs and latches and the living room mantel from the original residence are incorporated into the present dwelling.[2]

Robert and his son-in-law donated the land the Timber Ridge Presbyterian Church was built on in 1756. This church, about 200 feet from the site of the Houston family home, was still in existence in late 1984 and had 212 members. The main part of the sanctuary, approximately one hundred by sixty feet, is part of the original church. The front part of the church was added in 1902; the educational building in 1952.[3] The church is to be found on Route 11, about seven miles north from downtown Lexington, Virginia. The city is not only the county seat of Rockbridge County but is also the home of the Virginia Military Institute and Washington and Lee University.

Robert and his wife were the parents of Samuel who, when he grew to young manhood, joined the Continental Army of George Washington to do his bit in the American Revolution. He served in Daniel Morgan's Rifle Brigade from Virginia and was an excellent soldier, doing so well that when the war was over he returned to the plantation as a captain. After Robert's death, young Captain Houston inherited the plantation. Shortly thereafter, he married Elizabeth Paxton, daughter of one of the richest men in Rockbridge County. The new mistress of the plantation was a lady — tall, courtly, and attractive. In addition, she had enormous character, as later events were to prove. As was the custom in those days she brought her husband a dowry — a sizeable one. Together with her money she brought other qualities to the marriage that were to prove valuable assets to Captain Samuel and the nine children she bore him. She brought intelligence, industry, and a fortitude that stood her in good stead as mistress of the Houston household, which she dominated. Her Presbyterian Anglo-Saxon heritage helped her fulfill her duties in this still largely wilderness edge of the American frontier.

Captain Samuel enjoyed the military life so much he decided to make it his career. According to his son and namesake, it was his only passion.[4] With a rich wife he could afford to try it. He accepted an appointment as a brigade inspector in the Virginia Militia and lived the life of a typical gentleman-soldier-planter, occasionally dabbling in local politics. The pursuit of his military career frequently kept him away from his home and plantation. Consequently, it fell upon Elizabeth to manage the plantation and oversee the slaves as they tended the fields.

From time to time Elizabeth would take to her bed and produce a child. First there was Paxton, who died of consumption in Blount County, Tennessee, soon after reaching his majority. Then came Robert, a major in the War of 1812, who eventually took his own life. Next was James, then John, and the fifth child and fifth son, Samuel, named after his father. Sam was followed by William, then Isabella, Mary, and Eliza Ann.[5] Large families were common in those days when infant mortality was high, especially on the frontier.

The captain, a friendly and likeable man, was above ordinary size with a powerful physique. A lover of books, he indulged his taste with a well-stocked library. Unfortunately, he was not much of a businessman and neglected his plantation; consequently, he was frequently in debt and from time to time had to sell a slave or two or some of his land.

The purchase of the Louisiana Territory in 1803 from France by President Thomas Jefferson not only increased the size of the United States considerably, it also strained relations with Spain. That nation claimed Florida, New Spain, which included Texas, and much of the immense, uncharted area Napoleon sold Jefferson. There were many rumors of war, and in preparation for the anticipated conflict with the Spaniards Samuel was promoted to major. The promotion was welcomed with delight, but it presented several problems. With increased active duty he found himself away from home for even longer periods of time, and this depleted his cash. As an officer, he had to bear the cost of his travel. To meet his obligations he was again forced to sell some property and some slaves.

Young Samuel was by now ten and his character was forming. Every Sunday the Houston family — with the major when he wasn't making his military rounds — walked the few hundred feet to the nearby Timber Ridge Presbyterian Church. There is no record as to whether or not young Sam was baptized in the Presbyterian faith, inasmuch as early-day church records have been lost. He had little formal education, which was not uncommon for even the children of the propertied class in those days, especially those

6

living on the frontier. He attended the Liberty Hall Academy in Timber Ridge sporadically from 1801 until 1806 and, like the latter-day Sir Winston Churchill, proved a poor student, especially in algebra and geometry. To some degree arithmetic was conquered, and he learned to read and write. By his own admission he doubted if he had attended school six months in all by the age of fourteen, when his father died.[6]

The subjects in which Sam excelled academically were ancient history and his lifelong love, the ancient classics of Rome and Greece. This was no doubt due to the many books available in his father's well-furnished library. He could often be found lying on the floor reading Brown's *Gazeteer*, the two-volume set of Morse's *Geography*, or the eight volumes of Rollins's *Ancient History*. But his greatest delight was when he ran across Pope's translation of *The Iliad*. He memorized over 1,000 lines of this work and in time claimed to be able to recite from memory the complete book. This was no doubt true because he had a fantastic memory, as he proved later on when studying law.

There is no doubt that *The Iliad* had an enormous influence on the life of this young man. It helped develop his literary and oratorical style, both of which he used so effectively later on. In his maturity he was known to be able to speak extemporaneously for several hours and to hold his audience spellbound.

Sam and his brothers and sisters spent their childhood in the way all frontier children did. They swam in nearby Mill Creek; they spent hours fishing and hunting in the woods. In time Sam, like most of his companions, became an expert with the rifle. As latter-day youths played cops and robbers or cowboys and Indians, Sam and his friends played Redcoats and Redskins, with Sam using his father's second-best sword.

There was much visiting between families and relatives in the Timber Ridge Valley. Near High Bridge, now known as Natural Bridge, their cousin Matthew Houston resided in a palatial home. They visited their cousin the Reverend Samuel Houston, who had invented a grain reaper. He was unable to gain any benefits from his invention as another Rockbridge County lad, Cyrus Mc-Cormick, invented a better one and made a fortune from it.

All branches of the Houston family were doers, leaders of the community, men who gave their time, property, or money to help their fellow citizens. The Reverend Samuel was no different. He traveled frequently to Tennessee and was active in the formation of the short-lived State of Frankland, later Franklin, and headed a committee to draft a frame of government. His constitution was criticized as being so radical in character, however, that it was rejected.[7]

For several years after the Louisiana Purchase, a war fever spread from the eastern coast to the western frontier of the young United States and was increased by the so-called "Burr Conspiracy." Aaron Burr had been vice-president of the United States under Jefferson, but his political career had been shattered after he fought and mortally wounded Alexander Hamilton in a duel in 1804. He purchased land in the newly acquired Louisiana Territory, and in 1806 there were rumors he planned to lead an invasion of Spanish territory if war developed between Spain and the United States. It was said he planned to invade Mexico, or conquer Texas. Some say he wanted to become "Emperor of the West." In any case, on orders from Jefferson he was arrested and tried for treason but was acquitted. There was to be no war with Spain, but the purchase of Louisiana from Napoleon contributed to the later War of 1812 with England — a war that contributed so much to Sam Houston's destiny.

Houston's father was now in his fifties, in declining health, and virtually bankrupt due to his high manner of living and his constant neglect of his properties. The major decided to resign his commission, sell Timber Ridge and all his properties, and join the increasing migration to the West after paying off his debts. He started negotiations to purchase over 400 acres in eastern Tennessee, where there were other Houstons and Paxtons. For $174 he purchased a new "waggon with chain and gears compleat for five horses." He made his will, in which he left the majority of his estate to "my beloved wife, Elizabeth." In addition, he left his son John two horses, a dark bay and a sorrel, and Elizabeth was left instructions to give John and each of their three daughters a good feather bed and furniture when they married. John was also given one small sword, which upon appraisal was listed as being worth fifteen dollars. Elizabeth was also to give the other children horses and saddles when they needed them. Upon Elizabeth's death, John was to be given two shares of the estate with the other children receiving one share each.[8]

In September 1806 the major sold Timber Ridge Plantation and, although ill, rode away for the last time to inspect the Virginia Militia. He died at Callighan's Hotel, a celebrated inn, in what is now Allegheny County, Virginia. He was buried at High Bridge, near the residence of his cousin Matthew Houston. As a prominent person of the area, Major Houston's funeral brought forth a large number of local notables to pay their respects to the departure of this well-liked, amiable man.

After the major's death, his widow made preparations to move the family over the Alleghenies to Tennessee. An appraisal of his estate, which included five black slaves, totaled almost $3,600 — a considerable sum for those days; however, this included sundry bonds and notes amounting to $1,468 and much of the sum Elizabeth received was used to pay off various outstanding debts.[9]

Early in the spring of 1807 the widow Houston, her nine children, and their slaves started on the long, arduous journey to eastern Tennessee. Elizabeth and fourteen-year-old Sam were in the lead wagon, the new one the major had purchased. An older four-horse wagon followed closely, driven by some of the older sons. This was a formidable undertaking for a widow of fifty with six sons and three daughters, but this daughter of the landed gentry, who had grown up on the frontier, was equal to the task. As Sam later wrote, "she was not a woman to succumb to misfortune . . . she was nerved with a stern fortitude, which never gave way in the midst of the wild scenes that chequered the history of the frontier settler."

Several weeks later the small caravan reached Knoxville, the capital of Tennessee at that time. That this portion of Tennessee was still largely frontier was evidenced by the fact in 1800 the population of Knoxville was only 387, including 146 slaves.[10] Most of the homes were squared log cabins. Turning the wagon train south about fifteen miles, the Houstons entered Maryville, a settlement smaller than Knoxville, in Blount County, with homes built of unsquared logs and heavy shutters to stop Indian arrows and musket balls.

Turning east for a journey of a few miles, over streams and brush and rocks more difficult than had been encountered before, the Houston family and slaves finally reached their destination. It was here, on a tributary of Baker's Creek, that the redoubtable Elizabeth patented the 419 acres the major had purchased. Here she was to build a new home and rear her brood.

Although the Houstons were in a crude, rough land unfamiliar to them, far from the tidewater region where they had grown up, they were not strangers as new settlers. They had relatives and friends in the area nearby, and while they were building their new

9

home they accepted the hospitality of some of these relatives. James and John Houston were cousins of Major Samuel. Like him, they had served in the Revolutionary War; however, once the war was over they had moved immediately to this area, then still part of North Carolina. In the ensuing years they had become men of some substance. When Tennessee had become the sixteenth state and joined the Union on June 1, 1796, James Houston had been elected to the state legislature.

Cousin James was the owner of Fort Houston Blockhouse on Nine Mile Creek, five miles from where Elizabeth elected to build her home. This fort was like most forts — a stockade enclosing residences, outbuildings, and slave quarters — and had been built to withstand Indian attacks. The Creeks and Cherokees, who occupied these regions, had made no serious attacks on the settlers for almost twenty years. Over the years various treaties had been concluded between the white man and the Indians, giving the whites title to various lands.[11] But no matter how much land the white man acquired he was never satisfied, constantly wanting more and encroaching on the Indian lands. When the Houstons settled on Baker's Creek there were numerous Indian tribes in eastern Tennessee, and both they and the whites were exerting pressure on the federal government to settle their differences.

All the Houstons pitched in, with their slaves, to clear the land and build their new home. Sam in his later years was to refer to this home as "a cabin," but to the neighbors it was much more than a cabin as it had an upstairs, a real mark of distinction in those days. They were in the Great Smoky Mountains, and the Houstons, when their house was completed, were afforded a magnificent mountain view. Nearby was a cool spring. The family tilled the soil, planted their fields, and brought in the harvest. Their hard work produced prosperity. They bought more slaves and purchased an interest in a general store in Maryville, which brothers John and James operated.

Maryville was a typical small frontier town at the turn of the century. As the county seat of Blount County, it boasted a courthouse and county jail. Primarily a crossroads trading center where stage lines from Knoxville and Nashville met, the little village supported around forty families. Among the firms and businesses were a hattery, a hostelry and tavern, a tannery, the usual blacksmith shop, and a gristmill. There were a couple of other general stores in addition to the one John and James operated.

The new arrivals mixed well in the area with their relatives and other families. True to the family tradition of being doers and leaders in the community, it wasn't long before John became clerk of the county court, while brothers James and Robert became trustees of the Porter Academy when it opened in 1808.

There was only one problem: Sam, a likeable lad who made friends easily, had inherited an aversion to physical labor on the farm. He would disappear for days at a time with one of his books, and upon his return home be received with taunts by his brothers. Elizabeth reasoned that perhaps the boy, not being cut out to be a planter, would fit in behind the counter selling merchandise at the general store in Maryville run by brothers John and James. The result was the same. Unlike his brother James who enjoyed merchandising and later became a successful merchant in Nashville,[12] Sam had about as much liking for life behind a counter as he had for life behind a plow. Spare hours when he was not behind a counter were spent at the newly opened Porter Academy, but here once again Sam proved himself a poor student. His only interest seemed to be in reading the classics.

By the terms of the major's will, Sam had inherited a one-tenth interest in the family belongings. Due to the deaths of his brother Paxton and sister Isabella after moving to Tennessee, his holdings had increased to one-eighth. His father further stipulated:

> my executors are to be the guardians of my children until they shal arrive at lawful age and I would recommend that they put my sons to such trades as may seem most beneficial . . . and I do appoint as Executors . . . my wife Elizabeth and my sons James and John.[13]

As executors, brothers John and James, and Elizabeth thought young Sam should do something to earn his inheritance and were constantly reproving him for his lackadaisical air and frequent absences. Clerking at his brothers' general store bored him, and he did not take kindly to the constant incriminations from his family. Sam resented it so much that in later life he had little to do with any of them, including Elizabeth. He solved the problem by once more disappearing — this time for a much longer period of time. He became the original dropout, leaving to live among the Indians. What he didn't realize at the time was that he had just taken his first step in following his star on the road to his destiny.

11

CHAPTER 2

Adopted Son
of the Cherokees

The year was 1809, and Sam was sixteen when he first went to live among the Cherokees. Although still far short of his majority, he was six feet tall, stood straight as an arrow, and had inherited Major Houston's powerful physique. In addition to his resentment of the family's constant criticisms of his general aimlessness in life, he had other reasons to leave the bosom of his family. Later in life Houston described his youth as having been "wild and impetuous; but it was spotted by no crime . . ." [1] The lad was obstinate, and at an age when the young tend to resent authority, he was beginning to exhibit that restlessness and spirit of adventure that was to last a lifetime. Sam, like his compatriot Davy Crockett, definitely had the wanderlust.

Eastern Tennessee, still largely a rough, raw, wild frontier, was densely inhabited by Indians. Many trappers had come through Maryville trading their furs and pelts, and their tales of the Indians intrigued Sam. He had met many Indians and, unlike some of his counterparts, truly liked them. The Cherokees were "different," so Sam had much in common with them. They walked to the beat of a different drummer, as he did. They were not engaged in the hustle and bustle of the day, and this appealed to Sam's easygoing nature.

There were a number of Cherokee towns in Tennessee —

around sixty-five to seventy in the Cherokee Nation as a whole —
but young Houston headed for the domain led by Chief Oolooteka
(He Puts the Drum Away). Chief Oolooteka, or John Jolly, to give
him his American name, was head of a band of around 300 Cherokees who lived on Hiwassie Island, where the big Tennessee and
Hiwassie rivers merged. This island was a small one, approximately two miles long and a mile wide, located about fifty or sixty
miles southwest of Maryville. It was called Jolly's Island, after the
chief.[2] Why Sam headed for Jolly's Island is not known, but it is
very possible he had been informed of this island by some of his
trapper friends.

When Sam went to live among the Indians, he did not go off
into the wilderness to live among a group of illiterate savages residing in teepees and spending their spare time in war parties, seeking
the scalps of white settlers. The Cherokees were one of the five civilized tribes and the most highly developed Indians in America.
They had long ago given up their warlike ambitions and were a
peaceful people. They had achieved a remarkably high level of social and cultural development and were already advanced in the
fields of religion and education. In the eighteenth century Moravian and Presbyterian missionaries had entered the Cherokee Nation in their quest for Christian converts, and as early as 1801 the
Moravians established a school in Springplace, Tennessee.[3] In
1803 the Reverend Gideon Blackburn, a Presbyterian minister, established a mission school near Tellico, Tennessee.

The Cherokees had a complex tribal organization consisting of
seven clans. By 1808 they had adopted a written law and were in
the process of developing an intricate government, including a system of courts of law with a superior court at its head. In 1821 Sequoyah, a lame mixed-breed whose American name was George
Guess,[4] invented his syllabary of eighty-six characters. Sequoyah
was an unusual Indian who wore a turban; he had been trained as
a silversmith and blacksmith and was accomplished at both crafts.
He had worked on his syllabary for several years before finally per-
fecting it, and his invention made it possible for the Cherokees to
learn to read and write in their native language within a matter of
days. Shortly thereafter, the nation started printing its own newspaper in both English and Cherokee.[5]

In the Cherokee Nation women had status and were far from
subservient to the men. They took part in council meetings and had
their say in the election of chiefs. In the past, when the Cherokees
had been more warlike, the women frequently took part in the war-

13

fare. Land could only be inherited through the female side, and kinship was also traced exclusively through their side.

The Cherokee Nation spread over eastern Tennessee, North and South Carolina, Georgia, and Alabama, and there were many white traders living in the nation. A large number of these traders were Scotch, Irish, English, and German. They had fought in the Revolutionary War on the Tory side and had decided to stay in the New World after the hostilities were over. There was much intermarriage between the whites and the Cherokees, and even Chief Oolooteka, or John Jolly, had white blood in him. His sister had married Capt. John Rogers, a white trader of Scotch-Irish descent who had fought as a Tory in the American Revolution. It was the custom of white traders to import schoolteachers for the children of these mixed marriages, as they wanted them to be given an education. They also wanted them to be given religious instruction and therefore were supportive of the Moravians and Presbyterians in their efforts to Christianize the Cherokees.

The Cherokees did not live by fish and game alone, but had an agrarian culture. On their farms and plantations, which were worked largely by their black slaves, they grew corn, beans, squash, pumpkins, tobacco, and sweet potatoes. They grew peach and plum trees and had hog pens.

The towns throughout the nation varied in size. Some had as few as twelve or thirteen homes; others as many as two hundred. The majority of villages ranged from thirty to sixty dwellings. These rectangular homes were usually made of logs, with roofs of bark, one front door, and no windows. Some of the wealthier Cherokees, including Chief John Jolly and Maj. John Ridge, had European-style homes. The major towns had a council house in the center. This council house was seven-sided to correspond to the seven clans of the Cherokee Nation. Like the dwellings, it was built of logs, and it was used for many functions, including religious rites and civil and military council meetings.

This, then, was the setting in which young Sam Houston had decided to take a sabbatical. Here among the Cherokees Sam found the peace and contentment he sought. There was no one to criticize him; no hated farming or clerking to do. Sam was a free soul among other free souls and could lie indolently on the banks of the river reading books or could fish, if he so desired. Houston was liked by the Indians and he liked them, as they were kindred spirits. Sam studied their customs and their nature, and he learned to speak their language fluently. He became their lifelong friend, their ad-

14

viser, and in later life their champion — not only in Congress but in his private life as well.

Chief Oolooteka was easygoing, friendly, handsome, and very popular among his followers. Around six feet tall, he was born somewhere around 1770 and was old for an Indian, inasmuch as the life span of the Cherokees was usually from age forty to forty-five. He took a liking to this young, restless, fatherless boy who had come to his town and befriended him. Before too long he had formally adopted him as his son and had given him the Cherokee name of Colonneh — The Raven.[6]

Houston quickly adapted to his new life. He easily made friends, particularly with two half-Cherokee brothers named James and John, sons of Capt. John Rogers, and their much younger half-sister Diana. The Rogers brothers and Sam's other Indian friends taught him all they knew about the lore of Indian life. He learned to use the bow and arrow; he engaged in trapping and hunting and the playing of games. Chunkge, or chunkey, a game requiring sharp eyesight, skill, and the will to win, was a popular sport. But the most popular of all their games was the ball-play, a game somewhat similar to and probably the ancestor of modern-day lacrosse. This was a game played with as many as fifty players to a side and frequently many more. The object of the game was to capture a small ball in a curved stick, carry it down the playing field, and throw it over the goal. Simple enough, the game involved more mayhem than sport. There were no rules. Biting, gouging, and kneeing were common. No quarter was asked and none was given. A player running down the field was likely to be mauled, punched, or kicked — and sometimes even killed — by an opponent who would go unpunished.

The Cherokees were great gamblers, and when a ball-play was to be played between two towns everyone who could walk attended the contest. This was an event of great festivity and was celebrated by feasts and dancing. The wagering on the teams was so intense the onlookers frequently bet their entire possessions — including their clothes — on the outcome of the game.[7] Sam was never lacking in courage, and it is to be assumed he played both chunkey and the ball-play.

By now the disappearing Sam had been absent for several weeks, and Elizabeth began to worry about him. Some itinerant trappers reported having seen him on Hiwassie Island living with

15

the Cherokees. Elizabeth promptly sent brothers John and James to fetch the wanderer. When the brothers found their errant sibling, he was under a tree reading a book. He was deaf to their pleas to return home and later explained his reasons: "I preferred measuring deer tracks to tape and . . . I liked the wild liberty of the Red men better than the tyranny of my own brothers. I told them to go home and leave me in peace." [8] His brothers took him at his word and left him in his island paradise.

For about a year Sam had the time of his life living among the Cherokees and participating in their festivals, games, and dances, but then he returned home. He was received kindly by his mother and family, and because his clothing was in disrepair, Elizabeth and his sisters provided him with a new suit. When he had relaxed at home for a few days he went into nearby Maryville — and promptly got into trouble.

The Maryville militia, under the command of Capt. John B. Cusick, was having a muster. These musters were always popular as kegs of beer were opened and there was plenty of whiskey on tap. In addition, there was much merriment, kidding, and horseplay going on. Cusick and Sam both got drunk. This normally was no serious offense, but in a playful mood they compounded their error by getting a drum and beating on it underneath a court window while the court was in session. For this bit of frivolity they spent the night in jail. When the Blount County Court was in session next on September 29, 1810, Captain Cusick was fined ten dollars and his fellow culprit Sam was fined five dollars for "disorderly rioutously wantonly with an Assembly of Militia Annoying the Court with the noise of a Drum and with force preventing the Sheriff and Officer of the Court in the discharge of his duty . . . against the peace and dignity of the State." [9]

These sums were a fairly stiff penalty for that day and time; however, neither culprit paid his penalty inasmuch as the next court remitted the fines. By this time Sam had once more quarreled with his brothers and departed for the land of his beloved Cherokees, taking them many gifts and trinkets.

Again Sam enjoyed his stay among the Indians, learning more about their customs and absorbing their philosophy of life. He chased the deer in the forest and engaged in all the sports of his Indian friends. He was at an age when boys begin to notice and take an interest in girls, and he later related how he spent time "wandering along the banks of the streams by the side of some Indian maiden, sheltered by the deep woods, conversing in that universal language which finds its sure way to the heart." [10]

Undoubtedly, Sam was intrigued by these Indian maidens. According to William Bartram, who visited forty-three Cherokee villages in 1776 and kept a journal of his trip, the Cherokee women were "tall, slender, erect and of a delicate frame and their features formed with perfect symmetry. They were friendly and had cheerful countenances, and they moved with a becoming grace and dignity." Unlike women of other Indian tribes, they did not tend to get fat as they grew older.

It was easy to see why the Indian maidens would gladly wander along the banks of the streams with Sam and converse in "that universal language which finds its sure way to the heart." He had an excellent physique and could hold his own in any games his male friends might desire to play. In addition, he was the handsomest of the Houston sons — fair and tall with wavy, chestnut hair and friendly, blue eyes. These Indian maidens were early in discovering what many women discovered during the life of this remarkable man: it was mighty easy to fall in love with Sam Houston.

To Sam's brothers and friends in Maryville this carefree life among the Indians — living on the ground, participating in their ceremonies, chasing the deer, adopting the ways of the Indians, and showing little concern for his family — seemed odd. People began to remark that he would end up as either a great Indian chief, die in a madhouse, or be governor of the state; in other words, that some dreadful thing would overtake him. Although Sam's critics probably uttered these words in jest, they did not know how right their prediction was. He did not become an Indian chief. He did not end up in a madhouse. However, he not only became a governor of a state but became governor of two states, as well as president of the Republic of Texas.

During this stage of his life, Sam lived among the Indians three times for a period of about three years. From time to time he would return home to his family, no doubt to see what was happening back in "civilization." Elizabeth would always welcome her offspring warmly — as most mothers would under like circumstances — and try to talk him into staying home and learning a good trade or occupation. There were always clothes to be outfitted with or repaired, and it was nice to visit Maryville. But soon Sam was heading back to Jolly's Island and his adopted father.

Sam's three years among the Cherokees were during the most formative years a young man can have, when the body and mind are rapidly maturing. He had little formal education, but he had a quick native wit and a superior intelligence that was to stand him in good stead all his days. Those years among the Indians provided an unusual experience for a white youth, and he gained from it. The outdoor life hardened his powerful body as he grew to young manhood; he acquired the good qualities of the Cherokees and admired the patience they exhibited in their adversity. He sympathized with the Indians and his adopted father in their complaints against the federal government and its constant demands for the Indians to cede more of their territory to the whites.

In his eighteenth year, Sam decided to go back home. On his previous journeys home he had purchased, on credit, various gifts for his Hiwassie Island friends. All Indians liked gifts, and Sam was a generous friend. He presented his companions with needles, thread, powder, shot, blankets — all items prized by them. But his credit with the Maryville merchants had finally run out and he was in debt to them for one hundred dollars. The only solution was to go home and get a job. Sam always honored his debts.

The year was 1812 and there was war talk against England in the air. The doves of the Eastern states were opposed to war, while the hawks of the Western states supported the idea. Employment opportunities — at least the sort Sam would be interested in — were difficult; so difficult, in fact, that his brother Robert had already joined the army. No doubt Sam could have gone to work for his brothers, but that definitely did not appeal to him. He finally hit upon an idea. He would open a school.

No doubt many people in the Maryville area found it ludicrous that Sam, with his limited education, would have the temerity to open a school. A virtual stranger to the inside of a classroom, he could hardly have had more knowledge than his students. And, unbelievably, he was charging more than the going rate for tuition. But to Houston, who was always a larger-than-life figure on a very broad canvas, there was nothing ludicrous about it at all. It was in keeping with his character. He had confidence in himself. He was different. He had what it takes, and he knew it.

Sam had some announcements printed that he was opening an academy. The three R's would be taught, along with various other subjects, and the school would be on a farm about five miles east of Maryville. The school, built of squared logs, was slightly longer than twenty feet and almost eighteen feet wide. On two sides, part of the wall could be let down which, on props, formed a rough desk. In addition, this opening served as a window. Instead of the customary six dollars per term tuition being charged, his academy charged eight dollars: one-third in cash; one-third in corn at thirty-three and one-third cents a bushel; and one-third in calico of "variegated colors." The school opened in May 1812 after the spring corn planting, and his students ranged in age from six to sixty.

Sam gave his pupils their eight dollars' worth. His knowledge of the three R's might have been little better than elementary, but at least he knew more than his students did. He had read every book he had been able to put his hands on and he could quote Homer's *The Iliad* by the page to his students. And in one course he had no equal among his fellow schoolmasters. That course was Indianology, of which he was an undisputed authority. The Indianology course alone was worth the extra two-dollar fee he demanded.

His eager pupils were entranced with his stories about the Cherokee Indians. He could regale them with tale after tale about Indian lore, fascinating them with stories about Cherokee beliefs and customs, their six annual festivals, their legends and superstitions. The Cherokees, he taught, had many dances: the "Scalp" or "Victory" Dance, the Raccoon and Beaver dances, the Buffalo Hunt Dance, the Green Corn Dance, and others. All these dances had religious, sexual, or social significance in the Cherokee community and lasted for days, even for weeks, and in many of them their women took part.

Sam described the games of chunkey and the ball-play as his young pupils sat enthralled. He also described the homes his Indian friends lived in on Jolly's Island, how they farmed and grew crops, how they dressed. He sang the praises of Chief John Jolly, his adopted father, and told them about the simple wedding ceremony in which the groom gave the bride a ham of venison and a blanket, and she gave him an ear of corn and a blanket. Perhaps he even told them about wandering along the banks of the streams by the side of some Indian maiden, and conversing with them in that universal language which finds its sure way to the heart.

His critics might have laughed when Houston first announced he was going to open a school, but once the term was over Sam laughed last and longest. The school had been a success, with so many applicants he had had to turn many away. After the corn was gathered in November and the weather became too cold, he closed the academy. He had made more than enough money to pay off his debts, and he had gained some respect from the townspeople.

19

Many years later, after Sam had become General Houston, the governor of two states, a United States senator, commander-in-chief of an army, and the first president of the Republic of Texas, an old friend, in a casual conversation, asked him which, of all these offices, had given him the most pride. The general replied that as a youth in Tennessee he had kept a country school.

> With a "sour wood" stick in my hand as an emblem of ornament and authority, dressed in a hunting shirt of flowered calico, a long queue down my back, and the sense of authority over my pupils, I experienced a higher feeling of dignity and self-satisfaction than from any office or honor which I have since held.[11]

Once more Houston enrolled as a student at the Porter Academy, giving as an excuse the fact he wanted to learn more mathematics in order to qualify for a commission in the army. And once more he was defeated by Euclid. It was simply no contest. Sam didn't even try to solve the first problem.[12] He again dropped out of school. Later, the senior master of the academy, Isaac Anderson, commented about his student: "I often determined to lick him, but he would come up with such a pretty dish of excuses that I could not do it." [13] That would indeed have been an interesting sight, to see the master try to lick that strapping six-footer.

Sam was soon broke again, but he then took another step toward his destiny. He joined the army.

CHAPTER 3

Fighting For Old Hickory

On June 18, 1812, Congress had declared war against Great Britain. Although there was a great lack of enthusiasm in the East against such a venture, the war hawks, led by the formidable Henry Clay of Kentucky, John C. Calhoun of South Carolina, and Felix Grundy of Tennessee, finally had their way.

For a number of years there had been many disputes between the young United States and Great Britain. One of the points in dispute concerned the practice of the British impressing American seamen into the British navy despite papers of naturalization. In addition, the American government objected to the searching of its vessels off the American coastline. The U.S. accused, and rightly so, the British of intriguing their Indian allies to incite a frontier war. In 1803 Britain had forbidden any direct trade in American ships between the West Indian islands possessed by any European power and the continent of Europe. This had been a damaging blow to the economy of the United States. All too late, the British made concessions and agreed to stop the practices to which the Americans violently objected. They were unaware that just five days previously war had been declared by Congress.

Although the main reasons for a war had already been eliminated, the war hawks and the policymakers saw a great opportunity to seize Canada from the British Empire and incorporate it

21

into the United States. At the same time, it gave them an opportunity to settle a score against the Creek Indians who, under the terms of a treaty duly ratified by both parties, were claiming possession of most of what is today the state of Alabama.

On June 27, 1812, Governor Willie Blount of Tennessee received notification from Washington of the declaration of war against Great Britain. The document was given to him by Billy Phillips, a jockey who had ridden horseback 860 miles over mountains and poorly equipped roads to Nashville in nine days. The news of war was greeted with great enthusiasm by the Tennesseans, among them a lawyer-judge-politician named Andrew Jackson, who was also major general of the militia. Governor Blount promptly called for volunteers, and the response was so great that Tennessee ended up with its nickname of the Volunteer State.

The governor's volunteer force was raised in two divisions — one from the west and one from the east, with the West Tennesseans to be headed by Jackson. The fiery Major General Jackson, who was champing at the bit for action, offered President James Madison his well-trained division of 2,500 men for immediate action and declared he would have them facing the city of Quebec within ninety days. In spite of his offer, he received no orders to take to the field. In October 1812 the War Department bypassed Jackson completely and asked Governor Blount to furnish 1,500 men to reinforce Gen. James Wilkinson at New Orleans. This was an affront to Jackson. However, when his friend the governor diplomatically asked if he would object to serving under Wilkinson in a subordinate capacity, Jackson was so eager to get into the fray that he accepted. Even this attempt to get into the war left him thwarted. In the bitter cold of January 1813, Jackson, with two infantry regiments and Col. John Coffee's cavalry regiment, started off toward New Orleans. Thirty-nine days later, the army had traveled several hundred miles and reached Natchez. There Jackson was given mail for the army. Among his portion was a very polite letter from General Wilkinson giving him orders to halt his troops at Natchez.

After a month of idleness, Jackson was infuriated to receive a letter from Secretary of War Armstrong dismissing his command from service and ordering him to deliver to Wilkinson all articles of public property. To compound the insult, Wilkinson urged him to encourage his callously dismissed troops to enlist in the regular army.

Armstrong and Wilkinson underestimated the caliber of their

man. Jackson wasn't about to leave his troops stranded so far from home, ill and without sufficient clothing or rations. Politely and respectfully, he notified the secretary and Wilkinson that he was refusing to obey that part of the order calling for demobilization on the spot. As his command had volunteered to serve under him and were mostly boys, they were his responsibility and he would get them home at his own expense — even if they had to "eat their horses on the way." [1]

Wilkinson's quartermaster furnished Jackson with twenty days' worth of rations. At his own expense Jackson hired eleven wagons for the ill, being out of pocket more than $1,000. With the seriously ill riding in the wagons and the minorly ill riding horses, General Jackson placed himself at the head of his column and together they trudged off on foot for the long, perilous journey back home. The general proved himself a leader of men as he tirelessly led his ailing troops through the swamps and streams of the wilderness. As he marched up and down the line exhorting his weary men onward and sharing their hardships, someone muttered "he's tough as old hickory." The appellation stuck. It was a nickname that was to last the Tennessee militia general all his life with affection and admiration. Jackson had won the hearts of his soldiers.

Upon reaching Nashville the demoralized division was mustered out of service without having fired a shot in anger, and Jackson reverted to inactive duty. Once more he was in the backwater of the war. Then, on August 30, 1813, an event happened that brought him back into active service and gave him the battle for which he had been clamoring so long.

The Creek Indians owned practically all of what is now the state of Alabama, the land having been guaranteed them in a treaty with the federal government.[2] White poachers constantly violated this treaty, to the natural resentment of the Creeks. For years the great Shawnee Chief Tecumseh, a brigadier general in the British army, had been circulating among the Creeks and various other tribes. He was advocating a confederation of Indian tribes with the purpose of driving the whites back beyond the Alleghenies. His agitations had caught the receptive ear of a highly intelligent and well-bred mixed-breed Creek named Bill Weatherford, or Red Eagle to his followers. The Creeks hung their symbol of war, the crimson-dyed war club, or Red Stick, in their encampments, and Red Eagle called them to action against the hated whites. Their first strike culminated in an attack on Fort Mims, about forty miles north of Mobile, and resulted in a complete victory. About 400 people were slaughtered and scalped. When the news of the massacre at Fort Mims reached Tennessee, Governor Blount authorized 2,500 men to take to the field.

Through a series of misadventures involving being a reluctant second in a duel, General Jackson had been shot in a hotel gunfight. He barely escaped with his life, as a ball was fired deep into his upper left arm against a bone and his left shoulder was shattered by a slug. Physicians recommended amputation of the left arm, but Jackson would not hear of such a thing. To compound his physical distress he had a severe case of dysentery. Although he was far too ill to leave his bed, Jackson vowed to lead his troops in the field and did. He was not going to be denied his war. Jackson, like the latter-day Gen. George Patton, was a fighting general, and a minor thing like illness was not about to deter him when it was time to lead his troops.

Jackson had a worthy opponent in the wily Red Eagle, and his campaign was marked with frustration all the way. He had won his first two battles against the Red Sticks but fared far worse in the next two, when many of his troops took to their heels. In the severe winter of 1813 Jackson proved a genius as a leader of men when he was faced with a series of problems sufficient to make almost any commander resign his commission. There was a constant shortage of supplies, and the army was hungry, sometimes living on acorns alone. Jackson rarely knew how many men were under his command as enlistments were constantly expiring and men were either going home, threatening to go home, deserting, or mutinying. At one point the general stopped his horse in the face of an entire brigade that was about to desert. With his injured left arm still in a sling, Jackson rested his musket on his horse's neck and swore to shoot the first man who moved toward home. Physically, Jackson was a wreck, due to his still painful arm and shoulder, the dysentery, and lack of food and sleep, but he carried on through sheer will and determination.

Low ebb was reached when the general had only 130 men under his command. Then good fortune appeared. Eight hundred recruits from Tennessee marched into camp. They were undisciplined, raw troops and most of their officers were of the same caliber. But at least they were bodies to fill up his badly depleted ranks. He hoped to whip them into shape before the next engagement with the Red Sticks. Eventually, Jackson moved his troops to Fort Strother on the Coosa River in upper Alabama. It was there in February 1814 that he was reinforced by the Thirty-ninth Infantry, a regular army unit. Among the young officers of the Thirty-Ninth Infantry was Third Lieutenant Sam Houston. Soon Houston would meet the man who was to become a lifelong friend and mentor, and whom, but for a strange quirk of fate, he might have succeeded as president of the United States.

It was March 24, 1813, and Sam Houston was barely past his twentieth birthday. Some regular army recruiters were in Maryville giving a demonstration, showing muskets the recruits would use and a uniform of white pantaloons and waistcoats they would wear if they enlisted. The demonstration was accompanied by a rolling of the drums and parading of the colors, followed by a talk by the recruitment sergeant. Silver dollars were placed on the drumhead, and each person who intended to enlist was to pick up a silver dollar. Sam Houston, with a young friend, was standing on a corner watching the demonstration. He picked up a silver dollar. He wanted to fight the British.

The new recruit had not yet reached his majority of twenty-one so it was necessary for him to receive the consent of Elizabeth before he could put on those white pantaloons and waistcoat. She readily gave her consent and slipped on his finger a plain gold ring. Engraved on the inside of the ring was the single word "Honor." Sam wore that ring all his life and was wearing it when he died.[3] Later on Elizabeth gave her son another gift, a musket. According to Houston, she instructed him:

> There, my son, take this musket . . . and never disgrace it: for remember, I had rather all my sons should fill one honorable grave, than that one of them should turn his back to save his life. Go, and remember, too, that while the door of my cottage is open to brave men, it is eternally shut against cowards.[4]

Sam, in all his life, dishonored neither the ring nor the musket.

Houston's joining the army as a common soldier in the ranks was not without controversy. His brothers and friends raged at him, insisting he should have sought a commission. Houston lashed back at them, stating:

> And what have your craven souls to say about *the ranks*? . . . I would much sooner honor the ranks, than disgrace an appointment. You don't know me now, but you shall hear of me.[5]

Sam was assigned to the Seventh Infantry at Knoxville for

training purposes. His army records show that he was by now an impressive six feet two inches in height. From the first he showed he had leadership qualities. Within a few weeks, he was promoted to sergeant, then in July was commissioned as an ensign and transferred to the Thirty-ninth Infantry. By December he was promoted to third lieutenant.[6]

To some this might seem an extraordinarily rapid series of promotions for one who just a few months previously had been a backwoods youth with a meager education. But Houston did not receive his promotions through luck or influence. Many years later, from the floor of the United States Senate, Senator Thomas Hart Benton, who had served in the Creek campaign under Andrew Jackson, had this to say about Sam:

> I was the lieutenant colonel of the regiment to which he belonged, and the first field officer to whom he reported. I then marked in him the same soldierly and gentlemanly qualities which have since distinguished his eventful career: frank, generous, brave; ready to do, or to suffer, whatever the obligations of civil or military duty imposed; and always prompt to answer the call of honor, patriotism, and friendship.[7]

With the infusion of regular troops into his ranks, Jackson had some material to work with and promptly began instilling much needed discipline into his grumbling, nearly mutinous militia. Third Lieutenant Houston barely arrived in camp before he started receiving on-the-job training of troops in the field. Discipline is one of the first steps to any army's success, and Jackson was determined to get it. Those who did not want to conform began learning some of the hard facts of military life. Houston saw both officers and enlisted men arrested for drunkenness. Disciplined regulars by their example were helping the Tennessee militia shape up, and in the ensuing shakedown a major general and brigadier general were relieved of their commands and sent home.

Perhaps the one event that showed the civilian troops that their commander meant business was when a seventeen-year-old militiaman was shot for mutiny. Private John Woods had been involved in a fracas with an officer, refusing to obey an order. To compound his refusal, when the officer ordered him arrested, Woods threatened to use his gun on the first man to touch him. A court-martial tried him for mutiny, and the sentence was death by a firing squad. Jackson pondered the decision for two sleepless nights and then approved it. On March 14 at ten in the morning, a squad of regulars carried out the sentence, and by noon the army was on the march to have their final showdown with Red Eagle and his 1,000 braves.

Bill Weatherford had gathered his warriors of the Creek Nation at a bend on the Tallapoosa River, known to the Indians as Tohopeka and to others as Horseshoe Bend. Ten days of hard tramping south from Fort Strother through nearly fifty miles of Alabama wilderness brought Jackson's army on March 26, 1814, to the Creek fortifications. He immediately prepared for action.

Old Hickory's forces outnumbered the Red Sticks about two to one, as his army numbered approximately 2,000 men. This figure included about 600 Indians, of whom 500 were Cherokees and the rest friendly Creeks. Many of the Cherokees were commissioned officers, among them Sam Houston's friends from his days on Jolly's Island, John and James Rogers. Also among the Cherokees was the lame Sequoyah. Jackson's Indian allies not only served as scouts and spies but also performed valiantly in combat.

The formidable Red Eagle had chosen his defensive position well, as the Creeks had decided to risk their all on this battle. Horseshoe Bend, a peninsula of about 80 or 100 acres open on the north, was accurately named. Trees and brush grew on either side of the Bend, and it was further protected by a massive breastworks reaching down to the river on both sides. The breastworks were strongly and compactly built, composed of heavy pine logs five to eight feet high. There was a double row of skillfully arranged portholes, planned so that no enemy could approach without being exposed to a crossfire that allowed Creek sharpshootes to pick off their foe with a minimum of exposure to the white man's fire. An avenue of retreat was provided by a fleet of hidden canoes at the point of the Bend. The Creeks were armed well with rifles furnished by British and Spanish agents, and to bolster their determination they had been promised victory by their medicine men.

On the morning of March 27, Jackson deployed his troops and by ten o'clock had the peninsula surrounded. Gen. John Coffee, commanding the cavalry and all the Indians, had taken his troops to a position south of the Bend. Jackson, with the main army, had advanced to the north side. In the meantime, the Cherokee scouts under General Coffee swam the Tallapoosa and carried away the Red Stick canoes, thwarting any escape by that route. Red Eagle and his fanatical braves were completely encircled.

Jackson's entire artillery consisted of two small cannon, and he opened fire on the Indians only to see the round balls do no damage to the heavy breastworks as they sank in the soft pine logs. A lull in the fighting then occurred as a truce was arranged so the Creeks could remove their women and children — amounting to several hundred — from the battlefield. This took until around one o'clock and then the drums of the Thirty-ninth Infantry began their long roll as the foot soldiers began their charge.

The regulars of the Thirty-ninth Regiment were the first to reach the ramparts. At the portholes a bloody struggle ensued, man to man, muzzle to muzzle, and bayonet to bayonet. Maj. Lemuel P. Montgomery, the first to scale the ramparts, immediately fell back dead, pierced by a ball. His name lives on because the capital city of Montgomery, Alabama, was named in his honor.[8] He was followed immediately by Third Lieutenant Sam Houston, waving his sword in the air and urging his men onward. He cleared the fortifications and his platoon followed their leader. As Sam jumped down into a sea of screaming Red Sticks, an arrow pierced his thigh. He fell to the ground and engaged the Creeks with his sword. The Indians slowly gave way and the ramparts were taken. Sam tried his best to extract the arrow but it was of the barbed kind and would not give way. A fellow officer was nearby and Sam asked him to pull it out. The friend tried, but without success; he tried again and once more failed. He wanted to seek out a surgeon, but Sam would have none of it. Houston was in such pain that the lieutenant pulled with all his strength and finally succeeded in pulling the arrow out. The effort made such a gash it unleashed a torrent of blood that flowed so heavily Sam was forced then to seek a surgeon, who, after a great effort, managed to staunch the flow of blood. As he was lying on the ground recuperating, General Jackson rode by. Recognizing Sam, the general commiserated on his wound and ordered him to stay out of action for the rest of the day. Sam later remarked he probably would have obeyed those orders if he had not vowed that Maryville should hear of him.

With the breastworks taken, the Red Sticks retreated to the brush and numerous small battles raged, with the Creeks using not only their muskets but their knives, bows and arrows, and tomahawks. Sam disregarded his instructions to stay out of the fray and joined his comrades in the thick of the fighting. He later reported:

> Arrows, and spears, and balls were flying; swords and tomahawks were gleaming in the sun. . . . Not a single warrior offered to surrender, even while the sword was at his breast.[9]

Jackson's superior strength in numbers began to prevail, and his troops were whittling their opponents down; however, the Indians fought on with considerable courage. Jackson sent an interpreter to Bill Weatherford asking him to surrender and disarm. In return the Creeks would be paroled to their homes if they would promise not to take up arms against the Americans again. The offer was refused with a shower of arrows as the Red Stick medicine men moved among them, claiming the great spirit had promised victory. His sign would be a great cloud in the sky.

The carnage continued and finally the prophesy of the medicine men came true — the Creeks saw their cloud in the sky. Unfortunately, it brought for them not victory but just a mild spring shower. By early evening the Red Sticks had been wiped out with the exception of one large group entrenched in a fortress at the bottom of a ravine. Once more Jackson halted the fighting and sent an emissary asking for surrender. The Creeks, determined to fight to the last man, declined.

To take this last redoubt would be an extremely hazardous venture and undoubtedly would cost many lives of Jackson's troops. He hated to order his men forward in what for many would be certain death, so he called for volunteers. As his fellow officers and men fidgeted and hesitated, Third Lieutenant Houston limped forward and offered to lead a platoon of volunteers. He advanced down the ravine but found his men hesitating. Seizing a musket, he ordered a charge and ran forward. When he was within a few yards of the fortress an enemy musket ball lodged in his right shoulder and another smashed a bone in his right forearm. Sam staggered onward and, in turning, saw that his platoon had deserted him. He managed to get back to the top of the ravine and then collapsed.

Jackson, determined to lose no more men, had his Cherokee archers send their flaming arrows down on the log stronghold of the Creeks and set it on fire. By evening all resistance was finished. A body count by Jackson's men showed 557 lay dead at the battle site of Horseshoe Bend. General Coffee estimated his sharpshooters had killed from 250 to 300 in the water. In Jackson's opinion, not more than 20 Red Sticks could have escaped, with 26 dead and 107 wounded. His Cherokee allies counted 18 dead and 36 wounded, and the friendly Creeks totaled five dead and eleven wounded.[10]

The Creek War was over. Andrew Jackson's reputation as a general was made. He became a national figure overnight. The Battle of Horseshoe Bend was in the history books, and Sam Houston had honored his pledge — Maryville had heard of him.

CHAPTER 4

Wounds of War and Deceit

While the smoke was still smoldering from the last redoubt of the Red Sticks, Sam was carried off to a little clearing where the surgeons were treating the wounded. The deep gash in his thigh caused by the forced extraction of the arrow was given further treatment and bound. A surgeon removed one musket ball from his arm but the ball in the shoulder was left alone; another surgeon remarked it was useless to torture Sam as it was more than likely he would not survive until morning. Sam later said that it was the darkest night of his life.

The following morning, Sam was placed on a crude litter and transported sixty or seventy miles to Fort Williams. A week or so later he was taken to a field hospital in East Tennessee maintained by the Tennessee militia. Here he was given the very minimum of care but still managed to survive. Eventually, when this group of Tennessee volunteers was going home to be demobilized, he was transported with them in a horse litter. Finally, in May, weak, gaunt and haggard, and looking more like a scarecrow than a human being, he was delivered to the home of his mother in Maryville. Elizabeth scarcely recognized her son as he stood in her door.

That Houston survived his severe wounds with an almost complete lack of medical attention might be attributed to his strong build and the outdoor life he had led with the Indians, together with his tremendous will. Or perhaps it was because his Star of Destiny, which he followed all his life, was beginning to shine upon him. Nevertheless, various qualities of this young man, not yet twenty-one, were coming to the fore. He had earlier demonstrated his independence when he went to live among the Cherokees and his resourcefulness when he opened a school despite his lack of academic credentials. In arduous battle he had demonstrated his leadership and courage, and he was now demonstrating his indomitable will.

Sam's convalescence from his wounds was a lengthy and laborious one. In June, after a few weeks of rest at his mother's home, he felt strong enough to make the journey to Knoxville to consult a physician. The physician was less than useless and refused to handle his case, stating there was no point in Sam running up a medical bill inasmuch as he could not live more than a few days.

Houston would not give up. He rented a nearby room, rested for two weeks, and once more consulted the physician. By now his health had improved somewhat and the doctor, now believing he might live, accepted him as a patient. After a couple of months in Knoxville, Houston had recovered sufficiently enough that he mounted his horse and journeyed to Washington for further medical treatment, recuperation, and to see the capital for the first time. He arrived in August 1814, shortly after the British did, and found the White House and Capitol burned by the enemy.

The medical treatment he received in the nation's capital proved of little value, and once more Sam saddled his horse. This time he rode to the Timber Ridge area near Lexington to spend the winter visiting old friends and relatives. He was back in Tennessee by early March, shortly after Andrew Jackson's victory at New Orleans. Under date of March 1, 1815, he wrote Secretary of War James Monroe to apply for a commission in the regular army.[1] His request was granted, and on May 17 he was transferred to the United States First Infantry, which was stationed in New Orleans. His Knoxville doctor had told him that unless the ball that had lodged in his right shoulder was removed, he stood an excellent chance of losing the use of his right arm and shoulder. In New Orleans an army surgeon successfully probed and dug and finally retrieved the musket ball while Sam fortified himself with a generous slug of whiskey and held on to a chair. The wound bled copiously and, in Sam's already weakened condition, took what little strength he had left. Once more he was in for a long period of recuperation, which he spent in a barracks by the river reading books. The first-rate literature he brought included a Bible Elizabeth had given him, *The Vicar of Wakefield, Pilgrim's Progress, Robinson Crusoe,* works by Shakespeare, and Akenside's poems.

New Orleans was the ideal city for recuperation. This pleasant and beautiful city noted for its gaiety featured Saturday parades in the Place d'Armes, the twice-weekly masked balls at the French theater, and the quadroon balls. Sam, an imposing figure in his officer's uniform, took them all in. Further diversion was afforded by taking in the French Quarter, and it is not unlikely that he met the famous pirate Jean Laffite. The privateersman who so ably assisted General Jackson at the Battle of New Orleans owned a blacksmith shop in the Quarter — a building which still stands.

Sam's stay in New Orleans was marred only by a dispute with the War Department regarding the date of his promotion to second lieutenant. In a letter he wrote to the secretary of war in February 1816, he contended the correct date of his second lieutenancy should have been March 27, 1814, when he received a battlefield promotion from General Jackson. The army ranked him from May 20, 1814, and Houston referred the War Department to Jackson for confirmation of the correct date.[2] The affair was never satisfactorily settled and left Sam embittered.

His health showing little improvement, in the spring Sam boarded ship and sailed for New York for further treatment by army medical doctors. After several weeks in New York, he received a furlough and went home to Maryville. Eventually, he was ordered to report to the Southern Division of the army stationed at Nashville under the command of Andrew Jackson, who by now was a major general in the regular army.

Sam's furlough in Maryville was not long in duration but it was long enough for him to fall in love with one of the local belles and become virtually engaged. Sam, a gallant, was very discreet in his romances and her name is unknown to history. In various correspondence she is known only as M——. Apparently the affair had progressed to such a length that Miss M—— was ready and anxious to marry, but Houston called upon a boyhood chum to help extricate him from the situation. This accomplished, he settled down to his less-than-arduous duties shuffling papers in the office of the adjutant general of the division. He was promoted to first lieutenant, made application to join the Masonic Lodge, and on July 22, 1817, was raised to Master Mason in Cumberland Lodge No. 8 in Nashville.[3]

In his position in the adjutant general's office Sam came into frequent contact with Andrew Jackson, and it was during this period that the two men began developing a firm friendship that was to end only with Jackson's death. The general, a courageous man himself, admired courage in others. Seeing Sam in action on the battlefield, and particularly as he watched the final charge by Sam on the last redoubt of the Red Sticks, had filled him with admiration for this young lieutenant. Close contact with Houston revealed many other qualities in his subordinate that he admired, and it wasn't long before he became impressed with Sam's common sense and quick intelligence. Learning from him of his three years among the Cherokees, General Jackson became convinced that Houston was the perfect man for a task he had in mind.

The problem was the Cherokees. In 1816 Jackson had concluded a treaty with some chiefs and warriors of the Cherokee Nation in which the Indians ceded 1.3 million acres to the United States. For this they received $5,000, with the promise of an additional annuity of $6,000 to be paid for ten years. In addition, they were to move to new lands west of the Mississippi to territory the white man did not want.[4] As an inducement to sign the treaty, the reluctant chiefs were given "presents" Old Hickory thought it "well and polite" to offer.[5] As a number of chiefs and senior members of the nation had not been consulted on this treaty, there was great resentment against it and much reluctance to move to the west. Their resentment was so great, in fact, that there were rumblings and threats of war against the whites. Jackson, as commanding general of the Southern Division of the army, was busy making preparations for a campaign against the Seminoles in Georgia and Florida, but this time the Cherokees and friendly Creeks refused to ally themselves with him. As the general did not want to be distracted in a conflict with the Cherokees, his solution to the problem was to request the governor of Tennessee, Joseph McMinn, to ask the War Department to appoint Houston as sub-agent to the Cherokees. He was confident of Houston's ability to pacify the disgruntled Indians. McMinn honored this request, and Sam's appointment as sub-agent came through in October 1817.

Although Sam had asked for an assignment among the Indians, he approached his task with hesitation. His sympathies were with his Cherokee friends in their quarrel with the federal government; yet, as an army officer, he was obliged to follow his orders to the best of his ability. Those orders were to do everything in his power to persuade the reluctant Cherokees to swallow the terms of the Treaty of 1816, no matter how bitter the potion, and move westward beyond the mighty Mississippi. Sam doffed his uniform, donned his Indian clothes, and headed for Jolly's Island, where he was welcomed warmly by his adopted father and his many friends.

As an inducement to sign the Treaty of 1816, Jackson had promised that all those who migrated could draw various supplies such as a rifle and ammunition, a blanket, and a brass kettle, or in lieu of that a beaver trap. To date, the War Department, which held jurisdiction over Indian affairs, had neglected to carry out its share of the bargain. Sam not only spoke Cherokee fluently, but also spoke another language the Indians understood well: this was winter, and he quickly lived up to the government's defaulted promises by providing them with the blankets to which they were entitled. The promised kettles, traps, and rifles were also forthcoming.

Houston's knowledge of the character of the Indians and their thought processes began to pay off. In discussions with their chiefs in their council houses he reminded them that their honor was at stake. Despite the fact that many chiefs had not signed the treaty — and that it was a highly unpopular one — a treaty was still a treaty, and it was sacred.

There was another obstacle to removal beyond the Mississippi. The Arkansas Territory was west, and according to the Indians' superstitions and mythology "west" was to be feared as it was where the God of Evil resided. It was the symbol of death, darkness, and defeat. The east, where they resided, was the Sun Land, with the good under-Gods.

Jackson had chosen wisely in his appointment of Houston as his sub-agent. Sam was an eloquent speaker and finally convinced Chief Jolly and the others that it was in their best interests to abide by the hated treaty and emigrate to new lands. After all, he submitted, a military alliance among the five civilized nations and war against the whites might cause some trouble, but in the end the military strength of the United States Army would prevail as it did with the Red Sticks.

The Cherokees were faced with an extremely difficult decision. They had good reason to be resentful of the federal government in its demands to give up their homes and move west to lands occupied by many other tribes. Unlike the Indian tribes who owned little but their teepees and horses, they were people of property. Some of them were wealthy. A census of 1825 showed a total population of 15,160, including 1,377 black slaves; they had 22,531 black cattle, 7,683 horses, 46,732 swine, 2,566 sheep, 330 goats, 762 looms,

2,486 spinning wheels, 172 wagons, 2,843 plows, 10 sawmills, 31 gristmills, one powder mill, 62 blacksmith shops, 8 cotton gins, 18 schools, two turnpikes, 18 ferries, and 20 public roads.[6]

Oolooteka and his fellow chiefs finally decided to bow to the inevitable. To him it was not too difficult a decision to make, as he had long held the opinion the white man would never be content until he owned all the lands east of the Mississippi. Perhaps now the Cherokees and other tribes could move to the new land, join their brothers already there, and have the peace they sought.

The federal government agreed to pay for the cost of their travel. One of the first groups of Cherokees to depart was a contingent led by Capt. John Rogers in October 1817 with thirty-one in his party.[7] He was followed a few months later by Oolooteka and more than 300 of his followers, which included 108 braves who had been supplied with new rifles under the terms of their recent treaty. The government provided rations for seventy days and furnished sixteen flatboats, which remained the property of the government.[8]

There was no resting period for Houston. John Jolly and his band had barely started for the Promised Land when a new problem was thrown to Sam by Jackson.

In November 1817 the great Cherokee Chief Tahlontusky,[9] brother of John Jolly, was leading a delegation of Indians to Washington and stopped off in Knoxville to confer with Governor McMinn. He had a complaint to make — and it was a familiar one. Some ten years earlier, after the Treaty of 1808, he had led a band of more than 1,100 Cherokees west of the Mississippi to the Arkansas Territory, settling in what is today Dardanelle, Pope County, Arkansas. Since the government had consistently refused to honor the terms of that treaty, he and his delegation were on the way to the capital to present their case in person before the Great White Father.

The governor was highly impressed by the dignity, character, intelligence, and demeanor of Tahlontusky and his delegation, which included not only some statesmen of the Cherokees but some of their warriors as well. Among the warriors was Houston's boyhood chum John Rogers, who had fought in the war against the Red Sticks and was in the delegation as interpreter. John Rogers had the additional prestige of being Tahlontusky's nephew.

Governor McMinn wrote President Monroe and Secretary of War John C. Calhoun that the Cherokee delegation was on its way.

35

Then he and Jackson assigned Houston to accompany his friends to the capital to serve as an additional interpreter. Houston was in pain as his injured shoulder was giving him trouble. Nevertheless, he accepted the assignment and reported for duty to Tahlontusky, his foster-uncle. Once more Sam donned Indian regalia, and the delegation left Knoxville on their journey to Washington City.

The party traveled slowly since Tahlontusky was a very old man and there were many things he wanted to see in the white man's country. The group reached the capital on February 5, 1818, and was received by Secretary of War Calhoun. Sam interpreted for the aged chief.

Tahlontusky presented his complaints. The Treaty of 1808 had been made with the entire Cherokee Nation, the central government of which was located in Georgia. All payments of annuities by the U.S. had gone to Georgia, and the Western Cherokees had been getting very little of their share of the proceeds promised them for giving up their homes and making the long trek westward. The chief wanted to secede from the Cherokee Nation and establish his own Western Nation with himself as head. He desired Washington to recognize his government so that he could receive the promised annuities. His second complaint was serious but by no means as compelling as his first. Apparently, it had occurred to no one in 1808 that the land the government wanted the Indians to move to west of the Mississippi was claimed by many other Indian nations. Some of those tribes, and particularly the Osages, were giving the chief much trouble, though he thought he could settle their differences.

Secretary Calhoun, with his South Carolina charm, listened very courteously to the delegation and to the presentation made by Sam. Smilingly, he rose from his seat and told Tahlontusky that the Great White Father, President James Monroe, was waiting in another room to receive him. As the delegation was leaving Calhoun's office to be taken to the president, Calhoun asked Sam to remain behind for a moment.

To Sam's surprise and humiliation he was given a verbal blistering by Calhoun. The South Carolinian asked what an officer of the United States Army was doing appearing before the secretary of war dressed not in military uniform but in Indian clothes. Houston explained that his mode of dress was not chosen to show disrespect to the secretary, but as an endeavor to respect the dignity of the Cherokees. After all, he was a sub-agent to the Indians and thought he could be more effective with them by wearing their clothing than by wearing army attire. His explanation failed to mollify the enraged Calhoun. The secretary ordered him to wear regulation dress before appearing in public again and abruptly dismissed him.

As the wheels of bureaucracy grinded slowly, the Cherokee delegation was still in Washington when ten days later Houston was summoned to Calhoun's office. This time the charges against him were more serious than that of wearing Indian clothes. The secretary told him he had been accused of being part of a ring of white smugglers who transported black slaves from Florida and Georgia to various border states while he had been sub-agent to Chief Jolly the previous November.[10]

Sam had little trouble proving the falsity of these accusations. The truth was he had endeavored to halt the traffic by the smugglers once he found out about it, and in seeking revenge the smugglers themselves were the source of the charges against him. They chose an old ploy and charged Sam with their own crimes; hence the accusations against him. Houston was naturally resentful of the accusations. He protested to Calhoun his innocence and demanded his case be taken before President Monroe. Calhoun agreed to investigate the case and discovered that a senator who had lodged the complaint was involved with the smugglers. The charges were dropped.

Sam was not pacified. His career as an army officer would have been ruined, he told Calhoun, and he wanted those making the false statements against him punished. Nothing was done to those who had tried to damage Houston. He wanted an apology from the War Department but received none. Neither did he receive thanks for exposing the guilty persons. The whole affair was swept under the rug by the government. Sam fumed, but there was nothing he could do about it. He remained with Tahlontusky's delegation.

The chief's mission was finally over, and he was to return to his lands in the Arkansas Territory. In exchange for his promise not to bother the government any more, he had been given $1,000 in gold and his companions received $500. Sam succeeded in procuring government provisions for the delegation for their homeward journey and, wearing his Indian garb, accompanied them back to Tennessee as far as the Hiwassie River. On March 1, 1818, in a terse resignation requiring only one sentence, he resigned from the army.[11] He had been a soldier for five years to the day but had never accomplished his desire to fight the British. A brief postscript to his resignation read: "I will thank you [to] give me my commission, which I am entitled to by my last promotion." [12] Shortly afterward, he also resigned his office as sub-agent. The affair with Calhoun created an enmity between the two men that lasted all through their political careers.

In retrospect Sam's decision to resign from the army and his post as sub-agent might seem childish, but it was indicative of the impetuous nature of this remarkable man. He had liked serving with the army and fully intended to make it his life's career. But like many people, he could never take criticism gracefully. His honor had been impugned by the refusal of those in government to take action against his accusers of smuggling, and Sam was a man of honor. At this stage of his life he was somewhat naive and did not realize that politicians live in a different world. The bureaucratic processes of the army and the politicians did not conform to Sam's ideas, so his solution was to quit the army.

At age twenty-five he was out of a job, broke, and in debt — a familiar pattern that was to haunt Sam all his life. The government finally came through with $17.75 owed him. They still owed him $170 for expenses he had incurred as a sub-agent, and it was five years before he was paid in full. To help satisfy his creditors and avoid bankruptcy, he sold his interest in the Houston family belongings to his brother James. Having no idea as to what to pursue as a career, he rode to Nashville, where he had made many friendships over the years. Perhaps one of his friends would have a suggestion.

CHAPTER 5

Political Beginnings

When former First Lieutenant Houston rode into the thriving, bustling, growing city of Nashville, he had few prospects and less money, but he did have some assets. He had a good war record and an excellent reputation for paying his debts. He had charm, some relatives, and friends. Sam always had friends. Among the latter was Judge James Trimble, a lawyer Sam knew slightly.

Houston approached the judge with the request Trimble sponsor him in the study of law. In those days it was the custom for an aspiring lawyer to "read" law and study in a sponsor's office.[1] The judge readily agreed with Houston's request and prescribed a course of study that would last eighteen months before taking the required examination to practice before the bar. Sam, with his great self-confidence, remarked that "his circumstances precluded any such expenditure of time, and that he would be ready for the examinations in six months."[2] He began his studies in June 1818, reading the same books that had previously belonged to his fellow officer, the late Maj. Lemuel P. Montgomery.

Despite his studies, Sam still managed to have a social life and joined the Dramatic Club of Nashville, which was managed by Noah M. Ludlow. Many members of the Dramatic Club were prominent in social and political circles, and both General Jackson and Congressman Felix Grundy were honorary members. Among the officials of the club was John H. Eaton who, under President Jackson, became secretary of war. In his short-lived amateur acting career, Houston played several roles, his best probably being that of a drunken hotel porter in *We Fly By Night*. He also became an active member of the Tennessee Antiquarian Society.

As a law student Sam worked hard. With his quick, retentive memory he buried himself in the standard law books of the day and the Constitution of the United States. He grounded himself thoroughly in the basic principles of the law, and at the end of six months announced he was ready to take the bar examination and easily passed the searching test.

The fledgling lawyer decided to hang out his shingle in Lebanon, a town about thirty miles east of Nashville and the county seat of Wilson County. As usual, Sam had virtually no funds, and again his lifelong ability to make friends quickly and easily came into play. He came to the attention of Isaac Golladay,[3] who befriended him. Golladay was not only the postmaster but was also a merchant and one of the leading citizens of Lebanon. For one dollar a month he rented Houston an office at 109 E. Main Street, a small structure made of cedar logs.[4] In addition, he lent him enough money to purchase a law library and outfit himself with a comprehensive wardrobe, stating Sam could pay him back when he was able. His generosity did not stop there; it extended to introductions to prominent people who could throw legal business Sam's way.

Many years later, Golladay's generosity to a man he scarcely knew paid off in an unexpected way. Sam had a long memory and never forgot a friend or a favor, nor forgave an enemy. Years later, while living in Huntsville as a senator from Texas, he learned that a stranger who lay critically ill and unattended in a hotel room was Frederick Golladay, the son of his long-ago benefactor. Houston visited him in his hotel room and had the younger Golladay transferred to his home. He supplied medicines and nursed him, including personally washing his feet, and the care and attention he devoted to the young man probably saved his life.

A good mixer, it wasn't long before Sam could count some of the leading figures of the city among his friends. Invariably well-dressed, his imposing figure of over six feet combined with the Houston charm made him an easy man to remember and helped enable him to quickly build an excellent law practice. For relaxation and friendship there were many frequent trips to the Hermitage in Nashville to visit his former commander, General Jackson. The general's wife Rachel took him under her wing and soon he was calling her "Aunt Rachel." Houston admired the kindly wife of his chief and became her devoted lifelong friend.

The Hermitage was frequented by many important persons of the day, one being Governor McMinn, who knew Houston from having appointed him as sub-agent to the Indians some years previously. The governor was impressed with Sam and appointed him adjutant general of the Tennessee militia, a position which carried the rank of colonel. With his rising popularity and with Jackson's endorsement, he was nominated for the post of district attorney of the Davidson District and was easily elected. This necessitated a move to Nashville.

To the consternation and dismay of his fellow attorneys, Houston proved to be a formidable opponent in the courtroom. Those who derided him because of his youth — he was still only in his mid-twenties — found that although he had crammed his law studies into the brief period of six months, he had mastered what had been studied. As prosecuting attorney he proved to be the match of the ablest minds of the bar the region had to offer. Sam's good common sense, his flair for oratory and eloquence, and his commanding presence enabled him to successfully prosecute practically all of his cases. Criticisms of his youth and lack of legal knowledge quickly stopped.

Although his elective position brought in a steady salary to Sam, it was not enough. In the fall of 1820 he resigned and reentered private practice. He earned an excellent reputation as a trial lawyer and once more built up a lucrative practice. In 1821 he was elected major general of the Tennessee Militia by his fellow officers, and for the rest of his life was known by his military title.

As a York Rite Mason, Sam was an active member of the Cumberland Lodge No. 8 of Nasvhille,[5] and in 1822 served as Junior Warden. With increasing affluence he participated actively in many social affairs; as a bachelor and an enthusiastic as well as excellent dancer, he could always be found at the numerous balls in the city. His name was on an invitation to Miss Sally Fry dated December 20, 1822, as one of the managers of a ball his Masonic Lodge was sponsoring at the Nashville Inn.

Sam's wit, charm, good looks, and friendly personality produced many invitations to the homes of the Nashville mighty. One of his lifelong traits was not only his capacity to make loyal friends but to keep them. In a letter to Governor McMinn he stated:

I never quit a friend until I see a disinclination on his part to be

41

friendly with me. I dearly love my friends because they have been everything to me. I part with them as a Miser does his treasure with anguish and regret.[6]

His old army buddies frequently called upon him to pass the time of day. Indian friends never forgot him, and he was visited several times from the Arkansas Territory by his Cherokee chums of Hiwassie Island days.

On one occasion the half-white John Rogers made a special trip to Sam, complaining that as usual the government had failed to live up to the promises they made when urging the red men to move west of the Mississippi. The previous Indian agent had been removed from office on grounds of corruption, and Rogers wanted Sam to become the new agent. Houston considered the matter and through the influence of Jackson was tendered the appointment by John C. Calhoun, still secretary of war. After reflecting on the matter he declined the position. No doubt one reason for the refusal was that his long memory did not let him forget the difficulties he had had with Calhoun and the government during his previous term as sub-agent of Indian affairs. Also, in 1822 Sam had corresponded with the secretary concerning the $170 the government owed him for his services as sub-agent. He finally received the money; however, in these letters he makes it perfectly clear to Calhoun that he considers the latter to have a prejudice against him, and also makes it perfectly clear he will never forget what he considers to be "personal injuries" Calhoun has done him.

Sometime in 1822 Houston and some of his friends began taking an interest in Texas as a land speculation. In 1820 Mexico announced it would give permission to American and European citizens to settle on lands west of the Sabine River. This had drawn many emigrants to the region, among them the New Englanders Moses Austin and his son, Stephen F., who were trying to establish a colony in Texas. Houston made formal application for several grants of territory and then had a change of heart and let the matter drop.

As a rising man-about-town with some prestige — with his growing popularity and closeness to leading political figures of the day — it was perhaps inevitable that Houston enter politics. In 1822 the Tennessee Senate had proposed Jackson for the presidency. Sam, a Jackson man and high up in the political circles surrounding him, eagerly supported him. In 1823 several members of the Jackson hierarchy, including Sam, Senator John H. Eaton,

Governor McMinn, and William Carroll (who had been an officer in the War of 1812 and succeeded McMinn as governor of Tennessee), were all working hard to secure the presidency for Jackson.

A vacancy for congressman from the Ninth District of Tennessee to the United States House of Representatives was to occur at the end of the session, and with the backing of the Jackson machine Sam was nominated for the position. A few would-be candidates saw the formidable opposition they would face and threw up their hands in disgust. Thirty-year-old Houston was elected without opposition. When he went to Washington to take up his seat, he carried with him a highly laudatory letter of introduction from Jackson, by now the junior senator from Tennessee, to the aged Thomas Jefferson.

Only a few weeks after being sworn-in to office, Houston made his maiden speech in the House, January 22, 1824. With his usual oratorical style and flair for eloquence he supported the recognition of Greek independence. In April he engaged in another battle of correspondence with his old antagonist, Calhoun, over expense money owed him.[7] He represented the interests of his constituents vigorously and spent considerable time devoted to promoting the candidacy of his mentor, Jackson, for president. Socially, he spent many evenings at O'Neale's Tavern, a hostelry frequented by many of Washington's political elite, among them the renowned Daniel Webster.

The innkeeper had an attractive daughter named Peggy who was married to one John Timberlake, a pursor in the navy. Inasmuch as Timberlake was absent at sea for long periods of time due to his duties, the pretty Peggy was frequently seen in the company of Senator Eaton, a rich widower considerably older than herself. Several years later, when Timberlake cut his throat while on a voyage and Eaton was secretary of war in the Jackson cabinet, pretty Peggy became the new Mrs. Eaton. The resulting uproar created a scandal in Washington society as wives of Eaton's fellow cabinet officers refused to receive her.

The leading contenders for the presidency in 1824 were Jackson, John Quincy Adams, John C. Calhoun, Henry Clay, and William Crawford. Calhoun dropped out of the race shortly and ran instead for the vice-presidency. In the late summer of 1824, while Congress was out of session, Sam became ill, apparently with yellow fever. From Nashville on August 28 he wrote his cousin, John

H. Houston, that he was just out of a sickbed. After stating his health had been restored, he predicted Jackson would win the upcoming presidential election and that the tariff would not affect Jackson in the South.

Houston proved an astute prophet. When the November 1824 presidential votes were tallied, Jackson had 155,872 popular votes and had carried eleven states with ninety-nine electoral votes. Adams garnered 105,321 popular votes, seven states, and eighty-four electoral votes. Both William H. Crawford and Speaker of the House Henry Clay won three states, with Crawford receiving forty-one electoral votes and Clay only thirty-seven. With no candidate receiving a majority of the votes cast, the Constitution of the United States took effect and the contest was thrown into the House of Representatives.

The House would not cast their votes for the presidency until February. Crawford had no real national following, and it became apparent that Clay would be the swing man. Houston worked avidly for his friend. In a discussion with a fellow congressman he tested the waters: "What a splendid administration it would make," he said, "with Old Hickory as President and Mr. Clay as Secretary of State." [8]

In a letter to a friend dated January 22, 1825, he confidently predicted the election of Jackson. In the meantime, cloakroom maneuverings of the politicians had apparently created doubt in his mind. On February 7, two days before the House convened, Houston wrote Capt. W. V. Cobbs of Boston that there was no certainty in the election of either of the candidates, but that General Jackson was certainly the president of the people.

Perhaps Adams also thought Sam's remark about Clay as secretary of state was a splendid idea, but with himself as president. In any event, Clay threw his support to the Bostonian and on the first ballot Adams became the sixth president of the United States. Houston's old foe Calhoun was elected vice-president.

When Adams promptly appointed Clay as secretary of state, cries of "foul" and "corruption" were heard but soon died out. This was not the last time that a presidential candidate with the most popular votes failed to win the highest office in the land.[9]

Sam and others of General Andy's lieutenants immediately went to work to ensure the election of their man in 1828.

44

With the election over, Houston's thoughts turned to matrimony. In January 1825 he had written a friend:

> For my *single* self I do not know yet the sweets of matrimony, but in March or April, next I will; unless something should take place not to be expected, or wished for! [10]

After Congress adjourned, he hurried south to Cheraw, South Carolina, apparently to marry a Miss M—— (the second mysterious woman with the initial "M"). On April 20 he wrote his cousin John the marriage had been postponed until fall, and stated some of his friends at home were urging him to run for governor.

Apparently his letter brought a reply from his cousin inquiring as to the reason for the postponement. On June 30 Sam replied that the main reasons were he had not provided a house for his intended and, as he would be away from home so much, she would be among strangers, alone, and her situation would be unpleasant. He had agreed to return in the fall and also mentioned being retained in a legal case involving a will in which the fee was $1,000. For whatever the reason, the marriage never took place.

For the rest of his term Sam applied himself to the interests of his constituents, occasionally taking to the floor of the House where his oratorical prowess always drew an appreciative audience.

In his full life Houston was seldom a stranger to controversy, and in 1825 he was charged with making slanderous remarks against Gen. George W. Gibbs, a fellow Mason. This resulted in both of them facing charges of misconduct by their lodge. At a meeting held in October 1825 by the Grand Lodge of Tennessee, the Most Worshipful Grand Master stated to Sam: "You know there is a difference between you and Brother Gibbs; rumor has it all over town." Houston replied that "rumor had a thousand tongues, and that five hundred were slanderous." [11] A resolution was adopted by the lodge stating there was no cause for censure against Houston.[12]

Jackson had retired from the Senate and was back in Nashville at his beloved Hermitage. Although away from Washington, he managed to keep busy in politics and from time to time would assign a task to his disciple Sam. One assignment in 1827 was a request that Houston see John Randolph with the purpose of purchasing a filly from him if one could be had for $300 or under. This was quickly followed by a request that Sam find him a "free man of color" to look after some stud colts the general had turned over to one of his nephews. In a reply to him from Washington, Sam gives some political news and then states:

> I have spoken to Mr. Randolph on the subject of the ARCHY FILLY, that you wished to purchase of him. He says that he has none of the three year old nor, under four, as I understood him to say — perhaps he has yearlings — for his four year old Fillys he asks $400.00. I will expect you to write me on this subject. It has not been in my power to hear of a good Groom, which can be had. Shou'd I hear of any, I will forthwith apply to him, for Capt. Donelson.[13]

One assignment, however, embroiled Houston in a controversy far more serious than the one with fellow Mason Gibbs.

In 1826 the office of postmaster of Nashville became vacant. Jackson's old nemesis Secretary of State Henry Clay promptly urged President Adams to appoint John P. Erwin to the post. Erwin, in addition to being editor of the *Nashville Banner and Whig,* also happened to be brother to Clay's son-in-law. Adams granted Clay's request and made the appointment. General Andy had a candidate for this post, and in a brief letter to Houston wrote: "Attend to this business." [14] Sam, in whose congressional district the postmastership was vacant, promptly swung into action. In a letter to the president dated March 18, 1826, he requested B. Y. Curry be given the post; in addition, he bitterly denounced Erwin, stating he was not a man of upright moral character and claiming he not only did not pay his debts, but had also been caught eavesdropping late at night at the window of a gentleman of character. Then on the floor of the House he made various accusations against Erwin. Houston's opposition carried no weight with Adams and the appointment stood.

The matter did not end there. The victorious Erwin naturally took offense at Houston's remarks and on the latter's return to Nashville in August wrote him inquiring if, while in Washington, he had impeached the integrity of his conduct. Sam, in his reply, willingly admitted he had. Erwin then replied that owing to ill health in his family, further correspondence would be suspended.

At this early stage in the life of our nation, dueling to settle affairs of honor was still in fashion. The venerable Clay himself had not too long ago engaged in one with John Randolph. Under the *code duello,* one could not directly challenge an intended opponent; all negotiations had to be handled through a second. A professional duelist from Missouri calling himself by the odd name of "Col.

John Smith, T.," showed up and cornered Sam with a note. Sam refused to accept it and referred him to his friend Colonel Mc-Gregor. McGregor likewise refused to receive the note on the grounds that the whole affair was a local matter and that Smith, T., being from out of the state, had no legitimate interest in the matter.

Smith, T. left but returned shortly with Gen. William A. White, a lawyer from Nashville, and was armed. Instead of going through Colonel McGregor, as he should have according to protocol, he accosted Houston on a sidewalk of the Nashville Inn. As there were several persons present he requested Sam to step aside out of the hearing of those nearby. The two walked a distance of some fifteen or twenty paces and Smith, T. handed Sam the note. Houston refused to open it, and General White decided to get into the act.

"Colonel," White said to Smith, "I reckon he will not deny having received it."

"I have not received it," Houston insisted. "I do not know its contents. I will not open it, but will refer its contents to Colonel McGregor. But I will receive one from you, General White, with pleasure."

"I will receive one from you, General Houston."

"The saddle is on the other horse, General, and that is enough to be understood between gentlemen."

"If I call on you there will be no shuffling, I suppose?"

"Try me, sir." [15]

After a blast or two at Houston in the *Banner and Whig,* Erwin apparently decided discretion was the better part of valor and withdrew from the controversy. A few letters passed between Sam and Smith, T., then the latter departed for points west. On September 12, 1826, in an article in the *Banner and Whig* addressed "To The Public," Houston presented his side of the controversy to date as it pertained to himself, Erwin, Smith, T., and White. With Erwin mum and Smith, T. gone, White foolishly decided to challenge Sam.[16] Houston reluctantly assented. Being the challenged, he had the choice of weapons and selected pistols at fifteen feet. The date was set for a week hence and Sam promptly started practicing with his pistols. He asked the experienced Jackson for advice and was told to bite on a bullet; it would help steady his aim.

At sunrise on September 22, 1826, two men who had no valid quarrel with each other met on a farm owned by Sanford Duncan, just across the Kentucky border. The seconds quickly agreed on rules. Each principal could fire one shot. Whether biting a bullet

47

helped steady Sam's aim is unknown, but when he fired he put his bullet in his opponent's groin. As White sank to the ground, Houston rushed to his side. White, who thought he was dying, feebly whispered: "General, you have killed me."

Houston replied: "I am very sorry, but you know it was forced upon me."

"I know it, and forgive you," White responded.[17]

White survived, although it took him four months of convalescence to recover from his wound. Houston was indicted by a Kentucky grand jury but was never arrested, let alone tried. He was vastly relieved when his opponent recovered, but the whole affair left him with such a disgust for dueling that he never again engaged in one. Although challenged from time to time, he managed to make a jest to his would-be opponents and laughed them off with his quick wit. Later, in Texas, he quipped to a despised political opponent: "I never fight down-hill." [18]

Houston's duel with White had ramifications among the Masonic fraternity. While he was governor he was suspended from his lodge in Nashville. He appealed the suspension to the Grand Lodge, which upheld the suspension at a meeting on October 10, 1828.[19]

CHAPTER 6

Tennessee Governor

Although Sam was a faithful ally of Jackson, he was far from a subservient lackey and the relationship was not always one-sided. He gladly supported the older man when he thought he was right and never minded doing any errands requested. At the same time, when he thought Jackson in the wrong, he had no hesitation in opposing him. One such instance was the Southard affair.

In a private conversation, Secretary of the Navy Samuel L. Southard had expressed a view criticizing Old Hickory's defense of New Orleans. It was his contention the city had been saved by James Monroe. When this tale was carried back to the Hermitage, the hot-tempered Jackson exploded. Criticizing his military strategy was almost tantamount to casting aspersions on his beloved Rachel. He promptly penned a denunciatory letter to Southard and sent it to Houston with instructions to present it to the secretary for an immediate reply. As the letter was unsealed, Sam read it. He was shocked at its vehemence and could hardly see how Southard could avoid issuing a challenge after reading its contents. He knew Jackson had already killed one man in a duel and wounded another in a subsequent affair of honor. Jackson had his eye on the presidency in 1828 and another duel, even though not fatal, would seriously damage his credibility.

Sam consulted with friends, and the consensus was that the

letter was too hot to handle. Houston wrote Old Hickory and advised him to take a much more conciliatory tone to present to Southard. Jackson took the advice and the whole affair eventually blew over. Sam's prestige rose, and he acquired a reputation of being able to "handle" his patron.

As early as 1825, Houston had toyed with the idea of running for governor but eventually decided against it. Instead, he ran for a second term as congressman and was easily reelected. In 1826 he definitely decided to make the race for the governorship. The position would be vacant since William Carroll, the incumbent, had served the three consecutive terms permitted under the Tennessee constitution and was ineligible to succeed himself.

Houston campaigned hard for the post, with Newton Cannon as his major opponent. Willie Blount, who had previously held the office and was trying to make a comeback, was also in the race. Sam traveled across the state, appearing at all the functions vote-seeking politicians felt required to attend: barn-raisings, cock fights, barbecues, log-rollings. An imposing sight at six feet two inches,[1] he dutifully clucked babies under the chin and charmed their mothers with his handsomeness[2] as he smiled graciously at them. In his electioneering he paid special attention to the western portion of the state, and in a letter to his cousin John predicted victory by "a large majority, unless [there be] some vast accident . . ."[3] When the votes were tallied that hot August day, Sam was the victor with 44,426 votes to the 33,410 received by Cannon.[4] Blount, the third candidate, was a very distant also-ran. The first day of October 1827, Houston was inaugurated as Tennessee's chief executive in the First Baptist Church in Nashville.

Tennessee was largely an agrarian state and facility of transportation was a vital necessity to the inhabitants, not only to transport their products south to Mobile and other intermediate ports, but also to receive goods and other heavy articles of import. The many natural obstructions of the Tennessee River made such trade through Mobile difficult. Houston, in his message to the state legislature on October 15, 1827, anticipated the twentieth-century Tennessee Valley Authority by calling for various canals along the Tennessee to provide the essential outlet for goods.

For some time the federal government had been negotiating with the Cherokees to construct a canal over Indian land from Hiwassie to Coosa. Negotiations by the government representative, Gen. John Cocke, had failed largely because of the niggardly amount of $10,000 in specie offered by the government. Cocke asked Sam to secure the help of the Tennessee legislature in resolving the question, and from his executive office on October 27 Sam transmitted Cocke's letter, requesting that they consider Cocke's request.

Sam's administration as chief executive of Tennessee was a quiet one, conservative and successful. To a large degree he carried on the business principles initiated by his predecessor, Billy Carroll. He was a popular governor and had his eye on a second term, to the dismay of Carroll, who wanted the office back again. In this early footwork for a second term Jackson, the Sage of the Hermitage, was playing it close to his vest as he sincerely liked both men and was hesitant to commit himself to either one.

Houston proved himself an energetic worker in the campaign to make his old commander president and helped entertain the general at a public dinner for him at the Nashville Inn on Christmas Eve of 1827. Two days after Christmas, he joined the Jackson party on the steamer *Pocahontas* bound for a victory celebration of the Battle of New Orleans. On July 4, 1828, General Jackson and Governor Sam spent the anniversary in Lebanon. Two miles west of the city they were met by a military company, and 3,000 citizens escorted them to the town. In the backyard of Wynne's tavern a splendid dinner was served at a table bearing 250 plates. In the evening they were entertained at a ball.

The Jackson campaign for the presidency was in full swing against the incumbent Adams, and seldom has such villification, character assassination, name-calling, and ruthlessness been seen in American politics. Old Hickory was called a liar, a homicidal maniac, and a bribe-taker. He was depicted in the press as a murderer, a slave-trader, a drunkard, and a gambler. He was condemned for dueling and for having six deserters in the Creek campaign executed. In fact, he was accused of just about every crime in the book except peeking through keyholes. The old warhorse could take these scurrilous remarks in stride, but his fury was aroused when they called him an adulterer and accused him of bigamy and cuckoldry with his beloved Rachel. His accusers were referring, of course, to the marriage of the couple when Rachel had honestly thought her first husband had divorced her. The husband, either through laxness or deliberate design, had not done so, and the Jacksons had married illegally. When the error was discovered, and later corrected by a divorce, the couple had wed again.

In spite of the scandal, and the slime and mud thrown, this time Old Hickory proved a tougher nut to crack. When the votes were counted they showed Jackson once more the winner in the popular vote by receiving 647,276 to the 508,064 Adams garnered. But this time there was no question about the race being thrown into the House of Representatives because he also swamped his opponent in the electoral college, with 178 votes to 83. John Quincy Adams thus joined his father John as one of the first two presidents to serve only one term in the highest elective office in the land.

Unfortunately, Rachel did not get to accompany her husband to Washington to become the nation's first lady. Her health was poor; she had developed pleurisy after catching a cold and died. Sam was a pallbearer as she was buried Christmas Eve, 1828, in a garden at her beloved Hermitage. At last she was free of her attackers.

On January 18, 1829, the president-elect left Nashville on a steam packet to travel to Washington for his inauguration. Houston was at the wharf to see him off. The two friends discussed political matters, and Sam stated that shortly thereafter his candidacy for a second term would be announced. In addition, there was further important news of a more personal nature to communicate: in four days he would take unto himself a bride, a daughter of the Allen family. Jackson, who knew the family well, gave Sam and Eliza his blessings and wished them a happy marriage.

By candlelight on January 22, 1829, Governor Sam Houston stood beside Eliza Allen in the drawing room of Allendale, the home of her parents John and Laetitia Allen. The father of the bride smiled in approbation, and with the socially elite of the county as witnesses the ceremony was presided over by the Reverend Dr. William Hume, pastor of Nashville's Presbyterian Church. President Jackson sent the couple Rachel's prized silver service as a wedding gift.

Colonel Allen was a prosperous and politically powerful land-owner in Gallatin, a town about thirty miles northeast of Nashville. Sam had known him for some years and had even served in Congress with his brother Robert. Allen loved to entertain at his estate, and the Andrew Jacksons were frequent guests of the genial and gracious colonel. Through Jackson, Robert, and his own mixing ability, Houston was a welcome visitor to the Allens' spacious white home on the Cumberland River. He had originally met their eldest child when she was no more than thirteen or fourteen and a youthful student at the nearby Gallatin Academy, where she was studying literature, languages, and deportment. Already she was an excellent horsewoman.

Just when Houston's thoughts began turning from friendship to love with the petite Eliza is not known, but it could have started at a ball he attended in 1828 during a political campaign with Jackson at the Brittain Drake home on the Nashville Pike. The nineteen-year-old Eliza[5] attended this ball in the company of the Carutherses, some of her Lebanon relatives. Sam always had an eye for pretty women, and this grown-up creature with blonde tresses and blue-gray, almost violet, eyes was a far cry from the youthful girl in pigtails he had known so long. He was almost thirty-six, but apparently the almost seventeen-year discrepancy in their ages meant nothing to him. In any event, those horseback rides to the Allen residence became more frequent and Sam once more had matrimony on his mind. In a letter to his cousin John, dated November 10, 1828, he confided: "I am not married but it may be the case in a few weeks, and should it — *you* shall *hear* of it, before the newspapers can reach you." [6]

The newlyweds spent their wedding night under the roof of Eliza's parents. The next day they mounted their horses and started the journey to Nashville. Due to inclement weather they stopped short of their destination and spent the night at Locust Grove, the home of Martha and Robert Martin. It was a short ride the following day to Nashville, where they were put up for a few days at the home of one of Sam's many cousins, Robert McEwen. As Tennessee at that time had no governor's mansion for its chief executive, the couple established permanent residence at the Nashville Inn on the north side of Nashville's courthouse square.

Eight days after the marriage, the governor announced that he was a candidate for reelection. His predecessor in office, William Carroll, who was now eligible to run again, had announced his candidacy the day before the Houstons' wedding.

Now that he was married, Sam could look back with satisfaction to what he had accomplished since his resignation from the army. Just eleven years previously he had ridden into Nashville as a penniless ex-army officer. In the intervening years he had been admitted to the bar — after only six months of study. He had won the office of district attorney general and followed that by establishing a successful law practice. The state militia had elected him major general, and he had been accepted in the best circles of Lebanon and Nashville. The many powerful friends he had acquired had helped him with a political career that saw him serve two terms

53

as congressman, followed by his election to the governorship of Tennessee. The upcoming election would be hard fought against a strong opponent, but he was popular and had every confidence the voters would return him to office. With a beautiful and charming bride by his side as an asset, and with his patron Jackson to take office in the White House within a few weeks, his Star of Destiny was shining at its brightest — perhaps it would shine even brighter if he followed Jackson into the executive mansion in Washington.

Sam did not know it, but that star was soon to flicker out like a fading rocket bereft of its momentum.

It was Saturday, April 11, 1829, and the two candidates for the governorship met in a debate at Cockrell's Spring. To help draw an audience and to provide extra entertainment for the occasion, Sheriff Willoughby Williams had provided the local militia to hold a muster and drill. During the debate, the sheriff roamed through the large gathering, listening to the murmurings of the crowd and their comments regarding the two rivals. Afterwards, the sheriff reported to Houston with good news. The crowd, he said, was for Sam. Other sources also confirmed the governor was making excellent progress in his campaign and predicted victory. The two old friends conversed briefly, and Williams later reported to others he had left Houston "in high spirits." The sheriff then left on a journey, returning to Nashville on April 16. He proceeded immediately to the Nashville Inn and was greeted by the clerk, Daniel F. Carter. "Have you heard the news?" Carter inquired. "General Houston and his wife have separated, and she has returned to her father's home." [7]

The sheriff was a close and loyal friend of Sam's. Years previously he had stood beside him while he picked up the silver dollar and joined the army, and later on had met the stretcher bearers when they were bringing Lieutenant Houston home to die. As soon as he heard the news from Carter, he immediately went upstairs to Houston's suite and found him alone with Dr. John Shelby. Houston was depressed and highly distraught. He admitted the separation had occurred but beyond that was noncommittal. He would never discuss the cause to anyone. Williams then left his friend and the doctor alone and returned to his office.

At the time of the wedding, if Sam was under the impression his new bride was in love with him he was quickly disillusioned. From the first it seems evident that Eliza did not love Sam. At the time of Sam's courtship she was in love with another man and apparently had never told Houston. With as many women as he had known and affairs of the heart he had had, it is puzzling that he did not sense Eliza's true feelings toward him, or how he could mistake just friendship for love and realize the girl did not return his affections. There is no doubt that Sam loved Eliza, and perhaps this was truly a case of where the phrase "love is blind" came fully into play. Too, with Sam's superb self-confidence it is possible he thought that with time he could overcome her feelings and win her love.

Did Eliza tell her parents of her true feelings for her suitor? For the Allen family this handsome, popular man whose political star was on the ascendancy would be a fine match for their daughter. He was governor of the state and had an excellent chance of being reelected. He had the friendship and backing of the president of the United States and might well follow Old Hickory into the White House. The colonel genuinely liked Houston. It would not be to the Allens' disadvantage to have their daughter make an alliance with a man who could conceivably make her first lady of the land, and it would not be the first time parents have overridden the objections of reluctant daughters and pointed out the advantages of marrying someone of prominence and with still better opportunities in the future.[8]

Whatever the couple's feelings toward each other, matters seem to have come to a head after Sam unexpectedly returned from a campaign journey. There were all sorts of rumors and unsubstantiated suppositions: Houston had found Eliza weeping and burning old love letters . . . he had found her in the arms of another man (although there seems to be absolutely no credence to the latter). In any event, it seems she was told by Houston he did not expect her to be his slave and that she should return to her family. Some authors state that in a jealous rage he accused her of infidelity. Whether Houston actually made this remark or not, Colonel Allen later told relatives and intimates his daughter had been sent home because Houston questioned her virtue. Sam's version is unknown as he refused to talk in public or private. He was reported as commenting, "The marriage was as unhappy as it was short, owing to conditions about which far more has been conjectured than known by the world." [9] Sam, a superstitious man, later recalled that as he was going to his wedding a raven had fluttered, fallen to the ground, and died in the dust on the road as he approached Allendale. He considered the raven his bird of destiny, and its cries of distress were later interpreted as a note of forewarning to his short, unhappy marriage.

Whatever actually occurred, and whatever he might have said to Eliza or accused her of, he quickly regretted his actions. On April 9, 1829, he wrote to his father-in-law:

> The most unpleasant & unhappy circumstance has just taken place in the family, & one that was entirely unnecessary at this time. Whatever had been my feelings or opinions in relation to Eliza at one time, I have been satisfied & it is now unfit that anything should be averted to. Eliza will do me the justice to say that she believes I was really unhappy. That I was *satisfied & believed her virtuous,* I had assured her on last night & this morning. This should have prevented the facts ever coming to your knowledge, & that of Mrs. Allen. I would not for millions it had ever been known to you. But one human being knew anything of it from me, & that was by Eliza's consent & wish. I would have perished first, & if mortal man had dared to charge my wife or say ought against her virtue I would have slain him. That I have & do love Eliza none can doubt, — that she is the only earthly object dear to me God will witness.
>
> The only way this matter can now be overcome will be for us all to meet as tho it had never occurred, & this will keep the world, as it should ever be, ignorant that such thoughts ever were. Eliza stands acquitted by me. I have received her as a virtuous wife, & as such I pray God I may ever regard her, & trust I ever shall.
>
> She was cold to me, & I thought did not love me. She owns that such was one cause of my unhappiness. You can judge how unhappy I was to think I was united to a woman that did not love me. This time is now past, & my future happiness can only exist in the assurance that Eliza & myself can be happy & that Mrs. Allen & you can forget the past, — forgive all & find your lost peace & you may rest assured that nothing on my part shall be wanting to restore it. Let me know what is to be done.[10]

One sentence in the above letter strikes the eye: "But one human being knew anything of it from me, and that was by Eliza's consent and wish." Who was this "one human being"? Was it Dr. John Shelby, who was a close friend of both the Allen family and Houston and had attended Eliza since her birth? Perhaps Eliza, while denying charges of infidelity, asked Sam to discuss their situation with the physician in the hope he could clear up some of her husband's suspicions.

Apparently, his conversation with the good doctor did satisfy

Sam as to Eliza's virtue, and he wrote the letter to Colonel Allen. From this letter it is apparent Sam loved Eliza intensely and wanted a reconciliation with her.

Receiving no reply from Colonel Allen, Sam mounted his horse and followed his wife to Allendale. In a highly emotional state he requested an interview with Eliza. The colonel was not at home, but the interview was granted on condition an aunt stay in the room with the couple and monitor the conversation. It was not until years later that the world learned what happened at this meeting, when, in a letter to the *Louisville Courier Journal*, one of Eliza's nieces told the story. According to Mrs. H. C. Cantrell, the niece, Sam lost all composure. With tears streaming down his face he knelt on the floor and begged Eliza to return to Nashville with him. Perhaps it was because of her aunt's forbidding presence in the room, or due to her own injured pride, but Eliza refused to accompany him back to Nashville. And with her refusal she unwittingly changed the destiny of a nation and the direction of her own life. According to the niece, the family long regretted Eliza's decision, believing that if she had returned to her husband both she and the family would have been spared many years of unhappiness.

The exact date of Sam's emotional meeting with Eliza seems to be unknown, but it was apparently April 12, the day after the campaign speeches at Cockrell's Spring. This seems likely, because if Houston had interviewed his wife prior to then and had been rejected by her, it is extremely doubtful that he would have been in the "high spirits" his friend the sheriff reported him to be in after the political debate.

For years the wall of silence erected by the two principals in this romance withstood the best efforts of cracking, but slowly various chinks and crevices appeared in that wall. Many years after the event, some of Sam's thoughts on his wedding night came to light when the *New York Tribune* of November 13, 1880, carried an article written by the Reverend Dr. George W. Samson, Houston's pastor in Washington when he was senator between 1846 and 1859. According to Dr. Samson, Eliza had cried while putting on her wedding dress and Sam noticed that during the ceremony her hands were trembling as he slipped his ring on her finger. When alone in their bedchamber that evening he remarked on her nervousness, "which convinced him some secret had not been revealed." His sympathy and gentleness and his assurance that "he would work her no injury" prompted Eliza to confess that her "affections had been pledged to another . . . and that filial duty had

57

prompted her acceptance of his offer of marriage." According to Dr. Samson, the couple had "rested" apart that night, with Houston on a couch. In the morning the newlyweds agreed to act before the world as if theirs was a normal situation.

In 1884 Dr. William Carey Crane, former president of Baylor University, published his book *Life and Select Literary Remains of Sam Houston of Texas.* Dr. Crane had known Houston's third and last wife, Margaret Lea Houston, since 1839 when she was still Margaret Lea. About two years before her death, Dr. Crane had a long interview with Margaret and at her specific request undertook the task of writing Houston's biography. From Sam's lips, she told Dr. Crane, she heard the only clue he ever gave anyone as to what had transpired. The story was substantially the same as related in Dr. Samson's version with one addition: there was no charge of infidelity on Sam's part, and no admission of the same on Eliza's part.

In their book *Tennessee and Tennesseans,* published in 1913, the authors Will T. Hale and Dixon L. Merritt reveal an incident written by Martha Martin in her unpublished "Reminiscences." Mrs. Martin, hostess for the newly married couple, was glancing out the window as Sam was enthusiastically engaged in a snowball fight with the two young Martin daughters. As she later recalled, Eliza was coming down the stairs.

> I said to her: it seems as if General Houston is getting the worst of the snowballing; you had better go out and help him. Looking seriously at me, Mrs. Houston said: "I wish they would kill him." I looked astonished to hear such a remark from a bride of not yet forty-eight hours, when she repeated in the same voice, "yes, I wish from the bottom of my heart that they would kill him" . . . after breakfast they mounted their horses and went to Nashville, stopping at the Nashville Inn. We called several times at the inn, but never saw them together after their departure from our home.[11]

Martha Martin, a very tactful lady, never repeated to the governor this wholly unexpected statement.

We may wonder what in the world caused Eliza to make such an astounding remark. Was it because Houston tried to force himself on his young bride in an effort to secure his connubial rights? We shall never know. That disparaging remark may have passed Eliza's lips, but nothing of the sort occurred the few days the Houstons spent with the McEwens before settling in their quarters at the Nashville Inn. Mrs. McEwen later stated the couple seemed as affectionate toward each other as any married pair she had ever seen. Although they were not too gregarious, she assumed their reserve was due to the fact they had so recently wed.

Sam was close-mouthed about the affair, but what of Eliza? What were her thoughts, and did she confide in anyone other than her parents? She did to at least one person, and that under a pledge of strict secrecy. Balie Peyton was some six or seven years older than Eliza and a friend of long standing, although never a suitor. To his direct question of what happened, Eliza recounted her version of the romance and separation.

> I left General Houston because I found he was a demented man. I believe him to be crazy! He is insanely jealous and suspicious. He required of me to promise not to speak to anyone, and to lock myself in my room if he was absent even for a few moments, and this when we were guests in my own aunt's house! On one occasion he went away early to attend to affairs in the city of Nashville, and commanded me not to leave my room until his return. I indignantly refused to obey, and after he was gone, I found he had locked the door and carried off the key, leaving me a prisoner until late at night, without food, debarred from the society of my relatives, and a prey to chagrin, mortification and hunger. He gave additional evidence of an unsound mind by his belief in ghosts — he was timid and averse to being alone at night on account of these imaginary and supernatural influences, though ready to cope with any sort of foe in the flesh in the daytime. I should never have consented to marry him had I not been attracted by his brilliant conversation and his handsome and commanding presence. I parted from General Houston because he evinced no confidence in my integrity and had no respect for my intelligence, or trust in my discretion. I could tell you many incidents to prove this, but I would not say, or do, anything to injure him.[12]

Eliza had another reason which she did not tell Peyton, but which she did tell to members of her family, and many years later to her son-in-law Dr. William D. Haggard. The wound from the barbed arrow Houston received at the Battle of Horseshoe Bend had never fully healed. It left a running discharge through the wall of the abdomen, expelling an offensive odor. This was unpleasant for Houston and most likely revolting to a sensitive young woman such as Eliza.

CHAPTER 7

The Leader Steps Down

Billy Carroll was a successful Nashville hardware merchant and steamship owner who loved being governor. He had ably served with Old Hickory throughout the Creek War and had been second-in-command at the Battle of New Orleans. After the cessation of hostilities he, like Sam, had been close to Jackson and involved in the political arena. Having served three successive terms as governor, beginning with the 1821 election, under the Tennessee constitution he was ineligible to run in 1827 so had supported Houston for the position. He thought he had a tacit understanding with the latter that after one term in office Sam would step aside and let Carroll once again run for his beloved office. The news that Sam did not intend to relinquish the reins and was planning on running for a second term angered him. He felt betrayed and became Sam's lifelong enemy. He wanted his office back and was determined to get it.

In the early footwork for the governorship, Jackson was playing it close to his vest. He sincerely liked both men and was hesitant to commit himself to make a choice between them. Carroll was hoping for Jackson's support. At the same time, Houston was confident he would be the eventual beneficiary and receive Old Hickory's endorsement.

The news of Houston's marital difficulties was a godsend to

Carroll and his supporters, and they left no stone unturned in their efforts to take every advantage of Sam's misfortune. While Sam waited in vain for a reply to his letter to Colonel Allen, all sorts of tales and rumors suddenly were whispered about in the streets: Houston's loose living among the Indians . . . his previous broken engagements . . . his heavy drinking . . . the duel he had fought . . . all sorts of accusations of bed-chamber brutalities and worse.[1] The Carroll supporters made sure that all the malicious gossip was sped to all corners of Tennessee by the fastest means. What should have been a private matter was not kept private; it was sacrificed on the altar of public opinion and shamelessly exploited by a ruthless politician's ambition.

The usual fair-weather friends disappeared quickly from sight, but Sam had many loyal friends who stuck with him in his hour of agony. To none of them would he give an explanation as to what had occurred, and when he was urged by them to answer the gossip-mongers he refused. He later commented:

> Unfortunately for the peace of society, there is everywhere a class of impertinent busybodies, who make it their special business to superintend and pry into the domestic affairs of their neighbors; and as curiosity must be gratified at any expense of private character, and such persons always like to believe the worst, the secrets of no family are exempt from their malignant intrusions . . . this is a painful, but it is a private matter. I do not recognize the right of the public to interfere in it . . .[2]

Among those who came to offer their friendship and express their confidence in him was James P. Clark, whose friendship with Sam went back to their boyhood days in eastern Tennessee. Another old friend who dropped by was the respected chief justice of the Tennessee Supreme Court, John H. Overton. The judge, like Sam, was a veteran of the War of 1812 and the two men had much in common. They both belonged to Cumberland Lodge No. 8 in Nashville, and Judge Overton had twice been Worshipful Master. He came, he explained, "solely as philosophy and friendship could serve in an hour of need."[3]

Others who spent much time with Houston were Dr. Shelby and the faithful sheriff Willoughby Williams, who reported that crowds were clamoring to know what the whole affair was about, and that Sam was being burned in effigy. To the accusers, Houston's silence seemed to confirm all the base stories being circulated.

Williams urged Houston to speak out but to no avail. Sam responded:

> . . . remember, whatever may be said by the lady or her friends, it is no part of the conduct of a gallant and generous man to take up arms against a woman. If my character cannot stand the shock, let me lose it.[4]

Ironically, it was during this time that Jackson, who had been sworn in as president only a few weeks previously, finally made up his mind to give Houston his support for governor. He had known nothing of Sam's troubles, as it took two weeks for news of the happenings in Tennessee to reach Washington. He wrote a letter to Carroll with an offer of an ambassadorship to South America, calculating he would drop out of the race. He was too late. With the mud being thrown at Houston, Carroll was scenting an easy victory over his hapless opponent and would have none of Jackson's offer.

In these moments of despair the governor was spending all of his time in his quarters at the Nashville Inn. Like a punch-drunk prizefighter beaten beyond his endurance, he could not, or would not, defend himself. The entreaties of his friends to make some explanation to satisfy the demands of the public were refused.

Apparently, Houston's matrimonial problems had been weighing so heavily on his mind that he carelessly released some information to the wrong person. Donald Braider, in *Solitary Star*, relates how David Donelson, one of Andrew Jackson's numerous nephews, noted that in a conversation with Sam in March after the wedding the governor had discussed a "grand scheme" for stirring up a revolution of the white settlers of Texas against the Mexican authorities.[5] According to Donelson, one William Wharton was Houston's principal agent in this venture, and he had just returned from Texas where he had been active in such an undertaking. Wharton was to keep Sam apprised of the situation and let him know when the time was ripe to go to Texas and take personal command of the situation. It had long been known that the governor was interested in Texas. As early as 1822 he had engaged in some land speculation there, and only a couple of years previously had discussions with friends about that western area.

In the best of times Sam was a heavy drinker, and with a hard campaign at hand and matrimonial problems, he might have confided to Donelson more than he intended to about his Texas schemes while seeking surcease in the bottle. Donelson relayed the information to his brother, A. J., who had access to Jackson in the White House by virtue of being not only his private secretary but also his nephew. He suggested Houston be kept under surveillance. Jackson followed this advice and from then on Sam was under observation of one H. Haralson, who had met Houston previously in the tap room of the Nashville Inn. Regular reports on the governor's activities were made either to Donelson or the secretary of war, Maj. John Eaton.

From every street corner the yells of the mob became more frequent. Though no one knew anything, Sam's steadfast silence let the scandal-mongers and rumor merchants have full play. It was said that Sam had "wronged" his bride and a banner reading PURITY — IN DEFENSE OF WOMAN'S HONOR — PURITY was carried by the howling mob. Still the governor would make no explanation. Suddenly, placards appeared publicly "posting" him as a coward. This was more than Sam could take. He — who had risked his life and almost lost it at Horseshoe Bend, and had engaged in a duel over a silly matter — branded a coward?

With a few friends he left his quarters at the inn and slowly walked around the square, surveying the hostile crowd. They shrank back. No one had the courage to brand Sam Houston a coward to his face; if one did, it is doubtful that person would have seen the sun set. Houston later stated that "the streets of Nashville would have flowed with blood had I been attacked." [6]

The Reverend Dr. William Hume arrived at the Nashville Inn, summoned by his good friend Houston. In addition to officiating at Houston's wedding, Hume had been a fellow member with Sam in the Tennessee Antiquarian Society. He had also conducted the funeral services for Rachel Jackson at the Hermitage.

Houston outlined the reason he sought the interview. It was a personal matter. He was not a member of a church but he wanted the clergyman to baptize him. [7] As stunned as everyone else by the split between the couple he had so recently wed, Dr. Hume took the request under advisement. He would discuss the matter with the Reverend Obadiah Jennings, another pastor of the First Presbyterian Church. The two clergymen, whose job it was to save souls, decided not to save Houston's soul and declined to officiate at a baptism.

Who can imagine the emotional torment this unhappy man was going through as he awaited an answer from Colonel Allen — an answer that never came. Not only was he rejected by his wife and her family, but he was rejected by two members of the clergy when he sought religious solace. At low ebb mentally, he decided to resign the governorship and seek exile.

To historians decades after the event it is still puzzling to consider why Houston would not defend himself against the base charges and rumors flying about, and decided to relinquish his high office. One clue might be in the Houston character. Sam had many outstanding qualities — generosity, leadership, loyalty, honesty, personal magnetism, compassion. At the same time, he was a human being and had his faults. He was an impetuous man, given at times to impetuous acts for comparatively minor reasons. In his youth he had left his home for three years to reside among the Indians because he could not take his brothers' needling. His resignation from the army, in which he had intended to make his life's career, was due in large measure to minor matters that another man might easily have taken in stride. But perhaps George Creel, in his *Sam Houston, Colossus in Buckskin,* (p.36), has the correct answer. According to Creel,

> One of Houston's most marked characteristics was deep and almost childlike reverence for women. To him they were superior beings, and what wrongs and injustices they inflicted were to be borne by men without reply or reprisal. Any other course of conduct stamped a man as a scoundrel and a blackguard. Not for him to drag his bride through a divorce court, with its shabby business of charge and counter-charge, its public gossip and invitation to obscence surmise. Better the decency and dignity of oblivion, even though it meant the end of hope, the death of ambition.

Sheriff Williams was with Sam in his quarters and once again asked Sam to explain the situation. Once again, Sam refused. On April 16, 1829, Houston wrote his resignation of the office of governor at his desk and gave it to a clerk to be copied. When it was returned to him he signed it in a bold, quick hand and asked Williams to deliver it to Gen. William Hall, Speaker of the Tennessee Senate, who would succeed as governor. With that letter vanished his political career in Tennessee and, if he had ever had them, his dreams of residing in the White House.

> Sir: It has become my duty to resign the office of chief magistrate of the State, & to place in your hands the authority & responsibility, which on such an event, devolves on you by the provisions of the Constitution . . .[8]

After his resignation he spent a week in his rooms with various friends, his two most constant companions being the sheriff and Dr. Shelby. He put his personal affairs in order, burned all of his personal correspondence, and sold most of his possessions, keeping two saddles. To his old chum James P. Clark he gave his little white dog named Hero. He sent a thoroughbred colt to the Hermitage, to be kept with Jackson's thoroughbreds.

In the early morning of April 23, 1829, a group of silent men, including Sheriff Williams and Dr. Shelby, left the Nashville Inn and headed for the steamboat landing on the Cumberland River. One of the group was a tall man wearing an Indian blanket over old clothes. It was the resigned governor. Boarding the packet *Red Rover,* he signed the register as Samuels. He was headed for the Cherokee Nation in the Arkansas Territory and was accompanied by the mysterious H. Haralson. The following day Dr. Hume wrote: "*Sic Transit Gloria Mundi.* Oh, what a fall for a major general, a member of Congress, and a Governor of so respectable a state as Tennessee." [9]

Traveling in a northwesterly direction, the *Red Rover* was about sixty miles from Nashville when it stopped at Clarksville. Two men, heavily armed, boarded the ship. They were members of the Allen family and demanded an audience with Houston. Their excitement, they stated, was caused because Houston's sudden departure had given rise to the "rumor that he had been goaded to madness and exile by detecting our sister in crime." They demanded Sam either give his written denial to the story or else return and "prove it."

Abandoning his incognito, Sam declined their request. He called for the captain, and "in the presence of the captain and these well-known gentlemen," requested his visitors to "publish in the Nashville papers that if any wretch ever dares to utter a word against the purity of Mrs. Houston, I will come back and write the libel in his heart's blood." [10]

The former governor was a despondent man as the *Red Rover* slowly made its way down the river. With plenty of time to indulge in remorseful reflection, he contemplated the bitter disappointment his actions would give to General Jackson, and to the failure of his marriage. He even contemplated suicide by jumping overboard when, as he later wrote,

> at that moment . . . an Eagle swooped down near my head, and then, soaring aloft with wildest screams, was lost in the rays of the

65

setting sun. I knew that a great destiny waited for me in the West.[11]

Sam may have left Tennessee under vituperation and in disgrace, but in his refusal to defend himself against vicious accusations, to utter one word against the woman he loved, he proved himself a true Houston. Sam, descended from gentlemen, was undoubtedly a gentleman. He had class.

BOOK TWO

The Outcast

— Courtesy Barker Texas History Center,
University of Texas at Austin

CHAPTER 8

Colonneh Returns Home

The steamboat *Red Rover* slowly plied its northwesterly course on the Cumberland toward Cairo, Illinois, and Sam started growing a beard, vowing never to shave it off. Very little is known of his traveling companion, the congenial Mr. Haralson, except that he was an Irishman who had shown up at the Nashville Inn a few months previously and quickly became a frequent patron of that inn's celebrated bar. If it ever occurred to the former governor to wonder why a comparative stranger would want to accompany him in his exile, it was not mentioned in any of his writings.

The two friends kept largely to themselves, doing some heavy drinking, and Haralson soon proved himself the equal of Sam in his endeavors to reach the bottom of a bottle. Occasionally, the two would join some of the other passengers in a game of poker. It is reputed that Sam left Nashville with a male slave in tow and lost possession of him at a card table, but there are no definite facts concerning this.

Houston and Haralson disembarked at Cairo. For eighteen dollars they purchased a flatboat and hired a boatman with two dogs. They also hired a young, free, black man. After stocking the flatboat with provisions, they started down the Mississippi for their next port of call — Memphis. At Memphis fresh supplies were taken aboard, and the party continued southward down the Father of Waters until it reached Helena, a very small hamlet of some twenty cabins and six grog shops on the eastern border of Arkansas, just across the river from Mississippi. It was at Helena, and probably in one of the saloons, that Sam first encountered James Bowie.

Jim Bowie, reputedly the inventor of the famous Bowie knife,[1] was some six years Houston's junior and was already well known in the South. Born in Logan County, Kentucky,[2] he had moved westward and now he and his brother Rezin were the prosperous owners of a cotton plantation and sawmill in Louisiana. From time to time they supplemented their income by engaging in slave-running with the notorious pirate Jean Laffite. Although not making his permanent home there yet, Bowie had been to Texas several times and no doubt he and Sam discussed that area with all its future possibilities.

The Houston party embarked once more on their flatboat and went downriver until it intersected with the Arkansas River. Turning once more on a northwesterly course they reached Little Rock, the capital of the territorial government. In all, the trip from Nashville had taken about two leisurely weeks, and during the course of it Houston remarked to Haralson he had changed his mind; he was bound for the Rocky Mountains and would not be stopping with the Cherokees. He was going to create an empire out west. Secretary of War Eaton was promptly informed of this scheme by Haralson.[3]

At Little Rock the former governor dismissed the boatman, and he and Haralson surveyed the city for a few days. While there, Houston encountered Charles Noland, the son of a friend of his in happier times. Houston was still drinking heavily, but apparently was in a cheerful frame of mind. To young Noland he outlined his Rocky Mountain plan and stated he was going to be the first emperor. What Noland thought of Sam's idea is not known, but he promptly set pen to paper and on May 11 wrote his father, William, in Virginia a report of the encounter:

> General Houston arrived here three days since on his way to join the Indians — Merciful God! is it possible that society can be deprived of one of its greatest ornaments, and the United States of one of her most valiant sons, through the dishonor and baseness of a woman? He converses cheerfully, made a great many inquiries after you. He will stay this winter with the Cherokees and probably will visit the warm spring . . . this summer. He wishes to go to the Rocky Mountains, to visit that tract of country be-

tween the mouth of the Oregon and California Bay. He came with a rifle on his shoulder. General Jackson will certainly persuade him to come back from the woods.[4]

In Washington, President Jackson was following Houston's activities with puzzlement and sadness. "My God," he wrote his friend, Congressman John J. McLemore, on April 30, "is the man mad?" [5]

There is nothing in Houston's character or record to suggest that his planned "Rocky Mountain Alliance" was simply the ramblings of a man whose mind was clouded with drink. His eye had long been on the west, on Texas and Mexico, and he was a person of great intelligence and ambition. It was around this time he wrote a congressman friend that he expected "to conquer Mexico or Texas, and be worth two millions in two years." [6]

About the same time Noland was writing his father, Houston was composing a letter to Jackson. This letter was a lengthy one in which he stated he would be leaving in two hours for his old friend, Chief Jolly, of the Cherokees. He described himself as

the most unhappy man now living, whose honor, so far as depends upon himself, is not lost, I can not brook the idea of your supposing me capable of an act that would not adorn, rather than blot the escutcheon of human nature.

Sam apparently had been getting some feedback from Washington as to his plans for the future, because he continues:

This remark is induced, by the fact, as reported to me, that you have been assured that I mediated an enterprize calculated to injure, or involve my country, and to compromit the purity of my motives.

. . . to you, any suggestions on my part would be idle, and on my part, as man, ridiculous . . . you have seen my private and official acts — to these I *refer* you — To what would they all amount, and for what would I live? but for my own honor, and the honor and safety of my country? . . . Yet I am myself, and will remain, the proud and honest man! I will love my country and my friends . . .[7]

The letter continues with an offer to give information at any time he can of matters that concern the administration, and says he will cheerfully do anything he can to help keep peace between the Indians and the whites. He concludes by wishing "that Jackson may live long and his days be happy." [8]

Houston and Haralson, accompanied by the freeman, proceeded on the next stage of their journey to Fort Smith by a com-

71

bination of the steam packet *Facility* and horseback.[9] Along the way they picked up a new acquaintance, John Linton. Outside Fort Smith the three men indulged in a drunken orgy dedicated to Bacchus, the god of wine. They built a huge fire and, according to their rules, as each man took a drink he would then remove an article of clothing, throwing it into the blazing fire. By the time they were all devoid of clothing, they fell into a drunken slumber around the fire. The next morning when Sam and Haralson awakened they dressed in spare clothing and left the unfortunate snoring Linton to sober up as best he could. The fact that he was naked and without clothing or funds seemed a huge joke to them.

The steam packet *Facility* was primarily a cargo vessel which regularly plied its way from New Orleans to Little Rock, Fort Smith, and thence to Cantonment Gibson,[10] its furthermost point. Stopping at all the river towns to discharge or take on cargo, it brought to the frontier people the latest gossip and news from the outside world. To the cantonment the *Facility* brought supplies, provisions, new military personnel and, since 1827, displaced Indians from the East. On the return journey to New Orleans, the packet was laden with pelts destined for John Jacob Astor's American Fur Company. The last leg of the wandering Houston's journey was to Webber's Falls, a short distance south of Cantonment Gibson. As the *Facility* was approaching the falls, one of the soldiers aboard ship lighted a signal gun that was used to alert the soldiers at the cantonment that the supply boat was approaching. The gun exploded, killing several people and damaging much of the cargo.

The venerable chief, Oolooteka, was at the landing to greet his son Colonneh when the latter disembarked that moonlit evening in May. The old man was now in his sixties. His dwelling was at Tahlontusky on the east bank of the Illinois near its intersection with the Arkansas. He had been kept informed of the Raven's coming by Indian messengers, and with torchlights held by slaves, he and his retinue of many braves of the Cherokee Nation had proceeded to the landing.

The greeting between the two men was warm and affectionate. Charles Lester later described it in his book about Houston:

> The old chief threw his arms around him and embraced him with great affection. "My son," said he, "eleven winters have passed since we met. My heart has wandered often where you were; and I heard you were a great chief among your people. Since we parted . . . I have heard that a dark cloud had fallen on the white path you were walking, and when it fell in your way you turned your thoughts

72

to my wigwam. I am glad of it — it was done by the Great Spirit . . . We are in trouble and the Great Spirit has sent you to us to give us council, and take trouble away from us. I know you will be our friend, for our hearts are near to you, and you will tell our sorrows to the great father, General Jackson. My wigwam is yours — my home is yours — my people are yours — rest with us." [11]

Although eleven winters had passed since adoptive father and son had last met, the two had kept in touch through friends all those years and John Jolly was well aware of the great cloud that had descended upon the Raven.

When the weary Houston put his head to rest that night in the old chief's wigwam "after the gloom and the sorrows of the past few weeks," he said he felt "like a weary wanderer, returned at last to my father's home." [12]

To modern Americans the word "wigwam" brings to mind a teepee or thatched hut dwelling used by the Plains Indians. Such a description would not do justice to Chief Jolly's home. His residence, known as Wigwam Illinois, was a large and comfortable home of European style, very similar to the one he had previously owned in Tennessee. The latter had been described by Return Jonathan J. Meigs, agent to the Tennessee Cherokees, as "one of the finest homes in the South." [13] Another author described Jolly's lodgings as "magnificent, almost a palace in those days, with large porticos and yards tended by slaves." [14]

George Catlin, the distinguished American painter of Indians, spent several years traveling among various tribes in different areas of the United States. He met Jolly and painted his portrait. In his writings of the chief he made the following description:

> This man, like most of the chiefs, as well as a very great proportion of the Cherokee population, has a mixture of white and red blood in his veins, of which, in this instance, the first seems decidedly to predominate. [15]

His portrait of Jolly reveals an intelligent looking gentleman, quite handsome. Dressed largely in American-style clothes of the day, he is wearing a headband and easily looks the part of the chief he was.

Oolooteka, since the death of his aged brother Tahlontusky, was now principal chief of the Cherokee Nation West, a position he would hold until his death in 1838. He had prospered in his new surroundings. He had been a wealthy man in Tennessee and he was a wealthy man now. In addition to having a fine home, he lived well, as befitting the wealth, dignity, and position he held. Ten or twelve slaves took care of his large plantation, and he owned not less than 500 head of cattle. His wigwam was always open to the many visitors he had, and he fed them well at his bountiful table. He never slaughtered less than a beef a week for his welcome guests.[16]

This, then, was the home Houston had returned to in his hour of stress to lay his weary head.

There was good reason for Chief Jolly's greeting to be a warm and sincere one. He was truly glad to see Houston again after those eleven winters, and sorry he was troubled in mind and spirit. Twenty years had passed since Sam had first gone to Hiwassie Island as a youth in his early teens and not only been made welcome among the Cherokees but adopted into their tribe. Many of the chief's warriors had fought with Houston at the Battle of Horseshoe Bend and witnessed his bravery — and among Indians, bravery always commands respect. The chief had foreseen the good qualities Houston displayed and was proud that he had risen so high in the councils of the white man before resigning as governor. Indians are loyal to those they love and admire, and he meant it when he told Sam "my home is yours, my people are yours."

While the Raven was staying at Jolly's wigwam, he changed his appearance. Breaking his vow never to shave, he trimmed his beard into a goatee and kept a mustache, plaiting his chestnut hair into a long queue as he had done years previously while teaching school. Discarding white man's clothing, he wore a shirt of white doeskin, brilliantly decorated with beads. His leggings were of elaborately ornamented yellow leather extending to his thighs. For headdress he sometimes wore a circlet of feathers, sometimes a turban of figured silk, and over his shoulders was negligently thrown a bright blanket.[17] It is said that he "refused to speak English during his stay in the Cherokee Nation and to have used an interpreter upon occasion when he talked with other white men." [18]

Judge W. W. Oldham of Arkansas had known Houston in Tennessee, and from time to time visited Cantonment Gibson. He reported he "saw Houston dressed like a Cherokee; he would never then speak English to anyone, and a deep melancholy caused him to avoid all intercourse with white men." [19] If Sam did refuse to speak English, surely it was only temporarily, as his stay in the Cherokee Nation lasted nearly four years. At the beginning of his stay he was still emotionally drained from his recent unhappy experiences in Tennessee, and he probably wanted to become as much like his Indian brothers as possible. But in the next several years he simply had too much contact with whites at Cantonment Gibson, Indian agencies, trading posts, and on his many travels in the nation to keep up the handicap of having to converse through an interpreter. The inconvenience was just too great.

By no means was the Raven alone among strangers in his new surroundings. Many of the friends he had known in his sojourn among the Cherokees on the friendly banks of Hiwassie Island were here, among them Col. Walter Webber and Capt. John Rogers, who had been a trader among the Cherokees for forty years. And there were the captain's sons, James and John, Jr., Sam's boyhood companions of so many years ago. All these were prosperous men in the territory, owning vast plantations, trading posts, sawmills, and salt works, and having tremendous influence in the tribe.

It might have been Sam's original intention to use the Cherokee land as just a way station on his journey to the Rocky Mountains, but if so, he quickly changed his mind. Haralson lost no time in reporting that fact to Secretary of War Eaton.[20]

It was true that Jolly and his people had prospered in their new lands beyond the Mississippi, but they had many problems and they wanted help from Houston — help that Sam was more than willing to give. In 1818, when John Jolly had reluctantly been persuaded with his Cherokees to leave their eastern lands, he had moved his followers westward and settled close to his brother Tahlontusky on the Arkansas River at Lake Dardanelle, near what is today Dardanelle, Arkansas. It was thought this would be their last move; that they would have the hunting grounds to themselves and be out of the way of the white men. The assumption was false. Disregarding the numerous treaties previously made, the whites kept pushing farther west, encroaching on Indian lands. Other Indian tribes were under constant pressure as well to vacate and move beyond the western border — not only from Arkansas officials but also those of the federal government. In addition, the whites wanted Lovely's Purchase, near present-day Marble City, Sequoyah County, Oklahoma.

Tribal leaders vigorously protested. They pointed out that then Secretary of War Calhoun had promised white settlers would be kept out of Lovely's Purchase in order that the Cherokees would have a hunting outlet to the western plains.[21] The Cherokees had no desire to uproot themselves again. A succession of presidents from George Washington to John Quincy Adams had signed treaties pledging that if the Indians moved from where they were located, it would be the last time. In 1818 they had been assured their relocation to Arkansas would solve the problem to everyone's satisfaction; yet, various promises made in that treaty had been unkept.

On December 28, 1827, the chiefs and headmen of the Cherokee Nation West met in council. After deliberating solemnly, they sent a delegation from the Western Cherokee Nation to Washington to discuss the dispute between the government and the Cherokees. This group included some of the Cherokees' most prominent citizens, including the famed Sequoyah and John Rogers, Jr. In addition, there were Black Fox, Thomas Graves, Thomas Maw, George Morris, and Tobacco Will. Edward W. DuVal, their agent, accompanied them, and Sam's friend James Rogers was in the delegation as interpreter. The credentials of this group "authorized them to solicit from the Government a performance of the unsettled matters pending between the Government and the Indians; particularly they were directed to request a survey of their lands in Arkansas as promised in their treaties." [22] They were also instructed to seek solutions to a number of other problems, including their longstanding rivalry with the Osages, and were given strict instructions to cede no more territory.

In Washington the delegation met with James Barbour, secretary of war under President Adams. Barbour came up with a plan to give whites not only all of Lovely's Purchase but also all of the Cherokee lands in Arkansas. His plan was to exchange the Cherokee lands for an area beyond the western boundary of the territory, and to soften the blow, he proposed to move the western boundary of Arkansas approximately forty miles to the east.

President Adams was not very sympathetic to the Indian cause, and he complained that the tribe "had already more than they have any right to claim." He conceded that the promise made by his predecessor of a western outlet "is very embarrassing, and it is scarcely imaginable that within so recent a period the President and his Secretary of War should have assumed so unwarranted an authority and have given so inconsiderate a pledge." He decided that the promises made to the Indians must give way before the "just and reasonable demands of our own people." [23]

Then Adams came up with an idea. In a maneuver designed to make the Cherokee delegation more receptive to his secretary's proposal, he announced that the tribe was entitled to only 3,194,784 acres in Arkansas. As this was several million acres less than the

Cherokees claimed, they paused and reconsidered their objections. If they refused to leave Arkansas they were faced with the threat of the government actually reclaiming land already given to the tribe.

The president's strategy worked. Despite the wishes of John Jolly and the National Council of the Western Cherokees, on May 6, 1828, the delegates concluded a treaty with the government. According to its terms, they gave up their Arkansas lands and accepted a tract beyond the western boundary of the Arkansas Territory, which was moved eastward approximately forty miles to a line running from Fort Smith to the southwestern corner of Missouri.[24] For once more abandoning their homes and farms they were given seven million acres, including several million acres of choice land in Lovely's Purchase. John Jolly and the National Council were furious — not only at the terms of the new treaty, but at the members of the delegation who had signed it. The chiefs were well aware it was highly possible that bribes had been made to various members of the delegation and that some of the party were interested in promoting their own interests by acquiring mines and salt springs on Lovely's Purchase. According to Cherokee law passed in May 1825, anyone signing an agreement to cede tribal lands was subject to the death penalty. The treaty was denounced and the delegates were found guilty of fraud by the National Council, but in the long run no death penalty was imposed. The United States Senate ratified the document, and the Cherokees had no choice. They had sadly packed up their belongings and moved. This was their situation when Houston came among them.

For years the Cherokees had had problems with the Osages. Warfare between the two tribes had been continuous from the time the first Cherokees, under the leadership of Chief Tahlontusky, had emigrated to the Arkansas Territory after the Treaty of 1808 had been signed. To some extent the treaty had alleviated some of the problems between the two tribes and they had formed an uneasy truce. There was still some grumbling about the treaty, and a party of fifteen Cherokees, suspected as being from the Red River area, had killed eight Osages. These Red River Cherokees were led by the famed Cherokee warrior Tahchee, or "Dutch," and were not under the authority of the Cherokee Nation West. They resided south of the Red River, in Mexico, and had been harassing the Osages since 1823.

With the ratification of the Treaty of 1828 by the Senate, the government was doing everything in its power to spur removal of eastern Indian tribes in Tennessee, Alabama, and Georgia to the new territory. Seven hundred Creeks were located in the lower Verdigris valley by the spring of 1828 and another five hundred arrived in the fall. Choctaws were coming in as well as Chickasaws, and as early as 1826 the region around the Red River had seen the arrival of dissident Cherokees, Shawnees, Kickapoos, and Delawares. All this was beyond the small garrison of Cantonment Towson, which was near the Red River far south of Cantonment Gibson. This constant influx of immigrants was taking up valuable living space and, worse yet, encroaching on the hunting grounds supposedly reserved for the Cherokees. And all the tribes had to contend with the wild Pawnees and other Plains Indians.

The Raven was a popular figure among the Cherokees, and he had scarcely taken up residence at Jolly's wigwam before leaders and chiefs of the seven clans gathered to greet him and indulge in talks and feasts. As they set in their council house, smoking their pipes, Colonneh sat with them and listened to them deliberate. The Cherokees were faced with several serious problems, and there were differences of opinion between various factions as to their solution. In addition to their problems with the Osages, there were those of the corrupt agents, and the government's usual failure to live up to the pledges in their signed treaties. The Cherokees were also in dispute with the Pawnees and Comanches over ownership of hunting grounds to the west, as the government had failed in its promise to run lines to determine the boundaries of each tribe. To help provide a solution and reach a meeting of minds, a grand council of the tribes was to be held in June. As a respected friend Sam was invited to attend this grand council, as was Col. Matthew Arbuckle, commander of Cantonment Gibson.

As a sweetener to sign the latest hated treaty, the government had promised the Cherokees twenty-eight dollars per capita — in the aggregate, a huge sum. When the agents paid this money, or any other monies due the Indians, they always paid in certificates instead of the gold the Indians had been promised. To the Indians, paper money was worthless, and white traders, sutlers, and agents made enormous profits by taking advantage of the Indians' cupidity and discounting the paper money at exorbitant rates of exchange. Lester quoted Houston as stating:

> It is doubtful whether a fifth part of the money, secured to them by sacred treaty ever passed into their hands, and even this fifth

78

was wrung from them for whiskey, or in gambling. Preyed upon by abandoned speculators, whole tribes were robbed of the munificent grants of Congress.[25]

Although the Cherokee Nation extended from the Verdigris to the southwest corner of Missouri to the Canadian River fork, and thence westwardly to the forks of the Canadian nearly up to the old territorial line between the Arkansas and Canadian rivers, the five or six thousand Cherokees lived in small settlements scattered all throughout the territory. While many lived in feudal splendor, there were many more who were living in semistarvation.

The chiefs of the clans knew the Raven was friendly with the new white father in Washington. Perhaps he could use his influence with Sharp Knife,[26] as they referred to Jackson, in an endeavor to solve their problems. In the capital Sharp Knife was not very sympathetic to the cause of the Indian. In fact, he hated Indians and was doing everything in his power to push through Congress a bill for the forced removal of all Indians from the eastern states to the western frontier.

Once the Raven established himself at his father's house, the word quickly passed through other tribes, white traders in the region, Indian agents, army officers at nearby Cantonment Gibson, and white settlers. He had hardly settled himself comfortably in the council meeting of the seven clans when an Osage scout rode in on a horse. The Osage was an emissary of A. P. Chouteau, a highly respected white trader who, having lived among the Osages for thirty years or more, had won their affection and respect. Chouteau urgently desired Sam to come immediately to his home in the Six Bull River Valley, approximately one hundred miles away. Houston quickly accepted the invitation. With the Osage as guide and accompanied by Haralson, they covered the distance by horse path up the Arkansas in two and a half days.

When the grand council of the Cherokees met, Colonneh was absent, off on his mission to Chouteau's. Another absentee was the commander of Cantonment Gibson, Col. Matthew Arbuckle. In his place the colonel sent two officers as observers. To them Oolooteka handed a note which said:

> I invited my son Governor Houston here to listen to what I had to say on this subject but my son had promised to attend a council of my Neighbors the Osages and could not come. I must do the best I can without him.[27]

Houston's journey to the western frontier was still of great interest to Washington and Tennessee. Jackson had heard of Houston's scheme to conquer Mexico or Texas and be worth two million in two years, and had instructed the governor of Arkansas to adopt prompt measures to put down such an illegal scheme if it was discovered to be true; also, to give him the names of all those concerned.

From Tennessee, Sam's erstwhile opponent for the governorship wrote to Jackson on May 29, 1829:

> the fate of Houston must have surprised you . . . his conduct, to say the least, was very strange and charity requires us to place it to the account of insanity. I have always looked upon him as a man of weak and unsettled mind . . . incapable of manfully meeting a reverse of fortune.[28]

CHAPTER 9

A Leader Among Tribes

Auguste Pierre Chouteau was a white-haired Frenchman of forty-three years whose father had been one of the founders of St. Louis. Until 1802, the year before the United States acquired Louisiana from France in the Louisiana Purchase, he had had an official monopoly to trade with the Osages. In that year the governor-general revoked his monopoly. Not wishing to lose that profitable commerce, Chouteau induced a number of Osage chiefs to move their bands to the Three Forks area near the Arkansas, Grand, and Verdigris rivers. Like Houston, he was sympathetic to the Indian cause and, until the Raven came into the territory, had more influence over other tribes south of the Missouri River and west to Spanish territory than any other white man. His eminently fair treatment of all Indians as a trader had enabled him to become a wealthy man, and the many furs they brought to him were sent to the American Fur Company of John Jacob Astor. He owned a vast plantation and with his wealth had brought out a carriage from St. Louis and had built a racetrack. Married to an Osage named Rosalie, he had six half-breed children. A Jesuit missionary to the Osages had baptized them in the Catholic faith, and Chouteau had engaged a tutor to supervise their education.

When the famed novelist Washington Irving visited the Southwest some three years later, he visited the Chouteau plantation, which was presided over by Chouteau's Osage wife, assisted by her sister Masina. Irving passed on to posterity a description of the residence:

> . . . a large white log house, a room at each end. An open hall with Staircase in the center. Other rooms above. In the two rooms on ground floor two beds in each room, with curtains. Whitewashed log walls — tables of various kinds, Indian ornaments, &c. In front of the house ran a beautiful clear river.[1]

Many years later, in Huntsville, Texas, the Raven owned a home virtually identical to this description, except it was not made of logs.

As the Osage scout and Houston, followed by his Sancho Panza, Haralson, arrived at Chouteau's two-story log home, they were greeted by black slaves who took their horses. The courtyard was surrounded with horses, dogs of all kinds, giggling female slaves, hens flying and cackling, wild turkeys, and tame geese.[2]

Sam and his host took to each other at once as they had much in common. Both had lived among the Indians and not only liked them but respected them as human beings. They saw the good qualities of the Indians and resented the way they had been treated by the government and their fellow whites. After a supper of fricasseed wild turkey, roast beef, venison, cake, and wild honey, all washed down with coffee, the two men got down to business. To the ex-governor it was an old and familiar story as the French trader related to him how the Indians were being exploited and robbed by unscrupulous agents and traders. He, like John Jolly, wanted Houston to report this to his friend, President Jackson, and use his influence to get rid of the corrupt agents. He had a further suggestion: why didn't Sam become an Indian agent himself?

The surroundings were pleasant, the food delicious, and there was plenty of liquor to drink. Houston and Haralson enjoyed themselves and spent several days at the Chouteau plantation enjoying the hospitality of their host. They discussed Indian affairs in general and how to effect peace among the various warring tribes. These deliberations were suddenly interrupted by the arrival of a group of Osages at Chouteau's, complaining that their agent, John F. Hamtramck, was stealing their annuities, another installment of which was due. They had been "defrauded by every agent since Old Colonel Chouteau," they said, and were determined not to accept their annuity until justice was done.[3] In a letter to Secretary of War Eaton, dated June 23, 1829, Haralson reported the event:

They had concluded not to go to receive their annuity but hearing that some strangers were in the country (which was us) they came to see us. They insisted that Genl Houston . . . and myself go with them to the agency. We told them we would go and see what passed between them and their agent.[4]

Houston, accompanied by Haralson, acquiesced to the request of the Osages and went with them to their agency at Three Forks. Among the complaints of the Osages was one to the effect that their agent, Hamtramck, had purchased one of the wives of Chief White Hair. They believed part of their annuity was being used to purchase finery for their agent's squaw.[5] Both Houston and Haralson wrote letters recommending that agent Hamtramck be dismissed and replaced by Auguste Pierre Chouteau's half-brother, Paul. Sam then rode to Cantonment Gibson, just a few miles away, and arrived without Haralson, who had disappeared into oblivion.

Cantonment Gibson, established in 1824, was located three miles up the Grand River on its eastern bank near Three Forks. Col. Matthew Arbuckle, who commanded the post until 1841, had seen hard service in the Seminole War as a member of the Seventh Infantry. Arriving in the Southwest in February 1822, he had commanded the garrison at Fort Smith until ordered by the War Department to establish a post further west. He had selected the site of Cantonment Gibson partially because a rock ledge extending into the river formed a natural landing. For several miles up from the mouth of the Verdigris there were small settlements of fur trappers and traders. When Arbuckle led his men to the Three Forks, the Osages were the only tribe with permanent villages in the area. Then the government began subdividing the area among eastern tribes who were persuaded to negotiate removal treaties. The Choctaws were the first to arrive, followed by the Cherokees, the Creeks, and the Chickasaws. On the edge of civilization, the cantonment was the farthest military outpost in the United States. When Cantonment Towson, near the Red River, was abandoned by order of the War Department in June 1829, Cantonment Gibson remained the only military outpost of the frontier of Arkansas Territory. With the high incidence of deaths due to malaria and gastrointestinal maladies suffered by the five companies of foot soldiers stationed there, the post soon earned the unflattering name of the "Channel House of the Army." [6]

The Raven was quite an attraction at the cantonment, where he helped relieve the boring lives of the officers and their ladies. He drank heavily with the officers and engaged in their frequent poker games and horseracing bets. He formed an instant rapport with Colonel Arbuckle who, at fifty-three, was still a bachelor. The two men worked frequently together in their endeavors to keep peace among the various tribes in the territory. However, the colonel intercepted and read Houston's letters and, according to instructions of the War Department, kept him under surveillance. No doubt he read Sam's letter of June 24 from Cantonment Gibson addressed to his cousin John at Washington City, in which he introduced his good friend Dr. Baylor and stated he was worthy of John's friendship. He closed by making a request: "Write to me. My letters will reach my wigwam, and they will give me happiness." [7]

The pleasant interlude at the cantonment was suddenly interrupted by a large delegation from the Creek Nation. The full council of the nation was present, including a clerk and an interpreter. Headed by Roly McIntosh, son of the late Chief William McIntosh who with his band of Creeks had fought with General Jackson in his war against the Red Sticks, the group desired an audience with Colonel Arbuckle and General Houston.

The Creeks had a plaintive story to tell. Wild Indians to the south and west harassed and terrified them. In addition, the failure of the government to honor their treaty of 1826 was causing them great hardship. They had been promised a sum of money, together with rifles, guns and ammunition, beaver traps, butcher knives, blankets, and kettles, upon their arrival in the West. For more than two years after they migrated, this solemn pledge was not kept even in part, and without traps they could not catch the beaver whose furs they expected to barter for the necessities of life.

McIntosh handed Arbuckle and Houston a memorial of nine pages dated June 22, 1829, and addressed to President Jackson listing eleven specific charges against David Brearley, their agent. They complained, among other things, that the

> agent has not tried to make us happy . . . he has connived at the introduction of spiritous liquors into Creek Nation . . . intoxication and disrespectful language to the Chiefs . . . he has speculated on the Necessities of the Indians through his Clerk by permitting him to sell flour to the Indians at the enormous price of $10 the barrell.[8]

The lengthy memorandum requested agent Brearley be removed, but at the same time expressly requested that he not be replaced by John Crowell, agent of the eastern Creeks. They had good reasons to make this request. The eastern Creeks had the same complaints against Crowell as the western Creeks against Brearley and were petitioning Jackson to dismiss him. McIntosh and his fellow braves did not want Crowell foisted upon them as a replacement.

After reading the lengthy epistle and witnessing its signing, Houston was given the document by Roly McIntosh with the request it be forwarded to General Jackson. McIntosh informed him that previous communications sent through official channels had not reached their destination. Sam complied with the request and added a note urging the various complaints be investigated.

This conference with the Creek delegation proved a very useful tool for Houston while in the Cherokee Nation because it enabled him to meet many of the leaders of the Creeks; to size them up and to be sized up by them in return. No doubt they had heard tales of his matrimonial problems and his heavy drinking. But in the flesh, the Raven impressed them with his intellect, honesty, and character.

The government's policy of moving the eastern Indian tribes to the western frontier was causing great unrest among the tribes already there. In addition to inborn hostilities among some of the tribes, they were now having to contend with Plains Indians — including Comanches and Pawnees — for the hunting of buffalo, elk, deer, and other animals that provided food, clothing, and money for them. This problem of keeping peace among the various warring factions was a serious one for Colonel Arbuckle, who had only five companies of infantry at his disposal. Dissident elements of the Cherokees, Delawares, and Shawnees had taken up residence on the Red River beyond Cantonment Towson. The Osages and Pawnees had been in conflict for years, and hostilities between them were bad: government surveyors refused to continue running the boundary line for the new Osage reservation as they were so frightened.

Arbuckle had many worries. Over their bottles of whiskey he discussed them with the Raven, who listened eagerly. He mentioned the War Department's lack of interest in furnishing him the mounted troops he had requested; he complained about Indians in the nation being frequently drunk and disorderly on liquor sold them by not only white traders but by some of the Indian traders as well, including Houston's friend, John Rogers, Jr. The biggest problem of all, he said, was that of the traders coming into the territory from St. Louis to Santa Fe, along the Santa Fe Trail. The president had ordered a detail of four companies of infantry to accompany the traders. But the colonel, whose mission it was to keep peace among the tribes and white settlers, was worried because the traders would be going through the hunting grounds of the Osage, Pawnee, Kansas, Comanche, Arapaho, and Kiowa tribes, who were at war with one another. He foresaw much trouble ahead.

Houston was quick to offer assistance. From Cantonment Gibson on June 24, 1829, he wrote the secretary of war offering to assist in any capacity. Thus, he was redeeming the promise made in the letter he had written while en route from Fort Smith to the Cherokee Nation. In the letter, Houston mentioned that the Osages and the Pawnees had been engaged in war from time immemorial and that both sides still had a considerable number of prisoners. In his opinion, an exchange of prisoners would bring the two sides to peace on reasonable terms, and if that could be accomplished, there would be very little difficulty in making peace with the other tribes. Sam thought that treaties between the several tribes and the United States could be easily secured if the United States would select someone who understood the character of the Indians to present their chiefs some trifling presents. The presents should include medals from the president. According to Sam's best information, the only tribe of all those named which had received any medals was the Osage.

Houston closed his letter by presenting the name of Col. Auguste P. Chouteau as an agent to distribute the presents, as it was his opinion Chouteau was a man of fine intellect and had the best practical knowledge of Indians of any man with whom he had ever been acquainted. If Chouteau was appointed, Sam stated, he would be glad to accompany him on the mission and give him all assistance within his power, and would accept no compensation for any services rendered.

For some reason, Colonel Arbuckle was not receptive to this idea, and the War Department, probably on his recommendation, did not take Sam up on his offer. A man not easily discouraged, Houston persisted in his recommendation and in 1832 the War Department finally accepted his offer.

The commandant of Cantonment Gibson might have been less than enthusiastic about accepting Sam's offer to accompany Chouteau on a mission to dispense medals to the various tribes, but he lost no time in procuring the Raven's help in another emergency.

A group of impatient young Cherokees, he said, desired war with the Pawnees and Comanches — against the wishes of Chief

Jolly and other elders of the nation. They had approached Chief John Smith, a belligerent Creek, with their plan to form an alliance and attack the various Plains tribes. A council and war dance was to be held July 7, 1829, in Cherokee territory at a council ground located one-quarter of a mile east of Bayou Menard, six or seven miles east of Cantonment Gibson. Would Houston attend this council and use his influence among the tribes in an endeavor to prevent war? All the tribes in the West were discontented, and the colonel was afraid the whole frontier would be set ablaze with war if matters got out of hand.

As Chief Oolooteka was too ill to attend the council, Houston pointed his horse toward Bayou Menard and went to the council as the direct representative of his foster father. Arbuckle started out with him but for some reason turned back. Houston decided to face the young braves alone. The Raven, dressed in his Indian clothes and speaking in their language, addressed the assembled Cherokees and Creeks in his most persuasive and eloquent manner. He stressed the importance and advantages of peace between all the tribes, and urged them to discard their plans to go to war. It was to no avail. Infuriated by constant harassment from other tribes and harangued by Smith, the young braves did their war dance and decided to retaliate against their enemies. Sam's eloquence was not a total failure; he did succeed in getting the hot-blooded warriors to postpone any action for fifteen days. On July 8, Houston sent Colonel Arbuckle a lengthy letter relating some of the happenings:

> After you left me last evening I attended the Dance & Talk of the Cherokee [and the] Creeks and had the mortification to witness . . . the raising of the Tomahawk of War by 7 Cherokees. The Creeks did not join . . . tho' I am sensible that Smith will use every persuasive in his power with them to [join this] impolitic war against the Pawnees and the Kimanchies. It is the project of a few restless and turbulent young men who will not yield nor listen to the Talk of their Chiefs. The great body of Chiefs of the Cherokees are most *positively opposed* to the war: and I have pointed out to them the ruinous consequences which must result to them . . .
>
> The Creeks assured me that they would not begin a war without Genl Jackson's consent, but . . . I have some fears . . . I have been informed (but vaguely) that some Osage, Choctaw, & Delewares are to join the Party, and in all make it some 250 or 300 warriors. I will not yet give up the project of stopping the Cherokees until all hope is lost, and there are yet fifteen days . . . before they will actually start for home.

It is not difficult to perceive that the most turbulent among the Cherokees are very solicitous that Cantonment Gibson should be broken up and all troops removed without the I. T. I will predict that in the event of a removal of the U.S. Troops that in less than twelve months . . . there will be waged a war the most sanguinary and savage that has raged within my recollection.[9]

Houston's oratory might have caused the Indians to postpone their warlike plans, but in the long run his efforts failed. Early the next year, a Pawnee village in Texas was devastated by Cherokees.

There was still much work to do among the tribes. Immediately after the war council at Menard Bayou, Houston mounted his horse and headed for the Choctaw agency near Fort Smith, Arkansas. At the agency he met with the agent, Capt. William McClellan, and his wife, and had some discussions with them about the plight of the Choctaws. Once the Choctaws heard of Houston's presence in the neighborhood they came to him with their woes. On July 22 Houston wrote the secretary of war stating he had addressed General Jackson on the subject. He also wrote:

an old Choctaw Chief called on me today, and complained that the white people were on their lands, & were treating them badly. They take the Choctaws houses, and will not let them go *into* them. Some emigrants have lately arrived, and have not houses to go into, and complain that Genl Jackson, in a treaty with them E of the Mississippi told them if they would come west that they should be happy, and when they have come that the whites are on their land and they are not happy. Capt McClellan furnishes them with corn and does all he can to keep and content them, but he has no power, and acts from motives of humanity . . . I have assured him that you will soon grant relief to the Indians & take such measures as their situation requires.[10]

In a postscript, the Raven concludes his letter by stating that his post office is Cantonment Gibson.

The former governor had indeed been a busy man while in the Cherokee Nation West. In little more than six weeks he had established amicable and friendly relations with the Cherokees, Osages, Creeks, and Choctaws and had extended his influence over them. In his talks with them he had stressed the advantages of peace between the various tribes and urged them to patch up their differences. His relationship with two other powerful men in the region, Colonel Arbuckle and Auguste Chouteau, were harmonious. And then he almost became a victim of the "graveyard of the army."

It was around the first of August when the Raven, after a long, lonely ride from the Choctaw agency near Fort Smith, arrived at Chief Jolly's wigwam. Deep in the grip of malaria, with yellow skin and suffering chills, the trembling Raven was carried inside by some of Jolly's slaves and placed on a pallet of corn shucks. In addition to the chants of the medicine men to ward off evil spirits, Houston was given some tea made from the bark of a Peruvian tree. It was quinine. From various whites who had brought it into the wilderness, the Indians had learned of its curative properties.[11]

It was during the thirty-eight days that Sam was recovering from his fever at his foster father's home that he received a letter from Andrew Jackson, dated June 21. Jackson revealed to his friend he had been told that Sam had in mind the illegal view of conquering Texas, and that he had declared he would in two years be emperor of that country by employing the Cherokee Indians. According to Jackson, he did not believe the story inasmuch as Sam had given his pledge of honor never to engage in any enterprise injurious to the nation. He also suggested Houston consider either becoming a missionary to the Indians or building up his political influence in the territory as a political lieutenant for Jackson.

While convalescing, the former governor was cheered by another letter, this one showing he still had friends in powerful places who thought well of him. His old regimental commander, Thomas Hart Benton, was now a successful politician from Missouri. Writing from St. Louis under date of August 15, 1829, Benton stressed he was writing for the purpose of renewing old friendship, and he hoped Houston would call upon him if he could be of service. Benton also suggested that Houston had too much energy to remain idle, and that he expected to see him in active life before long.

Still weakened from his bout with malaria, on September 19 the Raven penned a reply to Jackson. Addressing his letter to his old mentor from Cherokee Nation, in Arkansas, he begins:

> I am verry feeble, from a long spell of fever, which lasted me some 38 days, and had well nigh closed the scene of all my mortal cares, but I thank God that I am again cheered by the hope of renewed health.

To Jackson's suggestion that he become a missionary to the Indians he rejects as follows:

> To become a missionary among the Indians is rendered impossible, for a want of that Evangelical change of heart, so absolutely necessary, to a man who assumes the all important character, of proclaiming to a lost world, the mediation of a blessed Savior!

Houston continues by commenting that his interest is in political events of the world, as well as his own country, and that it is increasing rather than diminishing. He then gives a clue that his thoughts are still focused on Texas:

> If we were to judge of the future by the past, it might so happen, were I settled in a state; that I might render my aid in some future political struggle between usurpation, and rights of the people in wresting power from the hands of a corrupt Userper, and depositing it, where the spirit of the constitution, and will of the people would wish it placed. These considerations are not without their influence, for I must ever love that country and its institutions, which gave Liberty and happiness to my *kindred* and *friends!* And these blessings can only be preserved by vigilance and virtue!

There is a postscript to the letter. "I hope to take, and send you, between this and Christmas, some fine buffaloe meat for your Christmas dinner, or at furthest, by the 8th of Jany." [12]

One wonders if Jackson was serious in his suggestion that Houston become a missionary to the Indians, knowing the vivid character and disposition of this man. Although it was only a matter of a few weeks before he became a citizen of the Cherokee Nation, Sam was probably uncertain as to whether to reside permanently among his Indian friends or eventually let his restless feet take him to Texas or beyond the Rockies. A self-confident man who firmly believed in his destiny, Houston was still floundering and trying to put the pieces of his life together. Undoubtedly resentful of the fact that two of the Lord's representatives on earth had refused to acquiesce in his desire for baptism, he knew that he had nothing to offer the Indians as a missionary. He could do his friends much more good trying to redress their wrongs than by trying to save their souls.

During his stay in the Cherokee Nation, Houston was frequently in conflict with the missionaries who lived around the Cantonment Gibson area. Primarily interested in converting the tribes to Christianity, the missionaries established three mission schools for the education of the Indian children. They were jealous of Sam's influence over the Indians — not only the Cherokees but the other tribes as well. In addition, they disliked his heavy drinking and his poker playing with the officers at the nearby cantonment. His unorthodox religious views and his later marriage to a Chero-

90

kee woman shocked them; his failure to seek additional funds for their work on his first trip east disappointed them.

The Reverend Cephas Washburn, missionary to the Cherokees for many years and head of the Dwight Mission, wrote a bitter letter concerning the Raven:

> We regard the residence of such a man as Governor Houston among the Indians, as a most injurious circumstance. He is vicious to a fearful extent, and hostile to Christians and Christianity. This I would not wish to have known as coming from me, as he has very considerable influence. As an offset to his influence, I am happy to inform you of the recent arrival of Captain Vashon, the new agent.[13]

Houston respected the missionaries for their personal honesty, their character and their dedication, but on the whole he distrusted them. On a trip down the Mississippi in the winter of 1832, he had a discussion with the famous French social observer, Alexis de Tocqueville, who was traveling around the United States. When asked about Christianity among the Indians, Houston replied:

> My opinion is that to send Missionaries among them is a very poor way to go about civilizing the Indians . . . Christianity is — above the intelligence of a people so little advanced in civilization . . .[14]

Many Indians distrusted the missionaries and their endeavors. They were suspicious of all white men as they realized their lot had drastically declined since the arrival of the whites in the New World. They continually complained about the missionaries' interference in their lifestyle, traditions, beliefs, and superstitions.

White Hair, chief of the Osages, wrote President Jackson complaining about the Reverend Benton Pixley.

> Father, he has quarrelled with our men and women and we hear he has also quarrelled with all the white men who our Great Father has sent here to do us good . . . Father, we have enough of white people among us without him, even if he was good . . . He forgets his black coat . . . disturbs our peace and many other things . . .[15]

For some time several Cherokee leaders, among them John Rogers, Jr., and John Drew, were actively seeking an independent school system completely separated from Dwight Mission, and Sam and the Cherokees were encouraging the abolishment or complete removal of Union Mission, which was located north of his wigwam. Sam was of the opinion the mission was unwisely located,

91

and in 1836, several years after he had left the territory, it was finally abandoned.

One clergyman with whom the Raven was on generally good terms was Dr. Marcus Palmer of the Fairfield Mission, which was located near Tahlontusky. In Sam's opinion, Palmer was the best of the missionaries in the Cherokee Nation. Despite their friendship and mutual regard for each other, the good Reverend failed in his efforts to convert Houston and to get him to stop his heavy drinking. Houston admired the clergyman so much he and his friends encouraged the expansion of the Fairfield Mission.

CHAPTER 10

Cherokee Ambassador

In October 1829 there was great excitement among the Cherokees. It was time for their annuity to be distributed at their agency, and they were expecting $50,000 in gold to be paid under the terms of the hated treaty of 1828. In addition, they were due a bonus of $2,000, plus various other sums due under earlier treaties.

From everywhere they came: high officials of the Cherokee Nation, the lesser chiefs, even tribesmen and their squaws and children. From Fort Smith they came, and from distant Little Rock; from Cantonment Gibson and Three Forks. Various functionaries of the Indian Bureau rode in. All the feather merchants, such as traders, speculators, and the usual contingent of camp followers and prostitutes were there, and so were the soldiers from the cantonment. Among the spectators was a huge white man in Indian dress. It was the Raven.

Maj. Edward DuVal, the Indian agent of the Cherokees, made his solemn announcement: there were to be no payments made in gold. In lieu thereof, certificates of indebtedness, of paper money, would be distributed. Disappointing to the Indians though it was, to them it was an old story. Once more they had been had by their agent.

Money, as such, to the Indians had an entirely different meaning than it did to the whites. Even hard money such as gold was

93

valued lightly by the red men, and paper money to them was totally worthless. Even property held a different meaning to the red men than to the whites. No Indian owned the land he lived on — it belonged to the tribe. The Indian wanted things — things such as blankets, beaver traps, guns and ammunition, pots, pans, kettles, needles, and thread. The fact that these were important to him helps explain why so many times various tribes were pacified or bought off with trinkets.

The unscrupulous merchants and traders, and even the agents themselves, were quick to take advantage of the Indians and discount the certificates for a mere trifle. Houston later wrote: "For the sacred obligation of our government, made under the sanction of a treaty, these deceived exiles often received a Mackinaw blanket, a flask of powder, or a bottle of whiskey." [1] The Cherokee agent, Major DuVal, himself maintained a partnership in a prosperous trading company and traded in the certificates. His brother William, in partnership with Peter A. Carnes, was notorious for selling whiskey illegally to the Indians. It is said that his store in one month sold more than 200 gallons of whiskey to them.[2] In May 1829, shortly before the arrival of Houston in the Indian Territory, Colonel Arbuckle had seized five barrels of brandy, rum, and wine from the firm of DuVal and Carnes. Not only that, but the firm could produce no trader's license. Political pressure forced the colonel to return the seized property to the merchants.[3]

The feather merchants did not completely swindle the gullible Indians. Col. Walter Webber, one of the prominent leaders of the Cherokee Nation and for whom Webber's Falls was named, emerged with some of the certificates. Ben Hawkins, a half-breed trader in the nation, also got some. The Raven ended up with $66,000 worth of certificates, which he turned over to the Cherokees.

Probably in retaliation for Houston getting away with so many certificates of indebtedness, and for his numerous letters to various authorities complaining about government agents, DuVal published an order requiring all white men who resided in the nation without the consent of the chiefs of the nation to comply with certain rules and regulations that he set forth in his order. He received a prompt reply from the Cherokees. They granted Houston full citizenship in the Cherokee Nation.

We do, as a committee . . . Solemnly, firmly, and [unrevocably] grant to him for ever all the rights, privileges, and Immunities of a citizen of the Cherokee Nation and do as fully impower him with all rights and liberties as tho he was a native Cherokee, while at the Same time the Said Houston will be required to yield obedience to all laws and regulations made for the government of the Native Citizens of the Cherokee Nation.[4]

Dated October 21, 1829, the document was signed by Walter Webber as president of the committee, Aaron Price as vice-president, and John Jolly, principal chief.

With his new citizenship in the Cherokee Nation, the Raven had severed a link to his past.

It was December and a chill was in the air, announcing the imminent arrival of winter. Chief Oolooteka and his foster son were conversing at the Wigwam Illinois. It appeared the venerable chief had an assignment for Colonneh, one that his son was more than willing to accept inasmuch as it was on a subject dear to his heart. The chief was highly disturbed that the Cherokee agent DuVal had not paid the Indians the various sums of money due them recently in gold, as their treaties provided. He was tired of the continual corruption of traders and agents and wanted the Raven to travel to Washington City to use his influence with the Great Father Jackson to have these wrongs righted. In addition, there were other matters of importance he wanted to be discussed. At his request, Houston wrote a letter to "Great Father." Chief Jolly glanced at it, approved it, and signed it with his mark.

> My son, The Raven, came to me last spring . . . at my wigwam he rested with me as my son. He has walked straight . . . His path is not crooked . . . He is now leaving me to meet his WHITE Father, Genl Jackson, and look upon him and I hope he will take him by the hand and keep him as near to his heart as I have done . . . He is beloved by all my people . . . We are far apart, but I send my heart to my friend Jackson, and the Father of my people.[5]

Under the various treaties with the United States, the Cherokee Nation was regarded as a separate nation. Chief Jolly gave Houston the rank of ambassador and appointed Col. Walter Webber,[6] who spoke, read, and wrote English, to accompany the Raven to the capital. John Brown, an eastern Cherokee recently arrived in the Indian Territory, was a third member of the delegation.

Two weeks later, on December 18, 1829, Jolly again wrote Jackson with another series of complaints:

More than a year ago, the last Treaty made by the great Father
and my Nation was to have been made good . . . and it is not yet
done — the lines are not run to show my people where to make
their houses and clear their fields. The Osage missionaries yet
live on the land given to my people and also a number of Osage
families live near to them. I wish them all removed. The Cherokees have missionaries of their own and want no more! . . . The
country containing the Reservations granted to Col. Chouteau
. . . was ceded to the Cherokees. They are in the midst of our
Country and many white people are settled upon them and I now
hope my father will have them — given to the Cherokees. If it is
not done I will have no peace, for troubles will arise with those
white men who have no laws . . . and blood may be shed and my
people blamed when not in fault.[7]

In Washington, Jackson was pushing for his Indian removal
bill. This bill provided for the removal of all eastern Indians to the
west, and it was apparent the bill's passage was inevitable. In his
letter to Jackson, Chief Jolly made it clear he wanted the newcomers to be given their own land to settle on, "for I have not more land
here than is necessary for my children who are here."

For some reason Houston's appointment as ambassador to
Washington was not made in open council among the Cherokees,
as such matters were usually done. Perhaps Jolly feared opposition
to his appointment, or to the delegation itself and their purposes.
Capt. John Rogers, Jr., Houston's boyhood friend and a future
principal chief of the Cherokees, wrote Secretary of War Eaton urging him not to listen to the designs of Houston and the delegation,
stating that fears of what the delegation might do "are creating
much anxiety and uneasiness amongst our people." [8]

John Rogers, Jr., had been a member of the 1828 delegation to
Washington that, contrary to the explicit orders of the council, had
ceded the Cherokees' Arkansas lands, thereby forcing the tribe to
move much farther west. Perhaps he was afraid Houston and the
delegation would try to undo the illegal treaty.

The Raven departed from his Wigwam Neosho in late December to fulfill his ambassadorial duties. Near Fort Smith, Arkansas,
he was approached by DuVal. The agent had been informed that
Houston was on his way to Washington to press charges against
various agents, and inquired if this was true. The former governor
admitted it was. DuVal then requested Houston to put his charges
against him in writing, and Sam complied, writing two copies. He
kept one for himself and gave the other to DuVal, receiving his

written receipt for it. Sam and the other members of the delegation then departed.

On December 28, as the *Amazon* was paddling up the Mississippi, Houston wrote his longtime friend, Judge John Overton. In this letter he told the judge he was on his way to Washington and perhaps New York before returning to the place of his exile, and stated that the purpose of his trip was "neither to solicit office or favors, either of our friend, the President, or the Government in any respect." He promised to deport himself in a manner that would in no way embarrass Jackson. The letter continued on by expressing his gratitude for the judge to offer his philosophy and friendship during Sam's "darkest, direct hour of human misery." He concluded by asking the judge to write him in care of Judge White, otherwise the curious would "open his letters as they have done the previous summer." [9] Old Hickory was promptly advised of the contents of the letter.

On January 11, 1830, Houston reached Fredericktown, Maryland, and promptly sent his first cousin, John Houston, a note, inviting him to take "Potluck" with him the next day at Brown's Hotel in Washington. "Don't say to *any one* that I will be in tomorrow," he concluded.[10]

When Sam arrived at the capital in the middle of January, 1830, he created a sensation. As ambassador from the Cherokee Nation to the White House, the Raven presented himself in the costume of the Indians. What a shock it must have been for official Washington to perceive this tall, powerfully built man wearing his beaded shirt, leather leggings with fringe, buckskin coat, and a brightly colored blanket over his broad shoulders. In case the city's hostesses were wondering what the president would do, they quickly found out. Jackson promptly invited his friend to a White House reception.

While Houston was furnishing entertainment to the gawkers and the curious who had heard so much about this flamboyant man, he himself was spectator to some entertainment that must have given him immense pleasure. His old enemy, John C. Calhoun, was the subject of much political in-fighting. Old Hickory was highly disturbed because Washington society, and the wives of his cabinet members in particular, would not accept Secretary of War Eaton's wife, Peggy, into their circle. They objected to her past as a barmaid in her father's tavern. That was not all. Peggy had been married to John Timberlake, whose duties as a purser in the navy kept him away from home for lengthy periods of time. Rumor was that the popular Peggy dated other gentlemen while her husband was away at sea, and that the then senator from Tennessee, John Eaton, a rich widower, was her frequent escort. Timberlake died, and Eaton and Peggy promptly married.

Jackson liked the comely Peggy. He had known her for some years, as he had been a frequent guest at her father's tavern. In his campaign to gain acceptance for her, he assiduously courted his vice-president, Calhoun, and his secretary of state, Martin Van Buren, who was a bachelor. The secretary of state cooperated and gave a party for Mrs. Eaton, and also had various friends be cordial to her. Calhoun's hands were tied. His wife simply would not receive Peggy.

Other anti-Calhoun forces were at play. Several years earlier a letter had surfaced stating that Calhoun, while secretary of war in 1818, had highly disapproved of General Jackson's conduct in prosecuting the invasion of Florida. Jackson was sensitive about his reputation as a military leader and had had an uneasy relationship with Calhoun ever since. Now the South Carolinian was in a predicament. The anti-Calhoun forces, including the Raven, got in their licks and reminded Jackson of the 1818 letter. When the whole affair was over, Calhoun's political career had reached its zenith, and any hopes he had of reaching the presidency had vanished. He later quarreled with Jackson over the spoils system and resigned the vice-presidency in 1831. Martin Van Buren was selected as Old Hickory's running mate in 1832 and succeeded him as president.

As Chief Oolooteka's emissary to the Great Father, Houston had not been a complete success; neither had he been a complete failure. He got nowhere in his endeavors to have Jackson stop efforts to have the Indian removal bill passed; the bill was passed May 28, 1830. He had more success in his efforts to have various Indian agents removed from their posts. Within a six-month period, Cherokee agent DuVal was dismissed, as was Osage agent John F. Hamtramck and Creek agent David Brearley. In addition, Thomas McKenney, chief of the War Department's Indian Office, was removed.[11] Sam was also successful in receiving Jackson's agreement that various Indian territorial lines would be clearly delineated.

The Raven, seldom a stranger to controversy, quickly became embroiled in one that in the long run had far-reaching ramifications. On February 18, 1830, a public announcement was made by the War Department, requesting bids to furnish rations for emigrant Indians to the west be submitted by March 20. The present cost per ration was twenty-one cents, and for all Indians the ration was delivered at just one point in the Cherokee Nation. This caused many Indians to travel a considerable distance to receive their rations. A fortune was being made by those holding the contract, inasmuch as the rations furnished were not only of such poor quality but in such insufficient quantities that many Indians were at a near-starvation level.[12]

On an evening in March 1830, Duff Green, editor of the *United States Telegraph*, strolled into the White House. There he found Jackson, Eaton, and Houston huddled over some papers. They were discussing, Secretary Eaton said, the Indian ration contract. Houston was proposing to bid eighteen cents and furnish the Indians a more superior quality of ration than the one being used. Houston's ration was to consist of a pound and a quarter of fresh beef, or a pound of fresh pork, with two quarts of salt to every hundred rations; if salted meat was used, one pound of beef and three-quarters of a pound of pork, with a quart of corn, or corn meal, to each ration of meat.[13] In addition, Houston proposed to have at least two and possibly three distribution points in the territory.

The next day Duff Green wrote a letter to the secretary of war protesting that Houston's bid of eighteen cents was far too high and might enrich a few. When the final bids were in, there were thirteen in all, ranging from eight to seventeen cents. In order to meet the competition, Houston's bid, submitted through a New York financier he was associated with named John Van Fossen, was thirteen cents per ration.

After receiving all the bids, Eaton was under considerable pressure from Congress. Charges of collusion between some of the bidders were voiced, and it was suspected that he was going to favor the Houston-Van Fossen bid, although it was not the lowest. Eaton at first postponed making a decision on the grounds that thirty days had been insufficient time for bidders from Illinois to submit their bids. Finally, he refused to let the contract to anyone, with the explanation that treaties providing for the removal of the Indians had not been ratified by the Senate; therefore, there was no need to let the contracts.[14] Two years later the whole affair blew up with charges of fraud and corruption against Eaton and Houston, and once again the Raven found himself in the national spotlight.

During his sojourn in Washington, Houston had a miniature

painted of himself in his formal Cherokee attire. With an open collar and a beaded Indian headdress, the portrait reveals a still-handsome man with a slightly haunted expression in his eyes. Still courtly, still courteous, and radiating his personality, it is not to be doubted that many a Washington society matron looked at this powerful man and wondered whatever in the world was the matter with Eliza Allen to reject her husband.

The Raven did not stay in Washington to see who received the ration contract but departed for the land of his exile with a planned stopover in Nashville. This visit was to be made in spite of a warning he had received that he would suffer "a fate most appalling to humanity" should he return to the West by way of Tennessee.[15] From Baltimore on April 4, 1830, he wrote his associate Van Fossen concerning their bid for the contract:

> To act in good faith with all parties, and to get just as much from the Government as will indemnify us for the use of the capital employed, and the labor bestowed, is what I wish; and further, to do ample justice to the Indians in giving to them full ration, and of good quality, should we get the contract, must be regarded as a "sine qua non" with us.[16]

It was April 21, almost a year to the day the Raven had resigned his post as governor of Tennessee. In spite of the warnings he had received not to return, Houston was in Nashville.

CHAPTER 11

A Lingering
Romantic Tragedy

It was spring in Tennessee and the dogwood was blooming. The skies were clear, but a bluish haze settled over the Smoky Mountains as Houston returned to Nashville, where he had been sworn in as governor with such a bright future ahead and left in disgrace under the darkest cloud. Who knows what the Raven's thoughts were as he arrived back in the city where he had taken his young, beautiful bride after their wedding? He had had such high hopes, and now they were all shattered.

Why did he go back to Tennessee at all? Was it to show his contempt for those who had warned him to stay away on pain of reprisal, and prove once more his courage? Was it due to some yearning to revisit the scenes of his youth, where he had grown to manhood and accomplished so much in such a short time? Or was it to visit his mother, brothers, and sisters? If Sam called on his immediate family, it was certainly never mentioned in his correspondence. Perhaps it was to test the waters of public opinion to see if there was enough of a following who would be receptive to a possible return to public life. Did Sam still love the woman who had rejected him? Perhaps it was a combination of all of these speculations. We do not know. Charles Lester's *Authentic Memoir* does not mention the month-long stay, and Sam's collected writings only briefly touch upon the subject.

One thing is certain: Sam's baggage had barely been unpacked before he found himself in the middle of a hornet's nest. There were two powerful cabals working against him. The Billy Carroll faction desperately wanted to keep Houston in controversy to prevent him making an attempted political comeback. In certain circles, feelings were still high against him because of his "treatment" of Eliza. At one of Houston's public appearances, a mother told her son: "Now, John, do you not go near him. The people have little to do to honor such a man." [1] At the same time he had been greeted by crowds who desired to show not only their confidence in him, but their respect. The last thing in the world the Carroll clique wanted was for the Raven to roost long in Tennessee. The other faction that looked with apprehension upon Houston's return from his exile was the Allen group. Eliza Houston was now a year older than the unsophisticated, immature, sheltered young lady who had exchanged wedding vows with the state's most popular man. What were the thoughts of this young woman scarcely out of her girlhood? As she strolled in her loneliness in the garden at Allendale, did she ever think of what might have been? It was true the general had his faults. Even if he was jealous and hot-blooded and had made accusations in anger, surely she knew the wreckage of their marriage rested to some extent on her shoulders. Perhaps she realized how shamefully she had treated her husband, entering into a sham of a marriage, and then, instead of trying to solve her problems with him, thoughtlessly and childishly running back to her parents.

Who knows what memories and regrets Eliza had of the previous year's events, when Sam had humbled himself at her knees, tearfully pleading for her forgiveness, a forgiveness she had withheld? No longer the governor's lady, the first lady in Tennessee, she was in limbo — a wife without a husband and as such unable to be courted by other men. We wonder if it ever occurred to this young girl that very possibly she kept her husband from becoming president of the United States.

Houston's conduct toward Eliza since her return to her parents was certainly irreproachable and gentlemanly in the extreme. Far from casting any aspersions on his wife, he had quickly absolved her from any blame in the whole sorry affair and had sacrificed his political career in preference to uttering one word against her. Did her conscience bother her for refusing Sam's pleas for a reconciliation? Did she in any way reproach herself or her father for the way the whole situation had been handled? We shall never know. Unfortunately, Eliza left no diary to let us know her version of the matter.

Perhaps Colonel Allen sensed the true feelings of his daughter because he sent her to Carthage to stay with her uncle Robert, the former congressman. Houston, ever close-mouthed on the subject of his separation from Eliza, in a letter to a friend gave a vague hint that the Allen family had attempted a reconciliation. But the Raven spurned their overtures:

> When they lost all hopes of a reunion, they came out with large *names* . . . They sent Mrs. H. to Carthage least she should come to Nashville, in spite of them and I would not receive her. If she had come this would have been the case, so I said to my friends from the time I arrived there. Great efforts, and strong hopes of fame were held out to me but, all of no use. Tho' the world can never know my situation and may condemn me God will justify me![2]

Why did Sam reject a reconciliation with his wife — the reconciliation he had so avidly sought only a year earlier? Was it because his self-confidence had been so badly shattered by his wife's refusal to forgive him? It was part of this man's personality to be hot-tempered, and perhaps his enormous pride would not let him forget how his wife of a few months had rejected his tearful pleadings when he had humbled himself at her feet. Perhaps it was in the makeup of this man, who "never forgot a friend or a favor, or forgave an enemy," not to forget how Eliza had refused to return to Nashville and their marriage when he had begged her to. Perhaps he could not forget that in those days a year past, when malicious gossip and rumors were tearing his reputation to shreds, his wife never came to his defense, and silence was the only voice he heard. For him the past was over. Apparently, on that fateful day when he had had his disastrous interview with his bride, she had returned to him the diamond engagement ring he had given her. For years he wore this in a little buckskin pouch suspended from a leather thong around his neck. Many years later he gave Eliza's ring to Sarah Jackson, the wife of Old Hickory's adopted son, Andrew Jr. The fires of Sam's passion had slowly cooled and were but dying embers of a once blazing love.

While the Raven was in Nashville — ten days were spent recovering from a recurrence of the malaria he had suffered in the Indian nation — a gathering of distinguished citizens of Sumner

County met at the Gallatin Courthouse. Rebuffed in their attempts at a reconciliation, the Allen-Carroll cabal went into action. They were fearful that public opinion might sway toward the former governor. A committee of twelve was appointed to draw up a report stressing the virtues of Eliza and once more laying the blame for the breakup of the marriage solely on the broad shoulders of Houston. Within two days the committee had drawn up its report; it was read and approved. A motion was then adopted requesting editors in the state of Tennessee who "feel any interest in the character of the injured female . . . to give the foregoing report and proceedings in their respective papers." [3] Perhaps the committee had visions of the hot temper of the Raven; they took precautions to see that the newspaper editors were not furnished with copies of the report until Houston had left Tennessee and was well on his way back to his Wigwam Neosho.

The committee published the letter Houston had written to his father-in-law a year previously. In addition, their report stated:

> very shortly after the marriage Governor Houston became jealous of his wife, and mentioned the subject to one or two persons, apparently in confidence; yet the Committee are not informed that he made any specific charges, only that he believed she was incontinent and devoid of affection . . . He rendered his wife unhappy by his unfounded jealousies and his repeated suspicion of her coldness and want of attachment, and she was constrained by a sense of duty to herself and her family to separate from her infatuated husband . . . since which time she has remained in a state of dejection and despondency.
>
> The Committee . . . are informed that Governor Houston had lately . . . returned to Nashville . . . and it has been suggested that public sympathy has been much excited in his favor, and that a belief has obtained in many places abroad that he was married to an unworthy woman . . . the committee have no hesitation in saying he is a deluded man; that his suspicions were groundless; that his unfortunate wife is now and ever has been in the possession of a character unimpeachable and that she is an innocent and injured woman . . .[4]

Houston stayed in Tennessee for almost a month before departing for the Cherokee Nation. He had quickly obtained a copy of the committee's report, and in a letter to Andrew Jackson dated Steam Boat Nashville 18th May, 1830, had written his mentor. To Jackson he denied some of the charges of the committee:

> They were anxious to publish my letter, and they have done it.

They state untruly when they say that it was after the separation, it was before it . . . It is stated that my treatment induced her to return to her Father's house for protection. This is utterly false, and without foundation . . .

This recent attack would not have been made upon me, if it had not been supposed that I was down in society. I am not down. The affections of the people of Tennessee are with me, and if I would present myself to them again, they would shew the world that they have confidence in me, and care nothing about my private matters, which they cannot understand.[5]

He concluded his letter to the president by stating that as soon as he reached home he would inform Jackson about the condition of the Indians, and whether the Mexican troops had reached the border of the United States.

On December 7, 1830, from his Wigwam Neosho, the Raven replied to the report of the committee. Writing to William Hall, who had succeeded him as governor, Houston did not mention any names but clearly intimated that his enemy Billy Carroll was the prime mover in the formation of the committee. His letter refutes certain charges against him and comments on the publication of his private letter to Colonel Allen. He complained, "When has society before witnessed the convention of a committee for the purpose of taking up the *private* and the *domestic* circumstances of a *Private* person, and in public and solemn manner reporting thereupon?" [6] He concluded by giving Governor Hall permission to publish the letter. For whatever his reasons, the governor suppressed Houston's reply to the charges of the committee of twelve, and the public was deprived of hearing Sam's side of the story.

The love-hate relationship between Sam and Eliza went on for years. It is known that after Houston exiled himself to the land of the Cherokees he visited Tennessee at least four times, and there is substantial evidence that at least twice he surreptitiously saw his wife. The first incident was related by a girlfriend of Eliza who was a bridesmaid at the wedding, and to whom Eliza related the incident. Eliza was in her garden one day when the housemaid announced that a stranger, a tall man, was in the reception room asking to see her. On entering the room she saw the stranger was the former governor in disguise. He arose and made a courtly salutation, not suspecting his disguise had been penetrated. The conversation was about the weather and the condition of the river, and during the conversation the visitor gazed at her as if to fasten her features securely in his memory. Eliza gave no hint that she recognized her husband. Finally, Sam gave a deep bow and left the house to go to the river. There he boarded a canoe and paddled to the opposite side.[7]

The second account is attributed to Dilcey, the black slave of the Allen family, and was supposed to have happened during Sam's last visit to Tennessee before departing for Texas. One day Houston suddenly appeared before Dilcey as she was busy about her cabin. By giving her some money he persuaded her to call Eliza to her cabin where, concealed, he gazed upon her face and heard the voice of his wife for the last time.[8]

It is a fair assumption that Eliza, as she grew older and had time for reflection, regretted her hasty decision to not return to Sam. She is said never to have mentioned his name but to have read every notice of his career and to have answered every harsh reference to him by turning her back on the speaker.[9] Although Eliza did not want her husband when she had him and rejected his pleas for forgiveness, she never bothered to divorce him. On the contrary. According to a distant cousin, some of her friends wanted her to get a divorce and she positively refused, saying she was not displeased with her present name; therefore, she would not change it, but would take it to the grave with her.[10]

As late as December 1836, Sam's cousin Robert McEwen, with whom the newlyweds had spent a few days before proceeding to their quarters in the Nashville Inn, wrote Houston stating Eliza was desirous of a reconciliation. But the Man of Destiny was following his star, and Eliza belonged to the past. He replied that reconciliation was impossible.[11]

Eliza never gave up hoping the Raven might fly back to her, and it was not until after Houston divorced her many years later that she remarried, although she had many suitors. Her second husband was Dr. Elmore Douglass, a wealthy widower much older than she and with several children.

Although the blighted romance was over and Sam felt he had been badly treated by the Allen family, he would never allow anyone to make a disparaging remark about Eliza. Soon after she remarried, Sam was visiting a cousin in Maryville. A group of his relatives were discussing Eliza while Houston was lying down to rest the leg that had been injured in the Battle of San Jacinto. When someone made a slighting remark about his former wife he jumped up instantly to defend her, his eyes flashing with anger.

106

By her second husband Eliza had two daughters, Martha and Susie, and was said by those who knew her to be a devoted wife and mother. She died on March 3, 1861, a little more than two years before the Raven. Shortly before her death she had all of her personal correspondence and portraits of herself destroyed. She lies buried in the Allen family plot in the Gallatin cemetery next to her daughter Susie Douglass. At her request she was buried in an unmarked grave and for years her request was honored. Somewhere around 1930 a marker was put up with the inscription:

Eliza Allen Houston
Douglass,
Daughter of
John and Laetitia Allen
Dec. 2, 1809
Mar. 3, 1861

Her death ended the saga of two thoroughly decent people caught up in a bizarre romantic tragedy that affected the destiny of not only their own lives, but of two nations.

CHAPTER 12

New Love and
Renewed Causes

The Raven had been gone from the Cherokee Nation for almost five months, and he decided it was time to return. He had heard that Gen. John Nicks, the sutler at Cantonment Gibson, was to be removed from his post. The licensed position of sutler was one of the most lucrative available, as the appointment gave its holder a virtual monopoly on the soldiers' trade. The Cantonment Gibson area was a prosperous one. The military road between Fort Smith and the cantonment had been completed in 1827, and the steamboat trade was flourishing. Over the road and via the steamboat many visitors and traders came to the area to take in such entertainment as the area offered in the way of weddings, community dinners, the always popular horseracing, and theater performances. There was a large army payroll to be dispensed, and the Indian tribes were frequent visitors to the community to sign treaties, negotiate, and receive their annuities.

From the mouth of the White River on May 20, 1830, Houston wrote Secretary of War Eaton, through Maj. William B. Lewis, second auditor of the treasury, a letter applying for the sutler's post. The letter was a lengthy one, and in it Houston gave various items of news, including some opinions on his erstwhile opponent for the governorship, Billy Carroll. "My honest belief is that if I would again return to Tennessee I would beat him for Governor, but I am too poor!!!"[1]

Possibly in anticipation of his becoming the new sutler, Sam ordered, while in Nashville, a keelboat of supplies and sent them up the Arkansas River to his Wigwam Neosho. Among the supplies were kettles, blankets, bridles, flour, soap, and rope — all items that the Indians needed. Also included in the assortment of goods were ten barrels of liquor.[2]

When Houston returned to his wigwam he quickly found out that news of his attempts while in Washington to secure the Indian contract for rations had preceded him, and that he was the object of considerable scandal as there were whisperings that he and his associates tried to receive the contract through illegal means. Sam also found out that sutler Nicks was not to be removed from his post. On June 13, Houston wrote the secretary of war withdrawing his application and at the same time intimating that the scandalous rumors concerning his ration venture had emanated from the secretary's office. The Raven denounced his accusers and mentioned that he would shortly commence a series of articles in the *Arkansas Gazette* signed "Talohntusky," in which he would be "showing in what manner the agencies have been, and are now managed in this quarter. The innocent will not suffer, the guilty ought not to escape."[3] In a postscript he informed Eaton that the claim of $50,000 due the Cherokees under the last treaty was in a fair way to be swindled from them.

Shortly thereafter, Houston made a public announcement he was opening a trading store at his Wigwam Neosho and was going to make his merchandise available to the Indians "at honest prices."[4] Bringing in his supply of liquor involved the Raven in a controversy with the commandant of Cantonment Gibson. When his shipment arrived, Houston wrote Colonel Arbuckle under date of July 21, 1830, informing him of the fact. He then stated:

> I ordered to this point for my own use, and the convenience of my establishment five Barrels of whiskey; four of Mongahala and one of corn. One Barrel of Cogniac, one Gin, one rum and two barrels of Wine, intended for stores, and for the accommodation of the officers, of the Government, and such persons, as are duly authorized to purchase, the same.[5]

As a citizen of the Cherokee Nation, he contended, he was not subject to the Indian Intercourse Law, and therefore not required to be bonded and obtain a license to trade with the Indians as were other traders. He proposed to store all of the liquor, with the exception of one barrel which he would keep at his wigwam for his personal use, at the establishment of the sutler. In addition, he pledged not to sell a drop of whiskey to either the Indians or the soldiers.

Colonel Arbuckle pondered the letter and then passed the buck to the War Department. The latter, in turn, consulted the attorney general's office, and in typical bureaucratic fashion the case dragged on for several months. Eventually, the ruling came down that Houston would have to be bonded and licensed, but he was permitted to take the nine barrels of liquor to his own residence for his personal use. Irrespective of the decision of the War Department, it seems that Houston had the final say in the matter of the license question, since government records of Indian trading do not show that a license was ever issued to him (although records do show licenses were issued to other traders during this period).[6] In any case, the question was largely moot, inasmuch as it was a small establishment and he never made much money from it. Due to his frequent absences the operation was left largely to others, and he stayed in business only about a year. He had many talents, but once more he proved that staying behind a counter was not one of them.

The Raven was a busy man in his exile, turning his knowledge of the law to good use. Earlier in the year he had successfully represented the Osages in an annuity controversy they had had with their agent, John Hamtramck. Now he had another case involving his friend John Rogers, Jr. Upon Houston's return to the Three Forks area in May 1830, he discovered Rogers had been dismissed from his post as official interpreter for the Cherokee Nation by agent Edward DuVal. Rogers had held that post since 1817 and was still the choice of both the chiefs and the national committee and council. Sam skillfully presented his client's case and Rogers was reinstated his post by order of the War Department.[7]

It was summer of 1830. Colonneh was still drinking heavily and, despite the fact that he was busy, was a lonely man. There were good reasons. This big, strong, virile man was a husband but had no wife. The girl he had chosen to be his lifelong partner had rejected him. Had not the Lord God said, "It is not good that the man should be alone"? Sam pondered his situation and took this admonition to heart. He took unto himself a bride, and of all the acts this strange, complex man of genius did, this through the years

110

has been one of the most controversial. Sam was a man of taste and, in the parlance of today, he traveled first-class. In his marriages he made no exceptions. The second bride he selected was Diana Rogers Gentry. When his liaison with Diana became known to the world at large, his enemies made open attacks in newspapers and magazines portraying him as a "Squaw Man," and jeered at him for living with a filthy Indian squaw. Far from being the latter, Diana was one of the socially elite of the Cherokee Nation, and if the Indians had had princesses in their culture, she certainly would have been one.

In actuality she was only one-sixteenth Cherokee. Her father was Capt. John "Hell-Fire Jack" Rogers, who had acquired his rank by being a Tory officer in the American Revolution and had later fought as a commissioned officer under Andrew Jackson at the Battle of Horseshoe Bend. After the Revolutionary War he had migrated to Tennessee and for years had been a trader among the Cherokees, first with them on Hiwassie Island and then later directing their emigration to the Arkansas Territory. Prospering in both the Cherokee Nation East and the Cherokee Nation West, he had become a wealthy man. His sons John, Jr., and James, Diana's half-brothers, were borne by his first wife, Elizabeth Due. With her demise he married Jennie Due, his stepdaughter, who was seven-eighths white and only one-eighth Cherokee. By her he had five children, including Diana. Diana's full brothers were wealthy in their own right as they operated profitable mercantile establishments and owned vast plantations. Her sisters and nieces were married to wealthy Cherokee merchants such as John Drew and Peter Harper, and she was also related to the famous Sequoyah, whose invention of the Cherokee alphabet made him an important figure in the Cherokee Nation. Her uncles, both of whom became principal chiefs of the nation, were the late Tahlontusky and the Raven's adopted father John Jolly. Her brother John became a chief, and his grandson William Charles Rogers became a principal chief. Will Rogers, the famous humorist and movie star from Claremore, Oklahoma, was Diana's nephew, three generations removed.

Once again Sam picked a mate younger than himself. There are no birth records available on Diana, but the best evidence shows that she was about seven to ten years younger than he. A widow, she had previously been married to a white blacksmith named David Gentry, who had been killed by the Osages. In those days blacksmiths had all the work they could handle, and Gentry

111

was not only prosperous but well respected in the community. Diana and her husband had had two children, but both had died.

Undoubtedly, Houston had known Diana during the formative years he spent living with the Cherokees on Hiwassie Island. The island and John Jolly's band of followers were so small it would have been almost impossible for him not to have known her, but because she was just a child at the time it is unlikely he had paid much attention to her. Now the situation was different. She was a grown woman. There are no portraits of Diana in existence, although there is a portrait of her drawn from contemporary accounts by the noted Creek-Cherokee artist Joan Hill. This portrait shows an exceedingly handsome, tall, slender woman dressed in a white gown and with black hair falling several inches below the shoulders. On her head she is wearing a small tiara. Other verbal descriptions confirm her beauty. It is a shame that the noted artist George Catlin, who lived among the Indians for several years and painted so many portraits of them, did not put Diana's likeness on canvas during the time he dwelled in the Cherokee Nation West.

Diana was prosperous in her own right. As a widow, according to Cherokee custom, she belonged "to herself" and could marry anyone she chose. Since the death of Gentry she had had numerous suitors but had turned them all down. Now came the Raven and she succumbed, as had many women before her, to the Houston charm.

It is not known exactly when Houston first encountered the matured Diana during his exile, but it was very probably at the Green Corn Dance held in July 1829, shortly after his arrival in the territory. As the Green Corn Dance was the most important social function in the Cherokee Nation, the entire tribe gathered for the celebration and undoubtedly both Sam and Diana attended this event. Perhaps they even joined around the fires for the dancing.

In the United States, Sam was still legally married to Eliza, but if he had any compunctions about taking another wife without securing a divorce, he reminded himself that he was a citizen of the Cherokee Nation and subject to Cherokee law. According to that law, their divorce would be clear, since they had "split the blanket" and no longer lived together as man and wife.[8]

As is the case with Eliza, little is known about Diana. She seems to have had a good education for a woman of those times, having been educated, according to family tradition, at a Moravian mission school in Tennessee before the family moved to the Arkansas Territory. Her father was interested in educating his children,

112

and it is not unlikely that they all had private tutors as well. Diana's younger sister Susannah attended the mission school at Dwight, operated by the Presbyterian missionary Cephas Washburn.

There is mystery surrounding Diana's name. In the official documents of the War Department and the Bureau of Indian Affairs her name is spelled both "Diana" and "Dianna" Rogers.[9] Among the Cherokees she was known as "Tiana" Rogers,[10] probably due to the Cherokees at that time having difficulty pronouncing the d in Diana. Other variations give her name as Talhina, Talihina, Tallahina, Talihena, Talahina, Tahlihina, and others. Houston is reputed to have called her "Hina."

In *The Only Authentic Memoir,* which was commissioned by Houston, Diana is not mentioned. Dr. Crane's *Life and Select Literary Remains of Sam Houston of Texas* also omits any reference to her. Among the Texas descendants of Sam there is considerable controversy as to Sam's relationship with her. Did he just live with an Indian woman or were they, according to Indian custom, actually man and wife?

To settle this question — at least to his own satisfaction — in 1919 a son of the Raven, William R. Houston of Dallas, Texas, visited Oklahoma. He went to the Cantonment (now Fort) Gibson area and talked with old settlers, newspaper editors, and historians. He returned home from his investigation convinced that Sam and Diana had been married, at least by Indian custom.[11]

So many white men living in the Cherokee Nation had taken Indian wives — at least temporarily while living in the nation — that as early as 1824 the national committee and council had passed a law making it unlawful for a white man to have more than one Indian wife.[12] In 1830 a resolution was passed establishing an intermarriage law that was designed to prevent whites from acquiring the rights of Cherokee citizens through intermarriage. For an Indian woman to be married to a white man required the service to be performed by a minister of the gospel or civil authority of the Cherokee Nation.[13] In 1830, at the home of Capt. John Rogers on Spavinaw Creek, now Mayes County, Oklahoma, Sam Houston and Diana Rogers were married.[14]

Many old settlers and full-bloods were of the opinion that Sam married Diana for power and position. They were in error. Through his adoption by Chief Jolly, Sam already had plenty of position and prestige, and, through his natural intelligence, leadership qualities, and still potent political connections in the white man's world, had even more power. He had already been given all the rights and privi-

113

leges of a Cherokee citizen by virtue of his certificate of citizenship. The fact was that he married Diana because he had great affection for her, desired her, and needed her. In the final analysis the exact type of ceremony by which Sam and Diana were united is immaterial. She was then and is still recognized by the Cherokee Nation as "Mrs. Sam Houston," and today, in the Officer's Circle at the Fort Gibson National Cemetery, lie the remains reputed to be hers. The inscription on the marker is a simple one:

Talahina R
Wife of Gen.
Sam Houston

The Raven established his new bride in his house, complete with trading store, near the Neosho River. Although his Wigwam Neosho was far from being a hut or shack, it was nowhere near the palatial estate John Jolly or other leaders of the nation were living in.

Sam planted an apple orchard and purchased two young blacks for house servants and field hands. In typical Indian fashion, the couple had a small herd of cattle and a garden. Under the influence of Diana, Houston began to take more of an interest in his personal appearance and was not as untidy in his grooming. Diana had an excellent reputation as a cook, and kept her house neat and clean. Also in Indian fashion, she supervised the running of the house and the care of the herds and the fields.

The Houstons entertained frequently. Their wigwam was on the heavily traveled Texas Road and was located only three miles from the cantonment, so many travelers stopped to chat with the ex-governor and partake of his hospitality. Sam was a gregarious man and the Cherokees have long been noted for their hospitality. Undoubtedly, Colonel Arbuckle, commandant of the cantonment, was a guest at their wigwam, and it is known that the novelist Washington Irving visited them. Diggings at the site of the wigwam have uncovered pieces of blue china, export porcelain, and glassware, presumably which were used by the Houstons when entertaining Arbuckle, Irving, A. P. Chouteau, and other friends.[15]

What sort of a social life the two might have had outside of their entertaining is questionable. The Raven's absences from home were frequent, but on his return to the Three Forks they could have enjoyed the theater and the professional horseracing in the area, and no doubt they visited Diana's numerous relatives and Sam's adoptive father John Jolly. At any rate, Houston's life with

114

the beautiful Diana was a far cry from his marriage with Eliza. She filled a need in this restless man during his lonely exile.

True to his word to Secretary Eaton, on June 22, 1830, Houston in the weekly *Arkansas Gazette,* in a letter headed "The Indians — Chapter First," commenced a series of articles indicating the various Indian agencies in their mismanagement of Indian affairs. Over a five-month period lasting into December, Houston had five articles published charging the agents with fraud and corruption against the Creeks and the Cherokees. Three articles were published under the name "Tah-lohn-tus-ky," one under the name "Standing Bear," and in the final article Houston used his own name.

In his articles, Houston gave a recitation of all the ills inflicted upon the Indians: the many unredeemed pledges given their leaders; how they had been cheated by being given short rations; the theft of specie certificates by agents and traders; the scheme of taking their lands; the illegal sale of whiskey to the Indians by their agents; and the open bribery in the War Department.

The former governor picked a potent weapon to use in his exposé. Although by 1829 the *Gazette* had a circulation of only around 500,[16] it was the most influential newspaper in the Southwest. It was read not only throughout the Indian country, but Eastern newspapers such as the *Niles Weekly Register* in Baltimore frequently reprinted entire items directly from the *Gazette.*

Regardless of the fact Houston used pseudonyms, it was generally known that he was the author of the articles. To the public at large and the Indian agents in particular, Houston was definitely on the wrong side of the Indian question. The reaction to the series was immediate and vitriolic, and each of his articles brought a sharp reply from one of his many detractors. The *Arkansas Gazette* of August 4, 1830, published a particularly bitter denunciation portraying him as "*a Greeneyed monster . . . a slanderer of man and deceiver of woman who opposed the views of the United States and fomented discord among the tribes by speaking disrespectfully of their Agents.*"

Perhaps the most vicious of the replies was by an author calling himself "Tekatoka." In his reply, Tekatoka referred to the Raven as "the turbaned Governor," and in a supplement to the *Gazette* of October 20, 1830, issued a broadside "To Standing Bear, alias Gen. Samuel Houston." In his article, Tekatoka called Houston a vagabond and a fugitive from the just indignation of an offended community. He closed his article by referring to Sam's new matrimonial alliance, and hoped that Houston's fair bride would awaken the Raven to a sense of his own degradation.

For some time no one knew who Tekatoka was, but eventually it turned out to be Maj. Edward DuVal, former Cherokee agent, who had been discharged from office following Houston's visit to Washington earlier in the year.

A supplement to the *Gazette* of December 8, 1830, included the last of Houston's articles. In a reply addressed to the editor, the Raven answered the counter-charges against him by Tekatoka and made the observation that his, Houston's, charges remained uncontradicted.[17]

With his series of articles in the *Gazette* Houston let the world know that although he might be in exile and not in the center of the stage, at least he was still in the wings. He wrote John Van Fossen, the New York financier:

> You will perhaps see in some of the northern papers, "chapters" signed Tah-lohn-tus-ky and every fact contained you may rely upon as true! The author you may guess at. They were written in great haste.[18]

In addition to trying to make some money by the operation of his trading store, Sam was looking about for other investments. On August 20, 1830, from "Wigwam, Neosho Territory," he wrote Van Fossen:

> I am just about to make a grand purchase of Salt Springs, and trust in God that I will be in a way to "do well." My fortune must not *wane*, it must *full*, if I live and meet with my deserts (in my humble opinion) . . .[19]

He concluded by asking, "How does 'Old Hickory' stand with you, and what is the political news?"[20]

Houston and his associates, David Thompson and John Drennan, on September 1, 1830, purchased the salt springs, or Grand Saline as it was known, and the land surrounding it from the Osage children of his friend Auguste Pierre Chouteau. Chouteau acted as guardian for his children in transferring the property in consideration of $3,000 — half in cash and half in goods. The "goods" consisted of one black boy valued at $500 and $1,000 worth of mer-

116

chandise to be selected from the Wigwam Neosho.[21] The Raven brought his legal talents to bear and acted as his own lawyer in drawing up the deeds to this property, which was on the east side of the Grand River, about twenty-five miles north of Cantonment Gibson.

Although normally on the western frontier the operation of a salt spring was one of the quick ways to wealth and power, Houston never did realize the potential he should have realized. Perhaps between his bouts with the bottle and his frequent absences from the Three Forks area he simply did not devote as much time to the springs as he should have. By the fall of 1832 he had transferred the operation of the saline to his brother-in-law, John Rogers, Jr. In spite of his lack of success in operating the saline, unlike most of the Raven's other business ventures this one turned out to be quite profitable. In 1832 he sold a portion of his acreage for thirty dollars an acre.

George Vashon was the new agent to the Cherokees, following the dismissal from office of Edward DuVal. He claimed Houston and his partners had made the purchase "with a view and expectation of prevailing on the government to purchase them out at an exorbitant price," and in a letter to Lewis Cass dated January 4, 1832, complained about Sam's purchasing the salt springs from "Chouteau's half-breed Indian Bastard Children." [22]

As busy a correspondent as ever, Houston had written on June 28 to one of his favorite cousins, John H. Houston, a letter of friendship and affection. With politics never far from his mind he wrote that Jackson would always be his friend, and that he and the War Department differed over various matters and gave as his opinion that Secretary of War Eaton would destroy himself by retaining unjust Indian agents.[23]

Apparently Eaton, who had been caught up in the fire of the controversy of the Indian rations, decided to defend himself concerning the awarding of — or, more appropriately, the non-awarding of — the contract. On July 28 he wrote the Raven at Cantonment Gibson explaining the circumstances which caused the rejection of the bids and denying any intended reflection on Houston's integrity. In November a Nashville paper had carried an article criticizing Eaton's handling of the Indian ration bids. Houston, always a generous person, from his Wigwam Neosho on December 23, 1830, wrote the editors of the *Arkansas Advocate* a

117

lengthy letter exonerating Eaton from censure in the matter of letting the Indian contracts.[24]

Always interested in his friends, on December 15 Sam had written one of his few letters to President Jackson requesting a favor, one that did not concern himself. A vacancy had lately occurred in the position of sub-agent to the Osages, and the Raven recommended for appointment to the post ". . . one of your old soldiers at the Battle of New Orleans. I allude to Captain Nathaniel Pryor, who has for several years past, resided with the Osages as a sub agent, by appointment of Govr Clark, but without any permanent appointment . . ." [25] Jackson honored the request, and Pryor received the appointment at a salary of $500 per year, but held the position for only a short time and died in 1831.

CHAPTER 13

Final Days in Exile

In spite of his efforts to keep busy while in his forest exile, the Raven was restless. Although he was married to the lovely Diana, perhaps some of his thoughts were back in Nashville and of his broken marriage with Eliza and his thrown-away political career. It would have been almost impossible in his surroundings to not brood over what might have been, and he was valiant in his endeavors to see the bottoms of those ten barrels of liquor he had imported into the Indian Territory.

In his restlessness Houston decided to enter politics once more. As an adopted citizen of the Cherokees, Sam was eligible to place his name in nomination for a position on the national council, which governed the affairs of the tribe. He was shocked when he was decisively defeated for the office. In fact, he was so bitter that he considered leaving the Cherokees and moving into the Choctaw Nation.[1] While drunk one day he got into an argument with his foster father and struck him. Nearby braves came to Jolly's defense and subdued Houston only after beating him unconscious. When Houston sobered up he publicly requested Jolly's forgiveness and apologized to the national council for his conduct. As to whether Houston was rejected for the council because he was a drunk or because he was a white man is unknown. Most likely it was partly for both reasons. Probably during this time, Jolly told Sam, "A man who is drunk is only half a man." [2]

During this period the Osages started calling Sam "Big Drunk," and some whites at the cantonment picked up the nickname. The Creeks still called him "Big-Holy-Person," and the Cherokees denied they ever called him Big Drunk, but Houston himself admitted he deserved the name.

Drunk or sober, his talents as a peacemaker were still in demand, and in May 1831 he was a participant of the negotiations between the Creeks and Osages, which resulted in two treaties being signed to guarantee peace between the Osages and the various emigrating tribes. A year earlier he had been appointed to a commission along with Chouteau and Colonel Arbuckle to investigate Osage charges against the Delawares and other nomadic tribes for killing eight of their warriors.

The Raven was still at loose ends, with neither his new wife, his trading post, nor his newly acquired salt springs being enough to keep this restless man busy and at home. He decided on another visit to Tennessee, possibly to see if there was any gold on some land he owned there in partnership with Ben Hawkins. It was probably on this occasion that he made one of his surreptitious visits to Eliza.

Leaving Diana home to tend to their wigwam and store, in June he boarded a paddle-wheeler and headed for Nashville. On board the boat he made the acquaintance of Matthew Maury, whose father was the American consul at Liverpool. During the voyage the men had many lengthy conversations punctuated with frequent drinks. Maury kept a journal of their conversation and was particularly fascinated by Houston's remarks concerning the Indians. He quoted the Raven as saying:

> They steal from friend & foe, & tho they were so friendly & so trusting to Genl. Houston, that they would not sign their treaty with the United States without consulting him, they sought all occasions of stealing his horses.

Maury recorded that he continued to pass the bottle to Sam, who continued to talk:

> My opinion . . . is that the U.S. can only hold together so long as there is an abundance of rich unoccupied wild land for settlers; because as soon as the population is at all dense we shall fall to pieces. I would run a line on the parallel of 33 or 34 to the Pacific Ocean, & say all north of it belongs to the U.S.; it would embrace

Santa Fe & N. California, but we could easily get them by conquest or treaty, & I would have the U.S. establish a fort & settlement at the mouth of the Columbia. And by God Gentlemen (said he, striking the table) if they don't do it, & if I can get some capitalists to join me, I would easily collect 2 or 300 volunteers on the Western frontiers, & I would proceed to establish a colony myself at the mouth of the Columbia; . . . I should get plenty of settlers, & from our great distance we could & would maintain an independence of any power on earth.[3]

Apparently, Sam's babblings did not impress Maury, as he commented in his journal that the former governor "gave no symptoms of that general knowledge & information which the imagination would consider indispensable in a Governor of a state."

Arriving in Nashville around the middle of July, Houston was not very well received, and no doubt caused considerable embarrassment to his friends by his heavy drinking and unkempt appearance. His friends must have wondered about his mental state when, in the July 13, 1831, issue of the *Nashville Banner and Whig*, the following proclamation appeared:

> . . . Now, know all men by these presents, that I, Sam Houston, "late Governor of the State of Tennessee," do hereby declare to all *scoundrels whomsoever*, that they are authorized to accuse, defame, caluminate, slander, vilify, and libel me to any extent, in *personal* or *private* abuse. And I do further proclaim, to whomsoever it may concern, that they are hereby *permitted* and *authorized* to write, indite, print, publish and circulate the same; and that I will in *no wise* hold them responsible to me in law, or honor. . . . I do solemnly propose, on the first day of April next, to give to the author of the most *elegant, refined and ingenious lie or [calumny]* a handsome gilt copy (Bound in Sheep) of the Kentucky Reporter, or a snug plain copy of the United States Telegraph, (bound in dog) since its commencement.
>
> Given under my hand and private seal, (*having no seal of office*) at Nashville, in the State of Tennessee.[4]

Shortly after having a Nashville artist paint his portrait in robes like those of the Roman general Gaius Marius, standing amid the ruins of Carthage, Houston headed back to the Three Forks and in August received a letter from Maryville that his mother was dying. He quickly returned to Baker's Creek and was at her bedside when she died. By October he was back at the Wigwam Neosho. The complex personality of Houston was such that he rarely ever spoke of his mother or his brothers and sisters or wrote to them, but

121

he later mentioned weeping by his mother's bedside as she lay dying. His mother's death apparently affected him greatly, and whatever bottom he had reached in his personal hell seems to have flattened out by the time he was back in the Cherokee Nation West. He started changing, getting his life back together.

That the Cherokees still had great affection for Colonneh was demonstrated when on October 31 once more they formally granted him citizenship in the Cherokee Nation. There had been talk that the resolution passed in October 1829 was invalid because the act was never approved by the council and because the chief himself was a party to the resolution. This time there was no question as to the legality of the measure, as it was passed by the national committee and council in general council, and was approved by John Jolly as chief.

Because Nathaniel Pryor, previous sub-agent to the Osages, had died after having served in the position only a short time, on November 19 Houston wrote the new secretary of war, Lewis Cass, recommending Thomas Anthony to fill the vacancy. Again Houston's recommendation was followed.

Once more Sam turned his thoughts toward Texas. Exciting events were happening in that land, and there was money to be made there. William H. Wharton, his friend from Nashville, some years previously had gone to Texas, married, and was prospering. Wharton's younger brother John, who had previously written Sam concerning a supposed expedition there, now had a law practice in New Orleans. He had visited his brother in Texas and was now preparing to move there permanently. He wrote Houston: "It is a fine field for enterprise. You can get a grant of land, be surrounded by your friends, and what may not the coming of time bring about?" [5]

In December 1831 Houston left the Three Forks with a delegation of Cherokees on their way to Washington via New Orleans, once more to present their grievances to the "Great Father." This time the Raven was not a member of the delegation, although he went along as an adviser and the instructions the delegates carried were in his handwriting. This infuriated agent Vashon, who wrote Secretary of War Cass, complaining about Houston's influence among the Indians being "pernicious." [6]

On this trip to the east Houston had other things on his mind than the affairs of his Cherokee friends; Texas was occupying more

122

of his thoughts, and he was planning on continuing on to New York to discuss possibilities in that Southwest area with some friends. Whether he knew it or not at the time, when he left his Wigwam Neosho to make this journey his life in the Cherokee Nation West was at an end.

On board the steamboat, Houston made the acquaintance of two French tourists, Alexis de Tocqueville, who was in the country on an official mission studying prison reform, and his traveling companion, Gustave de Beaumont. Over drinks Houston was questioned extensively about the characteristics and social customs of the Indians. At the same time, de Tocqueville noted Sam's seedy appearance and later made mention of it in his journal.

After a stop at Nashville, where Houston showed his Cherokee friends the Hermitage, the party arrived in Washington in early January and took up quarters at Brown's Indian Queen Hotel on Pennsylvania Avenue.

Houston spent some days in Washington renewing old friendships and then continued on to New York. Through John Van Fossen he was introduced to James Prentiss, a banker and principal of the Galveston Bay and Texas Land Company. The banker's firm was heavily involved in land speculation in Texas, and the two men had several discussions concerning Houston's plan to secure large acreages in Texas and sell them in parcels. It was agreed that Sam, under the auspices of Prentiss and his associates, would go to Texas in the future and survey the situation. Another subject of conversation between the two new friends was 10,025 acres Sam owned in Tennessee upon which gold had been found, and on March 27, 1832, he wrote Prentiss giving a description of his tract and stating where he derived his title to the property.

When Houston returned to Washington in early April, he found himself once more embroiled in a controversy that quickly became a *cause célèbre* and put him back in the national spotlight. It became known as "the Stanbery Affair."

CHAPTER 14

In the National Spotlight

The Raven had barely made himself comfortable in his rooms at Brown's Indian Hotel when he picked up a copy of the *National Intelligencer* dated April 3, 1832, which gave prominent space to a speech Ohio Congressman William Stanbery made to the House of Representatives on March 31 attacking the present administration. Stanbery inquired: "Was not the late Secretary of War removed because of his attempt fraudently to give Governor Houston the contract for Indian rations?" [1]

The truth was Eaton had resigned his position as secretary of war primarily because the vivacious Peggy had become an embarrassment to the administration. Jackson, in sympathy for his friend, had promptly appointed him governor of Florida. Stanbery knew the true facts of the resignation, or could very easily have found out. Houston resented the implication that he and Eaton were engaged in fraud, but he was shrewd enough to realize the attack was mainly an attempt to discredit the president.

There was a majority against Jackson in the Congress, and personal hatred against him had risen to a new high. As Sam later wrote:

> It was necessary in this last desperate crusade to hit upon a file-leader, who had distinguished himself for his malignant personal

hatred of General Jackson, and, at the same time, he must have no scruples against being the supple tool of wiser, but not better men, who pulled the wires behind the scenes . . . but the most supple, brazen-faced, shameless of all, was a certain politician, who had been elected as a friend of Jackson. He was chosen as the best instrument they could find.[2]

That man was Stanbery.

In his fury, Houston forgot about the proclamation he had issued in Nashville authorizing all scoundrels to defame him. His first reaction was to go on the floor of the House and have it out with Stanbery. He was intercepted by his friend James K. Polk, who dissuaded him from this action. He then sent Congressman Cave Johnson of Tennessee to deliver a note to Stanbery asking if he had been quoted correctly in the newspaper. The congressman refused to answer the note. Houston then started carrying a cane he had cut from a hickory tree at the Hermitage a few weeks previously. When Stanbery was advised by his friends that Houston was looking for him, he began to carry a pistol while on the street.

In the meantime, Texas was still on Houston's mind. He had received a letter from James Prentiss, written from New York on April 5, stating he was hourly expecting important intelligence from Mexico. Prentiss explained that the expected information may "require your sudden departure on the business of which we lately conversed" and requested Sam inform him how soon he could be in New York.[3]

Houston replied under date of April 8:

> If my presence should be required by those *interested;* it will be [convenient] for me to repair to New York at any time and with very little delay (say a few days) repair to TEXAS, and assume any duties in relation, to the Agency, which may be assigned to me. . . . Whether Santa Anna Succeeds, or not, is perhaps a matter of less importance to the company than what they are aware of.[4]

Sam concluded his letter by mentioning he had decided to visit Texas in the spring or summer, and would go by way of Nashville. However, if the company employed him he would forego passing through Nashville.

On the night of April 13, Houston, Senator Alexander Buckner of Missouri, and Congressman John Blair of Tennessee were visiting with Senator Felix Grundy in his quarters. The three left Grundy's together about eight o'clock in the evening and were walking on Pennsylvania Avenue. Suddenly, Blair saw a man he thought was Stanbery crossing the street. Suspecting trouble was about to occur and wishing no part of it, Blair promptly disappeared. Houston approached the man and asked if he were Mr. Stanbery. Upon receiving an affirmative answer, Sam cried out, "then you are the damned rascal" and began whacking the congressman with the hickory cane he was carrying.

The congressman from Ohio, a large man himself, cried out, "oh no!" and turned to run. Houston jumped on his back, and the two men fell to the ground. Sam continued to belabor Stanbery with blows but was having difficulty as he was weak in the shoulder due to the wound he received at the Battle of Horseshoe Bend. Stanbery finally managed to draw one of two pistols he was carrying, pressed it against Houston's chest, and fired. The charge did not explode. Houston then tore the pistol from Stanbery's grasp and continued whacking him. As a final gesture he lifted Stanbery's feet and gave him a couple of licks on the posterior.

The beating he had taken caused Stanbery to be bed-ridden. The next day he wrote Andrew Stevenson, Speaker of the House, complaining,

> I was waylaid in the street . . . and attacked, knocked down by a bludgeon, and severely bruised and wounded, by Samuel Houston, late of Tennessee, for words spoken in my place in the House of Representatives. . . . I am confined to my bed, and unable to discharge my duties in the House. . . . I request that you lay it before the House.[5]

Stanbery's letter was read to the House and a resolution was offered to arrest Houston. James K. Polk promptly jumped to his feet and protested the resolution, remarking the House did not have the power to arrest Houston in the matter involved. He was shouted down and the resolution passed by a vote of 145 to 25.

Houston was arrested and brought before the bar of the House. Walking down the aisle in custody of the sergeant-at-arms, nodding and smiling to his friends, the former governor was wearing his seedy buckskin coat and carrying his hickory cane. Responding to the charges filed against him, Houston denied that he assaulted Stanbery. He admitted that he had felt great indignation on reading in the *National Intelligencer* remarks stated to have been made on the floor of the House by Stanbery, "imputing to the accused, by name, a gross offence, of which he knew himself to be innocent, and the dissemination of which . . . was evidently calculated to affect his honor and character." [6] Houston stated he had

inquired of Stanbery whether the congressman had made the remarks attributed to him, but that Stanbery "refused to give any answer, in a manner calculated still further to injure the accused." [7]
Sam then admitted that under great excitement, when he acciden-
tally encountered Stanbery, he assaulted and beat him. But he
pointed out that he was carrying only a walking cane, while Stanbery was carrying pistols. He denied that his act constituted contempt for the House or a breach of privilege for a member of the
House. Houston's remarks were construed as a plea of not guilty,
and the trial was set to begin April 19.

When the trial began it was conducted before packed houses
every day. The newspapers created a sensation out of it. Sam had
retained the noted Francis Scott Key, author of "The Star Spangled Banner," as his attorney. Inasmuch as Key was ill throughout
much of the month-long trial, Houston virtually conducted his own
defense.

Stanbery, the first witness for the prosecution, displayed various bumps and bruises he claimed had been inflicted upon him.
On cross-examination by Houston he was asked upon what evidence he had to support his charge of fraud. Objection to this question was overruled by the House by a vote of 101 to 82. Stanbery
then replied: "It was no part of my intention to impute fraud to
General Houston."

The defense introduced Senator Buckner, who described the
events as he had witnessed them. The House roared with laughter
when he testified how Houston had raised Stanbery's feet in the air
and "struck him elsewhere." Stanbery then claimed the senator's
testimony was "destitute of truth and infamous," but then withdrew the statement and apologized.[8]

Although the evidence clearly brought out that Stanbery had
not only carried a pistol but had tried to fire it, the weapon was not
brought into evidence. On the other hand, Houston's by now celebrated cane was placed in evidence and passed around from hand
to hand. It was noted that the weapon that had inflicted so much
damage on Stanbery's person and pride was hardly larger in di-
ameter than a man's thumb.

Francis Scott Key made the opening address for the defense on
April 26. Ill at the time, he did not make a very good presentation
and from then on Houston took over completely.

President Jackson sent for the ex-governor and was in a foul
temper, lashing out at his enemies in Congress. He then told Houston he should build up his defense and asked him if he didn't have

127

some clothes to wear other than the buckskin coat. Sam confessed he didn't, as he had no money, so Jackson reached into a desk drawer, pulled out a silk purse containing some gold, and tossed it to the Raven with the admonition to go get a decent outfit. Houston immediately went to a tailor and was measured for "a coat of the finest material, reaching to my knees, trousers in harmony of color and the latest style in cut, with a white satin vest to match." [9]

Throughout the trial Sam continued his correspondence with his friend Prentiss in New York about Texas and Mexico. Prentiss had written him on April 15 stating the Vera Cruz packet had finally arrived bringing Mexican news, and that Santa Anna was firm and in full confidence of success. Houston answered this letter on May 1, commenting that his trial was progressing slowly, and expressed confidence that

> Congress can do nothing with me . . . My counsel is too indisposed to proceed in his argument until Thursday next. So soon as he is done . . . I will myself address the House. . . . Whenever I get thro I will repair to your city, and so soon as matters can be arranged, I will set out for the *land of promise*. . . .
>
> My Gold mine matters lay idle, as I expect my partner on to the Baltimore Convention, and I have no doubt, but he will have such evidence as will satisfy any person who may wish an interest, that it is truly valuable! [10]

Prentiss quickly replied to this letter, and under date of May 4 wrote Houston stating he had more news from Vera Cruz: Santa Anna was strong in power and increasing in strength and influence. He closed by asking Houston to let him know if he expected to be detained much longer. On May 6 Houston was notified he would have to close his case the next day.

At high noon on May 7, Speaker Stevenson looked down from his seat on the dais and called the House to order. At the back of the Speaker was a figure of Liberty, at whose feet a marble eagle spread its wings for flight. On either side were flag-draped panels, one hung with a portrait of Washington and the other with a likeness of the Marquis de Lafayette.

Every seat on the floor was filled; chairs had been placed in the aisles to take care of the overflow. On the first row was defense attorney Key, and near him sat Junius Brutus Booth, one of the foremost actors of the day. For hours the galleries had been packed with the diplomatic corps, the army, navy, and glittering society.

The Raven was dressed in the finery provided him by President Jackson's gold as he bowed before the Speaker. There was absolute quiet among his hushed audience as he slowly glanced around the chamber and with perfect composure began his lengthy defense. His defense was like a theatrical performance. Speaking in his rich, sonorous voice, he opened his speech by remarking on the embarrassment he felt by being arraigned for the first time in his life on a charge of violating the laws of his country. He denied that he had violated the law. He claimed that he had not attacked Stanbery for words the congressman uttered in the House charging him with corruption, but for publishing libelous matter in the *Intelligencer*. He cited the testimony of witnesses to the encounter that he had not been armed and that his meeting with Stanbery was accidental.

Attorney Houston then covered a wide range of subjects in defense of defendant Houston. He mentioned the respect he had for the House and its rights and privileges.

> Never can I forget the associations connected with this Hall. Never can I lose the remembrance of that pride of heart which swelled my bosom when finding myself, for the first time, enjoying those privileges and exercising those rights, as one of the representatives of the American people.[11]

He then attacked the legality of the proceedings, pointing out that he was not allowed the judgment of his peers, and that the House was acting as grand jury, prosecutor, jury, and judge. With his voice dropping, and then slowly rising, Sam quoted poetry:

> *I seek no sympathies, nor need;*
> *The thorns which I have reaped are of the tree*
> *I planted; they have torn me, and I bleed.*[12]

A recurrent theme in his summation was that he was a private citizen and that if the House could punish him they could do it to others.

With his vast knowledge of history Houston mentioned various tyrants such as Draco, Caligula, Caesar, Cromwell, Pompey, and Bonaparte and remarked: "Surely it cannot possibly be supposed that this court has a right to exercise powers which the Parliament of England does not claim for its members." He mentioned the Bible and the Apostle Paul; he quoted more poetry. Finally, there was a dramatic pause. As his hushed audience bent forward

129

eagerly to hear his next remarks, he flung out one arm and pointed to the American flag over the portrait of Lafayette.

> So long as that proud emblem of my country's liberties, with its stripes and its stars . . . shall wave in this Hall of American legislators, so long shall it cast its sacred protection over the personal rights of every American citizen . . . so long, I trust, shall the rights of American citizens be preserved safe and unimpaired, and transmitted as a sacred legacy from one generation to another, till discord shall wreck the spheres . . . and not one fragment of all creation be left to chafe on the bosom of eternity's waves.[13]

With a solemn bow to the Speaker, Houston was finished and took a seat near Francis Scott Key. His friend, the actor Junius Brutus Booth, embraced him. "Houston, take my laurels!" [14]

The spectators gave Houston a standing ovation.

The House deliberated for four days and then voted 106 to 89 that Houston was "guilty as charged." He was sentenced to be reprimanded by the Speaker on May 14. On the day of the sentencing once more the chamber of the House was packed to overflowing. Houston stood before the Speaker and bowed respectfully as he awaited the reprimand. Stevenson, a friend of the accused, began his unwelcome duty by praising Sam for his character and intelligence. He then added: "I forebear to say more than to pronounce the judgment of the House, which is that you . . . be reprimanded at this bar by the Speaker . . . and . . . I do reprimand you accordingly." [15]

The House then allowed Congressman William S. Archer of Virginia to present, on behalf of Houston, a protest in the *House Journal* about the entire proceedings of his trial, which Sam considered "unwarranted by the constitution." [16]

If Sam thought his troubles were over once he had been reprimanded, he was wrong. Stanbery proved himself a very vindictive man. As a former congressman Houston was entitled to the privileges of the House floor. His opponent presented a resolution to have Houston denied those privileges, but with future president James Polk leading the fight on Houston's behalf the resolution was defeated 101 to 90. Stanbery's next ploy was to have the House appoint a committee of seven to investigate the ration contract, with himself as chairman. Still not satisfied, in the federal court of the District of Columbia he had Sam indicted on a charge of criminal assault.

The congressional investigation of the ration matter dragged on for several weeks, with Houston once more acting as his own counsel. Witnesses were brought in from far away, and the Raven's friend Auguste P. Chouteau from the Indian nation testified on Sam's behalf. After six weeks, by a majority vote, Houston and Eaton were acquitted.

On June 28 Houston was found guilty in the federal court on the charge of criminal assault against Stanbery and was fined $500 plus costs. He was given until the following winter to pay the fine, but never paid it as it was later remitted by Jackson.

The trial and the congressional investigation of the Indian ration contract had enormous consequences for the Raven. It rescued him from obscurity and gave him a springboard to national prominence. He recognized this, and many years later in Texas he remarked to George W. Paschal:

> I was dying out, and had they taken me before a Justice of the Peace and fined me ten dollars for assault and battery, they would have killed me. But they gave me a national tribunal for a theater, and set me up again.[17]

Now that the Raven's tribulations with Stanbery were over, he could once more concentrate on Texas. During his lengthy trials a voluminous correspondence had been going back and forth between Houston, Prentiss, and others concerning the proposed trip there. On June 1, Sam had given Prentiss his note for $1,594.22 for a half-interest in 25,000 acres in Texas known as the Dominguez Grant and reached an agreement to go to Texas as the agent of Prentiss and his associates to purchase part or all of the shares of the Leftwich Grant.[18]

From the correspondence between Houston and Prentiss it is apparent that both were casting a wary eye on the volatile political situation in Texas, as Gen. Antonio Lopez de Santa Anna's ascendancy over Mexico had aroused the concern of Great Britain. In addition, there was great unrest among the Americans in Texas. Desiring a companion to go to Texas with him, Houston had written Charles Noland on June 10 asking him if he would be willing to accompany him there. He promised "if we should live, our wealth must be boundless." [19]

On June 2, John A. Wharton had written Houston from New Orleans, telling him that his conduct in the Stanbery matter "has been approved by a large majority throughout the Union . . . I do most sincerely and heartily rejoice at your whipping the puppy." [20] He went on to mention that he had given Dr. Branch T. Archer of Virginia a letter of introduction to Houston.

> Dr. Archer has been in Texas for upwards of twelve months, is intimately acquainted with matters and things there, and is in the confidence of all of their leading men. He is of opinion that there will be some fighting there next fall, and that a fine country will be gained without much bloodshed.[21]

Wharton then stated he expected to visit his brother William in Texas in August, and he asked Houston to procure him a passport. He also commented it was understood that Sam's old foe, Billy Carroll, was to be appointed minister to Mexico.

Before the Raven left the capital to go back to Fort Gibson[22] he had some unfinished business to take care of. First, as he had done a few years previously, he wrote the secretary of war recommending that medals be given various Indian tribes on the plains. This time the War Department acceded to his request. Then he struck back at some of his antagonists. On July 10, 1832, *The Globe* in Washington carried a lengthy statement he issued "To The Public." In this article he defended himself, President Jackson, and Secretary Eaton in the matter of the Indian rations and took several blasts at Duff Green and various Indian agents who had testified against him in the congressional hearings. He closed with a scathing denouncement of his oppressor, Stanbery.

> Insensible to every manly emotion, he is incapable of an attempt to rise in the scale of being, and seeks only to drag others to his own loathsome degradation. His vices are too odious to merit pity, and his spirit too mean to deserve contempt.[23]

Houston had planned to leave Washington July 12 for Fort Gibson, with a stopover in Nashville for a few days to await funds from Prentiss since his own funds were extremely low. However, severe chills and a fever delayed his departure for a day. His friend Noland, weary of the procrastination of the Prentiss group in furnishing money for the trip, had finally decided not to accompany Sam to Texas.

On his way to Tennessee from the capital, Houston stopped over in Cincinnati to visit with friends. On the evening of July 20, he and his party attended the theater, to be promptly greeted with hisses and boos. Apparently, the Ohioans could not forgive the Raven for his pummeling of their Congressman Stanbery. Sam rose and tried to calm the crowd down but it was no use. The manager was forced to bring the curtain down on the unfinished performance.

Houston's intention to spend only a few days in Nashville turned out to be a stay of six weeks, and the looked-for financing of his trip was never forthcoming. On July 31, Prentiss had written him there was a delay advancing him money as all the businessmen had fled New York on account of a cholera scare. On August 3, his friend John Van Fossen had written him from New York:

> I was informed . . . that there was reason to fear that your friends in New York would fail of their engagement to furnish the means of prosecuting your Texas enterprise. I do not believe that that portion of the country will long continue its allegiance to the Mexican Government, and I would much rather see it detached through your agency, as the consequences could not fail to be highly favorable to your interest . . .[24]

Van Fossen concluded his letter by predicting that General Jackson would be reelected in the forthcoming election.

From New York on August 18, Prentiss wrote Houston stating that the continuance of cholera in the city was preventing any movement in their Texas affairs, and on the same date from Nashville the Raven wrote Prentiss, asking that a draft for at least $600 be sent him. He also commented:

> I have seen several friends here lately from Texas, and all represent it in the most prosperous state, and say it is a lovely region! Thousands would flock there from this country, if the Government were settled, but will not venture without it!
>
> My opinion is that it would be of vast importance to have persons there who could look at matters, with a view to [make] changes, which are necessary, and must [take] place, before long in that country, and without which it can never be, what it ought to be, for the benefit of those interested. Several persons have said to me that I was looked for, and earnestly wished for by the Citizens of Texas. . . . The people look to the Indians on Arkansas as auxilliaries, in the event of a change — So I will pass that way and see my *old friends*. I will ride to the Hermitage this evening and see the Old Chief, General Jackson . . .[25]

In a postscript he added: "A population like that of Texas is in

133

perpetual liability to commotion, and tho it may be tranquil today, a storm may arise tomorrow."

All of his life Houston was short of funds, and there is a possibility that Old Hickory may have advanced him $500 for his trip to Texas. In any event, he instructed Acting Secretary of War John Robb to issue to the Raven a passport, which was dated August 6, 1832. The passport described Houston as "A Citizen of the United States, thirty eight years of age, six feet, two inches in stature, brown hair, and light complexion."[26] The passport requested all the tribes of Indians, whether in amity with the United States or as yet not allied to them by treaties, to permit Sam to safely and freely pass through their respective territories, and in case of need, to give him all lawful aid and protection. In addition, the War Department asked Sam to gather information on various plains tribes and report his findings to the newly appointed Stokes Commission at Fort Gibson.

Houston finally gave up expectations of receiving expense money from his New York sponsors. He wrote Prentiss on September 15, 1832:

> all considerations have certainly failed, on your part, which were held out as inducements to me and as your letters will shew upon their face. . . .
>
> The matter of Texas has, to my mortification, not turned out as I had hoped and believed, but I shall "cast my bread upon the waters, and look for its return after many days." Tomorrow morning I am to set out for there![27]

Before setting out "for there," the Raven flew back to the Wigwam Neosho and the waiting arms of Diana, arriving at the Fort Gibson area about October 8. A few days later he, Colonel Arbuckle, and Washington Irving spent a night drinking and talking. Undoubtedly, Houston's forthcoming trip to Texas was discussed; however, for some reason, perhaps at the Raven's request, no records or notes of any such discussion were made in either Irving's personal journal or his *A Tour on the Prairies*. But Irving did, in his journal, favor the world with his impression of his host:

> Gov. Houston, tall, large, well formed, fascinating man — low-crowned large brimmed white beaver — boots with brass eagle spurs — given to grandiloquence. A large and military mode of expressing himself. Old General Nix used to say God made him two drinks scant.[28]

Sam spent the rest of October and November putting his personal affairs in order. He deeded his Wigwam Neosho and his two slaves to Diana. Legend has it that he asked her to accompany him to Texas but that she refused, saying she could not leave her people.[29]

The first member of the Stokes Commission to arrive at Fort Gibson was Henry Ellsworth. Houston conferred with him, and then once more it was time for the Raven, that restless wanderer of the West, to move on. On his tailless pony, Jack, he headed toward the newly reactivated Fort Towson on the American side of the Red River for his first stop before entering Texas.

On his way to the Red River, the Raven encountered United States Marshal Elias Rector, who acquired some fame as the celebrated Arkansas Traveler, and the two traveled together for a day or two. Before they parted, the smooth-talking Houston managed to swap his bobtailed pony for Rector's full-sized horse. In addition, the Arkansas Traveler threw in a razor, and if legend is to be believed Houston thanked him for the gift with these words: "Rector, I except [sic] your gift, and mark my words, if I have luck this razor will some day shave the chin of a president of a republic." [30]

From Fort Towson in the Arkansas Territory on December 1, Sam wrote a lengthy letter to Commissioner Ellsworth, giving him a report on information he had received concerning the Pawnee and Comanche Indians, and asking him to forward a copy of his report to the secretary of war. The next day Houston wrote his cousin John telling him he was about to enter Texas and that "My health and spirits are both good, my habits sober, and my heart straight." He asked his cousin to congratulate Old Hickory on his recent re-election to the presidency, and mentioned some of his plans.

> It is reported that my friends have announced my name as a candidate for next Governor of Tennessee. Shou'd I live, I must be back by the first of April, or last of March and see how the land lies for such business. My friends are sanguine of my success. I do not doubt it, if I should run! as I think I shall. My business to Texas is of some importance to my pecuniary interest, and as such, I must attend to it![31]

The Raven then mounted his horse, and with a clear head and confidence in the future, pointed him south and followed his Star of Destiny across the Red River to Texas.

BOOK THREE

To Texas and Greatness

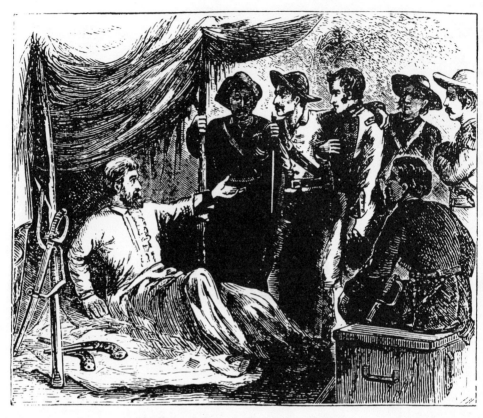

Houston and Santa Anna from an early print.
— Courtesy Texas State Library and Archives

CHAPTER 15

Discord in Texas

Although there were many Indian tribes in this bleak region, the first European settlement in what is now known as Texas was founded by the Spaniards at Isleta, near present-day El Paso. In an effort to strengthen their claim to the territory, from 1690 onward the Spaniards established numerous missions, military posts, and towns in the new territory.

The huge province of Louisiana originally belonged to France, but at the end of the Seven Years' War in 1763 it was passed to Spain. When the land was returned to France in 1800, a secret treaty clarified that if France ever gave it up it would revert to Spain.

When Thomas Jefferson consummated the Louisiana Purchase in 1803 for $15 million, the area purchased included Colorado east of the Rocky Mountains and Louisiana west of the Mississippi. Jefferson claimed both Texas and West Florida. In 1814 Gen. Andrew Jackson began the series of invasions of East Florida that led to the Treaty of 1819 when Spain, needing money, consented to President Monroe's offer to purchase Florida. As part of the deal the Adams-Onís Treaty of February 22, 1819, forfeited the American claim to Texas and fixed the boundary between Spain and the United States by a zigzag line, extending from the mouth of the Sabine River, dividing Texas and Louisiana, to the Pacific Ocean.[1]

Many Americans opposed the relinquishment of Texas in this fashion. One was Henry Clay, who filibustered against the treaty. Among those taking more direct action was Dr. James Long, a surgeon from Mississippi who had served in William Carroll's brigade under Jackson at New Orleans. Gathering some seventy-five followers, he marched into Texas with his army and captured the small town of Nacogdoches with little resistance. He and other leaders then declared Texas to be a free and independent republic. His invasion collapsed with news of the Treaty of Cordoba in 1821, declaring that Mexico had won her independence after three hundred years of subjection to Spain. He and some of his followers were captured and sent to Mexico City, where eventually he was freed. Shortly thereafter he was assassinated.

Moses Austin, a native of Durham, Connecticut, for some time had the idea of settling a colony in the province of Texas. On December 23, 1820, he arrived in San Antonio de Bexar, capital of the province, and made application to Governor Antonio María Martínez to colonize the area. At first Martínez turned Austin down, but through the intervention of Baron Felipe Enrique Neri de Bastrop he changed his mind and forwarded the application to his superior with the recommendation the application be approved.

At that time Texas was in an administrative division of New Spain known as the Eastern Interior Provinces, and its head as chief civil and military commandant was Gen. Joaquin de Arredondo. On January 17, 1821, Arredondo approved a grant permitting Austin to settle 300 families within an area of 200,000 acres.[2] A few days before Austin's untimely death due to pneumonia on June 21, 1821, at the age of fifty-six, he received this welcome news and virtually on his deathbed requested that his twenty-seven-year-old son, Stephen Fuller Austin, carry on the project.

Young Stephen was a brilliant man, educated in Connecticut and Kentucky. At twenty he had been a practicing lawyer and a member of the legislature of Missouri Territory, and at twenty-three, a United States district judge for the Arkansas Territory. Austin acceded to his father's request. Accompanied by several of the early colonists, he went to San Antonio de Bexar to confer with Martínez. After being received cordially, he was given a choice of where he desired to settle his colony. He selected a beautiful sight, watered by the Brazos, Guadalupe, Colorado, and San Antonio rivers, and named his capital San Felipe de Austin.

140

The governor and Austin discussed Stephen's plans for the new colonists: each male over twenty-one was to be given 640 acres, with an additional 320 acres for his wife, 160 acres for each child, and 80 acres for each slave. All settlers were to be of good character and industrious. In addition, the newcomers were to pay Austin twelve and one-half cents an acre for his expenses, and take an oath of allegiance to the Mexican government. The governor approved the plan, and newspapers throughout the Mississippi Valley carried advertisements for colonists.

Due to the turmoil in Mexico, Austin found it necessary to go to Mexico City and secure from the Congress a validation of his contract. Upon his arrival he found he was one of many seeking such a contract, and in addition there were the Cherokee chiefs Bowles, Nicollet, and Richard Fields. The chiefs were not seeking a contract to colonize but were seeking a grant of lands for members of their tribes who did not wish to settle in the Arkansas Territory. On April 27, 1823, the Cherokees were granted permission to stay in Texas with the understanding no more families of them should immigrate until the publication of the general colonization law.[3] Austin's contract was validated, and he was granted permission to bring in an additional 500 families.

The new Mexican government, far more liberal than the previous one, enacted laws designed to attract newcomers to Texas. The settlers could come on their own account or be introduced through *empresarios* such as Austin. Not less than 4,428 acres were to be given each stock raiser, and, as a further inducement, for a period of six years the newcomers were to be free from the payment of all tithes, taxes, and duties.[4]

In 1824 the government adopted a new federal constitution. It prohibited any religious faith other than Roman Catholicism and revoked the right to trial by jury. Subsequent decrees combined the provinces of Coahuila and Texas into one state to be known as Coahuila y Texas, with the provision Texas would become a separate state when sufficient population was attained. One clause of this new constitution gave preference to the Mexicans in the distribution of land; another clause required the would-be colonist to appear before the local *ayuntamiento,* the municipal government, and swear allegiance to the Mexican constitution. These two clauses raised the hackles of the Anglos and later on caused considerable friction between them and the Mexican government.

With the liberal colonization laws now in force, settlers from the United States started arriving daily. An official census in the fall of 1825 showed 1,800 people in Austin's colony, of whom 443 were slaves. By 1828 the population had grown to 2,021; the June 1830 census showed 4,248; and by 1831 the count was 5,665.[5]

The Fredonian Rebellion of December 1826 was the second attempt to establish an independent Texas republic, and it affected the relations between Mexico and Texas far more than the earlier ill-fated expedition of Dr. Long.

The principal figure of this rebellion was Hayden Edwards, who had been among those would-be empresarios Austin had met in Mexico City. Edwards was a wealthy gentleman from Kentucky who, after spending several years and many thousands of dollars in Mexico, finally secured a grant of one hundred square miles of fertile land in East Texas bordering Austin's colony. This included the area around Nacogdoches, not far from the Louisiana border. He asked his brother in Mississippi, Maj. Benjamin W. Edwards, to come to Texas and aid him in building up his colony. The major promptly accepted the invitation. The contract Hayden Edwards secured from Mexico required him to protect the rights of all who claimed to be original owners of land within the boundaries of his grant. In addition, he was authorized to organize and command militia to control the situation. In the late spring of 1825 he arrived in Nacogdoches and almost immediately became embroiled in controversy with both the Texans and the Mexican authorities. One of his first acts was to post notices announcing himself as military commander, which didn't please the settlers. Before the Edwards brothers arrived, there were about 1,600 squatters whose lands were in the Edwards grant or bordered it. These squatters were a mixed bag of American frontiersmen, speculators, and adventurers. There were fragments of a dozen Indian tribes in varying degrees of civilization. Some of the squatters were substantial planters, some were free blacks, and others were Mexicans. There was also a smattering of Spanish and French Creoles. Many of them had purchased what they believed to be valid claims to their land, although some of them lacked the documents to prove it.

Edwards quickly made it known that those claiming land within his grant were required to present themselves and show titles or documents proving their claims. Those with valid titles would have to bear the cost of such proof, and those unfortunates who could not comply with the requirements would find their lands sold to the first person who occupied them.

142

Among those who could not produce titles to their property was a Mexican named Ignatius Sertuche. Edwards promptly sold Sertuche's land to an American, and the furor began. Sertuche petitioned the legislature and other Mexicans sided with him. The acting political chief of that area, Don José Antonio Saucedo, ruled in favor of his compatriot and gave as his sole reason that Sertuche was a Mexican and thus entitled to preference. In other instances the same distinctions were made, and Mexicans were given preference over Americans.

In the early summer of 1826, Hayden Edwards returned to the United States to bring in more settlers. While he was gone, brother Benjamin wrote directly to Don Victor Blanco, the governor of the dual state of Coahuila y Texas, protesting Saucedo's action. Benjamin was shocked when the governor replied declaring the annulment of the Edwards contract, together with a decree calling for the expulsion of the two brothers from their colony. When the word was passed around that the Hayden Edwards contract had been abrogated, the Mexican population immediately set up claims to all the valuable places occupied by the Americans. The local *alcalde*, a position which combined the duties of a mayor, justice of the peace, and notary public, granted all the orders requested. A company of regulators was sent in to enforce the orders, and the Anglos were dispossessed and driven from their homes.[6]

The empresario Edwards and his brother Benjamin did not propose to take this action lying down. On December 16, 1826, Major Edwards and a handful of men rode into Nacogdoches. Carrying a red and white flag inscribed "Independence, Liberty and Justice," they seized and fortified the two-story stone house, a fortress-like building that was the seat of the ayuntamiento. Declaring the Texas portion of the dual state of Coahuila y Texas independent, they named it the "Republic of Fredonia."

When the Fredonians started their war it was with the hope and expectation all the Anglos and Indians in Texas would join them, and that volunteers from the United States would rally to their cause. Only a few Indian tribes could be induced to join the insurgents, as they had been badly treated by the whites. A few Cherokees aided them, but most of the Cherokees and their associate bands threw in their lot with the Mexicans when promised they would have the lands for which they applied.

An appeal from Edwards to Austin for help proved fruitless, as Austin was in a delicate position. To a friend he wrote, *"I am a Mex-*

143

ican citizen and officer and I will sacrifice my life before I will violate my duty and oath of office." [7]

When Saucedo and Colonel Ahumado reached San Felipe de Austin in early January 1827 and issued a conciliatory proclamation pledging the faith of the government and promising lands to those who were subordinate, Austin a: d his colony not only proved loyal to their oath to Mexico in their refusal to aid the Fredonians but joined in the war opposing them. Austin himself contributed two four-pounders to the Mexican army.

When the combined forces of the Indians and the Mexicans approached within ten or twelve miles of Nacogdoches on January 27, 1827, the Fredonians evacuated the city and crossed the Sabine River into Louisiana. The rebellion was over, and the Republic of Fredonia passed into history.

Although of short duration, the Fredonian Rebellion had long-term ramifications between the Texans and the Mexicans. To strengthen their hold on the frontier the Mexican government established a permanent military force at Nacogdoches. To many Anglos, the Edwards brothers had been cheated by the Mexican authorities, and from then on they were suspicious as to the reliability of the Mexicans when it came to a just administration of the law.

The history of Mexico had for years been a turbulent one, and for about a decade prior to obtaining independence from Spain, the country had been in a state of rebellion that was suppressed by terror. The leadership of Mexico changed hands numerous times, and like a thread running through a tapestry during those years was the name Antonio López de Santa Anna y Peréz de Lebron.

Born at Jalapa, Mexico, on February 21, 1794, Santa Anna was one of the most remarkable characters to step on the political stage of his country. At fifteen he had enlisted as a cadet in the Spanish royal army. Enjoying the military life, he did well in several engagements during Mexico's numerous revolutions, and with his intelligence and talent for changing sides at the right moment quickly won promotions. By the age of twenty-eight he was a general. He had great abilities and many faults, among which was an addiction to opium and pretty mistresses, preferably very young. Vain and capricious, he called himself "Protector of the People" and "the Napoleon of the West." An opportunist and a master of the double-cross, he was quick to betray his superiors — qualities which, added to a capacity for intrigue and treachery, saw him on

144

April 1, 1833, elected president at the age of thirty-eight.[8] In spite of his faults and betrayals, he was idolized by his followers, known as the "Santanistas," and became the master of Mexico eleven times.

Gen. Anastasio Bustamante had taken office as president of Mexico on January 1, 1830, and on April 6 a decree known as Bustamante's law went into effect and became the turning point in the relations of the Texas colonists and the government. The new law prohibited further American immigration into the colony but encouraged the immigration of Europeans, particularly the Swiss and Germans.[9] In addition, the law proposed to settle Mexican convicts in Coahuila y Texas after their release from prison and military service, and peons were encouraged to settle there in return for land given them. New customs duties that restricted trade with other nations were imposed; all land grants were suspended unless one hundred colonists had already settled in the areas allotted. Gen. Manuel Mier y Terán, an ardent royalist and stern anti-American, was appointed commandant-general of the eastern provinces and, with half a million dollars allocated by the Mexican government, promptly established military posts at Nacogdoches, Anahuac, Velasco, San Antonio de Bexar, Goliad, and other points.[10]

Col. John Bradburn was appointed both military commander and customs collector at Anahuac, at the mouth of the Trinity River near Galveston Bay. An adventurer from Kentucky who had been in Mexico and Texas for a number of years and had fought against Spain, he proved to be an unfortunate choice for the position tendered him. Irascible, tactless, and arbitrary, his pompousness made him the frequent butt of practical jokes and ridicule. Mild-mannered Stephen Austin was so appalled at the appointment that in a letter to a friend he remarked: "The fact is he is incompetent to such a command and is half crazy part of the time." [11]

In spite of the law prohibiting further immigration, new settlers were still arriving from the United States. Generally, they came on their own account instead of through an empresario and settled in the eastern portion of Coahuila y Texas. After their repeated applications for titles to their lands were ignored, the colonists in eastern Texas sent petitions to the state government asking for the appointment of a commissioner to extend titles. Their request was honored when Francisco Madero was appointed commissioner and dispatched to the Trinity, with José María Jesús Carbajal as his surveyor. Suddenly, both Madero and Carbajal were arrested and thrown into the prison at Anahuac by order of General Terán.

Under Commissioner Madero the municipality of Liberty, some thirty miles up the river from Anahuac, had been formed with its duly elected ayuntamiento. Colonel Bradburn dissolved the ayuntamiento of Liberty and placed both the town and Anahuac under martial law.

The militarization of Texas saddened Stephen Austin, who wrote the Mexican authorities:

> I have informed you many times, and I inform you again, that it is impossible to rule Texas by a military system . . . From the year 1821 I have maintained order and enforced the law in my colony simply by means of *civicos* [civil decrees], without a dollar of expense to the nation [Mexico] . . . Upon this subject of military despotism I have never hesitated to express my opinion, for I consider it the source of all revolutions and of the slavery and ruin of free peoples.[12]

In the past, the United States had made three proposals to Mexico concerning Texas. John Quincy Adams had hardly been installed as president when Joel Poinsett, minister to Mexico, on March 26, 1825, was instructed to sound that government out on making a new boundary. Mexico refused. On March 15, 1827, Poinsett was authorized to offer a million dollars if Mexico would accept the Rio Grande River as the boundary line between Texas and the United States, or half a million for its establishment on the Colorado. The final offer was made by President Andrew Jackson on August 25, 1829, for $5 million.[13] All attempts by the United States were rebuffed.

Mexico's foreign secretary, Lucas Alaman, in a lengthy report to the Mexican Congress in 1829 made harsh accusations against the United States and outlined what he believed were various methods the American government was using to stir up discontent in the Texas colony. Adding to the uneasiness of the Mexicans were the reports circulated for some time in American newspapers that American adventurers would invade Texas, and the ill-fated Long expedition and the subsequent Fredonian Rebellion gave credence to these reports.

The high-handed way Colonel Bradburn was governing his area was causing him great unpopularity. He was commandeering supplies for his troops and using slave labor in the erection of military buildings.[14] The colonists were dismayed when he encouraged the slaves to revolt, telling them it was the intent of the law to set them free. Worse yet, he refused to surrender two runaway slaves from Louisiana.[15] But it was the arrest of several colonists on various pretexts that brought the storm upon him in May 1832.

William Barret Travis, a red-haired, twenty-six-year-old lawyer from South Carolina, had been in Texas as early as April 1831. Travis lived in Anahuac and had attempted to recover the two runaway slaves for his client. He soon found himself in the guardhouse with Patrick C. Jack, who had organized a militia company and was arrested on an uncertain pretext, together with another man who had been jailed for no other reason than for playing a practical joke on Bradburn.

Outraged colonists elected Frank W. Johnson as their colonel, and with a force of over one hundred men they started marching from the Brazos River to Anahuac to release the prisoners. On their way they captured a contingent of Mexicans, and when they arrived at the fort at Anahuac they demanded the release of the Americans. Bradburn proposed a deal. If Johnson and his men would retire some miles from the fort and release the Mexicans, he then would release Travis, Jack, and the others. Johnson and his men then withdrew to Turtle Bay, about five miles from Anahuac on the Liberty Road. There, on June 13, 1832, they adopted what was called the Turtle Bay resolutions.

Bradburn then pulled a double-cross. He not only failed to release his prisoners but resupplied his troops with some stores from a house the Texans had occupied. He then sent word to Col. Domingo de Ugartechea at Velasco and Col. José de las Piedras at Nacogdoches, notifying them of the situation.

The Texans were furious at the treachery of Bradburn. Thinking it unwise to attack his fort without artillery, they sent to Velasco for two cannon and sent messengers asking for reinforcements. Colonel Ugartechea refused their request, but reinforcements came in to augment Johnson's forces until finally the Texans were several hundred strong.

While all this was happening, events had been transpiring in Mexico which greatly aided the Texans in their demonstrations against Bradburn. Mexico was once more engaged in civil war. Some months previously the wily General Santa Anna, in one of his frequent acts of betrayal of his leaders, had mounted a revolt against Bustamante in his assumed role as the "Protector of the People." In the resolutions adopted at Turtle Bay the Texans had condemned Bustamante for violating the constitution of 1824 and in their enthusiasm promised to support Santa Anna as he had promised to defend that constitution.[16]

At Velasco, at the mouth of the Brazos, a sharp battle had been fought between the forces of Capt. John Austin and Colonel Ugartechea on June 25.[17] After a bloody fight of eleven hours, in which the Mexicans suffered thirty-five dead and fifteen wounded, Ugartechea raised the white flag of surrender. The Texans had suffered seven dead and twenty-seven wounded. When Ugartechea and his men surrendered their arms, they were furnished with provisions and allowed to set out for Matamoros.

Colonel Piedras, commander of the fort at Nacogdoches, was advancing to the relief of Colonel Bradburn with a strong force, including a large group of Shawnees and Cherokees. Upon hearing of this the Texans sent a committee to meet him and lay before him their complaints against Bradburn. Piedras listened to them courteously and released the prisoners Bradburn was holding. In addition, he agreed to pay for the private property Bradburn had appropriated and very tactfully induced him to ask to be relieved from his command. Bradburn then sailed for New Orleans and later returned to Mexico.[18] Colonel Johnson and his forces, having achieved their objective, then went home and disbanded.

During the latter days of July 1832, the citizens of Nacogdoches, together with those of some nearby towns, decided to unite and present the Mexican forces there with a choice: to declare for the constitution of 1824 and for Santa Anna, or else to fight. A committee was appointed to call on Colonel Piedras and present him with their demands. The colonel chose to fight. When the committee reported his decision to the Texas forces, consisting of about 300 men, they elected James W. Bullock of San Augustine to the command. On August 2, 1832, they marched into Nacogdoches. Just north of the stone house they were suddenly attacked by Mexican cavalry numbering about one hundred. This charge was beaten off, but in the attack the Mexicans killed the alcalde of the town. The Texans took possession of the houses on the north and south sides of the square, and their accurate marksmanship took a toll on every Mexican showing himself. During the evening the Mexicans made one sortie and it was repulsed. Later that night Piedras and his troops fled, leaving behind his killed and wounded.

James Bowie, who was in this engagement, was dispatched with some men to pursue the Mexicans and caught up with them about twenty miles from San Antonio. After some gunfire, Colonel Piedras surrendered his command to Maj. Francisco Medine, who immediately declared in favor of the constitution of 1824. Colonel Piedras was sent back to Mexico, and Bowie and his men escorted the remaining officers and men to San Antonio.

Stephen Austin's policy was to remain aloof from Mexican politics and to take no sides in the numerous revolutions and counter-revolutions in Mexico. His motto of "adherence and fidelity to Mexico" had gained great benefits to the colonists, and one of his fixed rules of action for Texas had been "that with respect to her rights, she must always act on the defensive and never on the offensive." [19] He and his followers had no intention of breaking away from Mexico or starting armed rebellion, and they were known as the peace party. At the same time there were those in the war party who were clamoring for separation from Coahuila, even if it meant revolution. They were supporting Santa Anna in his uprising against Bustamante and were hoping that with his support the hated law of 1830 would be abolished.

On August 22, 1832, the alcalde of San Felipe sent out a call for a convention to meet on October 1. At the appointed time fifty-eight delegates assembled, representing seventeen townships. An influential settlement from San Antonio refused to participate, but a Mexican delegation did arrive from Goliad — after the convention adjourned. By a two-to-one vote over William H. Wharton, Stephen F. Austin was elected to preside.

Of the many reports of interest to the colonists that were adopted, two in particular seemed to be the most important. One called for the repeal of the hated article eleven of the law of April 6, 1830, which prohibited immigration from the United States and suspended practically all colonizing contracts. A petition to Mexican authorities calling for the separation of Texas from Coahuila was approved by a special subcommittee of three members, including Austin and Wharton. The Texans had many just grounds of complaint against their union with Coahuila, as the latter had three-fourths of the representation in the state legislature and its population was composed almost wholly of Mexicans. The administration of justice in Texas was neglected, and the right of trial by jury was postponed.

Nothing was done about the resolutions and petitions adopted at the convention. Ramón Musquiz, the political chief, wrote Austin that the ayuntamiento of San Felipe had acted illegally in call-

149

ing the convention. In a letter to Musquiz on November 15, 1832, Austin said:

> I give it as my deliberate judgment that Texas is lost if she takes no measures of her own for her welfare. I incline to the opinion that it is your duty, as chief magistrate, to call a convention to take into consideration the condition of the country.[20]

Musquiz did not see fit to call a convention. The central committee, a standing committee of citizens elected by the convention in October, then issued a call for another convention to be held April 1, 1833, with delegates to be elected on March 1.

This, then, was the situation as Sam Houston rode toward Texas and his destiny.

CHAPTER 16

Toward Independence

A question that has perplexed historians for years is why exactly Sam Houston went to Texas. To Charles Lester, Houston stated his intention "was now to become a herdsman, and spend the rest of [my] life in the tranquility of the prairie solitudes." [1] Surely he was pulling the legs of his readers. To picture this healthy, virile, restless man with his driving ambition settling down placidly to spend the rest of his life as a herdsman borders on being ludicrous.

To many of his critics Houston was a schemer and an opportunist whose sole reason for journeying to Texas was as Andrew Jackson's agent to wrench that area from Mexico so it could be annexed to the United States. It was certainly true that Old Hickory had long had his eyes on Texas, as he was farsighted enough to know that in order to grow, this still youthful nation must someday have its western boundaries at the Pacific Ocean.

To this day no one has uncovered any concrete evidence that Houston went to Texas as the agent of either Jackson or the United States government in order to foment a revolution. On the contrary, the groundwork for the coming revolution had been laid years before Sam crossed the Red River, and the fight for Texas's independence would have occurred if the world had never heard of Sam Houston.

151

In their talks at the Hermitage the previous summer, Jackson had expressed his worry to Houston about the Comanche Indians in Texas, whose war-like nature made them feared by all the other tribes. Many Americans by now were emigrating to that vast territory, and Jackson feared for them. He wanted Sam to use his good graces with the Comanches to sign a peace treaty with the other tribes. This Houston agreed to do.

When Houston entered Texas, the timing was right for a man with the opportunism, intelligence, leadership qualities, and ambition he had. His numerous letters to James Prentiss during the past year had shown he was interested in land speculation, and Texas had land aplenty — millions and millions of acres of it. Now he was actually in the promised land, and the opportunities for wealth were boundless.

From Fort Towson on the Red River to Nacogdoches, Texas was a long, lonely stretch of 180 miles, which Houston rode in solitude. After finally reaching his objective he paused to rest for several days and renew old friendships with various people. He then mounted his steed and headed southwest another 180 miles. After a journey of several days, during which he crossed both the Neches and Trinity rivers, he finally reached San Felipe.

The capital of Stephen Austin's colony, San Felipe, was a small village of some forty or fifty crude log cabins and pine buildings on the west bank of the Brazos River. For accommodations the town boasted two weather-beaten taverns — the Virginia House and the New England Retreat.

The empresario Austin was not at home, being engaged in business elsewhere in his vast domain. Houston's disappointment was assuaged when he encountered the sandy-haired Jim Bowie, who had added to his colorful reputation since Houston had first met him almost four years previously at Helena, Arkansas.

The former governor and Bowie liked each other immediately, as they had much in common. Bowie, like Houston, was a marvelous physical specimen; his 180 pounds were well distributed on his six-foot one-inch frame. As Houston had been adopted into the Cherokee tribe, so had Bowie been adopted into the Arapaho tribe.[2] The two men had other traits in common: both were men of courage and high intelligence, made friends easily and quickly, and, best of all, were natural born leaders.

Bowie had been a member of the ill-fated Long expedition some years before and had prospered since deciding to make Texas his permanent home. He had joined the Roman Catholic church

and in 1830 had taken as his bride none other than the beautiful
Ursula Veramendi, daughter of Don Juan Martín de Veramendi,
vice-governor of the state of Coahuila y Texas. In addition to two
children and a fine home near Saltillo, in the Coahuila section of
the dual state, he was the possessor of nearly three-quarters of a
million acres of land.

The two new friends rode together to San Antonio de Bexar, a
Hispanic city with homes of adobe and stone and several lovely
missions built by the Franciscan fathers. One mission, named San
Antonio de Valero and built around 1722, later became famous as
the Alamo — a site which would have an important impact on the
lives of Houston, Bowie, and all Texans.

In San Antonio, Houston was introduced and made welcome
by Bowie's father-in-law, the vice-governor. He then proceeded
along the Camino Real until he met with a delegation of Comanche
chiefs, to whom he delivered messages from President Jackson and
presented medals bearing Jackson's likeness. After a series of discussions with the chiefs, he secured their agreement to send a delegation to Fort Gibson in about three months to meet with the Indian commissioner and delegations of other tribes for a peace
conference. Houston later had little to say about his meeting with
the Comanches but described it as "a confidential mission with little known of its history." [3]

At San Felipe on December 24, 1832, Houston applied for a
league of land on Karankawa Bay, stating that he was a married
man. The application was approved by Austin, and for $375, with
an exchange of horses as part of the transaction, Sam became the
owner of approximately 4,428 acres.[4] Sometime later he was
granted a headright in the David G. Burnet colony, thus giving him
another 4,428 acres.

The peripatetic Houston then rode back to Nacogdoches for a
few days of relaxation. On March 1, an election of delegates was to
be held to meet at San Felipe de Austin on April 1. Houston readily
consented to a request that he stand for election as a delegate. He
then crossed the Sabine to Natchitoches, Louisiana, where on February 1, 1833, he wrote Henry L. Ellsworth, the Indian commissioner at Fort Gibson, reporting on his recent conference with the
Comanches. In his report, Sam gave his opinion that the chiefs
would reach Fort Gibson around May 15 or 20 and be well disposed to make peace. He was also of the opinion the Comanches
had a high regard for the Americans, while cherishing the most supreme contempt for the Mexicans.[5] He concluded by stating, "If

anything can defeat the present expectations, it will be the indirect influence of the Spaniards, who are jealous of everybody and everything."[6]

Old Hickory was the recipient of a letter written by Houston on February 13, in which Sam offered the president his frank opinions concerning Texas and the current situation there. It was Houston's opinion that nineteen-twentieths of the population of Texas desired the acquisition of Texas by the United States, as

> they are now without laws to govern or protect them. Mexico is involved in civil war. The Federal Constitution has never been in operation. The government is essentially despotic and must be so, for years to come. The rulers have not honesty, and the people have not *intelligence*. The people of Texas are determined to form a State Government and separate from Coahuila . . . .
>
> Mexico is powerless and penniless to all intents and purposes. Her want of money taken in connexion with the course which Texas *must and will adopt,* will render a transfer of Texas inevitable to some power, and if the United States, does not press for it, England will most assuredly obtain it by some means. . . . If Texas is desirable to the United States it is now in the most favorable attitude perhaps that it can be to obtain it on fair terms — England is *pressing* her *suit* for it, but its citizens will resist, if any transfer should be made, of them to any other power but the United States.[7]

Houston summed up his letter to his old chief by stating that after traveling 500 miles across Texas he considered it the finest country he had ever seen; that it could easily sustain ten million souls as the greater portion of it was richer than West Tennessee. He predicted that at the coming convention on April 1, at which he was to be a delegate, the Texans would form a state constitution and declare that country as Texas proper.[8]

The Raven then indicated that at last he had found his permanent nest: "It is probable that I may make Texas my abiding place! In adopting this course, I will *never forget* the Country of my birth."[9]

The last touches of winter were still lingering and the air was cool and crisp when slightly more than fifty delegates assembled in a rude, narrow apartment in San Felipe on April 1, 1833. Many, like Houston, wore buckskins and slept on the ground with a saddle for a pillow and a blanket for their sole covering.

Inasmuch as this group of unkempt pioneers had to pay their own expenses, they quickly got down to business and completed their work in thirteen days. By now the war party was in the ascendancy, and Houston's old friend from Tennessee, William H. Wharton, was elected president of the convention over Austin. When the requisite committees were appointed, Houston was elected chairman of the committee that framed a constitution for the separate state of Texas. Empresario David G. Burnet was appointed chairman of a committee to draw up a memorial to the supreme government of Mexico.

The constitution as adopted was modeled largely on the United States Constitution and called for the right of trial by jury and the writ of habeas corpus, as well as freedom of the press. A considerable debate was had over the banking clause, which Branch T. Archer favored and Houston opposed. On this issue Houston won. It was declared by the convention that no bank or banking institution should ever exist under the constitution. Nothing but gold, silver, or copper coins were to be legal tender.

In the selection of delegates to present the memorial and the proposed constitution to the authorities in Mexico City, Stephen F. Austin, William H. Wharton, and Dr. James B. Miller were chosen.[10] The emissaries were also instructed to do everything in their power to secure repeal of the odious eleventh article of the law of April 6, 1830, which prohibited natives of the United States from emigrating to Texas. In addition, they were to request the enactment of a law establishing regular mail service in Texas, the regulation of the tariff, and defense of the colonies against the Indians.

For some reason Austin was the only delegate to make the journey to Mexico City. He departed shortly after the convention adjourned, expecting to be gone only a few months; however, he was imprisoned and did not return for two years.

In May 1833, Houston arrived at Fort Gibson for the conference between Commissioner Ellsworth and the Comanches. After a wait of several days with neither the commissioner nor the Indians making an appearance, Sam rode to Hot Springs, Arkansas, to rest and recuperate, as his many arduous journeys through Texas and Arkansas wilderness had aggravated his old Horseshoe Bend wound. On July 31, 1833, he wrote Secretary of War Lewis Cass a brief letter billing the War Department in the sum of $3,520 for expenses incurred in his relations with the Indians. The War Department refused to pay that sum, but eventually settled $1,200 upon him.[11]

On the same day Houston wrote Cass, he wrote his cousin

John that he was practicing law in Nacogdoches and expected to return there in a few days. Sam proudly stated he had a retainer of $2,000 and had received fees of $750 just shortly before leaving Texas. With two other gentlemen who furnished the capital, he continued, he had purchased 140,000 acres of choice land, and in addition he owned and had paid for 10,000 acres that he considered the most valuable land in Texas. Houston closed the letter by stating Texas was the finest portion of the globe that ever blessed his vision.

After recuperating at Hot Springs, Houston returned to Nacogdoches and settled down to the practice of law. Among his many friends from Tennessee who were now in this area was Col. Henry Raguet, of Swiss descent and originally from Pennsylvania. Raguet had prospered in his new surroundings and was now a landowner, a solid citizen, and a prosperous merchant. Sam had known Adolphus Sterne, the alcalde of Nacogdoches, in Tennessee. And there was also Houston's lifelong friend Phil Sublett, who lived in nearby San Augustine close to the Louisiana border.

Exuding his usual charm and gracious manner, it wasn't long before Sam was invited by Adolphus and Eva Sterne to take up permanent residence in their hospitable white-framed home with its neat white picket fence and its French-speaking Louisiana black servants. Houston lost no time in accepting the invitation and leaving the flea-ridden tavern in which he resided. Soon afterward, Houston was baptized as Don Samuel Pablo in the Roman Catholic faith, with Eva Rosine Sterne standing as godmother and the alcalde himself standing as godfather. After the ceremony, Don Samuel Pablo presented Eva Sterne with a ring as a token of affection for her. There is little doubt that the conversion was simply due to the Mexican law that only Catholics would serve as lawyers or be landowners.

Not counting blacks, who were excluded from the 1833 census, there were 1,272 people in Nacogdoches — eighty percent Anglos and the remainder Mexicans. Socially, the two groups did not mix. On the issue of whether Texas should become a separate state or remain part of Mexico, the Mexicans were virtually unanimous in favor of the latter, while the majority of Americans were in favor of separation.

Houston suddenly found himself casting more and more glances on the pretty features of Anna Raguet, daughter of Henry.

156

Only seventeen years of age and the third of six children, she was the apple of her father's eye. She had been educated at some of the best schools in Pennsylvania; she played the French harp, and was a talented linguist, capable of speaking and writing in French, Spanish, and German.

Colonel Raguet was a generous man who lived in the best house in Nacogdoches, but not everyone was invited into his home to listen to Anna play her French harp. Don Samuel Pablo, in spite of the difference in their ages — he now having passed forty — by virtue of his leadership, popularity, and charm, was always a welcome guest. With some knowledge of Spanish being a virtual necessity for a practicing lawyer in this region, Sam eagerly took Spanish lessons from the beautiful Anna.

By now Houston had given up all thoughts of ever returning to Tennessee on a permanent basis. He loved Texas and he loved land. Later on he was to write, "you may escape the small pox, but you can never escape the contagion of land loving." [12] With events changing so rapidly from day to day, he was shrewd enough to realize that his destiny lay in Texas. Perhaps it was with those thoughts in mind — and possibly visions of the pretty Anna sharing in that future — that on November 30, 1833, he filed a petition for divorce from Eliza. The petition, presented by attorney B. Jonas Harrison in the free state of Coahuila y Texas, district of Ayish, was a lengthy one. The reasons given were the four-year separation between the couple and the impossibility of a reconciliation.[13] For some reason the petition was not acted upon, and it would be some years before the divorce was finally granted.

There was an air of tranquillity in the state at this time as the colonists were awaiting the results of Stephen Austin's journey to the Mexican capital. December found Houston in San Felipe, probably on a business trip, and in his diary dated December 15, 1833, William Barret Travis made the entry: "Genl. Houston [is] in town." [14]

In early 1834 Houston traveled east, visiting Baltimore, Philadelphia, New York, and Washington. In March and April he had an exchange of correspondence with James Prentiss concerning Texas. The New Yorker financier wanted Houston to represent the Galveston Bay and Texas Land Company, but he could not raise the fee Houston requested.[15] In a letter addressed from Washington City, dated April 20, 1834, Houston remarked:

Now as to Texas, I will give you my candid impressions — I do not think that it will be acquired by the U States. I do think within one year that it will be a Soverign State and acting in all things as such. Within three years I think it will be separated from the Mexican Confederacy, and remain so forever.. . . I assure you Santa Anna aspires to the *Purple,* and should he assume it, you know Texas is off from them . . .[16]

Houston wrote Prentiss again on April 24 and once more stated his opinion that Texas would never be acquired by the United States during the administration of Jackson; if it were acquired by treaty, the treaty would not be ratified by the present Senate.[17]

While in Washington, Houston stopped by the White House to visit Jackson. In later years Houston was extremely close-mouthed about his discussions with the president, but undoubtedly they covered Sam's conferences with the Comanches and the imprisonment of Austin in Mexico City. Jackson was still eager to purchase Texas but did not want to fight for it because he was certain it would mean war with England. As to whether he promised help to the Texans in the event of an uprising, or whether he would withhold American support, we do not know.

Another friend Houston managed to see in Washington was Junius Brutus Booth, who had given him so much support during the Stanbery trial. In an evening of drunken revelry at Brown's Indian Queen Hotel, Houston was heard to exclaim: "I am made to revel in the Halls of Montezuma." [18]

Returning to Texas, Houston stopped off in Little Rock, Arkansas. William F. Pope, in his book *Early Days In Arkansas,* gave his impression of the former governor:

Gen. Houston was one of the most magnificent specimens of physical manhood I have ever seen. . . . I first saw him on the public road a few miles out of town. He was riding a splendid bay horse, and his saddle and bridle were of the most exquisite Mexican workmanship and were elaborately ornamented with solid silver plates and buckles in profusion. He was enveloped in a Mexican "poncho" which was richly ornamented with Mexican embroidery work.[19]

In December 1834 the Englishman G. W. Featherstonhaugh, while visiting America, encountered Houston in Washington, Arkansas, a hamlet about thirty miles from the Texas border. He has left for posterity some of his impressions:

. . . General Houston was here, leading a mysterious sort of life, shut up in a small tavern, seeing nobody by day and sitting up all night. The world gave him credit for passing these waking hours in the study of *trente et quarante and sept 'a lever*; but I had seen too much passing before my eyes, to be ignorant that this little place was the rendezvous where a much deeper game . . . was playing. There were many persons at this time in the village from the States lying adjacent to the Mississippi, under the pretence of purchasing government lands, but whose real object was to encourage the settlers in Texas to throw off their allegiance to the Mexican government. Many of these individuals were personally acquainted with me; they knew I was not with them, and would naturally conclude I was against them. Having nothing whatever in common with their plan, and no inclination to forward or oppose them, I perceived that the longer I staid the more they would find reason to suppose I were a spy.[20]

What was Houston up to? He left us no hint of his actions or thoughts at this time, but there is little doubt that, like all leaders in Texas, he was keeping a wary eye on events and the continued imprisonment of Austin.

When empresario Austin had left the April convention for Mexico City to present the petition and the memorial to the authorities, he had expected to be gone a relatively short time. Due to a series of delays it was July 18, 1833, before he finally reached the capital. The scheming Santa Anna had been elected president without opposition by the legislatures of the several Mexican states on March 29, 1833. He had taken office but quickly retired to his estates to plot more schemes. In his absence Vice-President Valentín Farías was serving as the chief executive, so it was to him Austin presented the Texas petition.

While Austin was waiting for some action by the Mexican government, cholera broke out. Austin caught the disease and barely survived. The virulent disease quickly assumed epidemic proportions and spread into Texas, taking the lives of Austin's brother John, and the wife and two children of Jim Bowie, as well as both parents of Bowie's wife.[21]

Between the normal procrastination of the Mexican government and the cholera epidemic nothing had been done toward granting the requests of Austin. In addition, Farías conveyed the impression that nothing would be accomplished. Discouraged and

159

grief-stricken over the loss of his brother, on October 2, 1833, Austin wrote the ayuntamiento of San Antonio. It was his opinion that the fate of Texas depended upon itself, as he was firmly persuaded that his recommendation was the only means of saving Texas from anarchy and total ruin. He concluded by urging all the ayuntamientos to unite in organizing a local government independent of Coahuila, even though the general government refused to consent.

Austin's experiences in the Mexican capital had thoroughly disillusioned him. On the same date he wrote his brother-in-law, James F. Perry:

> I am tired of this government. They are always in revolution and
> I believe always will be. I have had much more respect for them
> than they deserve. But I am done with all that.

A few weeks later he wrote Perry again and remarked: "The fact is, this government ought to make a state of Texas or transfer her to the United States without delay."

Suddenly, events changed for the better. The Mexican Congress repealed the anti-immigration article of the law of April 6, 1830. Austin was informed that tariff exemption and improvement of the mail service had been referred to the treasury department. Also, a revision of the judiciary system that would allow trial by jury had been recommended to the state legislature. The government promised to do everything possible to hasten the development of Texas in preparation for statehood or territorial government.

With some of his missions accomplished and excellent prospects for the future, Austin departed on December 10 for his journey home. In the meantime, a copy of his October 2 letter to the ayuntamiento of San Antonio had reached the desk of Farías, who in a rage had Austin arrested at Saltillo on January 3, 1834. He was escorted back to Mexico City and placed in solitary confinement in a windowless cell measuring thirteen by sixteen feet. A slot in the door admitted food, and for a month he had no writing materials or books to read. On May 13, Santa Anna, who by now had returned to Mexico City and resumed the reins of government, had Austin released from his dungeon but kept him in confinement elsewhere. On Christmas Day, 1834, Austin managed to post bond of $300,000 and was released from prison, but his movements were restricted to the federal district. He was finally freed on May 3, 1835, by Santa Anna, who granted an amnesty to political prisoners. In all of his confinement Austin had never been tried; no tribunal to which his case had been submitted accepted jurisdiction over it.

Even though Austin was free, it was not until July 11, 1835, that he was issued a passport. Within a week he had left for Vera Cruz to return to Texas via New Orleans.

CHAPTER 17

Commanding the Texan Forces

When Houston returned to Texas from his travels in the East, he resumed his law practice between Nacogdoches and San Augustine, occasionally being employed by the state to prosecute a defendant. Socially, he was a frequent guest at the Sterne and Raguet homes. At the latter he continued his courtship of Miss Anna, though by now he was in competition with a twenty-seven-year-old doctor, Robert Anderson Irion.

Sam had a talent for making lifelong friends with men of substance, intelligence, and quality, and in twenty-nine-year-old Thomas Jefferson Rusk he found one who fit that description. At six feet and weighing better than 200 pounds, his red hair and blue eyes gave Rusk a commanding figure. As a successful young lawyer in the gold country of Clarksville, Georgia, he had invested his life savings in a mine but was swindled by the manager, who fled to Texas. Determined to get his money back, Rusk gave chase in the late winter of 1834 and was dismayed when he caught up with the swindler only to find all his money had been lost in a poker game.

The Georgian took a look at his new surroundings and liked what he saw. He promptly settled in Nacogdoches and set up a law practice, writing his wife Polly and their three small sons to join him. His application for a headright in the David G. Burnet colony was granted at a cost of approximately $200. On February 11,

1835, Houston was a witness when Rusk took his oath of allegiance to the Mexican government.

One night Rusk, Houston, and a mutual friend decided to have a few drinks and play poker. As the game progressed and the bottle was passed around, their spirits rose and — being without funds — they gambled their clothes. When each had won clothing of someone else they playfully decided to throw all the clothes in the roaring fire, as Sam and some friends had done years previously. The next morning Rusk's faithful servant Tom had to go out to find clothing for the three men to wear as they went about their daily business.

Rusk wrote his wife on February 15, telling her he had met Governor Houston: "He has made over $3,000 in the past twelve months. He is very dissipated and in very bad health." He also mentioned that Nacogdoches had about 300 Americans and 200 Spaniards living there.

On January 1, 1835, the opportunistic Santa Anna dissolved Congress and convened a new one whose members were loyal and subordinate to him. The new Congress quickly abolished the constitution and gave Santa Anna the powers of an absolute dictator. He then issued a decree abolishing all state legislatures, including that of Coahuila y Texas. In their place were appointed governors selected by the dictator himself, and the Anglo-Americans in Texas were alarmed when the Coahuila y Texas state government passed a land law opening Texas to gigantic speculation.

In 1833 the legislature had passed an act providing for the removal of the capital from Saltillo in the south to Monclova in the north. This caused a tremendous quarrel between the two sections. The Saltillo adherents set up a separate government, and in the resulting confusion it became impossible to hold the regular election of state officials in 1834. Opinion divided among the war party and the conservative elements, and a convention was called to meet at San Antonio on November 15, 1834. The meeting never took place.

Santa Anna had to keep the pot boiling as he was securing his grip on Mexico and had decided to force all Anglo-Americans out of Texas. He approved the moving of the capital from Saltillo to Monclova and virtually abolished the militia. This infuriated the colonists as they were surrounded by hostile Indians, who outnumbered them by large majorities. The colonists were further alarmed when they found out that Ben Hawkins, a half-breed Creek, was negotiating to purchase a large tract of land north of Nacogdoches with the purpose of bringing at least 5,000 Creeks into Texas, and that he had actually paid $20,000 down on the price of $100,000.

Santa Anna appointed his charming brother-in-law, Gen. Martín Perfecto de Cós, to become commandant of the northern and eastern provinces. Cós, in turn, appointed Col. Domingo de Ugartechea as commandant of Texas and then promptly disbanded the legislature and arrested the governor. In the meantime, Capt. Antonio Tenorio arrived at Anahuac with a detachment of soldiers and a tax collector to reopen the customs house and reinstate tariffs. A deputy collector was stationed at Brazoria.

When the Mexican dictator abolished the state legislatures, most of those south of the Rio Grande acquiesced, but Zacatecans resisted and refused to surrender their weapons. For their impudence Santa Anna placed himself at the head of his army and marched upon Zacatecas. After a bloody battle on May 11, 1835, his troops overwhelmed the Zacatecans, killing some 2,000 of them and taking 2,700 as prisoners.[1] Not satisfied, the victors marched into the capital and for the next two days engaged in the butchery of the unfortunate inhabitants and plundered their city.[2] When news of this atrocity reached the Anglo-Americans they were dismayed, and even in his native Mexico, Santa Anna was denounced. In his response to the criticism, he hypocritically announced his life was devoted to his people's freedom and to the federal system.

As an unofficial group of about twenty-five citizens gathered in San Felipe to discuss the new militarization of Anahuac and other matters, dispatches from General Cós to Tenorio were captured. The documents revealed that Santa Anna was sending into Texas a strong division of the troops which had butchered Zacatecas, and it was his intention to grind down the Texas revolutionaries and to expel all Anglo-Americans who had arrived in the colony since 1830.[3] These words inflamed the colonists, as they knew what had happened to the unhappy people of Zacatecas and were in no mood to have it happen to them.

In early June, Andrew Briscoe, a respected merchant, had been placed in the Anahuac jail with a friend due to a practical joke. The friend was released the next day, but Briscoe was retained. The impetuous William Barret Travis volunteered to head a twenty-five-man expedition to Anahuac to teach Captain Tenorio a lesson for imprisoning Briscoe. He and his small band of volunteers proceeded to Anahuac on the sloop *Ohio* with one six-pounder on board. They landed on June 29 and fired one shot, which hit the fort but did no damage. Wasting no time, Travis then boldly demanded the immediate surrender of Captain Tenorio and his troops. After a short bit of haggling, Tenorio surrendered. With the captain's pledge that neither he nor his troops would fight in Texas again, he and his men were sent back to Mexico and provided arms so they could defend themselves against the Indians.

There were still men of moderation in Texas who did not want war and expressed their loyalty to Mexico. To his surprise, Travis found his actions at Anahuac denounced by this group. But then the Mexican authorities again miscalculated the temper of the colonists. Orders were issued for the arrest of Travis and several other men, and with the orders for his arrest, Travis found public opinion turning in his favor. The Texas authorities never made any arrests, explaining that the wanted persons had left the area and were on their way to the United States.[4]

While these events were transpiring, Houston, as always a shrewd judge of political winds, was counseling moderation. Moseley Baker, one of the leading warhawks, visited Houston in August 1835 in Nacogdoches. Houston knew that warlike activities were extremely unpopular in the Redlands district of Ayish, where he lived, and he advised Baker to lie low.

On September 1, Austin had finally gotten back to Texas and on the eighth was the guest of honor at a banquet given at Brazoria. As he was the leader of the peace party, his views were looked forward to with great interest. A convention had been called to assemble October 15. What would Austin have to say about this? War or peace was in his hands, and the people would undoubtedly follow his lead.

Austin was in no mood to conciliate the Mexicans. Disgusted at Santa Anna's assuming a dictatorship and his butchery of the Zacatecans, he was convinced the Mexican dictator would not rest until the colonists were expelled from Texas. In his keynote address at the banquet he made his opinion known. He was in favor of the consultation. He told his audience he had frequently warned Santa Anna that "the inevitable consequence of sending an armed force to this country would be war, yet troops were coming in large numbers and a Mexican war vessel had already been ravaging the coast." [5] A few weeks later, in a circular, he said, "War is our only recourse." [6] Events rapidly got out of hand, and before the consultation convened, the Texas war for independence had begun.

In late September of 1835, Colonel Ugartechea, commandant at San Antonio de Bexar, had sent a force under the command of Lt. Francisco Castañeda to Gonzales, a small town seventy miles due east of San Antonio. Some four years previously the colonists at Gonzales had been furnished a six-pound brass cannon for their defense against the Indians. As part of a general plan to disarm the Texans, Lieutenant Castañeda was under instructions to take back this cannon.

When Castañeda asked the Texans to surrender the cannon they refused to give it up, so he positioned his forces on a small hill by the Guadalupe River and waited. By October 1, he had made no attempt to attack. The Texans, then about 150 strong, elected John H. Moore their colonel and that night under cover of darkness crossed the Guadalupe and took up position opposite the Mexicans. Filling their cannon with scrap iron, they painted "come and take it" on the cannon in large letters and placed it in full view of the enemy.

October 2, 1835, is generally acknowledged as the "official" date the Texas revolutionary war started, when at dawn Colonel Moore sent a messenger asking Castañeda to surrender. When the Mexican lieutenant refused, Moore ordered his Texans to fire the cannon and advance, whereupon the Mexicans panicked in a complete rout and ran back toward San Antonio to join the main body of their troops. The Texans suffered no losses and collected whatever booty the enemy had left behind.

On October 6, the committee of safety for the municipality of Nacogdoches, meeting in San Augustine, appointed Sam Houston general and commander-in-chief of the forces of the Nacogdoches Department and granted him full powers to raise troops, organize the forces, and do all other things pertaining to that office.[7]

Convinced by now that a general war was inevitable, Houston wrote his friend Isaac Parker offering liberal bounties of land to volunteers from the United States if they would join the Texans in their fight against Santa Anna. He urged each man to come soon and bring a good rifle and one hundred rounds of ammunition: "Our war-cry is 'liberty or death,' and our principles are to support the constitution, and *down with the Usurper!*"[8]

The letter to Parker was given wide circulation in the United States, as was the news that General Cós was at the head of 400 men marching on their way to San Antonio to confiscate the property of the rebellious citizens. Mass meetings, speeches, and public subscriptions were held. When Adolphus Sterne offered to buy rifles for the first fifty recruits, the "New Orleans Greys" were formed and claimed the rifles. Men formed in Georgia, Alabama, Mississippi, Kentucky, Tennessee, Cincinnati, and New York.

Needing money to defray some personal expenses — including the purchase, in New Orleans, of a uniform with a general's stars and a sword sash to adorn it — Houston placed 4,000 acres of Red River land on sale for $2,500 ($1,000 in cash). Sam needed no sword as he already had one, a "gift from an American army officer at Fort Jessup, Louisiana." [9]

After the imbroglio at Gonzales, volunteers to the army flocked there and on the evening of October 10 elected Stephen Austin their commander-in-chief, with the intention to set off in two days to attack San Antonio with a force of 500 men and the six-pound cannon they had retained. Austin accepted the command and departed to join his troops.

The army decided it might as well capture Goliad in addition to San Antonio and drive the Mexican army out of Texas. About forty planters under the command of Capt. George Collingsworth began a march to Goliad and on the way were joined by Ben Milam, a colorful bachelor who had been in Texas for many years and had just escaped from a Mexican prison.[10] Upon arriving at Goliad, the colonists attacked the quarters of Lieutenant Colonel Sandoval, the commandant, and after breaking his door down with an axe took him prisoner. Completely caught off guard by the attack, the Mexicans put up a short resistance and then surrendered. The Texans, with only one man slightly wounded, acquired military stores to the value of $10,000, some pieces of badly needed artillery, and 300 arms.[11] News of the capture of Goliad sent a wave of enthusiasm throughout Texas.

When the consultation convened on October 15 there were not enough delegates present for a quorum, so they adjourned until November 1 to meet at San Felipe, and leave was granted for those desiring to join the army. As a delegate from Nacogdoches, Houston arrived in late October to find that Austin was with his troops at Salado Creek, about five miles east of San Antonio, and many members of the consultation were with him. Houston decided he would ride to Austin, his chief, and bring back enough delegates so the consultation could get down to business. Upon arriving at the campsite he met a dispirited Austin, whose army was completely unorganized, undrilled, and without discipline. As volunteers with no regular enlistment or oath, they would come and go at will and sometimes left in squads to go home. Austin later wrote to the president of the consultation that his army was nothing but an undisciplined militia, and of very poor quality. It was his opinion that the officers, from the commander-in-chief down, were inexperienced in military service and that with such a force Bexar could not be successfully attacked. In his discouragement, Austin offered the command of the army to Houston, who declined in the interest of harmony.

Austin recognized the necessity of organizing a provisional government and providing means for its support, so he and Houston addressed the troops, informing them of the need for enough delegates to leave the army and return to San Felipe. After a discussion among themselves, the army voted to send all delegates in their ranks to San Felipe for the consultation. Houston and the delegates then returned to San Felipe, while Austin stayed with the troops.

Among the volunteers who joined Austin was James Bowie, who had come galloping into camp on a small gray mare with six volunteers from Louisiana, his famous knife secured in his sash and a rifle slung from his saddle. Austin gave him a commission and sent him and James Fannin at the head of separate detachments to select sites for an encampment nearer San Antonio. The mission Concepción was selected as the target. In an engagement on October 28, the Mexicans surrendered. Although the battle was a brilliant affair, operations slowed to a halt. The army of Cós was well protected by cannon, and the colonists had only five artillery pieces of small caliber. On November 2 at a council of war, Austin asked his officers for their opinion as to the advisability of a direct assault upon the Mexican positions. All but one voted against it. Houston himself thought the Texans should never have passed the Guadalupe River without proper munitions of war to reduce San Antonio, and that it would be folly to attack without heavy cannon. Thereafter, the army laid siege to Cós and his fortifications.

On November 3, with a quorum being present, fifty-five members representing the thirteen municipalities of Texas met in San Felipe in a narrow, one-room building. Sam was dressed in buckskin breeches and wore a Mexican serape.

Among the delegates from Harrisburg was Dr. Lorenzo de Zavala, a highly educated and cultured Mexican who had supported

168

Santa Anna in years past but had turned against him as the dictator increasingly ignored democratic principles. When his substantial Yucatán estates had been confiscated, Zavala, with his wife and son, escaped to Texas and had thrown in his lot with the colonists. He had been at Gonzales and fought valiantly to retain the six-pound cannon.

Once the quorum assembled, the delegates wasted no time in getting down to business and elected Dr. Branch T. Archer, a member of the war party, to preside. Houston was an active member and served on a committee whose purpose was to make declarations of the causes that impelled the Texans to take up arms.[12]

The war party, headed by William Wharton, was in favor of Texas declaring itself an independent nation. Zavala was opposed to this, pointing out that this action would offend all liberal Mexicans and prevent sympathetic Mexican states from giving Texas any aid in their dispute against Santa Anna. Another faction, led by the able Don Carlos Barrett, a lawyer, was opposed to even considering the idea of separating from Mexico.

Houston supported Zavala. At times an impetuous man, when the occasion warranted it, he could exercise extreme patience and caution, and he regarded a declaration of absolute independence at that time as ill-judged and ill-timed. He argued for support of the Mexican constitution of 1824 and introduced a resolution to this effect. By a vote of 33–14 on November 6, the delegates voted in favor of the constitution of 1824 and set up a provisional government. It provided for a governor and a general council with weakly defined and almost coordinate powers. In the election for governor, Henry Smith, a hot-tempered man from Brazoria, was elected by nine votes over Stephen F. Austin. James W. Robinson, a member of the peace party from Nacogdoches, was elected lieutenant governor. In a letter to the consultation, Austin requested he be relieved from command of the army. His request was granted and he, William H. Wharton, and Dr. Branch T. Archer were commissioned to go to the United States to try to enlist aid and sympathy — and to borrow $1 million. Houston was elected major general and commander-in-chief of all the forces called into public service during the war. With the departure of Austin to the United States, 400 men pledged themselves to remain at San Antonio and elected Edward Burleson as their commander. The convention adjourned on November 14 after agreeing to assemble again on March 1 at Washington-on-the Brazos.

Houston set up headquarters in the front room of the Virginia

House and quickly discovered that he had a title but no real authority. From the beginning there was dissension, intrigue, backbiting, confusion, and inefficiency among the various factions, and the council refused to cooperate in organizing the regular army. Houston later wrote that "All new States are infested, more or less, by a class of noisy, second-rate men, who are always in favor of rash and extreme measures. But Texas was absolutely overrun by such men." [13]

In an endeavor to man his army with officers, on November 13 Houston wrote James Fannin, who was serving as a captain with the volunteer army at San Antonio, and offered him an appointment as inspector general with the rank of colonel in the regular army. Houston was still of the opinion it would be unwise to try to dislodge General Cós from his well-entrenched fortifications at San Antonio without heavy artillery. In his letter to Fannin, he expressed his opinion that it would be better to fall back to Goliad and Gonzales and furlough most of the army until they had sufficient artillery: "Recommend the safest course! . . . Remember our Maxim, it is better to do well, *late*, than *never!*" [14]

Fannin, who had arrived in Texas from Georgia in the fall of 1834 with his family, was one of those men of dubious credentials who had enrolled in the Texas cause. Although he operated a plantation near Velasco, it seemed his main operation was as a smuggler of slaves from Africa and Spanish Cuba into the United States. In his youth he had attended the United States Military Academy at West Point for two years under the name of James F. Walker, but following a quarrel with a fellow student ran away from the academy. Apparently, his two years as a cadet gave him an exalted idea as to his military capabilities; in his answer to Houston he asked to be appointed a brigadier general, next in rank to the commander-in-chief: "I am well satisfied that I can fill either of the posts *better than any officer* who has yet been in command." [15]

Fannin quickly followed his letter to Houston's headquarters and protested that the position of inspector general offered him was not suitable for his experience and ability. Houston refused his demand to be made a brigadier general, but did ask the council to appoint him a colonel.

On December 3, the army at San Antonio had almost decided to go into winter quarters when the situation suddenly changed. The next day the Texans received information from an officer who had deserted Cós's army that the strength of the Mexican defenders was overestimated, their camp disorganized, and their morale poor. General Burleson was reluctant to go on the attack, but the grizzled veteran Ben Milam stepped in front of headquarters and cried, "Who will follow old Ben Milam into San Antonio?" Three hundred volunteers stepped forward.[16] Burleson gave his assent for the attack, but he stayed in camp with the reserve force.

The volunteer unit was separated into two commands, one being given to Milam and the other to Francis W. Johnson, and the Texans made their attack at about twenty minutes before daylight on December 5. In a side maneuver, Col. James C. Neill was directed to make a feint on the Alamo to divert attention. The siege lasted four days before General Cós surrendered his eleven hundred troops. On the third day the gallant bachelor Milam was struck in the head by a bullet as he entered the courtyard of the home of the vice-governor, Juan Martín Veramendi. Command of the force then passed to Colonel Johnson, and on December 10, 1835, a truce was signed. In the battle, the Mexicans suffered 150 killed and an untold number wounded, while the Texans had twelve killed with eighteen wounded.

General Cós gave his pledge to withdraw his weary troops to Mexico and never return against the Texans.

CHAPTER 18

General Without an Army

With the departure of General Cós and his beaten army, not a Mexican soldier was in Texas north of the Rio Grande. A wave of rejoicing swept the colonists. Many people thought the war was over. Burleson resigned his command and went home to his family. The time that should have been spent in organizing, training, and disciplining the troops was wasted as many soldiers followed Burleson's example and departed for home. The government also deteriorated as Governor Smith and the general council engaged in a series of disputes.

At San Antonio there were about four hundred men. At Velasco there were about two hundred, eighty at Goliad, and seventy at Washington-on-the Brazos. This was the Texas army at that time, and most of them were volunteers. Col. Frank Johnson, who had been elected to succeed Burleson as commander of the volunteers at San Antonio, placed Col. J. C. Neill, with a garrison of about one hundred Texans, in command of the Alamo.

General Cós had retreated to Laredo and halted with his troops, breaking his pledge to return to Mexico. He was shortly joined by Gen. Joaquín Ramírez y Sesma with 1,000 infantry and 500 calvary, and another army was concentrating at San Luis Potosi under the command of Santa Anna himself, the self-styled "Napoleon of the West." Preparations were under way by the Mex-

172

icans at Matamoros to not only defend that place, but to advance upon Goliad.

Friction between the governor and the council continued. The council continuously overrode Houston's authority and ignored his requests, and some of his military commanders were ignoring his orders. One of the particular trouble-makers in the army who irked Houston was Dr. James Grant, a Scot who had served valiantly during the Battle of San Antonio. Grant had never lived in Texas but for years had resided in the Mexican portion of Coahuila y Texas, where he had a splendid estate. He originated the idea of an expedition to Matamoros, located about 275 miles slightly southwest from San Antonio and across the Rio Grande, and then into the interior of Mexico where he could liberate his vast estates at Parras.[1]

The proposals of Grant fell on willing ears among the volunteers and adventurers at San Antonio, as he painted a rosy picture of the rich spoils to be taken from the cities of Tamaulipas, Nuevo León, Coahuila, and San Luis Potosi. Governor Smith opposed the proposed expedition and so did Houston, who considered the plan little short of piracy.[2] From a military standpoint he saw no reason why the army should be used to recover the confiscated estates of Dr. Grant, especially since Houston was trying to create an army capable of meeting the "usurper," as he referred to Santa Anna, in the field by the first of March. He knew Mexican pride would not allow the Mexicans to suffer the loss at San Antonio without an attempt at revenge, and he expected Santa Anna to put at least 10,000 soldiers in the field when he invaded Texas.

Despite the opposition of the governor and Houston, the council approved the Matamoros expedition and, when Johnson declined to lead the troops, appointed Fannin to the command to make the attack. Then Johnson changed his mind and wanted to lead the troops. In their indecisiveness the council authorized him to do so and did not bother to notify Fannin or rescind his instructions. Now the mission had two commanders. On December 17, 1835, Governor Smith ordered Houston to make a demonstration against Matamoros. Houston immediately wrote Jim Bowie to proceed to Matamoros and take the place, and reminded him that the port of Copano was important. He also instructed Bowie:

> If any officers or men who have, at any time, been released on *parole*, should be taken in arms, they will be proper subjects for the

173

consideration of court-martial. Great caution is necessary in the country of an enemy.[3]

Most of the members chosen for the original general council were men of substance and ability. Some competent members resigned to accept various appointments in the government or army, and others left to go home to be with their families. Under these circumstances it was not too long before the council was composed of inferior personnel who did as they wished, frequently acting without a quorum. They even passed an ordinance enlarging the membership of the council from thirteen to twenty-four.

When these noisy and second-rate men took over the government they could not wait to backstage Houston and plot against him. In an effort to get him out of their way they ordered him, on December 15, to transfer his headquarters from San Felipe to the small hamlet of Washington-on-the Brazos, about fifty miles away.

Houston transferred his headquarters on Christmas Day, and on the same date wrote William P. Smith appointing him surgeon for that post and commanding him to attend to all the sick and wounded, whether regulars or volunteers. He later wrote Don Carlos Barrett:

> I am myself as usual pressed with business; and thank God my Christmas times are over, and I am most miserably cool & sober
> . . . Instead of Egg-nog; I eat roasted Eggs in my office.[4]

Continuing their meddling into military affairs, the council decided to create an office known as "military agent" which would serve as a field commander and be responsible not to Houston as commander-in-chief but to the council.

Although the provisional government had authorized a regular army of 1,120 men to be enlisted for two-year terms under Houston's command, the council ignored this and gave its first priority to the volunteer army already in the field. In addition, when the provisional government had been set up, Article VIII had foolishly given the power to appoint regular army officers not to the chief executive but to the general council. As early as December 6, 1835, in a letter to Governor Smith, Houston had complained that the council was extremely slow in the appointment of regular officers for the army, particularly for the field units.

No officers are appointed, and it will be impossible for me ever to

174

enlist the rank and file of the Army until the Officers are appointed. An army never has been raised for Regular service until the Officers had all been appointed. The regiments of the U. States army were all completely officered before one man was enlisted in the ranks.[5]

Although the council was penurious in advancing Houston the funds necessary for recruiting or other military functions, it was liberal when it came to appropriating money for strange purposes. On several occasions it advanced several hundred dollars to three or four individuals of shady character for various purposes, who, when they received the money, promptly disappeared and were never heard from again.

The council finally acceded to one of Houston's requests, and on December 7 several field officers were appointed in the regular army: James W. Fannin as colonel; J. C. Neill, lieutenant colonel; William Oldham, major. As artillery officers, David B. Macomb was made a lieutenant colonel, and William Barret Travis was commissioned first major in the cavalry.

Fannin, who had so ardently sung his own praises to Houston when requesting he be made a brigadier general, immediately showed the stuff of which he was made. After he was sworn in and given his commission, he was ordered by Houston to report to Matagorda, on the eastern coast, open a recruiting station, and acknowledge receipt of the order in writing. Fannin did neither. When Sam sent orders for him to report to headquarters, he ignored them. Although a colonel in the regular army and sworn to loyalty, Fannin abandoned his position and was elected colonel of a volunteer regiment being formed by Alabama and Georgia troops that had arrived. William Ward, who headed the 112 men from Georgia, was elected lieutenant colonel. In the meantime, Francis Johnson was issuing proclamations of his own, calling for men to invade Mexico, and was labeling himself as head of the federal volunteer army.[6]

Houston was well aware of the treachery against him by some members of the general council, and he knew that the ringleaders were Wyatt Hanks, Lieutenant Governor James W. Robinson, and Don Carlos Barrett. Houston later wrote a friend that Barrett had exceptional ability but "was, in my opinion, the worst man that was ever in Texas." [7] Hanks, as chairman of the military committee, repaid Houston's support in getting him a job as army sutler (worth from $10,000 to $20,000 a year) by conspiring against his

175

authority as commander-in-chief. Knowing Houston's opposition to the proposed Matamoros campaign, he secretly wrote officers at San Antonio urging them to undertake the expedition. Houston later wrote about Hanks: "I do most seriously regard him as the *basest* of all mankind." [8]

In December the council had issued orders to Houston to visit the Cherokees and other Indian tribes and negotiate a treaty of neutrality with them. Houston then wrote Don Carlos Barrett that after he held his talks with the Indians it was his intention to "detail a competent officer to command the Recruiting station, while I proceed to the *frontier;* and organize the army for a prompt movement in the Spring." [9]

A few days later, Houston received a courier from Lieutenant Colonel Neill with the unwelcome news that Colonel Johnson and Dr. Grant were on their way to Matamoros, going by way of Goliad and Refugio. In their haste to leave San Antonio they had stripped the garrison of all horses, blankets, provisions, and medicines, taking over two hundred men with them and leaving behind only eighty sick and wounded.

On January 6, 1836, Houston wrote Governor Smith and enclosed Neill's report. He closed his letter by stating

> No language can express my anguish of soul. Oh, save our poor country! — send supplies to the wounded, the sick, the naked, and the hungry, for God's sake! What will the world think of the authorities of Texas? Prompt, decided, and honest independence is all that can save them, and redeem our country . . .[10]

By now Houston was in favor of complete independence from Mexico. On January 7, he wrote John Forbes that "there is but one course left for Texas to pursue, and that is, an unequivocal declaration of independence, and the formation of a constitution . . ." [11]

At ten o'clock in the morning on January 16, the general again wrote the governor.

> I will set out in less than an hour for the Army. I will do all that I can. I am told that Frank Johnson and Fannin have obtained from the Military Committee orders to proceed and reduce Matamoros. It may not be so. There was no Quorum, and the Council could not give power. I will proceed with great haste to the Army and there I can know all.[12]

176

It was a cold and windy winter day when Houston left for Goliad, accompanied by Maj. George Hockley, his aide. On the way they encountered an angry Capt. Philip Dimitt and his men, who related how they had been forced by Johnson and Grant's followers to surrender twenty of their horses, each the personal property of its rider. Arriving at Goliad on the night of January 14, they found no Fannin nor any supplies. They did find a posted appeal, signed by Fannin as "military agent" of the general council, calling for volunteers to join an expedition to "reduce Matamoros" and promising to pay the troops "out of the first spoils taken from the enemy." Johnson was also nowhere around. Major Morris of the New Orleans Greys was in command, and from him Houston learned that Dr. Grant had promoted himself to "acting commander-in-chief" and had departed for Refugio, an outpost about twenty-five miles to the southeast. He had taken about 200 soldiers with him.

The next morning Houston made an impassioned speech to the troops still in Goliad. He brought all of his powers of eloquence into play as he tried to dissuade the men from participating in the reckless venture of Johnson and Grant. For the first time these men heard the eloquence that had swayed juries, voters, and his colleagues in the halls of the United States Congress. Drawing himself up to his full height, Houston reminded them to expect little if any support from the Mexicans in the Coahuila section as those people had united themselves with Santa Anna. He reminded the troops that even the inhabitants of Zacatecas, the town that had been butchered by Santa Anna, was not showing them any support. "No other help," he said, "remains for us now than our strength and the consciousness that we have seized our arms for a just cause." [13] He admitted that there was general complaint about the negligence of the government in supplying the troops with war materials, but that situation was beyond the power of the governor.

While Houston was in the middle of his speech he was interrupted by a courier from San Antonio, reporting that two of Colonel Neill's scouts had discovered that two of Santa Anna's generals had led separate troops across the Rio Grande in an invasion of Texas and were on their way to attack San Antonio. Neill was calling for help to defend the Alamo, and he asked Houston for a furlough so he could visit his sick family. Almost immediately, Bowie rode up asking for men to go back with him to defend the Alamo. Houston was highly surprised as he did not think the enemy would invade Texas until the spring. Explaining the situation, he called for volunteers to go back to San Antonio with Bowie. Thirty men responded. Houston wrote out an order to Neill granting his request for a furlough but ordered him to remove all artillery from the Alamo and then blow it up "as it would be impossible to hold the town with the force there." [14] To Neill he gave some leeway, inasmuch as he was on the scene at the Alamo and knew the situation better than anyone.

Houston wrote Governor Smith on January 17 and enclosed Neill's letter. He told the governor that Bowie would leave in a few hours for San Antonio.

> In an hour, I will take up the line of march for Refugio Mission with about 209 efficient men, where I will await orders from your Excellency, believing that the army should not advance with a small force upon Matamoras with the hope or belief that the Mexicans will cooperate with us. I have no confidence in them . . . I would myself have marched to Bexar but the Matamoras rage is up so high that I must see Colonel Ward's men. [15]

Ward was the commander of a well-equipped battalion recently arrived from Georgia, and Houston had entrusted it to Fannin.

In a separate letter the same day, Houston informed the governor he had sent Col. Hugh Love to Nacogdoches to try to raise an auxiliary corps of 300 or more Indians from the Cherokee, Delaware, Shawnee, Kickapoo, and any other friendly tribes. Colonel. Love was authorized to offer them $7,000 in addition to one-half of all property taken by them if they agreed to serve six months. [16]

When Major Morris and his troops departed for Refugio to meet with Dr. Grant, Houston and his aide rode along with him. When they reached Refugio, once more they found no Fannin, no Ward, and no supplies — contrary to Houston's orders of December 30 and January 6. On the night of January 20, the intriguing Colonel Johnson galloped in and presented Houston with a set of orders from the general council relieving him as commander-in-chief of all volunteer forces. Fannin and Johnson had been appointed military agents, subject only to the orders of the council itself, and had been given joint command of all volunteers and instructed to proceed with the expedition to Matamoros. [17] Presumably, Houston was still in charge of the regular army, but there was no regular army — only a handful of officers and no enlisted men. In a rage he commented the army had been stolen out from under him.

Colonel Johnson had other unpleasant news for Houston. After a violent quarrel with the council in which he had called them corrupt scoundrels, the council had deposed Governor Smith from his office, appointing in his stead James W. Robinson to succeed him. Smith, furious, refused to give up his office. The confrontation between Governor Smith and the council had been caused when he received a letter from Colonel Neill at the Alamo describing the stark realism of the desperate military situation. The men had not only never received their promised pay but were also in a ragged and destitute condition and in dire need of medical supplies.

Houston addressed the troops and told them what had happened. His commission from the governor, he explained, gave him command of all the troops — regulars, militia, and volunteers. It was his opinion the council did not have authority to countermand those orders and had done so illegally. But, he added,

> I intend to recognize the authority of Governor Smith. Your new leaders — military agents — on the other hand recognize the authority of the council. You must decide for yourselves which you accept.[18]

After mulling this over, two hundred decided against continuing to Matamoros and left for home. The rest followed Johnson and Grant.

In February near San Patricio, about one hundred miles north of Matamoros, a force under Johnson was surprised by Gen. José de Urrea and wiped out, the only survivors being Johnson and one or two of his men. At the time, Grant was on a scouting expedition about twenty-five miles away with about fifty men. On the morning of March 2, in an ambush at a creek called Agua Dulce, he and his followers were slaughtered after being taken by surprise. So came an end to the ill-fated Matamoros expedition.

A dejected Houston, a general without an army, rode dispiritedly back to San Felipe with his aide Hockley and two other loyal officers. Later his biographer related his state of mind:

> During most of the day he rode along in silence and none of his companions disturbed his reveries. Deep in thought he was troubled by the most painful suspense, whether to withdraw once more from the treacheries and persecutions of the world, and bury himself deep in the solitude of nature ... or whether he should boldly mark out a track for himself, and in leading a new people to independence trample down all opposition. But men whom God raises up to become leaders of nations cannot be

crushed . . . in the midst of their adversities they may seem, for a moment, to bow before the blast, yet they never despair.[19]

After much contemplation he made his decision. Toward evening he addressed his companions and

> dwelt with enthusiasm upon the future prospects of Texas . . . He had fixed his purpose and the world could not move him. He was not going once more to retire from the world, but would cast his lot with Texas! [20]

At San Felipe, Houston presented himself to Governor Smith, who was still refusing to relinquish any of his authority. Sam asked for a furlough until March 1, and it was granted. He then went home to Nacogdoches and sought election as a delegate to the coming convention. Defeated by the Nacogdoches voters, he was elected as a delegate from Refugio. His next step was to take John Forbes with him and go among the Indians to negotiate a peace treaty with them.

CHAPTER 19

The Alamo Falls

"Washington-on-the-Brazos is a disgusting place," Col. William P. Gray wrote in his diary on February 27, 1836. "About a dozen cabins or shanties constitute the city; not one decent house in it . . . stumps still standing." The good colonel was there on a mission from New Orleans, where Stephen Austin had been successful in raising a $200,000 loan for the Texas cause. Gray was to be an observer at the March convention and report back to New Orleans whether, in his opinion, another loan to the Texans would be justified.

Among the assembled delegates were Governor Smith and Lieutenant Governor Robinson, both wanting to justify their previous actions in the provisional government. Don Carlos Barrett, who had shackled Houston in every way possible, never showed up. The delegates, once more composed of a superior quality of men, later refused seats to some of the troublemakers of the provisional government. Everyone was waiting for General Houston to put in his appearance. But Houston was with the Indians.

Sam was accompanied by his aide Major Hockley as he and his fellow commissioner, John Forbes, arrived in Peach Tree Village about the middle of February to confer with Chief Bowles and chiefs of other tribes.[1] Bowles, known as The Bowl, like so many of the Cherokee chiefs was of mixed white and Indian blood. Houston and his associates found The Bowl and chiefs of the tribes allied with them to be extremely restless and suspicious of the whites as the Mexicans had been agitating them and trying to recruit them to take part in the war on their side. It took Houston several days — together with many gifts of knives and tomahawks[2] — to calm the suspicious Indians before negotiations got under way. Houston pledged his sacred honor and authority as commander-in-chief of the Texas army to support the treaty which, he assured Bowles, would bring peace to the Cherokee people. Undoubtedly, one thing in his favor in gaining the confidence of the Indians was his distinction of being John Jolly's adopted son and a citizen of the Cherokee Nation.

The treaty contained thirteen articles, the first of which declared there should be a firm and lasting peace forever between both parties,[3] and that friendly intercourse should be pursued. Other articles specified that an area approximately fifty miles long and thirty miles wide would be set aside for the Indians as tribal property to be governed by tribal law, and provided for the establishment of Indian agencies.

On February 23, 1836, the document was signed by Chief Bowles, Big Mush, Corn Tassle, The Egg, Samuel Benge, Osoota, John Bowles (the chief's son) and Tenuta for the Cherokees, Shawnees, Delawares, Kickapoos, Quapaws, Buloies, Iowanes, Caddoes, Tamocuttakes, and Untanguous. Houston and Forbes signed for the Texans, with Major Hockley signing as witness.

As the neutrality of the tribe was the goal sought by Houston and Forbes, the question of whether the Cherokees would support a military campaign against the Mexican government was not discussed in the treaty. Apparently, the Cherokees had turned down his effort to enlist in the army for a six-month period.

After the signing, Houston presented to The Bowl a sword, a silk vest, and a sash, together with a military hat which the chief proudly wore for the rest of his life. In return, the chief's daughter Mary presented Houston with a gift of leather moccasins she had made especially for him. Houston wore those moccasins frequently in his war against Mexico until they wore out.

While these negotiations had been going on and the delegates were assembling at Washington for the convention, the stage was being set for one of the most thrilling events in the annals of military history. When Governor Smith had received Neill's desperate letter of January 6, he had transferred William Barret Travis from his position as superintendent of the recruiting service and ordered him to the Alamo.[4] When Travis arrived on February 3 with about thirty men, all but four of them regulars, he found Bowie had arrived a couple of weeks earlier with his volunteers from Goliad and was in command. A few days after Travis arrived, Davy Crockett and twelve other Tennesseans showed up.

Prior to Travis's arrival, Bowie and Neill had discussed Houston's instructions to blow up the fortifications, but, inasmuch as Houston had instructed Neill to use his own judgment, Neill decided he did not have enough draft animals to move the artillery and decided not to blow up the Alamo. Bowie concurred in this decision and on February 2 wrote the governor, "Colonel Neill and myself have come to the conclusion that we will rather die in these ditches than give them up to the enemy." [5] Several days later Neill left on his furlough.

From the first there was conflict between Travis and Bowie. Travis, who had been promoted to lieutenant colonel of cavalry of the regular army, thought he should have the command because he had been sent by the governor. Bowie, a colonel — and the best-known fighting man in Texas — at age forty did not fancy submitting to the orders of a man fourteen years his junior. The volunteers held an election and elected the popular Bowie as colonel. There was still resentment on both sides until finally, in the interest of harmony, the two soldiers arranged a truce and on February 14 wrote the governor a letter concerning the situation and the way they resolved it. The solution was for Bowie to have command of the volunteers in the garrison and for Travis to command the regulars and the volunteer cavalry. Until Colonel Neill was to return from his furlough, all general orders and correspondence would henceforth be signed by both men.

In any case, the quarrel became moot when on or about February 21, while helping with the construction of a lookout post or gun position, Bowie fell and broke his hip.[6] He subsequently developed pneumonia or typhoid-pneumonia, and was placed on a cot in his room.

After the treaty signing with Bowles and the other chiefs, Houston returned to Nacogdoches to visit the Raguets, particularly Anna. After leaving the Raguets, on his way to Washington-on-the-Brazos he ran into a blue norther,[7] and it was not until late on February 27 that he reached his destination and found the delegates in a high state of agitation. Santa Anna, to everyone's surprise, had managed to bring his army of 6,000 from Mexico through several hundred miles of scrub land in the cold of winter and had reached San Antonio. On the same day the Indian treaty had been signed, the defenders of the Alamo had retreated into the former mission and the siege was on.

The delegates showed Houston a letter that a courier had just brought in from Travis. Dated February 24 from the Alamo, the message was addressed "To the People of Texas & all Americans in the world":

> Fellow Citizens & Compatriots. I am besieged, by a thousand or more of the Mexicans under Santa Anna — I have sustained a continual Bombardment & cannonade for 24 hours & have not lost a man — The enemy has demanded a surrender at discretion, otherwise, the garrison are to be put to the sword, if the fort is taken — I have answered the demand with a cannon shot, & our flag still waves proudly from the walls — *I shall never surrender or retreat.* Then, I call on you in the name of Liberty, of patriotism and everything dear to the American Character, to come to our aid, with all despatch — The enemy is receiving reinforcements daily & will no doubt increase to three or four thousand in four or five days. If this call is neglected, I am determined to sustain myself as long as possible & die like a soldier who never forgets what is due to his own honor & that of his country. *Victory or Death.*

A postscript was added:

> The Lord is on our side — When the enemy appeared in sight we had not three bushels of corn — We have since found in deserted stores 80 or 90 bushels & got into the walls 20 or 30 head of Beeves.[8]

On the same day he wrote this message, Travis, knowing Colonel Fannin had 450 men at Goliad, had written him he was being besieged and called upon him to bring his troops to assist him.

As Colonel Gray recorded in his diary, Houston's arrival created a sensation. The delegates wanted his opinion of what should be done now that the Alamo had been attacked. Houston's advice was to organize the convention, set up a government, and declare complete independence from Mexico.

On March 1, 1836, fifty-eight delegates settled down to business in a crude shelter, an unfinished structure with cloth instead of glass in the windows. The building was owned by a gunsmith and part-time Baptist preacher named Noah Byars.[9] Richard Ellis was elected president of the convention and H. S. Kimble, secretary. A committee was instructed to draw up a declaration of independence, and on March 2, 1836 — Houston's forty-third birthday — the declaration was passed unanimously. During the initial discussions of the convention, Houston's treaty with the Indians provoked such general dissatisfaction among the delegates it was not presented to the convention for ratification.

Three days later, after Houston had told the convention under what terms he would accept the position, he was elected "Commander-in-Chief of all the land forces of the Texian Army, both regulars, volunteers and militia . . . and endowed with all the rights, privileges and powers due to a Commander-in-Chief in the United States of America." [10] Only one dissenting vote was recorded. The new commander was ordered to establish headquarters, organize the army, and continue in office until suspended by the government.

On Sunday, March 6, the convention was called to order in a special session while President Ellis read another appeal just received from Travis.

> I look to the *Colonies alone* for aid; unless it arrives soon, I shall have to fight the enemy on his own terms. . . . A blood-red banner waves from the Church of Bexar, and in the camp above us, in token that the war is one of vengeance against rebels, they have declared us as such, and demanded that we should surrender at discretion, or that this garrison should be put to the sword. Their threats have had no influence on me, or my men . . . *God and Texas — Victory or Death!!* [11]

In his letter Travis also mentioned he had repeatedly sent to Fannin for aid but had received none.

After Ellis read the passionate letter, a hush fell in the room. Then Robert Potter, a member of the peace party from Nacogdoches and the only member who had voted against Houston for commander-in-chief, rose. He proposed the convention be adjourned so all delegates could ride to the relief of the Alamo. Houston rose to answer him and spoke to the assemblage for over an hour. He called Potter's resolution "madness" as the delegates had declared themselves independent but no organization had been formed and no constitution had been written. The government to be formed must have an organic form, he said, "as otherwise we would be nothing but outlaws and can hope neither for sympathy nor the respect of mankind." [12] As the delegates listened in silence, Houston advised them to sit calmly and cooly pursue their deliberations.

185

> I pledge myself to proceed at once to Gonzales where we hear
> that a small corps of militia have rallied. I will interpose them be-
> tween this convention and the enemy. While you choose to sit in
> convention I promise you the Mexicans will never approach un-
> less they march over my dead body. If mortal power can avail I
> will relieve the brave men in the Alamo.[13]

He then strode from the crude hall and set out for Gonzales, about
115 miles to the southwest. With him were the faithful George
Hockley, now inspector general of the army; aides-de-camp Richardson Scurry and Albert C. Horton; and eighteen-year-old Verne
Cameron, who was to serve as Houston's courier.

After Houston left the convention the delegates remained in
session until March 17, setting up an ad interim government and
writing a constitution. For president they selected David G. Burnet, who neither swore nor drank, and Lorenzo de Zavala was selected as vice-president. The cabinet consisted of Thomas J. Rusk,
Houston's good friend, as secretary of war; Samuel P. Carson, secretary of state; Bailey Hardeman, secretary of the treasury; Robert
Potter, secretary of the navy; and David Thomas, attorney general.

After a few days on the road, Houston sent Cameron, his
young courier, to Fannin at Goliad. He told Fannin about his new
commission as commander-in-chief and ordered him to give up the
fort at Goliad and to meet him with all available troops on the west
side of the Cibolo. But Fannin was proving himself a master of procrastination, hesitation, and indecisiveness. He had received an ur-
gent appeal for aid from Travis and started out half-heartedly on
February 26. As horses were not available, he had used oxen to
haul the artillery and baggage wagons. Several hundred yards
away, while attempting to cross the San Antonio River, a wagon
broke down and Fannin decided to lead his men back to the fort at
Goliad, which he had christened Fort Defiance.

Houston rode into the volunteer's camp at Gonzales on March
11 at about 4:00 P.M. There he found 374 men, fifty of whom were
mounted. Among those present was James C. Neill, former commander at San Antonio, who had been prevented by the presence of
Santa Anna's troops from rejoining the forces at the Alamo at the
expiration of his leave. Also present were Capt. Sidney Sherman
and his troops from Kentucky and Ohio, who had just marched
more than 400 miles from Natchitoches, Louisiana.

The volunteers, led by the noted Indian fighter, Ed Burleson,
were in a pitiable state. Both weapons and ammunition were
scarce, and the men had provisions for only two days. Houston had

Burleson parade the troops and read them the declaration of independence, his commission, and his instructions as commander-in-chief. He realized he was in a delicate situation. In all of Texas this small force was the only army under his command, and they had not volunteered to serve under him but had volunteered to defend the Alamo. To be effective they must be organized into military units with discipline and training. His first step was to direct Burleson to organize the men into a regiment of battalions and companies, and in an election Burleson was elected colonel, Sidney Sherman, lieutenant colonel, and Alexander Somervell, major.[14]

Shortly after dark on the day of Houston's arrival, two Mexicans arrived at the camp with terrible news. The Alamo had fallen on May 6 after a siege of thirteen days. All 188 defenders were dead. By Santa Anna's orders, the bodies of those massacred had been burned in the public square.

Thirty of the women at Gonzales had lost husbands at the Alamo, and their screams and cries at the news created great excitement among the troops. Twenty men immediately left camp to go home and look after their families, and Houston ever after referred to them as deserters.

Once more Houston sent his messenger to Fannin, this time with orders to blow up Fort Defiance, dump into the river whatever artillery pieces he could not take with him, and to retreat to Victoria after sending one-third of his effective forces to join Houston at Gonzales.[15] Fannin not only ignored the orders to blow up the fort but once more procrastinated. When he finally decided to move, he committed several military blunders. On his march toward Victoria on the morning of March 19 he took along all of his nine brass cannon and 500 spare muskets — but no provisions. He then foolishly placed all of his ammunition in a single cart which broke down in the middle of a prairie where there was no protecting cover. Here they were struck by the superior force of General Urrea, who had disposed of Johnson and Grant. Fannin and his men put up a brave resistance, and the battle raged until the next day when the Texans surrendered.

Fannin and Urrea signed a formal agreement of surrender that stipulated all the Texans would be treated as prisoners of war and within eight days would be sent back to the United States via New Orleans. Fannin, who had been wounded in the thigh, and all his men were sent back to Goliad and confined. They were soon joined by Maj. William P. Miller with eighty volunteers from Tennessee. The major and his men had been captured while landing at Copano and had not engaged in any fighting at all. Next to arrive at the prison was Capt. William Ward and his eighty-five men, who had been captured at Victoria. A few days later, General Urrea left Goliad to proceed to San Antonio. Shortly after he left, the officer in charge, Col. Juan Portillo, received direct orders from Santa Anna to execute the prisoners.

On Palm Sunday, March 27, a large number of prisoners were herded into three groups and marched out of town. There are conflicting reports as to the number, but it is apparent there were well over 300 in all. Suddenly, the Mexicans swung to one side and opened a deadly fire. Surprising as it may seem, about twenty-seven Texans escaped by running away or feigning death. Fannin was not included in the general slaughter but was shot later in the day. He was the last of his command to be executed, and his last requests were that he be shot in the breast, that his body be given a decent burial, and that his watch be sent to his wife. All of his requests were ignored. He was shot in the head, his body was placed in a pile with the others and burned, and the Mexican to whom he entrusted his watch kept it.[16]

CHAPTER 20

Rising Above Dissension in the Ranks

On March 13, 1836, the scouts Erastus (Deaf) Smith and twenty-four-year-old Capt. Henry Karnes arrived at Houston's camp with a party of four: Mrs. Susannah Dickerson and her fifteen-month-old daughter Angelina; Joe, Travis's black body-servant; and Ben, the American black orderly of Santa Anna's aide, Colonel Almonte. Mrs. Dickerson confirmed that the Alamo had fallen and that the gallant Travis, Bowie, Crockett, and the other defenders had perished. She, her daughter, and two Mexican women had been in a small room to the right of the main entrance in the Alamo and had seen her husband, Lt. Almeron Dickerson, killed. She had also seen Maj. Robert Evans, master of ordnance, killed in an attempt to blow up the powder train leading to the ammunition. She, her daughter, Joe, and the two Mexican women were the only survivors of the frightful tragedy.[1]

According to Mrs. Dickerson, on the evening of March 6 Travis realized that his garrison was doomed and knew he must inform the men of their fate. He paraded them in single file before him and drew a line on the ground with his sword. He then asked every man who was determined to stay and die with him to cross over the line. With one exception, Louis Rose, all the men did. Bowie was on a bed, and it is said he asked to be carried across the

189

line. That night Rose dropped over a wall and successfully made his way through the Mexican lines.

On the personal orders of Santa Anna all of the 187 bodies of the soldiers were stripped, subjected to brutal indignities, and then thrown into heaps and burned.[2] After viewing the bodies, Santa Anna greeted Capt. Fernando Urizza and commented: "It was but a small affair." [3]

Shortly after Houston digested the horrible news from Mrs. Dickerson, another scout reported the news that Santa Anna was moving toward Gonzales and should reach there by late Sunday or early Monday morning. Now Sam had to alter his plans. It had been his intention to join up with Fannin at the Cibolo and advance on San Antonio to engage the enemy, but he had no idea where Fannin was by now. Besides, he had completely lost faith in him. Another fifty men had arrived to swell his ranks, so that Houston now had around 400 men in his command. With this small force he decided not to advance toward San Antonio but to fall back to Burnham's Crossing on the Colorado River, approximately fifty miles to the east. He gave orders to dump the artillery in the river and, followed by one ammunition wagon drawn by four oxen, the ragged army and a horde of civilian followers began to retreat. Deaf Smith was left behind with a mounted rear guard to send along refugees.

The scout who had reported that Santa Anna's army was moving toward Gonzales was in error. There were indeed about 600 infantrymen and 150 cavalry with light artillery on the move, but they were under the command of Gen. Joaquín Ramírez y Sesma. Convinced the war was over, the Napoleon of the West planned to return to Mexico City as he had learned that rebellion had broken out in Mexico.

Before leaving, Santa Anna outlined his plan of war to his commanders. It called for total devastation of Texas: homes and farms were to be burned and plundered, and civilians stripped of their possessions. All rebels found with weapons were to be executed, regardless of whether they surrendered or not, as this was part of the dictator's scheme to force the Texans to flee eastward across the Sabine River back into the United States. To be in overall command during his absence, Santa Anna selected Gen. Vicente Filisola, Italian-born but a citizen of Mexico for many years. General Ramírez y Sesma was to command the division in the central zone and, after routing the Texans at Gonzales, was to proceed to Lynch's Ferry, at the junction of the San Jacinto River and Buffalo Bayou, thence to Anahuac. Gen. Antonio Gaona was to proceed through Bastrop and Washington-on-the Brazos to Nacogdoches, and General Urrea was already on the move through the coastal area from Matamoros. The combined forces of the three armies would total about 6,000 men.

It took Houston and his army four days to reach the west bank of the Colorado River. The first night they spent at Peach Creek, about ten miles from Gonzales, where they were joined by Deaf Smith and the civilians he escorted. When Houston learned a blind woman and her six children had been left behind, he sent an escort back thirty miles to bring the mother and her brood to join the procession. The next morning, about 125 volunteers joined the army, but twenty-five of them quickly took to their heels when they heard what had happened to Travis and his comrades at the Alamo.[4] Houston then started having trouble with his troops as some of them wanted to go fight the Mexicans and others would desert at bad news.

Before reaching their destination, the last few miles had been slogged through chilling rain and mud, and when Houston and his weary caravan reached the swollen Colorado they found confusion. Alarmed by the defeatism spread by the Gonzales deserters, many citizens had abandoned their homes and were frantic to cross the river. To quell their fears the commander-in-chief went among them and gave his assurance they would all make the crossing before a single soldier crossed.

On March 17, Houston wrote James Collingsworth, chairman of the military committee of the new republic, reporting his arrival at Burnham's Crossing and telling about the frightened civilians he had encountered:

> It pains my heart that such consternation should have been spread by the deserters from camp. We are here; and, if only three hundred men remain on this side of the Brazos, I will die with them, or conquer our enemies. I shall raise a company of spies tomorrow to range the country from this to Gonzales.[5]

On the morning of March 19, the general moved his army southward about twenty-five miles to Beason's Ferry, at the present-day site of Columbus. He reached his new position the following day. Two days later, scouts Smith and Karnes rode into camp. They had sighted General Ramírez y Sesma on the opposite bank of the river about three miles north of Houston's camp. The Mexican general had two pieces of artillery and 750 troops, of whom

191

about 150 were cavalry. Some of Houston's army wanted him to attack Ramírez y Sesma at nightfall, but Sam was without artillery and refused. There were, however, a few minor skirmishes between patrols of the opposing forces.

News of the fall of the Alamo, tales spread by the deserters, and false reports that Santa Anna's cavalry had crossed the Colorado had had their effect on the officials of the provisional government. President Burnet and his cabinet decided to move the capital of the Republic to Harrisburg on Buffalo Bayou as it was considered a safer place than Washington-on-the-Brazos.

When Houston heard of the flight of Burnet and his cabinet, he referred to it sarcastically as "the flight of the wise men," and in a letter to Secretary of War Rusk expressed the opinion the retreat of the government would have a bad effect on the troops.[6] Then into camp rode Peter Kerr with the news that Fannin, refusing to obey Houston's order to leave his Fort Defiance, had encountered General Urrea's forces and been defeated. What had happened to them he did not know. This sorrowful news created such consternation in camp that Houston, afraid that more of his men would desert, had Kerr arrested as a spy and placed under guard.

Once more Smith and Karnes rode into camp with valuable information. This time they brought with them not only two prisoners but a captured communication addressed to Santa Anna at San Antonio from General Ramírez y Sesma. For the first time, Houston learned of the dictator's three-pronged plan to envelop him. In his communication, Ramírez y Sesma reported he had received reinforcements of several hundred men under the command of Gen. Eugenio Tolsa, and that he was planning to cross the Colorado toward Houston.

The strength of the Texas army was in constant flux as volunteers would report, while others would go home on furlough to take care of their families; others would simply desert. Houston, although desirous of fighting, knew he did not have strength enough to take on his opponents. Retreat was his only course, so retreat he did. His retreat and the ad interim government's flight to Harrisburg, together with the news of Fannin's defeat, caused a panic that began around the Colorado and spread into the Brazos and Trinity valleys. The mad scramble of the colonists to get out of the way of Santa Anna's advancing armies became known as the "Runaway Scrape," and so many people were heading for the Sabine River on

192

the Louisiana boundary that the trek was called "taking the Sabine Chute." [7]

The army grumbled as they had joined to fight, not retreat. The weather was miserable, and there was little food and ammunition. The troops slept on the ground with little covering, as did Houston, who used his saddle for a pillow. In his saddlebags he carried battered copies of *Gulliver's Travels* and *Commentaries of Julius Caesar,* a few ears of corn, and a generous supply of chewing tobacco. The general found the chewing of tobacco a good substitute for liquor; during the long retreat he did virtually no drinking. He also carried his lucky double-barreled pistols, which were decorated with his own dog and rooster carvings. [8]

Houston had learned much from Jackson about the leadership of men during the War of 1812. As he rode alongside his men, wearing his threadbare black cloth dress coat, he encouraged them while constantly urging them onward in the sloppy weather. The general would frequently apply to his nostrils some ammoniacal spirits made by distilling liquid from the shavings of deer horns. Mary Bowles, the granddaughter of Chief Bowles, had given him a vial of this concoction with the assurance it would prevent colds. She might have known what she was talking about: Houston never picked up a cold during that wet weather, even though he constantly slept on the ground. It was perhaps due to his constant sniffing of the spirits of ammonia that led some of his critics later on to accuse him of taking opium. [9]

It was still raining heavily and the Brazos was swollen when, on March 28, the ragged army made camp at Mill Creek, about one mile from San Felipe. The next day the general decided to lead his army about twenty miles up the west bank of the Brazos to the plantation of Jared Groce. As the region's richest man, Groce could supply them with provisions. Besides, the steamer *Yellow Stone* was there, which would solve the problem of how to cross the flooded river if it became necessary.

Along the march there had been so much discontent with the leadership of Houston that some were beginning to call him a coward for not seeking out the enemy and fighting them. Captains Moseley Baker and Wylie Martin were among the chief complainers and were leaders in talks about disposing of Sam as their commander. When Houston gave orders to march northward, Baker and his fellow grumbler Martin refused to move. Instead of court-martialing the two, Houston ordered Baker to stay behind at San

193

Felipe with his men to delay the enemy's advance. He then sent Martin with his company to Fort Bend for the same purpose.

Undoubtedly, Houston could have alleviated some of the criticism he received from the men under his command and from Burnet and his cabinet if he had confided his plans to them. Perhaps it was due to his living so many years among the Indians and acquiring some of their ways that he was secretive. He would take no one into his confidence, not even his officers. As he wrote to his friend Rusk: "I consulted none — I held no councils of war. If I err, the blame is mine." [10]

On March 31, 1836, Houston and his rain-soaked army made camp on a rise above the flooded river and creeks, on the west side of the Brazos near Groce's. It was a welcome respite after the three days the general had driven his men through mud and a driving rain.

It was around this time that several survivors from Goliad straggled into camp with news of the bloody massacre. The news of the fall of the Alamo had been bad enough, but the news of Goliad was worse and Houston's army was furious and thirsting for vengeance. They were aching for a fight, and Houston was hoping to keep them that way. He himself was depressed at what had happened to poor Fannin and his men, but all his life he was of the opinion that the battles of the Alamo and Goliad should never have been fought. Defense in fixed fortresses was not his way to fight a war. If the general council had backed him in organizing and training an army, and had not been engaged in the destruction of the provisional government, he could have taken to the field and defeated the Usurper of Mexico.

Houston had previously written Rusk:

On my arrival on the Brazos, had I consulted the wishes of all, I should have been like the ass between two stacks of hay. Many wished me to go below, others above. . . . There was on yesterday, as I understand, much discontent in the lines, because I would not fall down the river. If it should be wise for me to do so, I can cross over at any time, and fall down to greater advantage and safety. . . . I hope today to receive ninety men from the Redlands. . . . For Heaven's sake do not drop back again with the seat of government! Your removal to Harrisburg has done more to increase the panic in the country than anything else that has occurred in Texas, except the fall of the Alamo.[11]

Houston wrote Rusk again, telling him he had between seven

194

and eight hundred effective men, and asking him to send flour, sugar, and coffee on packhorses as soon as possible. He mentioned it had been his intention to attack and defeat the enemy at the Colorado on the second night after the day Peter Kerr reported Fannin's destruction, but he had information the enemy had had strong reinforcements during the night. Previous to that, the troops were in fine spirits and were keen for action.

The weather cleared and Houston used this time to train his raw troops in military tactics and to instill some discipline in them. He devoted time to creating a medical staff, and Anson Jones, a former druggist from New England who was now a physician serving as an infantryman, was made regimental surgeon. Two men were court-martialed for sleeping on watch, but the commander pardoned them. He was not so merciful when four men were caught robbing and raping women refugees. Those men were promptly hanged.

Houston's forceful personality and capacity for leadership was bearing fruit, and esprit began to revive among the soldiers. He was constantly checking the camp and making himself available to his men. One day, while making his rounds, the commander was asked by a young private if there were a blacksmith in the camp as he needed his gun fixed. Houston told him to leave the gun with him and return in an hour. When the young recruit returned, he found that the blacksmith who had repaired his weapon was the commanding general himself.[12] When tattoo and reveille were beaten on the drum in camp, the drummer was none other than Houston, who had learned the art of the drum in his youthful days in Maryville.

When Secretary of War Rusk first arrived in the camp, some discontented officers swarmed around him to complain about their leader. Rusk let them know he was backing Houston to the fullest and by that he did much to strengthen Sam's position. Soon the discontents were saying that Rusk had "fallen under the damned old Cherokee blackguard's spell." [13]

Criticism of Houston's strategy of constantly retreating was not confined to Baker and Martin and their fellow complainers. From his armchair redoubt, safely behind a desk at Harrisburg, President Burnet was screaming at Houston to get moving:

> The enemy are laughing you to scorn. You must fight them. You must retreat no farther. The country expects you to fight. The salvation of the country depends on you doing so.[14]

It was becoming apparent that this government, as the one before it, had a cabal against Houston. At Washington-on-the Brazos a great animosity had developed between Sam and Burnet, and he now discovered that Secretary of the Navy Potter had planted a spy in camp to report on Houston's every movement. To offset this, Rusk announced he was staying with the army for the balance of the campaign, and now Vice-President Lorenzo de Zavala, whose son had joined the army on the Colorado, arrived to give him added support.

On April 7, Santa Anna, with about 1,400 men, reached San Felipe. When Houston heard the news he knew the time was getting ripe to strike and immediately issued an army order:

> The advance of the enemy is at San Felipe. The moment for which we have waited with anxiety and interest, is fast approaching. The victims of the Alamo and the names of those who were murdered at Goliad call for *cool, deliberate* vengeance. Strict discipline, order, and subordination, will insure us the victory . . . the army will be in readiness for action at a moment's warning.[15]

When the Mexican president and his Santanistas rode into San Felipe, they found the town barren as Baker and the men under his command had burned it to the ground and crossed to the east bank of the river, where they had entrenched themselves. The Santanistas managed to capture one of Baker's scouts, who told *el presidente* that Houston was still on the west side of the Brazos, twenty miles upstream at Groce's.[16]

For some reason, the Napoleon of the West decided not to bypass Baker and ride upstream to engage the Texas army. Instead, he brought up two cannon and started shelling Baker's trenches. After a couple of days of fighting, in which the Texans lost one man, Santa Anna left General Ramírez y Sesma to deal with Baker and took about five hundred grenadiers and fifty dragoons and rode down the west bank of the Brazos heading for Fort Bend and Wylie Martin. Ramírez y Sesma joined him there on April 13. Martin realized he didn't have enough men to defend the river crossing and fell back.

When arriving at Fort Bend, Santa Anna learned that the new seat of the government was at Harrisburg. On April 14, he crossed the Brazos with his army of about one thousand, together with the numerous women camp followers. His destination was Harrisburg,

196

where he hoped to capture his old political enemy de Zavala, whom he swore to hang. It was not to be.

When Santa Anna and his advance guard rode into Harrisburg during the night of April 15, they found only Gail Borden, the newspaper publisher. He and two of his printers were busily engaged in putting out Texas's only newspaper, the *Telegraph and Texas Register*. Borden and his companions told them they were too late — Burnet and his government had fled to New Washington (now Morgan's Point, near modern-day Baytown) on Galveston Bay. The printers also gave them information about the Texas army. Houston and about 800 men had left Groce's plantation and, they thought, were heading for San Jacinto.

When Houston heard Santa Anna was crossing the river at Fort Bend, he knew it was time to cross the river. On April 12, he started putting his men on the steamboat *Yellow Stone*, together with two hundred horses and ten ox-drawn wagons containing baggage and ammunition. Houston crossed with the first contingent, and Rusk remained behind to supervise and follow with the last load. When Houston stepped ashore, the first thing he saw were two six-pound cannons in perfect condition, a gift from the citizens of Cincinnati. The men admiringly christened the cannons the "Twin Sisters," and Lieutenant Colonel Neill was made commander of artillery.

It took until April 15 before the army and its equipment was across the river, and that evening the army camped at the farm of a well-to-do settler named William Doniho, whose sympathies were with Mexico.

To add to his worries, Houston received another taunting letter from the government at Harrisburg. At the instigation of Burnet the acting secretary of war wrote Houston on April 12, calling attention that the commander-in-chief had assured the government that the enemy would never cross the Brazos. He then told him Santa Anna had also made the crossing, that there was nothing to stop him from marching to Harrisburg or Galveston, and that many families were exposed to the enemy.

> The country expects something from you. The time has now arrived to determine whether we are to give up the country, and make the best of our way out of it, or to meet the enemy, and make at least one struggle for our boasted independence. The government does not intend to control your movements; but it is expected that, without delay, you will take measures to check those of the enemy.[17]

To his aide Hockley, Houston dictated his reply to the acting secretary. In detailing the military reasons for his long retreat, he mentioned his lack of manpower and of supplies. He had submitted to the taunts and suggestions gratuitously tendered to him without any disposition to retort either unkindness of imputation. "I beg leave to assure you that I will omit no opportunity to serve the country." [18]

CHAPTER 21

In Pursuit of a Battle

On April 13, Houston, hearing rumors that Mexican agents were agitating the Indians, wrote his friend Chief Bowles, addressing his as "Colonel Bowl." Sam reassured his friend that he would get the land promised in their treaty and asked him to give his best compliments to "my sister, and tell her that I have not wore out the Mockasins which she made me." [1]

On the morning of April 16, he and his troops started marching from Doniho's with fourteen baggage wagons, accompanied by many civilians. The two perpetual troublemakers, Baker and Martin, had rejoined the army and were continuing their contributions to irritation and confusion. Houston, fed up with Martin, in salty language gave him a choice of going to East Texas to help fugitives or going to hell, so Martin and three or four hundred of his followers chose the former and left, reducing Houston's army to less than one thousand men. The next morning the army ran into a torrential downpour. Baggage wagons and artillery frequently broke down and had to be unloaded. When these emergencies occurred, Houston always dismounted and used his broad back and strong shoulders in helping his men maneuver the wagons and cannon out of the sticky mud.

Shortly after Houston left Doniho's, a black man rode up. He had been captured by Santa Anna but had been released to take

Sam a message: "Mr. Houston, I know you're up there hiding in the bushes. As soon as I catch the other land thieves [Burnet and the cabinet] I'm coming up to smoke you out." [2] The messenger also brought the information that Santa Anna had separated from his main army and was proceeding in advance of it with a force of seven or eight hundred infantrymen, one cannon, and a small force of dragoons.

About seventeen miles from Doniho's, there was a fork in the road. The settlers moving with the army expected Houston to take the left fork to Nacogdoches and the Sabine River border, where Gen. Edmund P. Gaines was commanding U.S. troops, while the mischievous Baker wanted the right fork to be taken to Harrisburg. Everyone wondered: what fork would Houston take? The commander-in-chief, as usual, was keeping his counsel to himself. When the fork was finally reached, the army turned to the right, and ever since, the move has been engaged in controversy. One version holds that Houston signaled a right-hand turn, while another holds that the front ranks of the army made the decision, turning down the right fork on their own and daring Houston to countermand the move.

In the meantime, Santa Anna had not been idle. Although he loved to consider himself the "Napoleon of the West," when it came to military tactics and strategy he had much to learn from his idol and during the campaign made many errors. He had passed up an excellent opportunity to catch Houston on the west bank of the Brazos when he had failed to bypass Baker and head north. Both his first-in-command, Gen. Vicente Filisola, and Colonel Juan Nepomuceno Almonte, Santa Anna's most trusted aide, disagreed with his three-pronged strategy as they realized no two armies would be within supporting distance of the others. When they made their objections known to *el presidente* and proposed an alternative plan, Santa Anna decided the rebellion in Mexico would have to be put on the back burner. He promptly resumed overall command, with Filisola his second-in-command, and made it clear he would adhere to his original strategy with two additional objectives. First, he would leave Harrisburg for New Washington, where he hoped to catch the fugitive government and its vice-president Lorenzo de Zavala; then he would backtrack and catch Houston somewhere in the vicinity of Lynchburg. But first he had to get some revenge. He burned Harrisburg to the ground and threw the printing presses of the *Telegraph and Texas Register* into the bayou.[3] Dashing for New Washington, he arrived there at noon on April 18, preceded by Colonel Almonte and about fifty dragoons. He flew into a rage when he found his prey once more was out of his reach. President Burnet and his wife had barely escaped Almonte's dragoons and were about 400 yards out in Galveston Bay in a rowboat heading for the schooner *Flash*. The other object of his vengeance, de Zavala, was not to be found as he was with Houston.

El presidente's trip to New Washington was not without pleasant results, however. He happened to notice a light-skinned mulatto slave named Emily loading some flatboats. She belonged to Col. James Morgan, and when she found favor in Santa Anna's eyes, the dictator promptly commandeered her and took her along as his "camp woman."

On the morning of April 20, the Mexican army had been ordered to transfer all supplies from the warehouses in New Washington to its own use. When this was accomplished, the order was given to burn the town, and as the Santanistas hurriedly carried out his excellency's orders, Santa Anna himself set the torch to the orange orchard of Colonel Morgan. Suddenly, a young captain named Marcos Barragan came galloping up, shouting the news: "Houston is on our rear and his troops have captured some of our stragglers and killed them."

The tattered Texas army, weary from being pushed fifty-five miles in two and a half days through cold, driving rains, had reached Buffalo Bayou on the morning of April 18.[4] Utterly exhausted, they rested for the night. Scouts Smith and Karnes swam their horses across the bayou, and when they returned they had three prisoners: one of Santa Anna's captains, a scout, and a courier from *el presidente*'s brother-in-law, General Cós, who had broken his parole and was with Ramírez y Sesma's army. The courier's mail pouch was a souvenir of the Alamo, inasmuch as it bore the name "W. B. Travis" — and it also bore a treasure of information for Houston. There was much mail from Mexico City, all congratulating Santa Anna, but much more important to Houston was the confirmation of his suspicion that the dictator was in the advance with his troops and was cut off from the main body of his army. The packet revealed Cós was racing toward Galveston to support Santa Anna in his chase of the elusive Burnet.

As a good commander should, Houston studied the facts as he knew them and the information his various scouts had brought him. He knew that generals Filisola and Ramírez y Sesma in the

201

central zone were still at Fort Bend. Gen. Antonio Gaona and his army in the northern zone were still west of the Brazos. That left General Urrea in the coastal area. After wiping out Johnson and Dr. Grant, he had proceeded to Matagorda where he had liberated supplies intended for the Texans. He had then marched to Brazoria on the Brazos River but was stopped by the high waters. From a study of his maps, Houston knew that Santa Anna must return from New Washington by crossing Vince's Bridge or Buffalo Bayou, just below the Texan camp at Lynch's Ferry.[5]

Undoubtedly, Houston thought of something Old Hickory had once told him: "When your enemy is superior to you in strength, extend him — lead him a chase until he exhausts himself — then close suddenly for the decisive blow." The chase was coming to a close, and now it was time for the decisive blow.

After analyzing the situation, Houston and Secretary of War Rusk retired for a private conference. They both agreed that a fight should be waged as soon as the enemy could be found.[6] Orders were given to the regimental commanders to prepare their troops for crossing the bayou, so that the army might begin its march upon the enemy the next morning.

On April 19, Houston penned a letter to his friend Henry Raguet.

> This morning we are in preparation to meet Santa Anna. It is the only chance of saving Texas. From time to time I have looked for reinforcements in vain. The Convention adjourning to Harrisburg struck *panic* throughout the country. Texas could have started at least four thousand men. We will only have about seven hundred to march with, besides the camp-guard. We go to conquer.[7]

When daylight arrived, in spite of the orders the commander had given to his officers the night before, no preparations had been made. Houston himself issued orders to the men, but it was nine o'clock before the troops could get under way.

The crossing of the bayou, some fifty feet wide and more than twenty feet deep,[8] was exceedingly difficult. First to cross were the scouts, headed by Smith and Karnes. Swimming their horses, they were followed by the cavalry. Houston was next, riding over on a crude raft, while Rusk stayed behind to make sure everyone got across safely. Left behind to guard some prisoners were a number of soldiers who had contracted measles.

When the crossing had been successfully negotiated, the commander assembled his haggard troops. Sitting on his white stallion, Saracen, he addressed his soldiers:

> Victory is certain! Trust in God and fear not! The victims of the Alamo and the names of those who were murdered at Goliad cry out for cool, deliberate vengeance. Remember the Alamo! Remember Goliad.[9]

His eager listeners responded with shouts of "Remember the Alamo! Remember Goliad!" When the shouting died down, Houston ended his speech by saying: "It is no use looking for aid. None is at hand. Colonel Rusk is with us, and I rejoice in this." [10] When Houston finished his remarks, the secretary of war addressed the troops. He said:

> Santa Anna himself is just below us, within the sound of a drum. A few hours more will decide the fate of the army. What an astonishing fact it is that when the fate of our wives, our children, our homes, and all we hold dear are suspended on the issue of one battle, not one-fourth of the men of Texas are here. I look around and see that many I thought would be first on the field are not here. . . . May I not survive if we don't win this battle.[11]

During all of Houston's retreat, while his ill-fed, ill-provisioned, and ill-clad troops were in near mutiny, and officials of his own government were carping at him and criticizing him, there was one man who stood fast in his faith. While most observers in Washington thought Houston was heading for the Sabine River and the protection of General Gaines's army stationed there, the man in the White House had a different opinion. Andrew Jackson knew Houston far better than his detractors did, and he knew he would fight. He was studying the reports from the Texas front with great intensity and was constantly referring to his maps. Finally, he put a bony finger on a map showing the western shore of Galveston Bay. Houston would fight *there,* Jackson said, or *there,* indicating a watery area called Buffalo Bayou.[12]

The general resumed his march with his troops through minor bayous, creeks, and treacherous marshes. Progress was slow over the difficult terrain as the column crept on, always on the alert to attack. Up and down the column rode Houston, from time to time putting the vial of spirits to his nose or spitting out a long stream of tobacco juice. At two o'clock in the morning, they crossed Vince's Bridge over Vince's Bayou, a tributary that flowed from the south into Buffalo Bayou. There they saw the cold, extinguished fires of

Santa Anna's army. The order came to break ranks, and the exhausted troops fell beside their arms in the damp grass. Houston let them rest for an hour, formed them again, then continued the march until daybreak, where the general hid them in a timber about half a mile from the ferry.[13]

The army had barely started their breakfast — steaks they had carved from some captured cows belonging to the Vince brothers — when some scouts came galloping in with news that Santa Anna had burned New Washington and was now on the march north toward Lynch's Ferry. Like any good general, Houston wanted to choose the time and place to fight to make his best thrusts count, and he wanted to fight before his opponent could receive reinforcements. If he could reach Lynch's Ferry before Santa Anna, he reasoned, he could have his choice of the best terrain and force *el presidente* to either fight or turn his force due west and lead his men over the terrible swampland Houston and his army had just passed through. No matter which choice Santa Anna made, Houston and his men would have the advantage as they were far more familiar with the terrain.

Tattoo was beaten and the virtually breakfastless army once more was on the march. About eleven o'clock they reached Lynch's Ferry, lying at the tip of a point of lowland where Buffalo Bayou flowed into the San Jacinto River. Across the river was a small hamlet, Lynchburg, consisting of unpainted houses. On a round hill behind the town stood a number of Mexican sympathizers, later called "Texas Tories," who had loaded a flatboat with supplies and provisions for Santa Anna. Some troops of Houston quickly liberated the supplies and made cakes out of the flour they captured.

Arriving at the point, Houston hid his soldiers in a heavily wooded oak grove festooned with moss. To his left was the San Jacinto, bordered by a swamp. Behind him was the bayou and in front was the plain of San Jacinto, a two-mile stretch of prairie covered with knee-high grass. Here and there were clumps of timber. If Santa Anna wanted the ferry, he would have to march on the prairie.

Houston deployed his troops with care, placing them in their order of battle: infantry, cavalry, artillery. He had his chief of artillery, Colonel Neill, place the Twin Sisters out in the prairie so they could be easily seen by Santa Anna and his troops. Then he established his pickets around the camp.

Once more Sam's hungry troops were trying to enjoy a meal of steaks when scouts rode into camp with news. Santa Anna and his army were approaching on the plain.

When the enemy's advance scouts discovered Houston's pickets and saw the Twin Sisters, they paused until Santa Anna caught up with them. *El presidente* studied the situation and formed his infantry and cavalry into position, then had the twelve-pound cannon known as the Golden Standard wheeled into its place. The Mexican dictator gave the order for the artillery to fire, and the first shot of the Golden Standard cut through the trees of the Texan camp. Colonel Neill answered with shots of canister, grape, and mangled horseshoes; several Mexicans fell. Some mules were also killed, and the ammunition chest was shattered. There was a brief artillery duel between the Twin Sisters and the Golden Standard and in the engagement Colonel Neill was injured. Houston was riding up and down among his troops when a ball glanced from a metal trimming on the horse's bridle.

Probably in an endeavor to force Houston to bring his main force out of the woods and into a battle, Santa Anna ordered his sharpshooters to return to camp immediately. The artillery was to follow as soon as they could gather up the ammunition for the cannon.

When Col. Sidney Sherman of the second regiment saw that the Mexicans were calling off the engagement, he asked Houston for permission to follow them and try to seize their twelve-pounder. Houston refused but gave him permission to take two companies of his regiment and reconnoiter with his cavalry. He gave Sherman "positive orders not to advance beyond the timber, or endanger the safety of his men." [14]

Sherman completely disregarded Houston's instruction, and with his men tried to capture the Golden Standard. Santa Anna's dragoons appeared, and there was a sharp skirmish in which several horses were killed, cavalryman Olwyn J. Trask was killed, and two others wounded. In the brief encounter Secretary of War Rusk, who was in the raiding party, almost lost his life. He had been cut off from retreat and was being attacked by several mounted Mexicans. Private Mirabeau Buonaparte Lamar, a Georgian and eventually the second elected president of Texas, came to the aid of Rusk by knocking down a Mexican cavalryman and his horse and making an opening through which Rusk was able to escape. Lamar further distinguished himself by dismounting under fire and lifting the wounded Walter P. Lane into his saddle, then taking him safely back to camp. When he arrived back at camp, Houston promoted him on the spot to full colonel. Rusk, as secretary of war and thus Houston's superior, promptly endorsed the battlefield promotion.

When the skirmish between the two opposing forces was over, Houston met the brown-bearded Sherman coming in and gave him a terrible blistering in front of the troops. Sherman had been one of the officers who had constantly connived against him and had been a leader in stirring up discontent and disobedience among the troops. It was Houston's belief that Sherman had deliberately disobeyed his orders in an endeavor to bring on a general engagement between the Texas forces and those of Santa Anna — an engagement which Houston did not want at that particular time. In addition, Sherman had not seized the cannon; in fact, he had accomplished nothing except to have one man killed and two others severely wounded.

That night, Houston, in conversation with his aide Hockley, confided:

> I do not doubt that we would have won today, but our loss would have been heavy. Tomorrow I will conquer, slaughter or put to flight the entire Mexican army, and it shall not cost me a dozen of my brave men.[15]

Houston passed the word down from headquarters for the camp fires to be put out and ordered the men to have their arms close at hand. The troops slept well because they knew that on the morrow they were at last to come to grips with the enemy they had sought for so long. Deciding to get his first good night's sleep in thirty-eight days, Houston appointed Hockley to take over for him. Hockley was to give the three taps on the camp drum for reveille the next morning, and if Houston was still asleep he was not to wake him. The commander then chose a spot under a tree for his resting place, lay on the hard ground under a chilling wind with not even a blanket between him and the earth, and went to sleep.

The dictator-general Santa Anna was proving himself a poor facsimile of the real Napoleon. Choosing a site for the battle he knew was coming the next day, he could hardly have picked a worse one. His position along the shore of San Jacinto Bay faced the northwest; Houston was on his right, and at the rear was an extensive grove of trees, bounded on the south and east by a vast marshland. Between the grove and the marsh was a miniature bayou. The site he selected was on slightly rising ground about

206

three-fourths of a mile from his enemy. It protected his flanks from an attack but left him little room to maneuver and no room to retreat. Two of his high-ranking officers thought the site chosen was ridiculous. Colonel Delgado, who survived the battle, later said, "Any youngster would have done better." General Castrillon, who did not survive, was equally skeptical.

> What can I do. . . . I know it well that we are in a dangerous position, but I can not help it. You know that nothing avails here against the caprice, arbitrary will, and ignorance of *that man*.[16]

Santa Anna placed his dragoons on the left and his infantry on the right, stationed in timber, about 400 yards from the enemy. In the center were breastworks with a five-foot parapet of pack saddles and baggage for the protection of artillery. Infantry supported them on each flank.

In sharp contrast to the earthbed his antagonist was sleeping on, the opium-indulging Santa Anna retired for the evening to much more luxurious quarters. His tent was a large marquee, lined with silk and floored with rugs. His fine bed was lined with elegant coverings. Contemptuous of Houston and the Texans, the dictator slid between his silken sheets and enjoyed a fine night's rest.

CHAPTER 22

The Decisive Blow is Struck

When dawn broke on the morning of April 21, 1836, Colonel Hockley signaled reveille, and the commander-in-chief slept on. The sun was shining and there was not a cloud in the sky. When Houston finally arose, he remarked that "the sun of Austerlitz has risen again." [1] His small army was restless, fidgeting to attack, and at this late hour reinforcements arrived — nine young men from the United States.

Houston was surveying the situation and planning his moves for the coming engagement when around nine o'clock Deaf Smith, his favorite scout, rode up with a message that General Cós was coming up to reinforce Santa Anna with about 500 troops. This raised Santa Anna's estimated strength to about 1,350 men, and Houston knew General Filisola was on his way with 3,000 more. The total strength of the Texans was less than 800 men. Houston told Smith to pick some men and destroy Vince's Bridge on the road to the Brazos, about eight miles from the Texas camp. This would not only prevent Santa Anna from receiving reinforcements from that direction, but would also prevent any retreat for the Texans.

Some of Houston's restless officers requested a council of war among the field grade officers, so between the hours of noon and 2:00 P.M. the commander had his first and only council of war during the entire campaign. Besides Houston and Secretary of War

208

Rusk, who had the rank of colonel and was participating as an active combatant, those present were majors Lysander Wells and Joseph L. Bennet, and colonels Burleson, Millard, Wharton, Somervell, Sherman, and Lamar. The only topic of discussion was whether to attack the enemy where they were, or to let them attack. As is customary in the military the junior officers spoke first, followed by their seniors. Houston listened courteously while every man present voiced his opinion, but the general expressed no preference of his own. When it was Rusk's turn to speak, he advocated letting Santa Anna make the attack. He pointed out the Texans were raw troops with few bayonets and would have to be sent out across a mile-long prairie against veteran Mexican troops behind fortifications.[2]

When the question had been thoroughly discussed Houston called for a vote, and of those present, only Millard and Wells voted to attack. Strangely enough, Sherman, Wharton, and Lamar, who had so frequently deplored Houston's caution during the campaign, voted to stay on the defensive. Once the vote was taken, Houston adjourned the council of war and still did not commit himself as to his plans. He had already decided not only that he would attack, but also at what precise moment the attack was to be made.

During the campaign, while some of Houston's subordinates had been scoffing at him for his caution, the wily general had not been idle. With little formal education in the art of warfare, he had nevertheless learned much under Old Hickory. In addition, he carried the *Commentaries of Julius Ceasar* in his saddlebags and constantly studied them. His years of living among the Indians had sharpened and honed his mind with the knowledge of how they made warfare, and from them he had learned to study the strength and weaknesses of an opponent. Since he first entered Texas he had observed and studied the Mexicans closely; he knew their customs, their character, and their habits. He had studied the life and campaigns of Santa Anna and thought he knew the character and temperament of his opposite number. Thus, by knowing that the Mexican dictator and his troops enjoyed a daily *siesta*, Houston planned to attack when the Mexicans were enjoying their afternoon slumber.

At three o'clock Houston called his army together. Seldom has there been seen a sorrier sight that called itself an army. Unwashed and unshaven, their long hair and beards and mustaches were matted, and their clothes were nothing but tatters and rags. Years later, Valentine Bennet, the quartermaster, was asked about the uniform the Texans wore that chilly day in April 1836. "Rags were our uniform, sir!" replied Major Bennet. "Nine out of ten of them was in rags. And it was a fighting uniform." [3] The army's commander was dressed appropriately to lead these ragmen, wearing a mud-splattered black frock coat with a velvet vest and snuff-colored pants. On his head was a slouch hat creased almost into the shape of the three-cornered headgear that was in style in revolutionary war days.[4] His army was composed of English, Irish, Scots, a company of twenty Mexicans and Texians headed by Capt. Juan Seguín, French, Germans, Italians, Poles, and Yankees from the United States. There were some blacks, including Private Hendrick Arnold, of the spy company, and Dick, a free black who served as a drummer. Among the volunteers from Tennessee was Capt. William J. Heard, who years before had been a student under the youthful Sam Houston during the one term that schoolmaster Houston taught at Maryville. Together they totaled 783 effectives.[5]

A motley-looking crew they were, but many were owners of large estates and some were distinguished in the fields of law and medicine. Some were important people back home and had graced famous drawing rooms. Coming from many backgrounds, they all had one thing in common: they were gathered together in the fight for the cause of Texas independence.

The commander assembled his men for the assault in the order of battle. He would lead the charge, followed by his company of thirty or forty spies and scouts under the command of Capt. Henry Karnes. On the extreme right wing Houston placed his newly appointed colonel, Mirabeau Lamar, and Lamar's sixty-one man cavalry. Next to them were Lt. Col. Henry Millard with two companies of regular infantry. Also with the infantry were Dick, the drummer, and three fifers. Lt. Col. George Hockley was in command of the artillery, since Neill had been wounded the day previously. Hockley and his thirty cannoneers were to the left of Millard's regulars and a few paces ahead of them. Next to the artillery was the first regiment, commanded by the famous Indian fighter, Col. Edward Burleson. At the extreme left wing of the line was the second regiment under the command of Colonel Sherman. With the second regiment was Col. Tom Rusk. The battle plan called for Sherman's regiment to attack the right side of the Mexican camp, which was in a grove of oak trees, and their movements would be

Sam Houston, the Patriot, in 1836.
— Courtesy Barker Texas History Collection,
University of Texas at Austin.

Sketch of Sam Houston in a Cherokee Indian costume, by Bernhardt Wall.
Taken from Following General Sam Houston, from 1793–1863.
— Courtesy Institute of Texan Cultures at San Antonio

Houston in uniform. From Yacht Voyage to Texas.
— Courtesy Barker Texas History Center,
University of Texas at Austin

Sam Houston — Governor of Tennessee, 1827–1829; Liberator of Texas and President of Texas from Tennessee — The Volunteer State, Vol. I, p.397.
— Courtesy Barker Texas History Center,
University of Texas at Austin

Photo taken in Kentucky, June 1845.

Governor Sam Houston, from a portrait by William Henry Huddle in the Texas State Capitol.

— Courtesy Texas State Library

Sam Houston
— Courtesy Texas State Library
and Archives

Photo of Sam Houston, 52, taken in Kentucky in 1845. Taken from The Houstons at Independence, *R. Henderson Shuffler, Austin, Texian Press, 1966.*

Photo of a painting of Sam Houston, wearing a waistcoat of leopard skin, and a chin beard, 1849.
— Courtesy Institute of Texan Cultures at San Antonio

Sam Houston in 1848 from a lithograph by F. Davignon.

Sam Houston. Photo by Morris, Galveston.
— Courtesy Barker Texas History Center,
University of Texas at Austin

Sam Houston. "Taken when he was Governor of Texas, ca. 1860."
— Courtesy Barker Texas History Center,
University of Texas at Austin

Sam Houston — Made in New York by Fredericks about 1849.
— Courtesy Barker Texas History Center,
University of Texas at Austin

"General Sam Houston" painting by Bernhard Gordon
— Courtesy Barker Texas History Center,
University of Texas at Austin

"General Houston from an old picture found in Tennessee."
— Courtesy Barker Texas History Center,
University of Texas at Austin

"Paint Me as Marius!" Painted at Nashville in 1831, during a brief excursion from the Indian country. Houston gave the original to Mrs. A. C. Allen, widow of one of the brothers who founded the city of Houston. This reproduction from a copy in the Senate Chamber, State Capitol, Austin.

— Courtesy Barker Texas History Center,
University of Texas at Austin

Margaret Lea Houston from a daguerreotype made in Galveston when she was a bride.

LEFT TO RIGHT:
Temple Lea Houston as he appeared as Senator of Texas 1885–89.
— Courtesy Sam Houston Museum, Huntsville

Photo of Temple Lea Houston, the youngest child of Sam Houston. He was a lawyer, orator, and plainsman.
— Courtesy Barker Texas History Center, University of Texas at Austin

Temple Lea Houston about age 40, as a successful lawyer and orator.
— Courtesy Mrs. Mary Henderson

Temple Lea Houston, cadet at Baylor Military Academy.
— Courtesy Mrs. Mary Henderson

Photo of Antoinette Power Houston, the daughter of Sam Houston. She became Antoinette Houston Bringhurst. Taken from The Houstons at Independence, *R. Henderson Shuffler, Austin, Texian Press.*

Mrs. Laura Cross Houston, wife of Temple Lea Houston.
— Courtesy Sam Houston Museum, Huntsville, Texas

Photo of Mary William Houston, daughter of Sam Houston. She married J. S. Morrow.
— Courtesy Barker Texas History Center, University of Texas at Austin

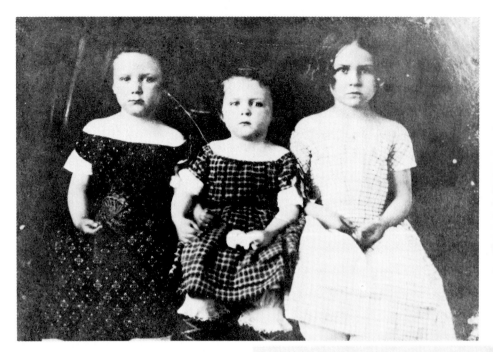

UPPER:
Copyprint of a Daguerreotype made in the 1850s. Houston's daughters Margaret, Mary, and Nannie.

RIGHT:
Possibly Andrew Jackson Houston.
— Courtesy Barker Texas History Center, University of Texas at Austin

UPPER:
*"General Houston, Santa Anna &
Co." Published June 1836 by H. R.
Robinson, New York. (Lithograph).*
— Courtesy Barker Texas
History Center, University
of Texas at Austin

RIGHT:
*"With a desperate effort he drew forth
the arrow, tearing the flesh as it came."
p.32. "Ensign Houston at To-Ho-Pe-
Ka," an engraving approved by Hous-
ton and first reproduced in* Sam
Houston and His Republic, *1846.*
— Courtesy Barker Texas
History Center, University
of Texas at Austin

"Sam Houston House, Huntsville"
— Courtesy Barker Texas History Center,
University of Texas at Austin

"Steamboat House (Old Sam Houston Home), Huntsville, Texas" photo taken
March 3, 1937.

— Courtesy Barker Texas History Center,
University of Texas at Austin

Sam Houston monument, Oak Grove Cemetery, Huntsville, Texas, erected by the State in 1911.

Bust of Sam Houston by Elisabet Ney.

"Bust of Houston by F. William Sievers, unveiled in the Virginia State Capitol, 1935."

Letter from Sam Houston to Secretary of State Robert Anderson Irion.
— Courtesy Sam Houston State University Library

screened from Houston and most of the rest of the army. Rusk's task was to ride with the second regiment at the start of the attack until it made contact with the enemy; then, he was to ride over to the center of the line and let Houston know how Sherman's regiment was doing.

It was around four o'clock when Houston, chewing on his customary wad of tobacco, trotted his white stallion Saracen in front of the first regiment. This was the moment the men had been waiting on for weeks, and with their eyes upon him and the battlefield hushed, the commander paused and glanced around in the bright sunshine. He slowly raised his right arm, saber in hand, and as he drew it down rapidly in a slicing motion the air resounded with his strong, vibrant baritone: "Trail arms! Forward!"

When the army of Texas marched off in columns toward the Santanista camp, the tobacco-chewing General Houston was at the point, riding from five to thirty yards ahead of his men. He had given strict orders to keep silent until after the first volley. While the troops were advancing, Deaf Smith rode up and announced he and his men had successfully accomplished their mission of burning Vince's Bridge. Houston rode to the front of Burleson's regiment and passed the news on, adding that the Mexicans' best avenue of escape was now closed. Smith rode up and down the ranks repeating the news.

Houston kept urging his men to keep low and hold their fire, and the Texans went rapidly through the tall grass on the plain. Mexican pickets discovered Lamar's cavalry, and a bugle blared away as Mexican artillery and infantry began firing. Houston was still ordering his men to keep low and hold their fire. Finally, the Texans reached the crest of the slight hill, and Houston gave the order for his artillery to fire. The Twin Sisters hurled their charge of cannister, balls, and horseshoes at the Mexicans while Dick, the black drummer, and the three fifers started playing "Will You Come to the Bower?"

The artillery was about ten yards ahead of the infantry when Houston almost got blown up by one of his own gunners. Ben McCulloch, one of the cannoneers and a future Confederate general, started to fire his cannon when Houston passed some thirty yards in front of him and every man in that part of the field.

With Houston's command to fire, a hurricane of unleashed fury swept the field as the Texans gave vent to their hate, rage, and frustration. Shouting "Remember the Alamo! Remember Goliad!" the infantry and cavalry went on the attack while the Twin Sisters

211

under Hockley blasted away at the Mexican fortifications. Working in concert, Sherman drove the Mexican right flank into the center, while Lamar's cavalry advanced on the enemy's left, driving the dragoons toward the center where the Mexican camp was located.

Houston's plans had worked out to perfection as he had caught the Mexicans at their *siesta*; their guns were stacked, and the majority of them were asleep. Their officers, suddenly awakened, milled around in confusion while trying to organize their troops into some semblance of defense, but it was useless. The battle quickly became a rout and then a slaughter as the Texas infantrymen would fire their shots at almost point-blank range and then, reversing their muskets, used their rifles as clubs. In their pent-up rage many of the frontiersmen grabbed an opponent and slit his throat with a Bowie knife, and in a few cases even scalped them.[6]

When Houston was about forty yards from the Mexican line, a volley of shots caught the stallion Saracen, killing him. Houston landed on his feet as the horse sank to the ground and, catching a riderless horse, mounted it. As he was riding to the enemy breastworks a three-ounce copper ball struck him just above the right ankle and, simultaneously, his new mount was shot from under him. His aide, Alex Horton, dismounted and gave the wounded commander his third horse of the day.

Capt. Moseley Baker, one of Houston's severest critics during the long retreat, finally got the fight he had been aching for and, to his credit, performed valiantly until wounded. Secretary of War Rusk, having no command of his own, was all over the field, followed by his aide, Dr. Junius William Mottley. The aide was struck by a cannonball, knocked from his horse, and died soon afterwards.

On the Mexican side, General Castrillon and Lieutenant Arenal were in a tent enjoying champagne when they heard the bugle sound the alarm. Castrillon, a veteran warhorse of many campaigns and now commanding the Tampico Battalion, tried to rally his men but could not. Colonel Rusk rode up to him, shouting to his men not to shoot the Mexican general, but the enraged Texans paid him no heed and riddled Castrillon with bullets.

General Cós, Santa Anna's charming brother-in-law, had been resting in his tent when the attack started. The second regiment under Colonel Sherman routed his troops, and in the confusion Cós managed to escape.

212

And what of Santa Anna? He was literally caught with his pants down when Houston made his surprise attack. Between the silken sheets in his bed, he was being entertained by the light-skinned, voluptuous mulatto Emily. The dictator was clad only in a linen, diamond-studded undershirt and a pair of silken drawers. Emily, for her part in detaining Santa Anna, was later to become known as the "Yellow Rose of Texas." The "Hero of Tampico" took one look outside his marquee and saw the confusion surrounding him. Deciding discretion was the better part of valor, he did not even try to take command of his troops or put up a resistance. Instead, he hastily threw on a blue linen dressing gown, mounted a speedy horse, and dashed off in the direction of Vince's Bridge.[7]

Colonel Delgado, who later claimed he was the only officer in camp who was neither asleep nor having a party, was on duty and was watching his artillerymen repair the damaged Golden Standard. Suddenly, he saw the Texans charge over the rise in the plain, meeting no resistance as his fellow Mexicans fled in all directions. He tried to round up enough men to put up some resistance but gave up as it was impossible. When he saw Santa Anna mount his horse and dash off, Delgado decided to follow the example of his leader but was unable to mount his own steed due to its skittishness. Leading his horse to the grove between the battlefield and the march, he found what he later called "our disbanded herd" already there, seeking shelter from the slaughter. The site he picked for his escape was an unsafe one. To get to the grove the Mexicans had to pass a small bayou that was swollen by the tide and recent rains. Near shore the water was shallow, but at its center it was much deeper. Many of the runaways who had plunged in had become mired in the mud, to be picked off by sharpshooters on the shore. Delgado mounted his horse and tried to slowly maneuver the animal across to the grove, but near the middle of the bayou his steed got stuck in the mud. Delgado dismounted, abandoned his horse, and was lucky enough to reach shore without being shot.

As the slaughter continued, many Mexicans got down on their knees and imploringly cried out, "Me no Alamo! Me no Goliad!" But it was all in vain as the enraged Texans, showing no mercy, shot them, bashed in their heads with rifle butts, or killed them with their knives.

With the boot on his right foot filling with blood, Houston rode among his troops and ordered both officers and men to stop

213

the battle and the wanton killing. He told Col. William Allen to take a fifteen-man detail and catch up with the pursuing Texans to enforce his orders against killing and to bring into camp all who surrendered. Houston then rode to the little bayou where Delgado and Almonte had crossed. He was fatigued from his wound and his eyes were dimmed by pain and weakness. Suddenly, he saw Rusk come up, leading about 250 Mexicans. Houston must have thought they were General Filisola's army coming from the Brazos to reinforce Santa Anna. He cried out: "All is lost! All is lost! My God, all is lost!" [8] Then his officers told him it was the secretary of war leading in some prisoners Colonel Allen had pursued, together with Col. Juan Almonte, who had been discovered hiding in a tree. Houston then proceeded to his headquarters under an oak tree, where Rusk introduced him to Colonel Almonte, the aide and interpreter of Santa Anna. When asked by Houston where Santa Anna was, the colonel could only recount that he had seen the fleeing president ride from the battlefield on a black horse at about 4:45 that afternoon.

Dr. Alexander Wray Ewing, the acting surgeon general, took off Houston's blood-filled boot and pronounced the injury a serious one indeed. He diagnosed it as a compound fracture of the right tibia and fibula, just above the ankle.

The Battle of San Jacinto was over, although there was still minor resistance and the rounding up of prisoners was not completed until the next day. The entire fray had lasted eighteen minutes. The Mexicans suffered 630 killed and 208 wounded, together with 730 prisoners.[9] In the battle, two Texans were killed and twenty wounded, including six who subsequently died of battle injuries. Among the Mexican dead were one general, four colonels, two lieutenant colonels, five captains, and twelve lieutenants. The American battlefield dead consisted of one private and Dr. Mottley.

When the guns of the battle were silenced, the Man of Destiny's star was shining at its brightest. The Raven had risen up from his personal purgatory.

CHAPTER 23

The Personal Battle
Continues

From the battlefield on the morning of April 22, one of the first things Houston did was to send a short note to Anna Raguet, enclosing leaves from a laurel wreath. The note read: "These are laurels I send you from the battlefield of San Jacinto. Thine, Houston." He also penned the following:

> Nor should we withhold the tribute of our grateful acknowledgements from that Being who rules the destiny of nations, and who, in the time of our greatest need, has enabled us to arrest the powerful foe who was devasting our country.[1]

During the night, Deaf Smith and his men returned with several more prisoners they had captured, including Ramón Cato, private secretary to Santa Anna, and the urbane General Cós.

As the wounded conqueror lay on a cot taken from the enemy's stores, he surveyed the situation. An inventory of the spoils of war included 900 English muskets, 300 sabers, 200 pistols, 300 mules, 100 horses, plus a good amount of clothing, tents, and supplies. Santa Anna's war chest had been found, and it contained about $12,000, American valuation.[2] Included in the loot were the dictator's silver dinner service and a silver-mounted chamber pot, together with two six-foot-high mounds of baskets of champagne. Houston declared the money as part of the spoils of war and in-

215

structed his officers to divide it among themselves and their men. He declared that he would take none of it.

Houston had a worry more than money on his mind. Where was Santa Anna? The battle was over but the war could not be until Santa Anna was captured, as there were still armies of generals Filisola and Urrea with which to contend. Houston called in Colonel Burleson and instructed him to take a party and search for the elusive dictator.

> You will find the Hero of Tampico, if you find him at all, making his retreat on all fours, and he will be dressed as bad at least as a common soldier. Examine closely every man you find.[3]

Burleson and his men were instructed not to harm Santa Anna but to treat him courteously and bring him immediately to the commander.

All day, scattered bands of forlorn-looking prisoners were brought in, but no Santa Anna. Finally, late in the afternoon, a small squad of four men rode into camp. Riding behind twenty-one-year-old Joel W. Robison was a bedraggled prisoner wearing slave's clothes. The "common soldier" was Santa Anna.

The scouting party had been on the bank of Buffalo Bayou where Vince's Bridge had been destroyed. Suddenly, in the high grass, they saw a man moving toward the bridge. When the fleeing soldier saw them he tried to run but fell down and was captured. The scouts had no idea who the man was, but on their way back to camp they passed a group of prisoners sitting on the ground. The prisoners stood up and saluted. *"El presidente!"* they cried. *"El presidente!"*

When the Mexican dictator was brought before him, Houston was resting from the severity of his wound. Looking up, he beheld what he thought was a private in the Mexican army.

"I am General Antonio Lopez de Santa Anna, President of the Republic of Mexico and a prisoner at your disposition," the prisoner announced.[4]

Colonel Almonte was requested to act as interpreter between the two commanders, along with Lorenzo de Zavala. Santa Anna embraced Almonte and then said to Houston: "That man may consider himself born to no common destiny, who has conquered the Napoleon of the West; and it now remains for him to be generous to the vanquished." [5]

"You should have remembered that at the Alamo," [6] Houston replied.

216

A dialogue ensued between the two generals in which Santa Anna tried to justify the atrocities of the Alamo and Goliad on "orders from my government commanding me to exterminate every man found in arms in the province of Texas." Houston answered: "Why, *You* are the government of Mexico." [7]

The rest of the conversation was the same, with Santa Anna denying any responsibility for the slaughter of soldiers at the Alamo or Goliad, or else blaming everything on General Urrea. During the conversation, the Mexican dictator became extremely agitated and asked for some opium, which was furnished him.

After a respite during which it seemed the opium soothed the nerves of *el presidente,* he proposed a peace treaty to be signed by Houston and himself. Houston refused on the grounds that this was the responsibility of the civilian government. He countered with a proposal that an armistice be signed between the two, the terms being that all hostilities were to immediately cease and Texas was to be immediately evacuated of all Mexican troops. Santa Anna asked for his secretary Cato and dictated a dispatch to General Filisola instructing him to march back to San Antonio and to order General Gaona to do the same, both to await further instructions. General Urrea was to be ordered to proceed with his division to Victoria. Several copies of this document were made, and Deaf Smith and a small party were instructed to find Filisola and deliver the orders. To give Smith protection in case Filisola resorted to treachery, Colonel Burleson and 250 men followed him.

During a lull in the activities, Almonte moved closer to Houston and engaged him in conversation, asking why he had not fought the day before but waited until Cós had arrived with reinforcements.

"Because," replied Houston, "I *knew* you expected me to fight that day . . . besides, why take two bites for one cherry." [8] When Almonte translated his conversation to Santa Anna, his chief became furious and cursed Almonte for losing the battle.

Santa Anna's marquee was set up near Houston's headquarters and his personal baggage restored to him. In a subsequent conference with Houston, he inquired as to the whereabouts of the Texas government. Houston sidestepped the question but later commented the government had "fled from the scene of danger, and scattered to the four winds of Heaven." [9]

Later, Houston wrote Rusk a letter outlining what he thought the terms of a peace treaty between Santa Anna and the Texas government should include. He suggested that the recognition of the independence of Texas should be *sine qua non,* with the boundaries of Texas extending to the Rio Grande, from the mouth of its most northwestern source, and from thence northeast to the line of the United States. General Santa Anna was to be retained as a hostage until the terms were recognized or ratified by the Mexican government. There was to be instantaneous withdrawal of all the Mexican troops from Texas.[10]

While dealing with these matters, Houston was confronted with an unexpected problem. Mrs. Peggy McCormick, who owned the property on which the battle had been fought, came into camp and furiously accosted Houston, demanding that he take "those stinking Mexicans off my farm." Sam, in an effort to mollify her, retorted: "Madam, your land will be famed in history."

The furious Peggy replied: "To the devil with your glorious history. Take off your stinking Mexicans."

Houston sympathized with her as the bloated corpses were beginning to smell in the heat of the day, and he gave orders for the Mexican prisoners to dig graves and bury the dead.

Although Houston had started writing his formal report of the battle to President Burnet on April 23, it was not sent to the president at Galveston until two days later.

The first of the absent government to arrive at Houston's headquarters was Lorenzo de Zavala the vice-president, who arrived on the twenty-third, bringing in not only fresh supplies to augment the army's meager diet but also James Morgan, the master of the mulatto Emily. Morgan promptly reclaimed his property. Several days later, the army moved toward Vince's Bayou to the plantation of Dr. George Moffit Patrick. The men were put up in rude shelters while the officers found quarters in some frame houses. Houston, who had developed a fever from his ankle injury, was given a cot.

Now that the campaign was over, once more Houston was forced to endure the slings and arrows of petty men. Burnet and some of his cabinet arrived on May 4 and could not wait to show their resentment toward and jealousy of him. Burnet and Secretary of the Navy Robert Potter were angry because Houston had allowed the spoils of war to be divided among the men, whereas the cabinet thought the money should have been saved for the government. Inasmuch as the cabinet had never paid the troops for their services, the spoils were the only pay the soldiers received. After the silver found in Santa Anna's war chest had been counted several times and the law of diminishing returns had taken its toll, there was so little left that hardly anyone received more than ten or twelve dollars. Some of the unlucky ones received less than that.

Instead of heaping praise and congratulations on the victorious general, Potter declared Houston should be court-martialed for mismanagement of the campaign. Houston had friends at court, including Rusk and de Zavala, who supported him, so nothing came of Potter's grumblings. Houston's critics in the cabinet also had to contend with the army. The rank and file which had once so severely criticized Houston had changed their opinion of him since the victory and now idolized him. They simply would not have tolerated a court-martial of their commander.

By May 5, Houston's ankle had not improved. Dr. Ewing was afraid a serious infection might set in if he did not receive better medical attention and suggested Houston be sent to New Orleans via Galveston.

As Burnet was leaving for Galveston in a couple of days, Houston recommended Rusk be made acting commander, and the president approved the appointment. Rusk was given the rank of brigadier general; Mirabeau Lamar, who only a few days previously had been a private, was appointed to replace him as secretary of war.

In their attempts to denigrate Houston, the cabinet did not even ask him to attend a cabinet meeting to discuss the future of Santa Anna. And when the *Yellow Stone* was being readied to take Burnet and his cabinet, together with Santa Anna, Cós, and others back to Galveston, the mean-spirited Burnet even refused to give permission to let Houston ride along. When Surgeon General Ewing, who was going to accompany his patient to New Orleans, reported this to Capt. J. E. Ross, master of the *Yellow Stone*, Ross refused to sail unless Houston was aboard. The government did not try to prevent Sam from boarding the ship, but in a fit of pique told Dr. Ewing he was not authorized to go to New Orleans with Houston. If he did, he would be dismissed from the army. The good doctor, a man of integrity and honor, decided to stick with his patient.

In the Galveston harbor, the schooner *Liberty* was readying to sail to New Orleans. Once more the government refused Houston and his doctor permission to ride on a government vessel. An American schooner, the *Flora*, was about to sail for New Orleans. Houston sent for the captain and explained he needed passage but was broke because neither officers nor soldiers had been paid during the recent campaign. The captain assured him he could make payment later.

The little schooner *Flora* docked at New Orleans at noon on Sunday, May 22, to be met by a tremendous throng of people who had been alerted earlier. The general was greeted enthusiastically by cheering crowds who had previously received reports of the Battle of San Jacinto and knew that Santa Anna was a prisoner of war. As he was being moved from the *Flora* to the dock, Houston fainted.

The conquering hero was among friends and was taken to the home of Col. William Christy, an old comrade with whom he had served as a lieutenant in the army years previously. There they immediately called for Dr. Kerr, who as a young army surgeon had removed the bullet Houston had received at Horseshoe Bend. Houston was more dead than alive, weak and thin from lack of food and for weeks without medicines or poultices. Dr. Kerr and his associate, Dr. Cenas, quickly operated on Sam's injured right ankle and removed twenty pieces of bone and splinters. They then drained the wound. The doctor later said that if Houston had not been treated at that time he would have certainly died in a few days.

While the general was recovering at the home of Christy, he was the hero of the hour. He was offered a testimonial dinner but regretfully declined on the grounds of his health. Any resentment he might have felt about the shabby treatment rendered him by Burnet and his associates was quickly alleviated by a personal letter of congratulations from President Jackson.

As usual, Houston was strapped for money. For all his efforts he had not been paid a cent of salary, and during his long retreat he had given away more than $300 of his own funds to widows who had lost their husbands at the Alamo or Goliad. As he recuperated he was contacted by John T. Mason, agent for a New York land company, and was advanced $2,000 to be attorney and agent for the company in Texas.

Daily reports were coming in to Houston from Texas. After the government had arrived at Galveston with Santa Anna, it had proceeded on to Velasco, a port south of Galveston. The cabinet changed daily, and Burnet had just about lost control of his government. The army was rapidly becoming the real ruler of Texas. Burnet, as did Houston, believed Santa Anna should be held as a hostage for peace. This produced much wrangling within the cabinet: Secretary of War Lamar and Secretary of the Navy Potter wanted to charge Santa Anna with murder and execute him immediately, while Rusk and the rest of the cabinet sided with Burnet.[11]

On May 14, Burnet and Santa Anna signed two peace treaties — one public and one secret — in which were incorporated virtually all the terms and conditions Houston had expressed earlier in his letter to Rusk. In the secret treaty, Santa Anna acknowledged the independence of Texas with the Rio Grande from its mouth to its source as boundary between the two countries. The second treaty was kept secret at Santa Anna's request, as he carefully explained he did not desire to have an adverse public opinion aroused at home until he was on the ground to combat it.[12] The provisional government of Texas pledged to give the Mexican president safe return to his country. The disgruntled Lamar and Potter refused to sign either treaty.

Against the wishes of his host Christy and doctors Kerr and Cenas, the still-ailing Houston left for Texas around the middle of June. At Natchitoches, Louisiana, he was met by Dr. Robert Irion, his competitor for the affections of Anna Raguet. The doctor cleaned and dressed Sam's draining and swollen leg, and the two men then rode on horseback to the home of Houston's old friend, Phil Sublett of San Augustine. He stayed there as a guest while he convalesced.

Still on crutches, Houston attended a barbecue on July 4, and in response to a welcome address made by Jonas Harrison replied "in his happiest manner." Later the same day he wrote Henry Raguet a long letter and closed by remarking, "My wound is worse than when we parted but do not, I pray you, let it be known but say that business detains me here." [13] On July 10 he wrote a letter to Rusk informing him Dr. Alexander Ewing, surgeon general of the army of Texas, had been ordered to the headquarters of the army for the purpose of organizing the medical and surgical department of the army.

More disturbing news reached the convalescing Houston. By now Burnet's government had just about collapsed and the army was taken over completely. In early June, Santa Anna and several of his officers had boarded the Texas vessel *Invincible* for passage to Vera Cruz. Suddenly, Thomas Jefferson Green, claiming to be a general, arrived with several hundred followers and in spite of the protests of Burnet and other officials boarded the *Invincible* and forcibly removed Santa Anna from the vessel. The unhappy dictator was rescued by Capt. William H. Patton, an aide-de-camp to

Houston at San Jacinto. He was then taken to Velasco and thence to Columbia, twenty miles up the Brazos. Burnet and various members of his government then moved to Columbia and set up the capital of Texas.

The weak, petty Burnet had been blaming Houston for many of his troubles and now accused Sam of fomenting the army against him. He then promoted Lamar to major general and commander-in-chief, over both Houston and Rusk. When Lamar arrived at Rusk's headquarters to take over command, he apparently sensed the sentiments of the army and had them vote as to whether they would accept him as their commander. Out of a total of almost 1,800 men, Lamar secured the votes of only 170. Discouraged, he left camp and resumed his seat in the cabinet.

From Rusk, Houston received a letter dated July 2, asking him to return to the army:

> First they mounted you and tried to destroy you. Finding their efforts unavailable they have been hammering at me and really trying to break up the army. A vast deal depends on you. You have the entire confidence of the army and people.[14]

Four days later he wrote again with the news 4,000 Mexican troops were at Matamoros and 6,000 at Vera Cruz waiting to invade Texas.

The army, still running out of control and wanting to execute Santa Anna, dispatched colonels Millard and Wheelock to the cabinet. They not only wanted Santa Anna to be turned over to the soldiers and executed, but demanded that Burnet be arrested and brought to the Texan camp. When Houston heard about it he wrote a lengthy letter dated July 26 to Rusk, as commander in the field, and protested the proposed action. He correctly pointed out that a live Santa Anna would certainly be more advantageous to the republic than if he were executed. Any examination of his character showed that Houston was a gentle, compassionate man with true feelings. In addition, he had brains and vision enough to know that a dead Santa Anna would be a distinct liability. The Mexican leader's death would not only enrage an already hostile Mexico, but would flout the laws of international decency and bring great disapproval from the chancelleries of the world upon the head of Texas and seriously impair future relations with those governments.

The so-called "general," Thomas Jefferson Green, was proving himself to be an obstreperous man. Not content with interfering in governmental affairs and seizing Santa Anna, he next showed up in Rusk's camp with the information that it was his intention to march into Matamoros and destroy the town and its people. Rusk concurred[15] but then received a lengthy letter from Houston, dated August 8 and signed in his capacity as commander-in-chief, in which he vigorously opposed the move. Houston gave many reasons for his opposition as he could find no reason in support of the project, and could not see anything to be gained by it. "If the Enemy chooses, let them run [the] risk. A wise man will wait for the harvest, and prepare the reapers for it when it comes." [16] The letter to Rusk put a stop to the project for the time being.

The government of Burnet had finally run its ill-starred course, so the weary president called for a general election under the constitution to be held September 5, 1836.

BOOK FOUR

Forging a Nation

"Samuel Houston. Engraved by W. J. Edwards, from a Daguerreotype." circa 1848.
— Courtesy Barker Texas History Center,
University of Texas at Austin

CHAPTER 24

The Presidency

Though Houston's many detractors in both Texas and the United States called him "power mad," "ambitious," or credited him with the desire to become dictator, emperor or president, the subject of their scorn showed little inclination to grasp the reins of government. From the beginning, he made no effort to seek the presidency and announced he did not intend to run for office, as he wished to be happy and free in retirement from public life. He suggested that Rusk should run for the presidency. Rusk considered the matter for ten days and then declined, writing Houston:

> I feel flattered that you should think me worthy of filling the Presidential Chair, but my age precludes me from running [he was 33 years of age]. . . . I would rather vote for you than any other man in the country, but we cannot spare you from the army.[1]

Among those who were willing and anxious to run for the presidency were Henry Smith, the former governor, and Stephen F. Austin. The latter, who had been in Washington as a commissioner from Texas seeking aid, had left that city on May 24 to return to Texas. From New Orleans, on June 16, Austin had written Houston:

> I shall do all I can to procure the annexation of Texas to the

United States, on just and fair principles. . . . I am of opinion that our independence will be acknowledged, and that Texas will be admitted into these United States, if they are regularly asked for.[2]

To the army, Houston was their overwhelming choice for the office of chief executive. Friends demanded that Houston enter the contest, and petitions were circulated urging that he run. But Houston still played it cool, studying the capabilities and weaknesses of both announced candidates for the post. Finally, just eleven days before the election, he consented to run. To his former aide Hockley he wrote:

> You will learn that I have yielded to the wishes of my friends in allowing my name to be run for President. The crisis requires it or I would not have yielded. Duty, I hope, will not always require this sacrifice of my repose and quiet.[3]

The army was ecstatic.

In addition to the election of a president, a vice-president, senators, and representatives, there were three proposals on the ballot: adoption of the constitution, annexation to the United States, and authority of the Congress to amend the constitution.

Although he did no campaigning at all, Houston won the election overwhelmingly with 5,119 votes. Smith had withdrawn from the race but still received 743 votes, and Austin finished third with 587. Mirabeau Buonaparte Lamar was elected vice-president. The constitution was adopted unanimously and provided that the first president should serve two years; the term thereafter would be three years, and the president could not succeed himself.[4] More than 6,000 favored annexation, with only ninety-three opposed. The proposal to give Congress authority to amend the constitution failed.

Two days after the election, Houston wrote his cousin Robert McEwen in Nashville, forwarding to him as a present the saddle and bridle owned and used by Santa Anna at the Battle of San Jacinto. The saddle and bridle had been presented to Houston by General Ramírez y Sesma, and Houston made the gift to McEwen as an evidence of grateful affection. McEwen was instructed to present the equipment to either Andrew Jackson or Dr. John Shelby if he did not want it; otherwise the mementos were to remain in the McEwen family.[5]

Although the constitution provided the president was to take office on the second Monday of December, Burnet resigned on October 22 and by four o'clock that afternoon General Houston, still limping badly from his war wound and still on crutches, was sworn in as the first elected president of the new republic. Presumably, he used the razor that Ellis Rector had given him almost three years previously when he shaved that morning.

In his inaugural address, the new president called for treaties of peace and amity and the maintenance of good faith with the Indians. He mentioned the unanimous vote of the people for annexation to the United States, and questioned:

Will our friends disregard it? . . . . We are cheered by the hope that they will receive us. . . .

He paused and dramatically disengaged his sword. His listeners quietly leaned forward as he then resumed his speech.

It now, Sir, becomes my duty to make a presentation of this sword — this emblem of my past office. . . .

Here the old warrior was so overcome by emotion that he paused for some minutes before resuming.

I have worn it with some humble pretensions in defense of my country, and should the danger of my country again call for my services, I expect to resume it, and to respond to the call, if needful, with my blood and my life.[6]

The chief executive of the fledgling republic entered into his duties with vigor and enthusiasm. A brand new government was being started from scratch, and the machinery of government had to be established. The judiciary was organized, and judges were elected for the supreme and subordinate courts. The army and navy were organized, and provisions were made for defining and paying the civil lists. Congress authorized Houston to contract a loan of $5 million.

In his newly formed cabinet, Houston found places for his two opponents in the recent election. The ailing Austin was selected as secretary of state and Henry Smith accepted the portfolio of secretary of the treasury. Once more Thomas Rusk found himself secretary of war, and his opposite as secretary of the almost nonexistent navy was Samuel Rhodes Fisher. The attorney general post went to James Pinckney Henderson, a lawyer from North Carolina, after the post was turned down by James Collingsworth.

Houston was once described by a friend as "a man commissioned for leadership by God. He needed no gewgaws or artificial decorations of rank. He had an extraordinary and forceful personality." [7] As chief executive it required all the leadership and personality Houston had to cope with the enormous problems he was faced with daily. The republic had an exhausted treasury with neither money nor credit; the ever-present Indian problems had to be disposed of; a system of public education had to be established; and there was the question of what to do with the one greatest asset of the country — its public lands, which now held a population of about 30,000 Anglo-Americans, 3,470 Mexicans, 14,200 Indians of various tribes, and about 5,000 blacks.[8] The army was sullen and resentful as they had not been paid for months. There was the lack of suitable chambers for the senators and representatives — two rooms in an unfurnished shack comprised the halls of Congress. The presidential quarters consisted of a one-room office with a small fireplace, and when Houston had an overnight guest he let his guest occupy the one cot while Sam slept on the floor.[9]

Two of the chief executive's most pressing problems were the annexation of Texas by the United States and the disposition of Santa Anna. As long as the latter was in Texas he would be nothing but a liability and embarrassment; there were still some people demanding his execution. During the Mexican president's incarceration, Houston had visited him in his prison and treated him with great kindness.[10] The two generals had a friendly conversation and Santa Anna expressed interest in going to Washington to discuss with Jackson the possibility of transferring possession of Texas to the United States in exchange for enough cash to eradicate a Mexican debt to Great Britain. He hoped he then would be permitted to return to Mexico. As early as July 4, 1836, he had written Jackson urging him to act as mediator in having the treaties of Velasco carried out.

Santa Anna's proposal had great appeal to Houston. There was an exchange of letters between Jackson and himself, and an appeal to Congress to release Santa Anna. When Congress refused, Sam took matters into his own hands. In late November, the citizens of Columbia awoke one morning to find their noted prisoner was on his way to Washington, escorted by Col. George Hockley, Col. Barnard E. Bee, and Maj. William H. Patton, aide to General Houston at the Battle of San Jacinto. Among the items Santa Anna carried was a new set of clothing he had bought with a loan of $2,000 from Colonel Bee, and a letter of introduction to Jackson from Houston. The party arrived at their destination on January 17, 1837.[11]

In Washington, Santa Anna was received with kindness and

courtesy by Jackson, and the two men had several friendly interviews. The Mexican president was entertained at a dinner given by Jackson and his cabinet, and he later had his portrait painted. On January 26, he left Washington via the *Pioneer* for Vera Cruz, but in the meantime the Mexican government had informed the United States that *el presidente*'s functions as president had been suspended. When his excellency docked at Vera Cruz, he was treated coldly and discovered he was the original forgotten man. He hurriedly retired to his vast estates.

Escort Hockley carried a much more important communication to Jackson from Houston than a letter of introduction to Santa Anna. The letter was confidential and in it Houston said:

> My great desire is that our country Texas shall be annexed to the United States and on a footing of Justice and reciprocity to the parties. It is policy to hold out the idea (and few there are who Know to the contrary) that we are very able to sustain ourselves against any power who are not impotent, yet I am free to say *to you* that we cannot do it.[12]

Houston also mentioned that he had dispatched an emissary to Jackson who would doubtless arrive before General Santa Anna. The emissary was William H. Wharton, whose goal was to secure the recognition of Texas as a nation and its annexation to the United States. He was also instructed by Houston to cultivate both the British and French. Subsequently, he was joined by Memucan Hunt.

Early in his term, Houston suffered a loss among his personal friends, and Texas suffered a loss among its true patriots. Dr. Lorenzo de Zavala, the intelligent, cultured Mexican who had chosen to join forces with the Texans in their quarrel with Mexico, and who had served as vice-president of the ad interim government, died on November 15. One of the few officials of the Burnet cabinet who had not made Houston's life miserable during his campaign against Santa Anna, de Zavala died by drowning when a boat capsized while he was crossing the flooded Buffalo Bayou. Next, Houston suffered his first loss among his cabinet. Rusk, who had served scarcely a month in office, resigned due to a difference of opinion with Houston over the Matamoros expedition question. He was succeeded in office by William S. Fisher, a participant in the Battle of San Jacinto.

In early December, Sam sent some representatives to the Comanche chiefs with presents, and in a letter expressed the mutual advantages of peace between the Indians and the Texans, and the advantage of trading and swapping between the two peoples.[13]

In spite of the lengthy days Houston was putting in to handle affairs of state, he was never too busy to take pen in hand and write the pretty Anna. Columbia, as the site of the capital, simply had no accommodations for the government. The Allen brothers, John Kirby and Augustus, proposed to build a new city near Buffalo Bayou and name it Houston. It was decided to make Houston the new capital of the republic, and in a letter to Anna dated December 7, 1836, Houston wrote: "By the month of *May*, war or no war, I hope we will meet, at the new city." [14]

On December 17 Houston vetoed a bill establishing the post office. The bill provided the postmaster general should be elected by joint ballot of both houses of Congress, and it was Houston's opinion that that official should be appointed by the president. After being given that power he promptly selected Robert Barr for the position. Shortly thereafter, a mail service was established.

Houston next asked the Senate to ratify the treaty he and John Forbes had previously made with the Cherokees almost a year earlier, and the matter was referred to a committee for study. A year later, the Senate refused to ratify the treaty and on December 26, 1837, it was declared "null and void." [15]

Another member of the cabinet was lost when Secretary of State Stephen F. Austin died. Austin had proved an excellent choice for the position he held because he was hard-working, intelligent, and industrious. He and Houston had developed a relationship of trust and mutual respect. In frail health, he had developed a chill on Christmas Eve and three days later was dead of pneumonia. The sorrowful president ordered newly appointed Secretary of War Fisher to issue general orders to the army:

> The Father of Texas is no more! The first pioneer of the wilderness has departed! General Stephen F. Austin, Secretary of State, expired this day at half past twelve o'clock, at Columbia.[16]

All officers, civil and military, were required to wear crepe on the right arm for thirty days, and all officers commanding posts, garrisons, or detachments were to fire twenty-three guns at intervals of five minutes. He then urged Rusk to return to the cabinet, this time as the new secretary of state. Rusk, anxious to get back to Nacogdoches where he could devote more time to his family, reluctantly agreed to accept the position but resigned after serving a short period. Houston then appointed J. Pinckney Henderson as acting secretary of state.

On January 26, 1837, the chief executive wrote a personal letter to Henry Raguet asking him to forward any letters or newspapers from Fort Jesup until the mails were established to the Sabine. He also asked Henry to inquire about a horse Houston had left in Nacogdoches sometime previously, as the horse had never been returned to him.

The poor Austin had hardly settled in his grave when newspapers from the United States brought the chief executive a further blow. In a State of the Union message to Congress on December 22, President Jackson, after discussing the question, expressed his opinion that "it would be *impolitic,* yet, to recognize Texas as an Independent State!" [17]

Old Hickory was a staunch advocate of not only recognizing Texas, but of annexing her as well. Yet the man in the White House had political problems. For years he had been pressing Mexico to pay some debts she owed the United States, and he did not want to antagonize that nation south of the Rio Grande. In addition, annexation was a political hot potato. To the abolitionists in the North, recognition automatically meant annexation — and that meant another slave state in the Union with its two votes in the Senate. To the abolitionists, that was an anathema.

Emissary Wharton was an industrious negotiator on behalf of Texas and was constantly pressing both Jackson and his Congress for recognition. Finally, on Houston's instructions, he informed Jackson that Texas would not ask again but would enter into negotiations with Great Britain, as Houston had received assurances from the British that they would go far in the matter of friendship and aid in return for commercial benefits. In a private interview with Wharton, Jackson told him he would leave the matter up to Congress and would approve recognition if Congress so approved.[18]

March 2, 1837, was the first anniversary of the Texas Declaration of Independence, as well as Houston's forty-fourth birthday. Houston and others celebrated this event with a dinner and ball at Washington-on-the Brazos held at Gray's "new building." [19] A toast was proposed by Stephen R. Roberts, owner of the local Roberts' Hotel: "To Sam Houston, the man who is contented to be called Sam, and who has proved a Sam's son to the enemies of Texas." [20]

A few days later, Houston and Texas received the welcome news they had been waiting for: on February 28, 1837, the United States House of Representatives voted for recognition, followed by the Senate on March 1. The last official act of Jackson as president was to sign the bill on March 4. To his office Jackson called Wharton and Memucan Hunt, whom Houston had appointed to assist Wharton in his negotiations. "I propose a toast to the independence of Texas," the president said. "I have nominated Alcée LaBranche, of Louisiana, to be Charge d'affairs of the Republic of Texas." [21]

On January 29, Houston wrote Anna that he had heard reports she was to marry Captain Edwards and asked her if it was so. Apparently, Sam was contemplating matrimony with Anna, as he said:

> I will not marry until I can once more go to Nacogdoches and see how my matters are there! and if my tenants have erected me comfortable cabbins; why then I may look out for a "spare rib" to appropriate to myself. [22]

The republic's capital was moved to the new city of Houston — now a city of some 500 souls — in the middle of April. The president's mansion consisted of a two-room log cabin with a lean-to in the back of Houston's bedroom serving as a kitchen and living quarters for Sam's two servants.

To celebrate the first anniversary of San Jacinto, a grand ball was held in the new capital. Guests from fifty and sixty miles away and from Oyster Bay, Caney Creek, and Brazos Bottoms came on horseback and by ox-drawn cart. According to a letter Sam later wrote Dr. Irion, out of more than one hundred ladies resident in the new city, seventy-three attended the ball. [23]

The president, dressed in velvet coat and trousers trimmed with broad gold lace, led the grand ball with Mrs. Moseley Baker to the strains of "Hail to the Chief." Houston, always a gallant with the ladies, told Mrs. Baker he had selected her to be his partner because she was the most beautiful woman there. The festivities were interrupted by one unpleasant matter when a mounted messenger arrived with news for the two Cooper sisters. Their brother had been killed by the Indians on the Colorado River.

234

In addition to his official duties, Houston found time to attend to a few personal matters. On June 24, he sold Lot No. 3, Block No. 43, in the city of Houston to Dr. David C. Kerr, one of the physicians who had treated his wound in New Orleans. However, another matter far more important than the selling of a lot was now to be taken care of.

While living in Nacogdoches before the revolution, the general had petitioned for a divorce from Eliza. This petition had been lost and the attorney who had filed it had subsequently died. Sam now retained the services of attorney W. G. Anderson to check into the matter and determine his marital status. Anderson located the original petition and discovered nothing had happened. A new petition was presented before District Judge Shelby Corzine in San Augustine, and the case was tried in the judge's private chambers. An attorney represented Eliza and the Allen family. Sam complained of abandonment, the length of separation, and the impossibility of reconciliation. He was granted the divorce.

The opening of Congress was delayed for five days while a temporary covering was erected. The president's message to Congress was delivered by Houston in person, and in it he gave a report on the government and outlined some of its problems. The treasury was completely without funds and could not meet the many demands upon it. Due to the financial panic of the Van Buren administration, the money market was poor, and the commissioners sent to the United States to negotiate a loan of $5 million had seen their efforts fail. Congress had adopted a land grant policy which made it almost impossible to sell much of the 180 million acres of public lands for the benefit of the treasury's empty coffers, and to alleviate this situation Houston recommended the land grant law be changed.

In his message, Houston also mentioned the problems the citizens were having with the Indians, particularly the Caddoes. The army, he said, "has never been in a more favorable condition than that at the present." He brought up the subject of the African slave trade and the fact thousands of Africans had been imported to Cuba with the design to transfer them into Texas, and called upon the governments of the United States and Great Britain to stop that traffic.[24] The subject of annexation to the United States, he reported, had undergone no important change since the last adjournment of Congress.

A newcomer to Texas was in the audience during Sam's speech to Congress. Sitting next to his friend J. Pinckney Henderson was Dr. Ashbel Smith, a practicing physician from North Carolina who had graduated from Yale with A.B and A.M. degrees and a Phi Beta Kappa key. Smith, a bachelor, had recently arrived in Texas but as yet had not determined to make it his permanent home. After Houston concluded his remarks, Henderson escorted Smith to the executive mansion, such as it was, and made the introductions. Houston took an immediate liking to Smith, the two men became friends, and within a short time Houston had forwarded to Congress the nomination of the doctor for surgeon general of the army. Later on, the two became charter members of the Philosophical Society of Texas.[25]

In his message to Congress, Houston had not been entirely candid in his remarks concerning the army. Far from being in a "favorable condition," the army was one of his biggest headaches. It was a severe drain on an almost nonexistent treasury and had a size of almost 2,500 men, mostly volunteers, who had arrived in Texas after the fighting was over.

When Rusk left command of the army to take over the portfolio of secretary of war he had been succeeded by Felix Huston, a Kentuckian and a lawyer by profession who, to his men, was known as "Old Long Shanks." He was an ambitious man and, with a restless army behind him, began giving consideration to the old scheme of marching against Matamoros. On December 31, Houston had written Gen. James Hamilton of South Carolina to see if he would accept command of the army. Hamilton wanted to accept the appointment but circumstances of a private nature prevented him.[26] Houston then appointed Albert Sidney Johnston as commander. Johnston was an honors graduate of West Point who had resigned from the U.S. army at the request of his wife and moved to Texas. After her death, he joined the Texas cause and had fought in the army as a private.

The new commander reached camp on February 4, but Old Long Shanks refused to turn over his command and promptly challenged Johnston to a duel. Johnston foolishly accepted the challenge, and when the two met on February 7, four or five shots were fired and Johnston was severely wounded but did not die. While Johnston was recovering from his wounds, Huston remained in command.

Under the command of Huston the army had grown progressively more rambunctious, ruffianly, and disobedient. After the duel a Colonel Rodgers, a henchman of Huston, suggested the army march upon the capital at Columbia, chastise the president, kick Congress out of power, and "give laws to Texas." [27] When news of these remarks reached Houston's ears, the wily old campaigner proved that he was more than a match for the malcontents.

In a move that his enemies loved to characterize as his Indian cunning, in the middle of May the president invited Old Long Shanks to the capital to be his guest and entertained him at the executive mansion. Rushing through secret orders, he had Secretary of War Fisher go to the field and deliver them to the army. With the exception of 600 old reliables, the rest of the army was given unlimited furloughs by companies, subject to recall at any time. Secretary Fisher lined the men up and marched them off to various destinations on the coast while Colonel Rodgers stood helplessly by. The men scattered to the winds. When Felix Huston returned to camp, he found himself a general without an army. In disgust, he left Texas for New Orleans and the United States.

To some of Houston's critics his method of furloughing and reducing the size of his army might have been evidence of his "Indian cunning," but in other quarters he received much approbation. Francis Lubbock, a future governor of Texas, described it as "one of the most marked evidences of statecraft I have ever known." [28]

The furlough ploy still did not solve all the problems with the army. Those remaining were poorly fed and unpaid, and many were threatening to mutiny. Along with all this were the constant threats of an invasion by Mexico. Three times the Mexicans gathered troops to march into Texas, but all three enterprises foundered when so many of their troops, most of them convicts released from prison, deserted. At one time the threat of invasion was so serious that Houston had written Anna that in a few days he would be setting out for the army, and

> if I am not mistaken you shall have more laurels . . . If the enemy are not about to advance, I will return to the seat of Government, which will be at Groce's retreat until the first of May.[29]

The ever-popular Matamoros expedition idea simply would not die. In this matter, Houston must have compared himself with Hercules and his cleaning the Augean stables. Every time he thought he had this problem solved it came up again.

Maj. Thomas G. Western had served valiantly in the revolution and was now commander of the cavalry at San Antonio. He suddenly began broaching an expedition against Mexico as all the others had, with visions of spoils and riches for the troops. Next, he began muttering against overthrowing Houston and his "one-horse" government. Once more Houston resorted to his Indian cunning. To his office he called William H. Patton, a former aide of his whom he knew to be a talkative man and who was leaving soon on a business trip to San Antonio. He wanted Patton's advice. He was thinking of sending an envoy to England and France, and was seeking a man of cultivated manners and diplomatic skill. Strictly in confidence, he was considering Major Western for the post. Did Patton think Western was qualified for the position? Of course, nothing of this sort was to be mentioned to the major.

The president gave Patton time to reach San Antonio, and then issued orders for Western to meet with him. Houston welcomed the major cordially and the two men discussed odds and ends, but no mention was made of an appointment to London. After several days had passed and the anxious Western had heard nothing official, he asked the new surgeon general, Ashbel Smith, if he knew anything about him being mentioned as ambassador. To Western's dismay, Smith replied that, on the contrary, to his information J. Pinckney Henderson was to receive the appointment. A few days later it was announced that Henderson was to be the envoy to Great Britain, whereupon Western mounted his horse and rode back to San Antonio and another surprise. He found orders transferring him to an outpost, and another officer was now in command of the cavalry.

On June 6, Houston sent a message to Congress and presented documents showing the army's various liabilities that had to be met immediately or the credit of the government would be entirely destroyed. On his own, the president had been required to give his individual guarantee before credit would be given for supplies.[30] In his message, Houston mentioned that since the beginning of the constitutional government no public officer had received any salary and that many had resigned from the government inasmuch as their individual means were exhausted. Sam himself was so strapped that he had had to turn down an offer to go into a partnership with Philip Dimitt as he had no capital.

> I am without funds and [m]iserably poor; The first cent I have
> not yet drawn from Government for any of my services rendered,
> and I can form no idea; when I will be able to do [so].[31]

The treasury was so exhausted that Memucan Hunt, who had succeeded William Wharton as commissioner to Washington, could not pay his room and board bill. Neither could the vessels in the navy be properly maintained. To bring money into the coffers, various import duties were imposed, ranging as high as forty-five percent on liquor and fifty percent on silks.

Mexican agents were still infiltrating the Indians, trying to stir up trouble. In December 1836, laws had been passed calling for a chain of blockhouses, forts, and trading houses to protect the frontier from Indians. In addition, Houston was doing everything in his power to defuse any potential harmful situation with any of the tribes. He wrote Thomas Rusk on June 7, stating that Congress had passed a law authorizing the employment of the northern Indians in Texas service to operate against the Plains Indians.[32] The rank-and-file Indian would receive eight dollars per month; lieutenants, twenty dollars; and captains, twenty-five dollars per month. In July he wrote his friend The Bowl, chief of the Cherokees, asking him to meet him at Nacogdoches in four days and bring Big Mush and chiefs of other tribes with him.

> I have a Talk, that you will like to hear. I want you to bring in with you the copy of the Treaty which I last sent to you. Don't forget to bring it. It has ribbons and a seal on it.[33]

Adding to Houston's problems were his troubles with Mexico. That nation had received news of United States recognition of Texas with less than enthusiasm. The Mexican secretary of war made a speech of denunciation against both Texas and the United States.

Deaf Smith and a mounted force of twenty-one men set out in March to plant the Texas flag at Laredo, and about five miles east of that city he encountered about forty Mexican cavalry on the march. Smith and his men hid in a thicket of mesquite and held their fire until they were sure of their aim. After a skirmish lasting about forty-five minutes, the Mexicans retreated with a loss of ten dead and about the same number wounded, while the Texans had two men wounded.[34]

After Commissioner Wharton had resigned his office to be succeeded by Memucan Hunt, he was on his way home on the Texas warship *Independence* when about thirty miles from Velasco the vessel was intercepted by two Mexican brigs of war.[35] After a severe fight, Wharton and the crew were overpowered, taken as prisoners of war to Matamoros, and confined in prison. Many people demanded action against Mexico, but Houston was opposed to it due to the weakened condition of the navy and the country. He tried to solve the problem by sending Wharton's brother John, together with thirty Mexican prisoners of war, to Matamoros under a flag of truce to secure the release of William. The Mexicans ignored the flag of truce and threw John in jail to keep his brother company. The Whartons saved Houston from further embarrassment by escaping from the prison and getting back to Texas.

To the president, who was now presiding over a nation virtually bankrupt, there was one solution to all his problems: annexation to the United States.

CHAPTER 25

New Life and Another Love

In his efforts to persuade United States officials to annex Texas, Memucan Hunt had no more success than had his predecessor. On January 4, 1838, United States Senator W. C. Preston offered a resolution in favor of annexation, only to have it tabled by a vote of 24 to 14. When a similar measure was later brought to the floor of the House, John Quincy Adams filibustered the measure for three weeks, claiming annexation would divide the North and the South and would bring on war with Mexico. When he ended his filibuster, the session of Congress closed and no vote was taken on the measure.

Houston decided to play a game of political chess. If America was not interested in Texas, England and France surely would be. He sent instructions to Commissioner Hunt to withdraw the proposal of annexation unconditionally, but before receiving the instructions Hunt had resigned his office and was on his way home. Anson Jones, who was named as his permanent replacement, called upon Secretary of State John Forsyth and made it clear Texas was withdrawing their proposal.

While these efforts were going on, J. Pinckney Henderson, the North Carolina lawyer Houston had appointed as envoy to England and France, was in London. In a series of conferences with Foreign Minister Lord Palmerston, he was presenting interesting reasons why Her Majesty's government should recognize and sign commercial agreements with the republic. After several weeks he was finally informed Great Britain could not extend recognition but would allow Texas to have her ships enter British ports. Henderson's next stop was Paris to discuss with Foreign Minister Count Molé the republic's recognition, commercial treaties, and a loan. As had Palmerston, Molé offered no hope for immediate recognition.

The vision of the Allen brothers in developing Houston City on Buffalo Bayou was paying off. The city was growing daily and now had a population of around 2,000, including about 100 Mexicans who had been captured at San Jacinto and had chosen to stay in the new republic. A channel had been cleared in the bayou, and the two steamboats that plied between Galveston and Houston were bringing in new settlers frequently. For the citizens, there was much in the way of entertainment: billiard rooms, horse races, saloons, and — for those a little more discriminating in their quest for entertainment — a theater where plays were being performed. The future of the city seemed so assured that Houston, who all of his life speculated in land, purchased several lots and gave one to Anna.

The future of the republic, however, did not seem so bright. The trials and tribulations of the infant nation brought welcome news to the enemies of Houston, foremost of which were Vice-President Lamar and Burnet. Both men had their eyes on a future presidency, and every measure Sam undertook or any private thing he did was subject to their critical scrutiny. Burnet, a teetotaler, was quick to point out Houston's drinking habits. Other disgruntled opponents were publishing anti-Houston pamphlets alleging his cowardice in battle and criticizing his personal habits. There were threats of impeaching him, and even rumors of assassination plots.[1]

Perhaps it was due to his drinking, or a recurrence of his malaria, but in October the president became ill. Still ill on November 1, he wrote Congress a letter of apology for having failed as yet to deliver to them a message on the State of the Union.[2]

In spite of Houston's illness he managed to send to the Senate a stream of correspondence, and on November 8 requested that body to confirm his nominations of Dr. Robert A. Irion as secretary of state and Barnard E. Bee as secretary of war.[3] on November 15, he had published in the *Nacogdoches Chronicle* his denial to a charge by one Peter E. Bean that he had forfeited on a contract made with

242

him[4] and on the same day wrote his first personal letter since his illness. This was to Henry Raguet. To his friend he reported his recent illness and commented on the stream of abuse against him:

There is a systematic opposition to the President, and, it grows out of the very *Laudable* feeling, of envy, and a disposition, to put him down that they may have it in their power to establish all the fraudulent land claims with *corruption* has originated.

He gave generous praise to his friend Rusk, stating he had been "the most efficient, advocate of the true policy, of our country, in the House of Representatives." Plaintively, he continued:

My situation ever since I came to office has been most disagreeable. I have been kept at the Seat of Government, and not one comfort — not even a shelter for my head, and subject to every exposure of season, and weather — At last a house has been purchased by [the] Government, and is ordered to be fitted up, for future use — so you see I will be in order for a *Levee* or Soiree.[5]

Houston closed his letter by saying: "I will write to Miss Anna very soon."

By November 21 the president's health had improved to the extent that he delivered his annual message to Congress in person.[6] Much of his message referred to the depleted condition of the treasury, and he recommended a conservative policy in the issuance of paper money. He thought it would be safe for the government to issue $500,000 in treasury notes.

Houston had promised to try to go home to Nacogdoches for Christmas but was unable to make it. On Christmas Day, 1837, he issued a "Proclamation Recalling Certain Land Scrip" and revoked the authority of all agents in the republic to sell land scrip. As no agents had ever been authorized to sell land scrip on credit, the proclamation stipulated that all scrip previously sold on credit should be returned, the land relinquished, and the scrip cancelled. The proclamation also specified that in the future only promissory notes of gold or silver would be received for any debts or dues payable to the republic.[7]

The new year rolled in with a blast of wintry weather. The new executive mansion was not yet completed, and Houston was freezing in his two-room cabin. He wrote Anna:

It is late at night and I am freezing in a miserable open house. Four windows in it and not one pane of glass nor shutter — three doors and shutters to but two — no ceiling and the floor loose

243

laid. Is not this a "White House" with a plague to it? The Palace is not finished, but it is said to be in progress and will soon be completed. I have sent to New York for magnificent furniture, and when it arrives, what a beautiful contrast shall I enjoy! [8]

The new year also brought a challenge. Houston, who had been drinking heavily to the consternation of his friends and the delight of his enemies, decided to start the new year off with a resolution: he would stop drinking. On January 7, 1838, Sam and August C. Allen, one of the founders of Houston City, entered into an agreement whereby Sam would abstain from the use of "ardent spirits, wines and cordials" until December 31, 1838. The winner of the wager was to receive a suit of clothes worth $500 from the loser. Both parties signed the agreement, and it was witnessed by James S. Holman.

How long Houston stuck to his resolution is not known, but he evidently did for at least several weeks, as on January 23 W. T. Brent wrote his brother in Virginia that while in Houston City he had called on the president and found him in good health and perfectly sober. Sam, according to Brent, told him that he was determined not to "touch, taste, or handle the unclean thing" until the first of the coming January.

Brent was not the only person who had been impressed by Houston's health and abstinence. On February 4, J. Wilson Copes wrote Ashbel Smith, who had gone back east to purchase medical supplies for the army: "The President is now in fine health and has not tasted strong drink since you left." [9]

There is some evidence, however, that Houston fell off the wagon at least once, as Ben Fort Smith, a Houston hotelkeeper, presented the president with a bill for board from April 20 through April 25. Among the various charges were three dollars for a bottle of champagne on April 21; twenty-five dollars for champagne, liquors, and breaking glasses at a champagne party on April 22; and three dollars for three bottles of whiskey on April 25. Although on a note written on the back of the bill Houston said "furnished 3 dozen champagne — broke no glasses — the bill I never will pay as I am satisfied it is unjust," it is endorsed by B. F. Smith, per Jas. M. McGee, that payment was received in full.[10]

Houston was still buying property. On January 12, he wrote Anna that he had made a splendid purchase of Cedar Point. He had not seen the property, but Dr. Irion had declared it was the only Eden on earth. He could not refrain from passing on a little gossip, mentioning that, with one exception, everyone in the cabinet was either a bachelor or a widower and they were all "deranged" by the arrival of a rich and pretty widow from Alabama who was young and only worth a hundred thousand.[11]

All through the year Houston carried on an extensive correspondence with Anna, letting her know what was happening in the capital and giving little gossipy bits of information about mutual friends. In one letter he said,

> My friend Wright has completed my portrait for your father's parlor until I have as good a mansion. It will be taken to you, because it is said to be the best likeness ever taken of me.[12]

He had given Anna a horse named Whalebone and was delighted to know that she was charmed with it, "but I can't retake him," he wrote, "as I have now only four very fine horses, and none a good match for him." [13]

Although the president was busily occupied with governmental affairs, he still was active socially. In 1837 the Grand Lodge of the Republic of Texas was organized and he became a charter member, and on November 13, 1837, he affiliated with Holland Lodge No. 1 at Houston City.[14]

On February 23, 1838, Houston, who had never received any salary for his services during the revolution, submitted an itemized bill in the amount of $5,905.27 for services from the period November 11, 1835, to October 22, 1836. The items listed showed his pay for the rank of major general to be $200 per month, and the total included sums for subsistence, rations, and forage for seven horses; pay, clothing and rations for four servants (not soldiers); and transportation at ten cents per mile for 1,748 miles. The account was audited the same day, approved, and draft No. 8031-Z issued.[15] It is not known what Houston did with this windfall, unless he used it to pay for the furniture for the new executive mansion, but it wasn't long before he was strapped for cash again. On May 31 he wrote Dr. Ashbel Smith: "If you have cash, purchase the note which my friend Wilson may present on such terms as may be just, as so soon as I can, I will pay and lift it. My cash is exhausted!!!" [16]

For five years Sam had been courting the pretty, popular Anna Raguet and suddenly he became aware of a coolness in her. She had heard an exaggerated version of Houston's divorce that displeased her — apparently, she had been led to believe the divorce was not legal — and she was angry because Sam had paid "addresses" to her while not free to do so. In an endeavor to get

245

back in her good graces, Houston wrote her a letter on June 4 that was a masterpiece of obfuscation. To support his contention he was legally divorced, he enclosed some letters containing the opinions of "gentlemen eminent in the profession of the law" as to the legality of his divorce. It was of no use.[17] The romance was all over, although the couple continued their correspondence and their friendship.

The republic had been in existence for over a year now, and slowly things began to get better as various problems were being solved. A commercial treaty with Great Britain had been signed, allowing ships of either country into the ports of each other, and Henderson was having serious talks with other governments about similar arrangements.

The financial condition of the country was greatly improved as immigration had enhanced the value of lands, and those who had to sell found a ready market. Steadily increasing revenues from various taxes, land fees, tonnage dues, and port fees were paying the running expenses of the government.

The nation was at peace except with various Indian tribes. The Indians, still constantly being agitated by Mexican agents, were disgruntled because the treaty Houston had negotiated with them had never been ratified by Congress and because surveyors and locators were encroaching on their lands. During the latter half of the year there were several engagements between units of the Texas army and the Indians, primarily the ferocious Comanches and some Cherokees, but through the personal efforts of Houston and some of the older chiefs things had simmered down — at least for the time being.

Perhaps the strain of his office and the constant criticism of his activities were getting the best of Houston. During a visit to Nacogdoches on August 11, he wrote his old friend Jackson at the Hermitage and gave vent to some of his trials and tribulations. He mentioned some of the differences between their respective presidencies: When Old Hickory had become president he had had an "organized government and men who were accustomed to civil rule." On the contrary, Houston had to command a government from chaos with men who had never been accustomed to any rule but their passions.

The first term of the president, vice-president, and Congress was to expire on December 10. On July 11, Houston issued a proclamation calling for an election of those officials on September 3. He was ineligible to succeed himself, so the three leading contenders for the presidency were his old foe, Mirabeau B. Lamar, James Collingsworth, and Peter W. Grayson. David Burnet entered his name for the vice-presidency.

Lamar ran on a platform completely opposite to everything Houston stood for, and before election day rolled around, the three-man race had dwindled down to one as both Grayson and Collingsworth committed suicide. When the votes were counted, Lamar garnered 6,995 out of 7,247 cast.[18]

At the inauguration ceremonies for the new administration Sam, ever the actor and knowing how to stage a scene, had little difficulty in stealing the show. He attended the ceremonies wearing a white wig and a costume of George Washington's day, down to knee breeches with silver buckles.[19] When called upon to make a speech, he responded with a three-hour oration. In his speech he reminded the audience that he had vetoed more than eighty bills and that he was leaving office while Texas had a debt of less than $2 million. At his conclusion he gestured for the incoming president to give his address. Lamar knew when he had been upstaged. He weakly handed his address to Algernon Thompson, clerk of the Senate, who read it to an exhausted audience.

Now that Houston was no longer encumbered with governmental duties, he could devote some time to his personal and business affairs. On January 8, 1839, he entered into a law partnership with John Birdsall, who had served as chief justice under his administration. The partnership never really got off the ground as there was money to be made in land speculation. Sam quickly joined George Hockley, Philip Sublett, and four others in a real estate enterprise to develop Sabine City in East Texas.

On February 4, Sam was a guest in Houston City at a dinner given in honor of Dr. John Shackelford. In a number of toasts, Houston took particular offense to one given by Thomas Rusk. A few days later he wrote to Anna how Rusk was "claiming the laurels of San Jacinto." [20] This further strained relations between the two friends. Four days later, he wrote Anna from the capital city that he was considering a trip to the United States on business and to see his sisters and Eliza's little ones.[21] He told Anna he regarded Nacogdoches as his home and had paid for a lot and house, which was to be completed by mid-summer.

The former president, having more invitations in Houston than he could handle, had to decline a farewell dinner and ball in his honor. However, on February 25 he attended a "frolic" on the British bark *Ambassador*. He left Houston around mid-March for New Orleans and arrived there around April 1. Before leaving Houston, however, he was guest speaker at the first meeting of a temperance society that had recently been formed. Sam offered a resolution "favorable to the cause."

In New Orleans the former president spent several days as the guest of William Christy and looked for investors in his land venture. His former commissioner to Washington, Memucan Hunt, was also in the city and took great delight in keeping Lamar apprised of Sam's activities. In one letter he passed on the information that Houston had become intoxicated and burned off his coattail,[22] and later on he wrote Ashbel Smith that Houston had been drunk almost every day while in Nashville.[23]

By May, Houston was in Alabama where he wrote a friend "there are five things on earth which I love. A fine woman, a fine Horse, a fine dog . . . A Game Cock, and fine arms." [24] On this combination pleasure-business trip, Houston found three of his great loves: from Hickman Lewis he purchased seven fillies for a total price of $6,000; in the autumn Tom Edmundson delivered to him on Galveston Bay "one dog and two bitches"; and in Mobile he found his fine woman. While in that city, Houston called upon William Bledsoe to discuss the wealthy merchant's investing in the Sabine City project. Bledsoe listened with interest to Sam's presentation, was charmed by him, and invited him to his home, Spring Hill. Bledsoe's wife Antoinette was having a strawberry festival in honor of her mother, Nancy Lea, who was on a visit from Marion.

Mrs. Lea was the widow of a Baptist preacher and was also a shrewd businesswoman. It happened she was looking for a good investment as she had recently sold her large plantation, the Cane Brake, at an excellent price.

At the Bledsoe estate, Houston met the lovely Antoinette, who was entertaining the ladies of the local Baptist church. Suddenly, Antoinette's sister Margaret strolled by carrying a plate of strawberries, and any thoughts Sam may have had concerning matrimony with Anna Raguet disappeared from his mind. When he looked upon Margaret's lovely face he fell fast, he fell hard, and he fell forever.

When introductions were made the general bowed low over Margaret's hand and said: "I am charmed." There were a large number of guests and many introductions to be made. Apparently, Houston confused Margaret with her married sister, because he is said to have remarked to another guest: "If she were not already married I believe I'd give the charming lady a chance to say 'no'." The other guest replied: "But that's not Mrs. Bledsoe. That's the older unmarried sister, General, so you're free to give her that chance." [25]

The general then had an interview with Mrs. Lea in which he discussed properties at Sabine Pass on the Texas Gulf Coast near the international boundary east of Galveston Island — properties in which his townsite company was involved. When the interview with Mrs. Lea was concluded and Houston returned to the party, he and Margaret spent the rest of the afternoon strolling in the azalea garden.

Margaret Moffett Lea, born April 11, 1819, had just passed her twentieth birthday when she met Houston. Three years previously she had been one of those on the dock when the general disembarked at New Orleans to seek treatment for his injured leg, and had had a presentiment that one day she would meet him. Tall, with beautiful dark brown hair quite full of waves, her face was an oval and her arresting eyes violet.[26] A daguerreotype taken in her early twenties shows her to be an extremely pretty young woman, and, according to Dr. William Crane who first met her at that time, she was regarded as the most attractive and fascinating young lady in that part of Alabama. A student at Judson Female Institute, she loved to read books, particularly the romances, and she composed poetry and played the piano extremely well.

Houston stayed in Mobile for a week and twice addressed audiences on land values in Texas, while at the same time putting in a plug for annexation. During the evenings he would stroll with Margaret in the azalea garden. Once, he pointed to a star in the heavens. "That," he announced, "is my Star of Destiny." It might have been that he asked her if she would be willing to follow his star with him, because before he left for Tennessee he had proposed to her.

There is one strange thread that seems to have run through the tapestry of all Houston's romances. In every case he was considerably older than his sweetheart: with Eliza there was a virtual seventeen-year discrepancy in ages; with Diana there had been a seven- to ten-year gap; with Anna, the belle of Nacogdoches, a twenty-three-year difference. But now Sam was forty-six — twenty-six years older than his intended. To Margaret, the discrepancy in ages made no difference at all.

In Nashville, Houston was the guest of Jackson at the Hermitage, and the two old friends spent many hours discussing the Texas revolution, Houston's strategy during the campaign, and politics, particularly the ever-present question of the annexation of Texas. Alone in his room he took pen in hand and wrote Margaret. Like all lovers he anxiously awaited the reply from his beloved and when it came it was all he had hoped for — there was no doubt his love was returned:

> I have heard from you and the tidings are truly welcome, I assure you. My answer may be taken as strong evidence of that, for it is the first I have addressed to any gentleman. My heart . . . is like a caged bird whose weary pinions have been folded for weeks and months — at length it wakes from its stupor, spreads its wings and longs to escape . . . . Last night I gazed long upon our beauteous emblem, the *Star of my Destiny,* and my thoughts took the form of verse, but I will not inscribe them here, for then you might call me a romantic, star-struck young lady.[27]

The questions arise as to what Margaret saw in a man so much older than herself and why she was so determined to marry Houston. Part of the answer is that she loved him — but that is not all. With his romantic history, commanding figure, winning manners, and vivacious personality, Sam never lacked for the attention of the ladies. But with Margaret it was more than that. A gentle woman, she was also a strict and devout Baptist, and her religion gave her a sense of purpose. She had a will of iron and knew what she wanted. When Dr. Crane asked her why she ran the risk of unhappiness and misfortune by consenting to link her destinies with those of General Houston, at a time when he gave way to such excesses as drinking, she replied that "not only had he won her heart, but she had conceived the idea that she could be the means of reforming him, and she meant to devote herself to the work." [28]

Houston had won the heart of Margaret with ease, but in the person of Nancy Lea he faced a more formidable opponent. Nancy liked Houston personally, but she was a pious, practical woman who necessarily possessed the toughness and business acumen required to run a fifty-slave plantation since the death of her Baptist preacher husband. She wanted her daughter in a happy, successful marriage, and when she looked at Sam through her Baptist teetotaling eyes, she saw not only the charming war hero and former president of a republic, but she saw the warts: a man twice as old as her daughter, a man with two previous marriages already behind him, and a known drunk. She was far too smart to forbid the marriage outright, and although she did nothing to discourage the romance, she certainly did nothing to encourage it.

In June, Nancy and Margaret returned to Marion. Nancy was satisfied of Houston's honesty. It was decided that her son-in-law William would go to Texas and, if he was satisfied there were possibilities of a good investment there, then she and Bledsoe would go to Galveston to further inspect the land. Before they left Mobile to return home, Margaret had told her mother that Sam had proposed. Nancy disapproved, but strong-willed Margaret was determined and without her mother's permission agreed to marry Houston.

While Sam was still in Tennessee there was an exchange of letters between himself and Margaret. She was willing to marry him, but she made it plain she wanted her fiancé to visit her in Marion so that he could meet the rest of her family. In one of her letters she wrote,

> I stated to you . . . that it was the wish of myself and relations that you should visit Marion . . . our opinions are unchanged. I have never yet taken sides in any affair of moment without being guided in a great measure by my relations. In this case . . . I shall rely entirely on their discretion.[29]

Houston was reluctant to make the journey but finally agreed to go to Marion in July, and when he visited Alabama he was greeted by a radiant Margaret. For their engagement he gave her a cameo portrait of himself, to which Margaret fastened green ribbons and hung it around her neck.

When Houston left Marion for Texas, his fiancée, an expert in needlework, started working on her trousseau.

251

CHAPTER 26

Again a Congressman;
Again a President

Upon Houston's arrival in Texas in September, in San Augustine he was told he had been elected to Congress as a member of the House. Short of funds, on the twentieth he borrowed fifty dollars from O. B. Hill and gave him a note for repayment on Christmas Day. To his sorrow, Houston learned John Birdsall, his law partner, had died of yellow fever. He was further dismayed when he learned that the capital was being moved from Houston City to a new township called Austin, situated on the east bank of the Colorado River and about 200 miles west of Houston City.

There was other bad news. Lamar, who hated Indians, had boasted that he would kill off "Houston's pet Indians" and was determined to run the Cherokees out of Texas.[1] In a two-day battle beginning July 15, 1839, on the western side of the Neches River, the Texas army under the command of Thomas Rusk killed over 100 Cherokees, including Houston's friends Chief Bowles and Big Mush. Houston was so angered about the affair when he heard about it that in a blistering speech at the town hall in Nacogdoches he denounced Lamar's Indian policy and those responsible for the murders.[2] His remarks so infuriated the listeners that when he left the hall his life was threatened, and for some time there were strained relations between him and some of his best friends, includ-

252

ing Henry Raguet and Adolphus Sterne. His relationship with Rusk, already strained, was further damaged.

On November 11, the Fourth Congress convened for the first time in Austin. Senator Anson Jones and "a cavalcade marshaled by three colonels" rode to meet Houston three miles from the capital.[3] A few evenings later, Jones presided over a dinner held in Houston's honor and "handsomely served." The weather was terrible and with the roads muddy there were many absences, but still over 200 people attended. Of the forty-three toasts given, the first — to the United States — brought "three cheers"; the second — to General Houston — brought "3 times 3."[4] In his response, Houston offered the sentiment "Texas — if true to herself, she can be false to no one!" The third toast — to the president of the Republic — evoked no cheers. Lamar was not embarrassed by the silence because although he had been invited, he had chosen not to attend the function.

Whenever the former president took the floor to speak on any subject dear to his heart he could speak long and eloquently and cover a wide range of subjects. And so it was on December 2 when he rose from his seat in the House. In a speech carrying over until the next day, he bitterly opposed the removal of the capital to Austin, claiming the government had speculated in city lots and the people of Texas had been defrauded. He defended the claims of the Cherokees to the lands they had been driven from, as they had been in the country long before the white man, and condemned the government for not living up to their treaties with the Indians. As to his own Indian policy, time would tell whether he was right or wrong. The day previously during debate he had been criticized for his conduct of the war once he took over at Gonzales and for his failure to attack Santa Anna sooner, so he answered his critics on that score. A few days later he wrote a letter to Anna Raguet in which he described the new capital city as "the most unfortunate site upon earth for the Seat of Government."[5]

On December 22, Houston introduced a bill providing that the lands lately owned and occupied by the Cherokees be divided into 640-acre tracts, and in another lengthy speech once more reminded his audience the Cherokees had just title to those lands. However, as they had been driven off, he proposed the funds brought in from the sale provide a sinking fund for the redemption of bonds for a $5 million loan.[6] Continuing his attacks on the government's Indian policy, in an hour-and-a-half speech on January 8, 1840, he lambasted both Lamar and Vice-President Burnet.

253

By January 1840, the presidential campaign for 1841 was well under way. George Hockley, who was to offer a toast to his old chief at a Washington's Birthday celebration, sent Houston three proposed toasts and requested he pick the one to be used. The wily old campaigner chose "Houston — He whose very battlefield is holy ground which breathes of Nations saved, not worlds undone." [7]

The Fourth Congress ended its session the last of February, and the eager swain hurried to Galveston to await the arrival of his bride-to-be. Mrs. Lea and Bledsoe were coming to Texas so that Nancy could inspect the property her son-in-law had recommended she purchase, and Sam had been imploring Margaret to come with them so they could be married. James Love, who was one of many who always kept President Lamar aware of Houston's movements, wrote the president: "*The Great Ex* . . . awaits the arrival of his bride to be." [8]

To Houston's friends the idea of their old chief contemplating matrimony — and especially with one so much younger than he — left them dismayed. Barnard Bee, who had the dubious honor of having been stiffed by Santa Anna for $2,000, was skeptical about the marriage and wrote Ashbel Smith "in all my acquaintance with life I have never met an individual more totally disqualified for domestic happiness — he will not live with her six months." [9] His opinion was more or less shared by George Hockley, who was disturbed and doubted if the marriage would ever take place.

When the boat from New Orleans, bearing passengers from Mobile, anchored at Galveston harbor shortly after dawn, the general went out to the vessel in a dory to greet his beloved, her mother, and her brother-in-law. On the deck were Mrs. Lea and Bledsoe, but no Margaret. Just then a cannon boomed and Houston announced it was the way his friends in the garrison were announcing their pleasure in the arrival of his bride-to-be. "And," he asked, "where is Margaret? Not indisposed from the voyage, I hope?"

> General Houston, my daughter is in Alabama. She goes forth in the world to marry no man. The one who receives her hand will receive it in my home and not elsewhere.

With those words Nancy Lea gave up her opposition to the marriage of her daughter to this man of destiny, and it is to Sam's credit that for the rest of his life he had nothing but the warmest regards and highest admiration for Nancy Lea.

With the Reverend Peter Crawford of Siloam Baptist Church officiating, General Houston and Margaret Lea were married on Saturday, May 9, 1840, in the parlor of the home of her oldest brother, Henry, in Marion, Perry County, Alabama. The groom was forty-seven; the bride, twenty-one, wore a white satin dress.[10]

Houston's close friend Dr. Ashbel Smith had been invited to serve as best man but had replied that "the unsentimental obstacle preventing his attendance was money," [11] so Margaret's brother Martin filled in for him. Barnard Bee had also been invited to the wedding but he, like Smith, was broke and could not attend. Sam himself, always with the shorts when it came to money, had had to borrow $250 while in New Orleans to pay for his trip to Alabama.[12]

After the ceremony the wedding party attended a luncheon, after which the newly married couple went to the Lafayette Hotel where they stayed for a week while Margaret's possessions were packed for the journey to Texas. At a barbecue held in honor of the newlyweds in the oak grove adjoining the church graveyard, a Major Towns rose to propose a toast to Margaret. In the toast he named her the "Conqueress of the Conqueror." [13] The good major may have spoken his words in jest, but he was absolutely right. Houston had met his conqueress, and under Margaret's influence and strong personality he was to be thoroughly domesticated.

Accompanied by Margaret's slave Eliza, the Houstons arrived at Galveston where Sam was building a log residence on his farm, Cedar Point. Until the new home was completed, which Margaret was to name "Ben Lomond" from one of the Sir Walter Scott romances she had read, she and the general moved in temporarily with her mother. Mrs. Lea had invested heavily in Texas land and was staying in Texas permanently to oversee her investments. For her part, Margaret was enthusiastic about the salt air's healing powers and considered it as her ally in restoring Sam's health.

Always available for a speech, Houston made an oration in Houston City on July 6, and on July 25 he made a speech at Henry Corri's Theater to celebrate impending construction on the Houston and Brazos railroad.

The newlyweds made a trip to Nacogdoches and San Augustine so Houston could keep his political fences mended; there was an election coming up September 7 for the new Congress. Sam proudly showed his new wife off to all his friends in the Redlands. To his delight, with her charm, beauty, and natural warmth Margaret made a highly favorable impression. He spoke at many barbecues and dinners and his friends were delighted to note he did not touch any of the liquor that was so prevalent at these affairs. He was so happy and relaxed that those who had made such pessimistic predictions as to his marriage were forced to admit they had been mistaken. Ashbel Smith noted the changes in his friend and wrote Barnard Bee:

> His health is excellent, as good or *better than* I have ever seen it. He indulges in no conviviality with his friends — but strange to say is a model of conjugal propriety. . . . Will it last? I always hope for the best.[14]

Hockley was also amazed at Houston's abstinence and noted that Houston did not touch liquor while campaigning, even if Margaret was not with him.

Houston easily won reelection to Congress. While waiting for the reconvening of Congress in December, he and Margaret moved to Houston City, where they stayed with the Frank Lubbocks in their two-story home. Houston was asked by the Galveston Bay and Texas Land Company to handle some title suits coming up in the San Augustine court. As Margaret had a slight touch of fever the couple were separated at length for the first time as Sam went to handle the suits while Margaret stayed behind with the Lubbocks. Sam's intense feeling for his wife is revealed in a letter he wrote to her:

> . . . Every hour that we are apart, only resolves me, more firmly, not again to be separated from you. . . . I cannot be happy, but where you are! [15]

Houston won his cases and sent the substantial fee he was paid to Margaret for expenses and purchases at Ben Lomond.

When the Fifth Congress convened in the new capitol in Austin that cold, wintry day in December 1840, the government was rapidly becoming nothing but a shambles under the presidency of Mirabeau Buonaparte Lamar. Lamar, of medium height, muscular, and with blue eyes and long black hair, had many good qualities. He was an expert horseman, an accomplished fencer, and was of undoubted courage. He "had a facility with the pen, an innate speaking ability and a skill at oil painting" and had been one of the founders of the Philosophical Society of Texas.[16] Unfortunately, he was a dreamer and a visionary and had absolutely no talent as an administrator. He was completely out of his depth as chief executive of the nation. From the first day in office the Georgian had swung the ship of state on a course 180 degrees from that steered by Houston. Declaring Texas could go it alone, he was opposed to annexation. Due to his ruinous fiscal policies, trade was at a standstill and the nation was millions of dollars in debt. While Houston had practiced economy due to limited funds, governmental offices under Lamar were swollen with unneeded employees while mail routes, courts, and schools for settlers' children were neglected.

Whereas under Houston the republic had spent only $190,000 for the defense of the nation, Lamar spent $2.5 million.[17] Imports during the year had exceeded $1.3 million, while exports amounted to a little over $200,000.[18] Lamar's solution to the nation's problems was to reduce taxes, abolish duties, and to print paper money — large sums of money — which was noninterest-bearing currency unsupported by any kind of security. These were known as "red backs," in the first year dropping to sixteen cents on the dollar and twelve and one-half cents the second year. Eventually, they dropped to as little as three cents on the dollar.

As Mexico was still refusing to acknowledge the independence of Texas and Lamar had failed in his efforts to persuade them by diplomatic means, he asked Congress to declare war against Mexico. A joint committee of the House and Senate gave a favorable report on this measure, but on the House floor Houston fought the resolution, declaring a war was folly and that Texas needed peace and prosperity. Congress agreed and Sam's viewpoint prevailed. The public had lost so much confidence in Lamar that in the elections of 1839 only ten of his supporters who had been elected in 1838 were returned to office.

Worn out by the complete failure of all of his policies, the stress of his office, and public ridicule, Lamar asked Congress for a leave of absence to go to New Orleans for medical advice. He suggested Vice-president Burnet act for him during his absence. The leave was granted, and it was proposed Burnet's salary be increased by $5,500 as compensation for his extra duties. Houston opposed this, but the resolution passed when it was proposed to make the extra compensation not a "salary increase" but a deserved donation.

On December 16, 1840, Acting President Burnet gave a highly inflammatory message to Congress and demanded war against Mexico. Once more Houston rose to denounce such an undertaking

257

and demanded to know why Texas did not develop its current resources instead of starting out on new conquests. Once more Congress postponed action on a declaration of war.

The war spirit attracted some followers, however, and from New Orleans Houston's former secretary of war, William S. Fisher, made himself heard. After his service in Houston's administration Fisher had wandered south of the Rio Grande into Mexico and for a while had served as a colonel in the Mexican army. Now he was back in the United States and had fallen upon hard times. Although his pockets were bare his mind was full of dreams of glory, and writing to Gen. Felix Huston on January 28, 1841, he claimed Mexico was planning to invade Texas with a force of 20,000 men. He said it was his intention to go to Texas and raise a force of five or six hundred men, take up a position commanding the valley of the Rio Grande, and strike when the opportunity presented itself. Fisher expected no commission or authority from the government of Texas, but the thousands of adventurous spirits who would flock to the banner would be rewarded with the riches of the land and the fatness thereof. He said Huston was the one person named by everyone as the leader who must conquer Mexico. "I [write] for the purpose of ascertaining your views," [19] he said.

Two days before Congress adjourned on February 4, 1841, Houston wrote to Anthony Butler complaining about the state of affairs:

> We are in debt — we have nothing to pay with. It will be impossible for the Government to go on without the most burthensome taxes. . . . The truth is that useless extravagance and the most unprincipled profligacy have characterized the present administration.[20]

Houston was now eligible to run for the presidency again, and on Texas Independence Day a public dinner was given for him at Galveston. In early April, he was nominated for the presidency at a Harris County meeting and made a speech at San Augustine on April 19, following up with a speech at the Old Stone Fort at Nacogdoches on San Jacinto Day.

As expected, David Burnet announced his candidacy opposing Houston, and on May 19 the *Telegraph and Texas Register* endorsed him with the observation that Houston was a "noble wreck of humanity — great even in ruins."

The two candidates had long been enemies, and the campaign developed into one of unlimited vituperation and mud-slinging, with Sam calling Burnet "Wetumka," the Cherokee name for hog-thief, while Burnet retorted with "drunk" and "half-Indian." An anonymous pamphlet entitled "Houston Displayed, or, Who Won The Battle of San Jacinto?" had appeared sometime previously. Now it was given wide circulation. This bitter anti-Houston tract claimed that Houston had exhibited cowardice on the San Jacinto battlefield; that he was an opium addict; and that he had sold the consulship of Texas at New Orleans for a price. Houston, always quick to take to his pen, wrote a series of articles attacking Burnet and signed them "Truth." Burnet responded with extremely vitriolic articles denouncing Houston, signing them "Publius" and "Texian." Houston got so under the skin of his opponent that the peppery Burnet sent Dr. Branch T. Archer to Sam, challenging him to a duel. Houston, giving four reasons why, declined.

While relaxing at Cedar Point for a short time during the campaign, Houston took time out to write his friend Gen. William G. Harding in Nashville, apologizing for his inability to repay a loan of $500 due the general. He had $25,000 due him, he said, but could not collect enough to pay one-fourth of his land taxes. "In addition, two valuable negro boys for which I had paid in cash $2,100 previous to my visit to Nashville, ran away last spring to Mexico." [21] Several days later he wrote Samuel Williams, stating "my health is pretty fine, but Mrs. Houston's is not good, but better than it has been." He also mentioned "we have no liquor, and I do not taste one drop of it, nor will I do it!" After some political observations he asked Williams for a loan of "sixty or $80.00." He then asked Williams to see if his partner McKinney could buy him a one-horse buggy — on time.

On election day, September 6, 1841, Houston beat his opponent by a three-to-one margin, garnering 7,508 votes to the 2,574 Burnet received. The noted Indian fighter, Edward Burleson, was elected vice-president over Memucan Hunt.

The new president-elect and his lady were guests of honor soon after at a dinner in Washington County celebrating the victory. In a letter to Ashbel Smith on September 17, Henry Gillette reported on the affair:

> *thirteen* barbecued hogs and two thundering big beeves well roasted with lots of honey, *taters,* chickens and goodies in general . . . it was a cold water*doins,* for the Old Chief did not touch or handle the smallest drop of the ardent during his stay in this county.

Apparently, Margaret's campaign to lead Sam to the wells of temperance was bearing fruit.

Before inauguration day, Sam and Margaret spent a couple of months traveling around East Texas. Houston loved having Margaret with him on these trips and introducing her to his friends. Among those Margaret met was Dr. Robert Irion and his new bride, Anna Raguet. The two had eloped and been married on March 29, shortly before the Houstons married. Sam and Anna remained the best of friends, and when the Irions had their first child — a son — they named him Sam Houston Irion.

When Houston was inaugurated as president of Texas for the second time on that cold, windy day of December 13, 1841, he was wearing a linsey-woolsey hunting shirt, pantaloons, and an old wide-brimmed white fur hat.[21] In his mind he was assuming what he considered a receivership of a bankrupt enterprise, remarking that the situation was worse than it was on April 22, 1836. About the only thing in the nation's favor was that J. Pinckney Henderson, as minister to France, had gotten that nation to recognize Texas as independent on September 25, 1839, to be followed by Holland in September 1840 and Belgium in 1841.

As Margaret had not accompanied Houston to Austin, having elected to stay in Houston City, Sam chose to stay in the cramped quarters of the Eberly House Hotel instead of the executive mansion. This was probably a wise choice, inasmuch as there was not enough money in the treasury to buy firewood for the executive mansion.

Anson Jones was selected secretary of state after Houston had asked him not to refuse on the grounds that he was "poor." Houston admonished:

> I am — all are so! The officers shall have salaries, and in good money. It can be done — and shall be done!!! [22]

Houston's former aide Hockley was appointed secretary of the army and marine; William Daingerfield, secretary of the treasury; and George Terrell, attorney general. Ashbel Smith, who had proven himself an astute man with diplomatic skills and a fluency in French, was nominated as minister to Paris with the understanding he would fill the same post in London when Texas won recognition from Great Britain. It was also understood that because the treasury was so empty, Smith would have to pay his own expenses. Washington D.

Miller once more became Houston's private secretary, and Gail Borden was named collector of the port at Galveston.

In his first message to Congress, Houston outlined some of the serious problems confronting the nation. He made it plain that Texas was broke. "There is not a dollar in our Treasury. . . . We are not only without money, but without credit," [23] and he estimated the nation was in debt from ten to fifteen million dollars. He recommended that direct taxes be reduced by one-half and that the government accept only gold, silver, or "paper of unquestionable character" in payment of money owed it. He proposed to outlaw the previously authorized currencies and to issue $350,000 in new currency, in what was called the exchequer system, issued in increments of less than $50,000 a month and backed by a million acres of land previously owned by the Cherokees.[24] Of the $350,000 requested, Congress only authorized $200,000.

Houston pointed out that relations with Mexico were in poor shape as overtures made by Lamar to secure an amicable adjustment of existing difficulties had been rejected. He explained Indian relations were far from satisfactory and recommended a number of posts be established at suitable points extending from the western border to the Red River, and that treaties be concluded with the various tribes.

In an effort to economize, Houston's salary was reduced from $10,000 a year to $5,000, along with substantial cuts in the salaries of cabinet officers and various other officials. So many jobs were abolished that in some cases there were not enough clerks to handle necessary governmental business. Economy measures even forced the curtailment of mail service.

Always looming over Texas like a black cloud upon the horizon was Mexico, with the chameleon-like Santa Anna once again in power. Houston had been receiving reports that Mexico was planning an invasion, and in an address to the House of Representatives on December 30 he asked for authority to fortify Galveston and Matagorda bays. To add to his troubles, just a few weeks later news of the ill-fated Santa Fe expedition came filtering back home.

This expedition was a grandiose scheme dreamed up by Lamar in 1841, in an effort to revive his sagging popularity and to bring riches into the Texas treasury. The expedition, ostensibly on a peace mission, was to go over 1,000 miles through wilderness, prairie, and mountains on the Santa Fe Trail. However, troops were to accompany its members and the real object was to enforce Texas claims to 2,000 square miles of territory in New Mexico ceded by the Treaty of Velasco but still not occupied by Texas settlers. When the scheme was first proposed to Congress, Houston put aside his knife and pine stick — which he used to whittle toys for children while listening to debates — and violently opposed the measure. He pointed out the scheme would be regarded as an invasion of Mexico and that nation would undoubtedly resume hostilities against Texas by the unprovoked attack upon one of their states. Congress then refused to authorize the measure.

Lamar had proceeded on his own, however, and without consulting Congress ordered a New Orleans printer to print a half million dollars of money, which he used to purchase uniforms and horses (at $1,000 each). Money was snatched wherever it could be found. Supplies were commandeered and arms and munitions were taken from government arsenals, the prize confiscation being a cannon that bore upon the breech, stamped in glaring letters, the magic name of Mirabeau B. Lamar.

In June 1841 the procession, under the command of Brigadier General Hugh McLeod, Lamar's brother-in-law, marched off from Brushy Creek with twenty-two wagons carrying the expedition's supplies. There were five companies of soldiers totaling 265 men, accompanied by merchants, financiers, diplomats, gamblers, a young English lawyer named Thomas Falconer, and assorted adventurers. To cover the events for his newspaper, the *New Orleans Picayune,* a young editor named George Wilkins Kendall went along.

For months there were no reports of the expedition, then on January 18, 1842, the shattering news came in. The expedition had been an unmitigated disaster. The men had been betrayed by a Mexican guide who had purposely and consistently wandered off course and finally deserted them. They had been harassed by Indians, who killed five Texans and ran off with eighty-three horses, and under the hot summer sun of the Texas skies the group ran out of food and water long before they reached the borders of New Mexico. In a search for food the famished party broke up in various groups and eventually all groups were captured by units under the command of General Manuel Armijo. When Armijo read captured documents which showed that the true nature of the expedition was to set up a territorial government with a governor, customs officers, and military commandant, he was furious. Under conditions of extreme brutality the prisoners were marched off to Mexico City and those unfortunates who tried to escape, or fell by the wayside due to exhaustion, were ordered shot and their ears cut off. Eventually, the weary survivors landed in the hideous castle of Perote in Vera Cruz.

When news of the expedition's capture and their treatment and imprisonment in Mexico City became known, there was a fearful outcry among citizens not only of Texas but of the United States as well. United States Secretary of State Daniel Webster immediately sent special instructions to the American minister in Mexico City to procure the release of American citizens captured, and to tell the Mexican authorities any undue punishment of the Texans would foment in the U.S. a bitterness of feeling prejudicial to Mexico.[25] Houston, for his part, immediately asked Capt. Charles Elliot, the British commercial agent at Galveston, to ask the British minister in Mexico City to intervene in order to prevent the execution of those involved in the expedition. He also asked the United States and France to use their good offices in securing the release of the prisoners.

The Texas Congress sought reprisal and passed a bill authorizing war against Mexico, together with the annexation of upper and lower California, all of New Mexico, Chihuahua, Sonora, and portions of the states of Tamaulipas, Coahuila, Durango, and Sinaloa — in all, an area far larger than the United States.

Houston vetoed the bill as a "legislative jest," as he thought it was utterly ridiculous to talk about invading Mexico when the army had no munitions and the government's credit so poor that he had to give his personal guarantee for $250 before coffee and sugar were released to the troops in Galveston. The treasury's coffers were so empty that George McIntosh, the Texas chargé d'affaires to France, whom Ashbel Smith had replaced, had not received any salary or expense money since the preceding fall and had had to pawn his watch and other valuables. Only his diplomatic status had prevented him from being placed in jail; the kindly Dr. Smith came to his rescue by assuming his debts.

Congress promptly overrode the veto and then adjourned on February 5. Houston mounted his chestnut brown mule, Bruin, and headed for Houston City and Margaret. He later wrote his secretary, Miller, that he made the trip in two hours less than four days, "so you can see the mule did me honest service." [26]

CHAPTER 27

War Resurfaces

The clamor for an all-out invasion of Mexico went on, and from Galveston on March 3 Houston wrote to George William Brown outlining his opposition to such a venture. In Houston's opinion, it would take a minimum force of 5,000 men, and at least two and a half million dollars for any hope of success.

> To defend a country requires comparatively but little means. To invade a nation requires everything. — To conquer Mexicans in Texas is one thing — to battle with Mexicans in Mexico is a different kind of warfare. The true interest of Texas is to maintain peace with all nations and to cultivate her soil.[1]

Santa Anna, apparently in retaliation for the ill-fated Santa Fe expedition, struck back on March 5, 1842. On that date Gen. Rafael Vasquez crossed the Rio Grande with 1,400 troops and quickly marched to San Antonio. Receiving no resistance from the citizens, he seized 100 prisoners and returned with them to Mexico. Smaller Mexican forces entered Refugio and Goliad, took a few supplies and beeves, then retreated back across the Rio Grande. When Houston received news of the raid, he responded quickly. On March 10, he issued orders to Col. Alden A. M. Jackson at Galveston to place the fort at the east end of the island in an efficient state of defense in case of an invasion of the enemy by sea. To Brigadier General Edwin Morehouse he issued orders to hold his troops in readiness to march at a moment's warning, with emphasis that "system and order must be preserved."[2] Brigadier General Alexander Somervell was to proceed to San Antonio and take charge of the army and organize it under the laws regulating the militia.

> You will maintain the strictest discipline in camp . . . If a man is taken asleep at his post, or on guard, let him be shot . . . Maintain subordination: it will inspire confidence . . . If the invasion proves to be a formidable one, I will be at the army in person.[3]

To Secretary of War and Marine Hockley on March 10 he issued orders to remove all the public archives of the republic to the city of Houston.

On March 22, Houston wrote Somervell he had information there was a considerable force at San Antonio and on the frontier, and that they were anxious to advance upon the enemy. That being the case, Somervell was authorized to go to Laredo and cross the Rio Grande. The president emphasized that Somervell was not to advance upon Matamoros with an insufficient force, as in previous communications to Somervell he had made it plain Texas would not be in a position to invade Mexico before 120 days. He reminded the general to conduct civilized warfare. These instructions were followed up with an order on March 26 to blockade Mexican ports.

Many voices were still urging war, and on March 30 the *Austin City Gazette* demanded an immediate invasion of the northern Mexican provinces. On April 14, Houston issued a proclamation to all of Texas advocating a policy of retaliation against Mexico on account of repeated invasions. "Texas," he said, "was compelled to make war; a war not of agression, but one which the civilized world will justify."[4]

Once more Houston found himself in the position of trying to raise an army without money or supplies. In a letter dated March 15, he wrote: "I have not one dollar at my disposition, either to purchase horses or the equipment necessary for one man."[5] Previously he had appointed various agents in New Orleans to process any volunteers desiring to come into Texas, but made it perfectly clear to the agents they were to send no volunteers to Texas unless they were prepared to serve for six months. In addition, they were to equip themselves at their own expense with sufficient clothing for that amount of time, a rifle or musket with 100 rounds of ammunition, a cartridge box, and food for eight days. The agents completely disregarded these specific instructions, and Texas was flooded with unequipped volunteers who swarmed into the state with nothing except the clothes on their backs. They were nothing but a strain on the already meager resources of the government. Charging they had been deceived by the government, they became insubordinate and refused to obey orders; they complained of poor rations and hard conditions; and they stole what they could from private citizens. Houston was disgusted and wrote Adj. Gen. James Davis, commander of the troops in Corpus Christi, a strongly worded letter on June 15 denouncing the activities of the unruly troops. He made it clear that he expected Davis to establish discipline in the army and place in irons those men who had stolen horses, and to punish them as a court-martial may think proper. Several weeks later, the president wrote Congress that he despaired of the reformation of the troops and suggested it would be more politic for Texas to rely upon its own militia and to discharge the foreign volunteers.

When General Somervell had arrived in camp to take command of the army as ordered by Houston, he found to his surprise that Vice-president Burleson had forsaken his governmental duties and taken to the field, arriving in camp before him. Burleson had been elected by the troops as their commander, but had no orders from Houston. As the troops refused to obey Somervell, he had no alternative but to withdraw. Some days later, after thinking the matter over, Burleson offered to yield the command to Somervell, who declined the offer. Burleson then disbanded the troops on April 2. A number of his militiamen were still so restive and anxious to march against Mexico that Burleson started complaining that Houston had placed shackles on his movements. Five days later, the president wrote his vice-president: "To oppose the orders of the Executive, when he is in the exercise of his constitutional functions, is insurrection." [6]

Houston was undergoing great criticism in not ordering an immediate invasion of Mexico. He wrote William Daingerfield:

> You would be amused and miserably provoked at some of our "Heroes." It has been reported by rumor (for that has been the only official) that Burleson was at San Antonio with 1500 men & Clark L. Owen with 1000 at Victoria, all burning with revenge to cross the Rio Grande and "damning the President" that he would not let them go on. Oh, they were snorting! [7]

To compound Houston's difficulties with Santa Anna, both

James Hamilton and Barnard E. Bee had written the dictator letters offering $5 million for a peace treaty between the two nations. In addition, a side sum of $200,000 was offered to Santa Anna as a bribe. This was a wonderful propaganda coup for the Mexican dictator, and in individual letters he wrote both men, indignantly refusing their offer. He made angry references to the Santa Fe expedition and declared their offers of bribery were insults unworthy of a gentleman. Then, to maximize his fury, he released copies of the correspondence to newspapers throughout Mexico and the United States. Houston, although having absolutely nothing to do with the matter, was horribly embarrassed by the affair as it blackened his government. In a lengthy reply to Santa Anna dated March 21, he remarked:

> You have threatened to plant your banner on the banks of the Sabine . . . believe me, Sir, ere the banner of Mexico shall triumphantly float upon the banks of the Sabine, the Texian standard of the single star, borne by the Anglo-Saxon race, shall display its bright folds in Liberty's triumph, on the Isthmus of Darien.[8]

A call was issued by the president for a special session of Congress to convene June 27 at Houston City. Before Congress met, word was received from Ashbel Smith in London that Great Britain had recognized Texas as a republic and that Capt. Charles Elliot was to be accredited as its chargé d'affaires.

In his message to Congress, Houston asked that the capital be moved to Austin, leaving the choice of a new site to the legislators. He mentioned the lack of discipline among the troops and the conflict over command, and he told how the lack of funds had put the executive department in a bind. Appeals for contributions from the United States had brought in less than $500.

Houston pointed out that the government could not exist without revenue. He had recommended that the direct tax be reduced by one-half, but instead it was cut so low that it could not pay for its collection; for want of appropriations by the last Congress, mail transportation had entirely ceased.

On July 23, a law was passed requiring customs collectors, sheriffs, clerks, and postmasters to receive exchequers only at the current rates at which they were sold on "change" in open markets. As a consequence, gold and silver flowed into the treasury, and at the close of Houston's second term exchequers were on a par with coin.

Margaret had gone with her brother Martin in May to spend

time with her family in Alabama, so immediately after submitting his message to Congress Houston left for Galveston to await her return. After receiving word that she had been too ill to make the journey home, he returned to Houston City.

In a series of messages to Congress that July, he gave an estimate of the number of troops needed for the coming campaign, together with an estimate of the cost of equipping four companies of cavalry for six months and the amount required to support the navy at sea for six months. He also reported to the House of Representatives he had tried to ameliorate the condition of the Santa Fe prisoners, and that Mexico had released some of them.

Finally, Congress finished wrangling and passed a bill authorizing an offensive war against Mexico. Houston was empowered to head the army with dictatorial powers and to conscript one-third of the population able to bear arms; in addition, he was authorized to sell ten million acres of land to finance the undertaking and to proceed across the Rio Grande.

Once more Houston played his cards close to his chest. As a whole, the public rejoiced at the war measure. Sam's enemies who backed the bill thought the people would turn against him if he vetoed the measure. Nevertheless, he refused to disclose his intentions. He had patience, and as a military man he knew it took more than empty words to conduct a successful campaign. It also required money, munitions, and trained manpower, and Congress had given him none of those.

Congress was to adjourn July 23 and the bill would become law if Houston did not veto it. Although many of Sam's friends wanted him to sign the bill, J. Pinckney Henderson was hoping he would veto the measure. There were threats of revolution and assassination in the air, and angry groups paraded in front of the president's house. Houston paid them no mind and would not place guards around the building. Margaret, by this time back from her trip to Alabama, gave him her full support. At night the playing of her harp and piano was heard coming forth from the open windows of their dwelling.

A day before Congress was due to adjourn, Houston vetoed the war bill. Among his reasons were that an invasion would require at least 5,000 men, who should be enlisted for a period of not less than one year, as it would require at least six months to train and discipline the troops. Although Congress had authorized the sale of ten million acres, the sale would not result in enough money to carry on a war.

Although the veto was unpopular, Congress did not try to override it. But threats of assassination were renewed. As people read Sam's veto message and reflected upon it, however, the clamor against him finally died down. As James Morgan reported to Ashbel Smith in August, "Old Sam is more popular than ever." [9]

The general was heartened to know that one longtime friend — a man whose views he always respected — approved of his veto. Old Hickory, now feeble and with not too many years to live, from the Hermitage wrote Sam under date of August 17:

> I approve your veto fully. To make offensive war without ample means both in money and men would be the height of folly and madness, and must result in defeat and disgrace. To invade a country with drafted militia for a limited time, without a regular army enlisted and for and during the war, would be the height of folly and lead to the destruction of the army attempting it, and the disgrace of the general leading it. . . . [10]

Thus spoke the voice of experience, for Andrew Jackson, reflecting upon his campaign against the Creek Indians, certainly knew what it meant to lead an ill-equipped, ill-disciplined, and ill-fed army of volunteers with short-term enlistments.

To some, "Old Sam" might have been more popular than ever — but not to all. Secretary of War and Marine Hockley, one of Houston's closest friends, was so disgusted by the president's vacillation in defense, his attacks on the volunteers, and his plans to sell the steamer *Zavala*, that on September 1 he wrote a bitter letter of resignation. Houston was hurt and tried to get Hockley to withdraw the letter, but to no avail. It was a strange facet of Houston's personality that he seemed to have a genius for creating antagonisms and losing friends, and Ashbel Smith commented that he acted on one of Talleyrand's strange maxims, "Would you rise, make enemies!" [11] No doubt, part of the antagonisms were created by Houston's lifelong habit of never discussing his plans with anyone and never taking anyone into his confidence. He and Hockley later patched up their quarrel, but the friendship was never as solid as it had been.

Gail Borden, customs collector of the port at Galveston, offered his resignation but Houston had better luck with him by appealing to his patriotism. He succeeded in getting Borden to withdraw his letter.

On September 1, Houston wrote to a chief of the Apaches a message of peace and friendship, stating, "The tomahawk shall never be raised between us." The same date he wrote Castro and Flacco, two chiefs of the Lipan tribe, stating he was sending doctors Tower and Cottle on their way to the Apache nation and asking the Lipans to furnish horses to the doctors.[12]

Houston had never cared for Austin as a site for the capital, as he considered its location to be dangerous. A few days after elections for the Seventh Congress were held on September 5, Richardson Scurry, one of Houston's strongest supporters in Congress, wrote him advising the president to consider Washington-on-the-Brazos as a compromise between those who wanted the capital at Houston City and those who desired Austin. Houston thought the matter over and agreed with the suggestion.

The sleepy little village of Washington-on-the-Brazos, with a population of around 250, had little to offer except a racecourse, some faro banks along Main Street, and the inevitable saloons.[13] It did have one advantage, though. The city fathers, led by Judge John Lockhart, were so eager to get the capital located in their city that they promised to provide free transportation for all government property and to furnish rent-free accommodations for government offices until existing buildings could be remodeled. Houston City would not match this offer, so the president accepted the offer of Lockhart and his associates.

On September 28, with Houston riding his pacing mule Bruin, a caravan of six wagons and teams rattled down Main Street into the forest, transporting the government's property but leaving the archives in Austin. In one of the wagons rode Margaret with all of the Houston home furnishings, including her beloved harp and piano. Until new quarters could be provided, the Houstons and Secretary Miller would live with the Lockharts; other government officials and employees would live with private families.

Once more Santa Anna struck at the Texans. At daybreak on September 11, a force of around 1,200 men under the command of Gen. Adrian Woll, a French soldier of fortune, attacked San Antonio. Approximately fifty Texans resisted but eventually found themselves completely surrounded and, having been assured they would be treated as prisoners of war, surrendered. The district court was in session, so among the prisoners acquired by Woll was Judge Anderson Hutchinson, the jury, and three lawyers.

When the reports of Woll and his troops in San Antonio reached the citizens of Gonzales, they sent a force of eighty men

270

under the command of Capt. Matthew "Old Paint" Caldwell, an Indian fighter, to seek out Woll and his men. When they reached the Salado, a creek about six miles east of San Antonio, Capt. Jack Hays was dispatched with about fifty men to draw out the Mexicans. Woll took the bait and about 250 cavalry and 600 infantry pursued Hays until he fell back on the Salado. Caldwell, whose force by now had increased to about 240 men, was well positioned behind the bank of the creek. Here, around eleven o'clock in the morning, he was attacked by Woll's entire force and the battle raged until sunset, when the enemy fell back. The Mexicans had sixty killed and as many wounded, while the Texans had but one killed and nine wounded.[14] And then a tragedy occurred. Capt. Nicholas Dawson and fifty-three volunteer infantrymen were coming from La Grange to join Caldwell when they were discovered and surrounded by Woll's cavalry. After a brief resistance Dawson sent out a white flag, but it was fired upon. During the battle thirty-two of Dawson's men were killed and a few escaped. When the others surrendered after being assured they would be treated as prisoners of war, they were lined up and shot.[15]

At daybreak on September 18, Woll's army departed for Mexico. Caldwell and his force pursued them for thirty or forty miles and twice caught up with them but did not attack, as they supposed Woll had been reinforced. Consequently, the Mexican force got safely back across the Rio Grande.

Once more there was a demand by citizens, Congress, and editors for a march on Mexico City, but Houston still played it cool. The government simply was unable to support an invasion of Mexico without supply wagons, weapons, or ammunition –– and it had none.

More as a sop to public opinion and to play for time, on October 13, 1842, from the new capital at Washington, Houston issued orders to Brigadier General Somervell to proceed to the Southwestern frontier and select the most eligible position on the Cibolo or elsewhere and then to organize and drill all troops reporting to him. Houston was fed up with undisciplined, unruly troops who did not have the slightest respect for authority, and several times he emphasized to Somervell that he was to recruit and accept only those who would be obedient to orders. Houston further emphasized that all movements should be conducted in secrecy, and when the strength and condition of the troops warranted a movement upon the enemy, it was to be executed with promptness and efficiency.

President and Mrs. Houston and their entourage reached Washington-on-the-Brazos on October 2 and were cordially welcomed by Judge and Mrs. Lockhart as their guests. The president and his first lady were furnished a comfortable bedroom-sitting room with a small fireplace and a large mahogany bed, which Mrs. Lockhart had brought from Alabama. To furnish the Houstons with maximum privacy, the Lockharts had had a side door cut into the room so Sam and Margaret would not have to go in and out through the house.[16]

Good news was an event Sam seldom celebrated during his two terms as president, but around the middle of October Margaret whispered in his ear an item that left him overjoyed. She announced she was going to have a baby. Margaret's mother was informed of the coming event, and shortly afterward arrived at Houston City. Nancy Lea had decided to take Margaret to the home of her daughter and son-in-law Antoinette and William Bledsoe, who owned property up the Trinity River near the inland village of Grand Cane.[17] Her son, Vernal, and his wife, Mary, were staying with the Bledsoes, and in the peaceful surroundings of her kin Margaret would await the birth of her baby. Houston protested to Nancy Lea as he wanted his wife with him. He was used to command, but in Mrs. Lea he met his match. She was a woman of powerful will and would not be swayed from her decision.

After Margaret had been at Grand Cane several weeks, she was surprised to see her husband ride up. When they were alone Sam told her he had a humiliating confession to make. He had not only fallen off the wagon but in addition had made a fool of himself. Since his marriage, Houston had drunk only bitters, flavored with orange peel. During Margaret's absence he had been given a jug of extra-fine Madeira and had taken it home, intending to make a gift of it to Mrs. Lockhart. That estimable lady was away from her home for the evening and, in his loneliness for Margaret, Sam's old thirst got the better of him. He proceeded to get drunk. In his stupor he decided that one of the bedposts interfered with his vision and summoned one of his slaves. The slave was told to bring an ax and chop off the righthand post at the foot of the bed. Judge Lockhart was awakened from a sound sleep and finally broke the door down, thinking an assassin was after the president. Mrs. Lockhart arrived home in time to see the last strokes of the ax cut off the tall bedpost.

The next day the Houstons returned to the capital. Once more

272

under the influence of his wife and her stern opposition to alcohol, Houston gave up his drinking.

Brigadier General Somervell had had his troubles organizing and disciplining his complaining troops as clothing, food, powder, and guns were inadequate and slow in coming, but on November 22 he finally started for the Mexican border with 750 men. Among his captains were Houston's former secretary of war, William S. Fisher, and Thomas Jefferson Green, who had tried to kidnap Santa Anna from the *Invincible* some years previously.

After an unpleasant march the army reached Laredo, on the Texas side of the Rio Grande, on the morning of December 8.[18] The next day a portion of the troops visited Laredo and, in direct violation of the orders of Somervell and Houston, plundered it. When the troops brought back their booty, Somervell was so disgusted he had all the plunder thrown into a pile, sent for the alcalde, and directed him to return the articles to the owners.[19]

On December 10, Somervell permitted all soldiers who desired to do so to return to their homes, and some 200 men, disgusted with the unruly actions of the plunderers, took advantage of this offer. Somervell and the remainder of his army crossed the Rio Grande and went downriver, arriving opposite the Mexican town of Guerrero on the fourteenth. For several days the Texas army camped near Guerrero and requisitioned supplies from the Mexicans, then they recrossed the river to the Texas side. On December 19, 1842, Somervell, as commander of the Southwestern Army, issued Order No. 64 for the troops to march back to Gonzales, where they would be disbanded. Five companies of men, totaling about 300 and under the leadership of Fisher and Green, decided to invade Mexico and refused to accompany Somervell back home.

The troops of Fisher and Green crossed the Rio Grande on December 22 and marched into the town of Mier, six miles inland from the river and second in size to Matamoros. They handed the frightened alcalde a requisition for supplies: cannon, muskets, powder, lead, flour, sugar, coffee, shoes, blankets, and pantaloons — all of which the alcalde promised would be delivered the next day at the river, but below the Texan camp. As the supplies were piling up, Fisher and Green took the alcalde with them across the river as a hostage and left several Texans behind to guard the supplies. On Christmas Day, scouts reported that Gen. Pedro de Ampudia and General Canales had arrived in Mier with 750 soldiers and two cannon, and had captured the five-man Texas guard, together with the accumulated supplies.

The Texans voted to attack, and by four o'clock they had crossed the Rio Grande and were on the march toward Mier. Captain Baker and his company of spies were in the advance, and as they encountered Mexican pickets, the pickets fired on them and ran. After some difficulty in semidarkness and a cold drizzle, the Texans managed to cross the Alcantra, a wide stream. They advanced on a street leading directly to the plaza square, the entrance of which was protected by artillery. Taking shelter in houses, the Texans started opening passages through the stone houses until they got within fifty yards of the artillery where, opening portholes, they poured a destructive fire upon the Mexicans. When daylight appeared and the attackers could see the artillerymen, they silenced the enemy's pieces with their unerring rifle fire. The Mexicans then took to the rooftops and the fight continued until noon of the twenty-sixth.[20]

During a charge by the enemy, Captain Fisher received a bullet in one of his thumbs, and although not serious, the wound was terribly painful, sickening him so much that he vomited. Green then took over the command, and when he counted his men he found that out of 261 Texans in the battle, sixteen were killed and twenty or thirty wounded.[21]

In the midst of the confusion, General Ampudia sent Dr. Sinnicton, one of the captured prisoners, under a flag of truce to the Texans. The general, said the doctor, gave the Texans a choice of surrender or death and gave his word that if they surrendered they would be treated as prisoners of war and not sent to Mexico City. He assured them that they would be kept on the frontier until a peace was made or an exchange effected.

Fisher had served in Mexico with Ampudia and thought he was a man of honor. The Texans decided to surrender, and Ampudia and Canales promptly violated the terms of surrender. The prisoners were tied together and put on the march for Mexico City, going by way of Matamoros, Monterey, Saltillo, and finally Hacienda Salado, a hundred miles from Saltillo, where they arrived on February 10 and were imprisoned.

At sunrise on February 11 a group of prisoners led by Capt. Ewing Cameron overpowered one of the guards at the prison and managed to escape and seize horses and weapons. During the skirmish, the Texans suffered five men killed and several wounded, and by ten o'clock left for home by way of Monclova. Unfortunately, they abandoned that road and took to the mountains. For five days they wandered through the barren mountains seeking the Rio Grande. Through the heat of the day and the cold of the night they suffered without food or water and to survive killed and ate their horses. On February 18, they discovered smoke from a campfire and, approaching it, discovered a troop of Mexican cavalry. As they had thrown away their arms, were dispirited, weak with hunger, and helpless, once more they surrendered and were prisoners.

The captured troops were then marched in chains back to Hacienda Salado, and along the way a few more stragglers were picked up by the Mexicans. Upon reaching Salado, orders from Santa Anna were awaiting them that every tenth man should be shot. Accordingly, 159 white beans and seventeen black beans were put in a pot. The prisoners, still manacled and in twos, passed by the pot and drew their beans from a pitcher that was held up so those drawing could not see into it. Manacles were taken off the unfortunate ones drawing the black beans, and they were taken to the courtyard which was to be their place of execution. Bound together with cords, their eyes bandaged, they were forced to sit down on a log with their backs to their executioners and then were repeatedly shot.

The next morning the survivors were marched to Mexico City. About eighteen miles from the city, at Huchuctoca, General Canales received an order from Santa Anna to execute Captain Cameron in spite of the fact he had drawn a white bean. The remaining prisoners, still in chains, were then marched into Mexico City and placed in prison.

Ever since April, Houston had been endeavoring to get not only the national archives but the archives of the French government removed from Austin as he feared for their safety in that frontier town. On December 10 he instructed Col. Thomas I. Smith and Capt. Eli Chandler to proceed in the utmost secrecy to the General Land Office in Austin, where Col. Thomas William Ward, commissioner of the land office, was instructed to give them every available assistance in the removal of the records. Around noon on December 30, as the archives were being loaded in some wagons, a howitzer loaded with grapeshot was discharged on the land office. Smith and Chandler escaped with what records they could, but at Kenney's Fort on Brushy Creek in Williamson County they were captured by an unruly mob of over twenty people. The boxes of rec-

275

ords were taken from them and returned to Austin. The archives were then placed in tin boxes and stored at the boardinghouse of Mrs. Angelina Eberly.

On January 10, 1843, Houston made a report on the whole affair to the House of Representatives:

> If the representatives of the people have failed to sustain him, he feels acquitted of his trust. Whatever of evil may befall the nation from the loss or destruction of its archives must *fall upon the people* and not on the President.

He concluded by remarking he could no longer entertain a hope for the safety of the archives and no longer felt it was his duty to use any exertions for their preservation.[22] For Houston, the Archives War was over, and he washed his hands of the whole affair.

CHAPTER 28

The Annexation Debate

As Houston had his troubles with his army, so he was also having troubles with his navy. In May 1842, the naval vessels had returned from Yucatan and had been ordered to report to New Orleans and Mobile to refit in preparation for the enforcement of the blockade of the Mexican ports. By July the navy was still not ready for action. An appropriation of $19,000 was made with the understanding four ships could be gotten to sea. When the ships still remained in harbor, Capt. E. W. Moore, commodore of the small fleet, was ordered to sail the ships to Galveston. Moore disobeyed the orders and stayed where he was. As the blockade against Mexico had never been enforced, other nations protested to Texas about its existence and asked that it be discontinued. Houston obliged and on September 12 issued orders revoking the blockade.[1]

In a secret message to Congress on December 22, Houston outlined his problems with the navy. In his estimation it would require over $200,000 for the current year to support the navy, and the nation simply did not have the money. In addition, although a large portion of the public debt had been incurred in their purchase, the vessels were still unpaid for. Therefore, he recommended the ships be sold and suggested that the person from whom they had been purchased could be induced to take them again.[2] Congress concurred with Houston and, in a secret act, authorized him to dispose of the vessels.

Commodore Moore had been ordered to turn over the command of his fleet to the senior officer present and report in person to the Department of War and Marine. Once more he disobeyed his orders. Houston sent some commissioners to New Orleans to take possession of the vessels, but the commodore proved himself a wily man. He came up with a scheme to sail down the Gulf Coast and capture the Mexican fleet, blockade the whole coast, and levy contributions in the amount of $8,000. Half of this sum would be turned over to the treasury of Texas. Commissioner James Morgan thought this was such a good idea that he forgot his instructions from Houston and sailed with Moore. Houston then published a proclamation practically calling Moore a pirate and asking all nations in amity with Texas to seize Moore. Eventually, Moore showed up at Galveston — in July — and was promptly court-martialed and given a dishonorable discharge by Houston.[3] Moore was outraged and challenged Houston to a duel, but the president, as he had done with similar challenges by the disgruntled Albert Sidney Johnston and David Burnet, ignored the challenge.

Houston was very fond of William Henry Daingerfield, his secretary of the treasury and general troubleshooter, who had served well and faithfully on various assignments. On January 28, 1843, Sam wrote Daingerfield informing him that he and Ashbel Smith had been created Knights of the Order of San Jacinto, with the ensign of the order to be "a Green Ribbon, in the left breast, or Button hole of the coat opposite the heart." There was nothing in the constitution prohibiting this, and, as Houston told Daingerfield,

> This I have a right to create, and as I am a friend to "Order," I surely have a right to start an order, and then to create some reward for the *worthy,* as we have no cash, to encourage Gentlemen in preserving order.[4]

Perhaps in an attempt to revive his friendship with George Hockley, on January 18, 1843, Houston requested that Hockley call on him in Washington to discuss a plan for fortifying Galveston, Velasco, and Matagorda Bay, as $9,000 had been appropriated for that purpose. Later on he wrote Asa Brigham, the treasurer, to authorize the payment of $689.25 to Hockley as acting colonel of ordnance while in command of the post at Galveston from September 24, 1842, to January 10, 1843.

Suddenly, James W. Robinson showed up. This was the same Robinson who had been lieutenant governor in the provisional government and a leader in the anti-Houston group that had done everything in its power to tie Sam's hands as commanding general in 1836. Robinson had been among those captured by Woll in his attack against San Antonio and had been languishing in a Mexican prison for some time. Concocting a scheme to extricate himself from prison, he wrote Santa Anna claiming he had always been a loyal subject of Mexico. He suggested to Santa Anna that after seven years of war most Texans were anxious for peace and would accept a reunion with Mexico. It was his opinion that peace could not be had without an armistice, and he suggested that he be sent to Texas as a commissioner to talk to Houston about the matter. Santa Anna fell for the proposal and released Robinson.

When Robinson arrived with an offer from Santa Anna to end hostilities if Texas would acknowledge the sovereignty of Mexico, most Texans were for lynching him. But Houston decided to use him. Under date of April 15, 1843, Houston dictated to Robinson a crafty letter to the Mexican president that Robinson signed. "Robinson" informed Santa Anna his peace proposals had created less stir than he had anticipated; that Texas had been recognized by several foreign powers as an independent nation and had formed treaties with these nations; that for Texas to act independently of those powers would, in his opinion, be treating them with disrespect. He then went on to state that many people were clamoring for an invasion of Mexico and that Congress had given Houston authority to accept the services of 40,000 volunteers, which could easily be increased with 10,000 citizens, besides the immigrant volunteers. General Rusk at that moment, he said, was raising an expedition to cross the Rio Grande. In addition, Houston had succeeded in making peace with the Indians.

"Robinson" then favored Santa Anna with a few suggestions.

> The first is, that if your excellency had thought proper to have released all the Texas prisoners and let them return to their homes, and declared an armistice for some months . . . it would have had a good effect upon the people.[5]

He then went on to tell the Mexican president he thought Houston would prefer peace, if it could be had on honorable terms.

In his letter to Santa Anna, Houston played his cards skillfully. He dangled an armistice between the two nations and brought up the release of the prisoners. Then he cleverly tied in the threats of an invasion of Mexico, while in reality an invasion of Mexico was the last thing he wanted, as Texas was simply not prepared to invade. Far, far better to stay on the defensive and let Mexico assume all the risks of an invasion.

After reflecting on the matter, the Mexican president agreed to an armistice, and with the news of the armistice Sam's popularity in Texas increased.

On April 24, Houston wrote Dr. Cornelius McAnelly, asking for a personal favor. As Mrs. Houston had a sore breast and expected soon to have to nurse, would the doctor obtain "nipple guards" for her?[6] He also mentioned to the doctor there was a report that the Mier prisoners were safe within the Texas borders.

On May 25, 1843, Margaret gave birth to a boy, whom the proud parents christened Sam Houston, Jr.

In spite of his official duties, Houston was still a prolific letter writer and was keeping in touch with his Indian friends in the Cherokee Nation West. On May 30, he wrote a friendly letter to his former brother-in-law, John Rogers. Most of the letter concerned his efforts to make peace with the various tribes in Texas and toward that line he was calling for an Indian council to be held at Bird's Fort on the Trinity in early August. It was his hope to be there in person.

Thomas Rusk had been elected major general of the militia, and when he wrote Houston regarding an invasion of Mexico he received a highly unsympathetic reply. "The wise man would wait for the harvest and prepare the reapers for it when it came. If the enemy chooses, let them run the risk." [7] To his friend Dr. Robert Irion, Houston wrote he had heard Rusk would soon be on the march with the advance of "The Grand Armie for the reduction of the palaces of the Montezumas," and commented that Rusk had fallen upon evil companionship and would regret it when it was too late.[8]

On June 15, Houston acknowledged Charles Elliot's letter of congratulations by remarking, "Mrs. H. and the boy are doing well. He is stout, and I hope will be useful to his kind. May he be anything but a loafer, an agitator, or in other words, a demagogue." [9] On the same day he issued a proclamation of an armistice between Texas and Mexico with the hope of achieving peace between the nations. A few months later, George Hockley and Samuel M. Williams, a former partner of Stephen F. Austin, were appointed as commissioners to meet with representatives of Santa Anna at the Rio Grande to agree upon the terms of the armistice. The armistice was signed February 18, 1844, but was rejected by the Texas Congress because it referred to Texas as a department of Mexico.[10]

In spite of the bad press Texas was getting in some papers in the United States, Houston had his admirers. The Nu Pi Kappa Society of Kenyon College and the Philomathesian Society of Wake Forest College voted him an honorary membership in their organizations, and in October the president wrote the secretaries of those bodies expressing his thanks at the tribute paid him.

Not everyone in Texas was pleased with Houston's announcement of the armistice between Texas and Mexico. A large number of the citizens desired an aggressive war against Mexico because they thought Texas could expand its territory all the way to the Pacific. Some of Houston's loud detractors were now accusing him of selling out to England and of being bribed by Santa Anna, and the constant criticism and sniping of the *Houston Telegraph* and a few other newspapers was getting under the president's skin.

On November 8, Sam delivered a speech at the Presbyterian church in Huntsville and took the opportunity to denounce his critics:

> . . . I have been assailed for years without mitigation, malice never relaxing its anxiety, nor vengeance staying its hand. Every arrow has been shot that it has been deemed could wound, and poisoned by rancor and malice. . . . I am denounced as a villain, a drunkard, a blackguard and a wretch.[11]

When he finished his lengthy speech, the audience gave him a standing ovation and cheered him.

The Eighth Congress was getting ready to assemble, and on November 23, 1843, Gen. Edwin Morehouse wrote Anson Jones: "The Old Dragon, family & Co., leave this morning for Washington." [12]

When the "Old Dragon" addressed the Eighth Congress in December, he did so with an air of optimism and confidence. He reminded the senators and congressmen that when he took office Texas was without currency, credit, or a mail system; Mexico was harassing the fledgling republic; Indians were hostile; and foreign governments regarded the new republic with apathy. Things were now improving in the nation. The republic had its most abundant harvest, fine farms were dotting the countryside, and cattle were

281

multiplying. Relations with the various Indian tribes were excellent. Houston himself had traveled more than 500 miles to visit a grand council of Indian tribes, and all but two — the Comanches and Kiowas — had signed peace treaties. The recent armistice between Mexico and Texas was brought up, and Houston reminded his listeners that in foreign affairs France was establishing a line of royal steamships direct to Texas. The chargé d'affaires in Paris, Ashbel Smith, was negotiating with Spain for trade between Texas and Cuba. In addition, Texas had sent a chargé to Holland and Belgium to stimulate trade on the European continent. The United States, unfortunately, had neglected since 1842 to ratify a commercial treaty with Texas.

All this was true, and there was no doubt Texas was prospering, but there was still the question of annexation.

Annexation to the United States was Houston's goal, and he pursued it with diligence, tact, patience, and extreme shrewdness. Although annexation was popular with many people in the United States, there were many powerful forces opposed, led by the abolitionists. In Europe the two great powers of Great Britain and France were opposed; it was to their interest to keep Texas as an independent nation as that would provide a buffer between the United States and Mexico and hamper the growth of the United States to the Pacific Ocean. In addition, England was highly anti-slavery and resented America's consistent anti-British policy.

Secretary of State Anson Jones was no admirer of his chief and in his diary remarked "cunning, Indian cunning, is the secret of his success. Old Bowles . . . learned him all he knows though he has native tact, was an apt scholar, and learned *Indian* well." [13]

Houston was an astute judge of human nature and decided to apply some of his "Indian cunning" and play a little bit of international chess. To the United States he decided to appear indifferent about annexation and led officials to believe the republic was planning an offensive and defensive alliance with England, as he was of the opinion that if "anything could crystalize annexation sentiment in the United States, the specter of a British satellite on the southwestern border west of the Sabine would do it." [14]

To England and France, Houston gave the impression the United States was about to annex Texas. On excellent terms with British chargé Charles Elliot, Houston wrote him asking him to intercede on behalf of the Mier prisoners. He then brought up the subject of annexation to the United States. The majority of the people in Texas were in favor of it, he said, as it would assure peace, but in the United States the question was both a political and sectional one. He intimated that he preferred Texas to be a separate nation, but that Mexico must recognize the independence of the republic.[15]

On October 15, 1842, Houston had George W. Terrell, now acting secretary of state as well as attorney general, write a lengthy memorandum to the governments of the three powers. The memorandum pointed out it had been nearly seven years since Texas won its independence, but Mexico was still making predatory raids against the republic. He asked the three powers to either require of Mexico the recognition of Texas independence or to make war upon her according to the rights established and unanimously recognized by civilized nations.[16] The United States responded by proposing concerted action, but Great Britain insisted it would be better if each nation acted separately.

In August of 1837, Memucan Hunt, then chargé to the United States, had presented the subject of annexation to Martin Van Buren, then president of the United States. Van Buren declined and Texas withdrew the offer. John Tyler, who had become president in April 1841 on the death of William Henry Harrison, was in favor of annexation, which was becoming increasingly popular with Congress. On December 23, 1842, Isaac Van Zandt, now Texas chargé to Washington, wrote Houston that Tyler and a majority of his cabinet were in favor of annexation but feared they would not get a two-third vote in the Senate to ratify a treaty. Houston decided to whet the appetite of Joseph Eve, the American chargé d'affaires, and in February 1843 wrote him that some of the oldest settlers of Texas, even some of Austin's "Old Three Hundred," were in favor of annexation.[17] In September, Abel P. Upshur, secretary of state under Tyler, told Van Zandt that Tyler contemplated early action upon the subject of annexation and wanted Van Zandt to inform his government of that fact. Houston played coy and told Van Zandt to make it appear that Houston was indifferent to the subject. The next month, in a discussion with Elliot, Sam stated categorically that "with the independence of Texas recognized by Mexico, he would never consent to any treaty or other project of annexation to the United States, and he had the conviction that the people would sustain him in that determination." [18]

283

Upshur again brought up the subject of annexation with Van Zandt in mid-October of 1843 and told him Tyler was ready to present the matter in the strongest terms to Congress. This was welcome news to Houston; however, he thought he could get better terms if Texas independence was first acknowledged by Mexico. Still playing hard to get, he then instructed Van Zandt to inquire of Upshur if, after a treaty was signed and before it was ratified, the United States would order a military and naval force to the proper points on the Gulf of Mexico to protect Texas from foreign aggression.[19] The answer was yes. Tyler agreed to send a fleet to the Gulf of Mexico and army troops to the border. In March, John C. Calhoun became the new American secretary of state when Upshur was killed in an explosion on the sloop *Princeton*. On April 11, 1844, Calhoun wrote Van Zandt and Henderson confirming this pledge.

From the Hermitage the ailing Jackson was keeping a close eye on events in Texas, and Houston's many conversations with the British were giving him fears Houston was becoming pro-British. In a letter to his former protegé dated January 18, 1844, he wrote:

> You know, my dear General, that I have been, & still am your friend. I have put down everywhere I heard them the slanders of British intrigue circulated against you. You never could have become the dupe to England, and all the gold of Santana . . . could not seduce you from a just sense of duty & of patriotism. . . . My strength is exhausted and I must close.[20]

Five days later the aged general once more wrote Houston:

> I tell you in sincerity & friendship, if you will achieve this annexation your name & fame will be enrolled amongst the greatest chieftans of the age. . . . Now is the time to act & that with promptness & secrecy & have the treaty of annexation laid before the United States Senate where I am assured it will be ratified. Let the threats of Great Britain and Mexico then be hurled at us. . . .[21]

From Washington-on-the-Brazos Houston replied to his old chief on February 16, addressing Jackson as "Venerated Friend." In his reply he stated:

> I am determined upon immediate annexation to the United States. Texas, with peace, could exist without the United States, but the United States can not, without great hazard to the security of their institutions, exist without Texas. . . . Now, my venerated friend, you will perceive that Texas is presented to the United States as a bride adorned for her espousal. But if, now so confident of the union, she should be rejected, her mortification would be indescribable. She

has been sought by the United States and this is the third time she has consented. Were she now to be spurned, it would forever terminate expectation on her part, and it would then not only be left for the United States to expect that she would seek some other friend, but all Christendom would justify her in a course dictated by necessity and sanctioned by wisdom . . .[22]

In Washington, the impression Houston was trying to convey that he was indifferent or even opposed to annexation was bearing fruit, but in Texas there was one man that easily saw through him. On February 9, 1844, James Morgan wrote a friend concerning the letters Jackson had written Houston, and commented:

The impression at W. City is, that Genl. Houston is opposed to annexation, and Old Hickory has been written to from that, to use his influence with Houston to bring him over it is surmised! "Old Sam" has managed his cards in this affair very well, but he is no more opposed to annexation than Genl. Jackson yet the English & French agents here think he is![23]

In the belief that the United States Senate would vote down an annexation treaty, on December 13, 1843, Houston wrote Van Zandt instructing him to suspend negotiations with the American government. Faced with the knowledge that England was pressing her powerful and friendly offices upon the young republic, these instructions to Van Zandt alarmed American officials and the annexation movement was greatly accelerated.

In order to keep his Congress informed of the current state of negotiations, on January 30, 1844, Houston appeared before the Senate and House of Representatives in secret session. To them he mentioned he had carefully abstained from expressing any opinion regarding annexation and did not think it desirable now to express any preference. He pointed out that if Texas sought annexation and failed "it would have a seriously prejudicial influence upon the course which England and France might otherwise be disposed to take in our favor, as well as being mortifying to Texas." Houston admitted the annexation was desirable and requested an appropriation of $5,000 to pay the expenses of another representative to Washington to assist Van Zandt.[24] Consequently, the trusted James Pinckney Henderson was appointed to the legation in Washington to assist Van Zandt in handling the treaty of annexation. Henderson was instructed to go immediately to Washington-on-the-Brazos for instructions before proceeding to the United States. Two clauses in particular were among the instructions Henderson received: the treaty was to provide that sometime in the future Texas might be divided into four states; also, the United States should acquire the naval vessels of Texas and pay the builders the price Texas would have paid for them.[25]

On January 29, 1844, Houston started a letter to Van Zandt, but due to interruptions did not finish it until February 15.[26] In his letter Houston told the chargé the previous instructions to suspend negotiations toward annexation would be revoked, and should the indications on the part of the Congress of the United States justify the course, to open negotiations and conduct them with the most profound secrecy, as news would prove greatly prejudicial to future negotiations with other governments. Van Zandt was further instructed that if there was no possibility of successful negotiations then, if possible, to bring about a treaty of alliance offensive and defensive toward Mexico. He went on to say he was sending General Henderson to Washington to assist him and that his own private secretary, Washington D. Miller, had been appointed a secretary of the special legation.

Both Great Britain and France were aware of the ongoing treaty negotiations, and both protested to the United States against annexation. Elliot even wrote Anson Jones he did not think the Senate would possibly ratify a treaty, and in his opinion Houston's real interest was to see the Texas republic remain independent.[27] On April 7, Elliot had an interview with Houston and immediately thereafter wrote Foreign Minister Lord Aberdeen that in his view Houston expressed little confidence in the success of annexation.

On April 12, 1844, the annexation treaty was signed, and ten days later President Tyler placed it before the Senate for ratification, where it became a political football.

The day before the treaty was signed the general and Margaret were guests at the home of Mary Rhodes, an old friend of Houston. The affair was a birthday party for Margaret, who was now twenty-five. Shortly thereafter, Houston began negotiating to buy some property near Huntsville, one hundred miles northwest of Grand Cane, as a home for himself and Margaret when he retired from the presidency. Then in May he moved to Houston so he could receive news from the United States capital thirty hours sooner than he could at Washington-on-the-Brazos.

To Washington politicians there were other things equally as important — if not more so — than the annexation of Texas. This was an election year and it was time for both parties to nominate their candidates for presidency. Tyler had broken with his party shortly after he assumed the presidency; consequently, the Whigs nominated Henry Clay, "The Great Compromiser." For the Democrats, Martin Van Buren was expected to be the candidate and he, like Clay, was opposed to annexation. At this time the United States was having a difference of opinion with England over the boundaries of Oregon, and both parties hoped to keep the two national issues — annexation and the Oregon boundary question — out of the campaign.

Old Hickory decided otherwise. Although getting feebler by the day, he still kept an interest in politics and retained powerful influence in the Democratic party. Through his influence, Van Buren was shunted aside and James Knox Polk, an ardent proponent of annexation, became the nominee of the Democrats.

On May 6, Houston wrote William Murphy a lengthy letter and in it stated, "If the Treaty is not ratified I will require all future negotiations to be transferred to Texas." He then predicted that if the treaty was not ratified, Texas would eventually become an empire that would reach to the Pacific Northwest, taking in the friendly northern provinces of Mexico, Chihuahua, and Sonora; upper and lower California; and Oregon. All of this was "destiny," he wrote, and would occur "in thirty years from this date." [28]

On June 8, 1844, the Senate rejected the treaty by a vote of 36 to 16 and Mexico abruptly ended the truce and renewed threats of invasion. Houston recalled Henderson, and Van Zandt was permitted to resign. Texans were bitterly disappointed at Mexico's action, and various newspapers supported Houston and urged him to cultivate England and France.

The United States was not the only nation engrossed in an election. Texans were to go to the polls on September 2 to elect a new president and vice-president, and under the constitution Houston could never be president again. His enemies tried to persuade former President Lamar or David G. Burnet to run for the office, but they both knew "Old Sam" would take to the stumps in opposition to them, and they decided to sit on the sidelines. Anson Jones and Ed Burleson threw their hats in the ring and the contest between the two became exceedingly bitter. Naturally, everyone wanted to know who Houston preferred, but he was close-mouthed on the subject until about a month before election, when he finally endorsed Jones. The public had no enthusiasm for Jones, who was a colorless individual and had no following of his own as he was walking strictly in Houston's shadow. Houston had spoken, and when the votes were counted Jones won handily and his running mate, Kenneth L. Anderson, was elected vice-president. As James Morgan wrote to Samuel Swartwout in New York: "Jones rode in on Old Sam's shadow. . . . Old Sam can make anyone president." [29]

George Gordon, the Earl of Aberdeen and Queen Victoria's foreign minister, acted quickly when he heard about the rejection of annexation by the United States Senate. Calling in Ashbel Smith, he presented the Texas envoy with a tentative draft of a document he referred to as a "Diplomatic Act." The document proposed that Great Britain, France, the United States, Texas, and Mexico join together to work for peace between Texas and Mexico, with Mexico recognizing the independence of Texas and the establishment of the Rio Grande as a boundary line between the two nations. Texas would exclude forever the possibility of annexation. Smith was given assurances by Lord Aberdeen that England and France were prepared to use force against Mexico if that nation proved unwilling to go along, and the two countries would go to war with the United States if she refused to sign the act and would not stand aside.

By the time the proposed diplomatic act was received by Houston, Jones was president-elect. Houston gave instructions to Jones to have Smith sign the act, but Jones procrastinated. Houston repeated his instructions and once more they were ignored. Finally, Houston put his orders in writing and rode off to a series of Indian councils and Jones, without the president's knowledge, instructed Smith to return to Texas. When Smith arrived at the capital he was told by Jones that he was to be his secretary of state and any negotiations would take place in Texas as Jones wanted the honor of concluding the diplomatic act for his own administration.

With his refusal to obey Houston's instructions, it is very likely that Anson Jones, the former New England druggist, changed the destiny of Texas. Texans wanted peace and were furious at being snubbed twice by the United States. With the guarantees established by both Great Britain and France, plus recognition by Mexico, there is little doubt the people of Texas, the House and Senate, would have backed Houston if he had signed the act. But Jones, that small man who in his diary consistently denigrated Houston, did not give them the chance to express their views.

On December 5, 1844, the outgoing president's message to the Ninth Congress was a brief and conciliatory one. He reported that England and France were friendly in spite of annexation agitation and that both were working for an independent Texas; the United States still declined to ratify a commercial treaty. Although the armistice had failed, Mexico had liberated all but one of the Mier prisoners. The Indians were peaceable, but best of all "the finances of the country are in the most healthy and prosperous condition," and there was a balance of $5,948.91 in the treasury.[30]

Four days later Houston, together with his cabinet and the chaplain of the House of Representatives, followed the president-elect and the vice-president-elect on a rough, wooden platform in front of Independence Hall. To the assembled dignitaries, the outgoing president spoke first, and in his valedictory address commented on the annexation problem:

> If Texas goes begging again . . . she will only degrade herself. . . .
> If the United States shall open the door and ask her to come into her great family of states, you will then have other conductors, better than myself, to lead you into the beloved land from which we have sprung. . . . If we remain an independent nation, our territory will be extensive — unlimited.[31]

A few minutes later Anson Jones was sworn in as president and assumed the burdens of the office. Houston left office as a very popular leader with the people, and his star of destiny was shining brightly. He held no public office, but his huge body was still to cast a giant shadow upon the affairs of his nation.

BOOK FIVE

The Statesman

Engraving copied from Daguerreotype by B. P. Paige, Washington, D.C.
— Courtesy Barker Texas History Center,
University of Texas at Austin

CHAPTER 29

Senator of a New State

The former president spent a few days in Washington attending to some personal affairs, and on December 13, he wrote Old Hickory. Polk had defeated Clay overwhelmingly for the presidency, receiving 170 electoral votes to 105 for Clay, and Houston commented:

> The recent election in the United States, seems to indicate pretty clearly that the people are in favor of the annexation of Texas, and if the preliminaries of the measure should be properly adjusted, I should not interpose any individual obstacle to the consummation.

He was leaving for home the next day, some 160 miles distant, and also commented to his old friend that he and Margaret intended to visit Jackson at the Hermitage during the coming spring.[1]

Houston reached Grand Cane on the nineteenth of the month and two days later, in a letter to Anson Jones, reported he had had a joyous meeting with Margaret, and she was "gratified that my probation had passed." In closing he told the new president, "Money matters gave me more trouble in my administration than all others. With them right, you can have no trouble of serious character." [2]

Margaret, who was almost ecstatic now that Sam was back in

private life, as a Christmas present wrote her husband a poem of ten verses. Entitled "To My Husband — December 1844 — On Retirement from the Presidency," the first verse read:

> Dearest, the cloud hath left thy brow,
>   The shade of thoughtfulness, of care,
> And deep anxiety; and now
>   The sunshine of content is there.[3]

In the spring of 1845, with a wagon train of belongings, including Margaret's piano, Houston, Margaret, and Sam, Jr., moved to their new home fourteen miles from the small city of Huntsville in Walker County. It was similar in design to Ben Lomond in Cedar Point but larger, with two large square rooms flanked by an open hallway. There was an upstairs room, and in the yard the kitchen and various farm buildings were still under construction. Houston gave his plantation the name "Raven Hill." [4]

Although John Tyler would retire from the American presidency in March 1845, he was still determined that Texas would be brought into the Union before the close of his administration. Annexation by treaty had failed to be ratified once, so the best solution to the problem was to recommend to the House and Senate annexation by a joint resolution in accordance with the terms of the treaty. Consequently, since December, several different bills or resolutions were introduced in both the Senate and House and were debated, with Jackson directing from the sidelines. In February 1845 the House voted 120 to 98 to annex. Texas "was to keep her debts and public lands," and boundaries "were to be adjusted by the United States." In addition, there was to be no slavery north of 26°30'.[5] The Senate met in a night session on February 27 and, with the lobbies jammed with spectators eagerly watching the proceedings, voted 27 to 25 to approve a resolution which would bring Texas into the Union. On March 1, 1845, three days before his term expired, Tyler signed the resolution. The Mexican minister to the United States was promptly recalled and Mexico threatened war.

Ashbel Smith had hardly adjusted himself to his new office as secretary of state when private citizen Houston rode into Washington-on-the-Brazos and hitched his horse, Saxe Weimar, outside

Smith's door. Striding into the secretary's office, booted and spurred and with his riding whip in hand, he said:

> Saxe Weimar is at the door, saddled. I have come to leave [my] last words with you. If the Congress of the United States shall not by the fourth of March pass some measures of annexation which Texas can with honor accede to, [I] will take the stump against annexation for all time to come.[6]

Without waiting for a reply he embraced his friend Indian fashion, strode through the door, mounted Saxe Weimar, and was on his way.

On March 29, Capt. Charles Elliot and Count Alphonse de Saligny, chargés to Texas from England and France respectively, met with President Jones and Secretary Smith. Jones agreed to not assemble Congress or entertain any negotiation for annexation for a period of ninety days, with the understanding the British and French envoys would secure Mexico's promise for the independence of Texas. In addition, the two powers guaranteed to defend Texas. A preliminary treaty was drawn up and signed, with the stipulation that any agreement signed would not be binding if the people of Texas desired to join the United States.[7]

Immediately after the signing, Elliot and de Saligny were off to Mexico to secure the signature of the Mexican government. Andrew Jackson Donelson, nephew of Andrew Jackson and chargé to Texas, was hurrying to the republic, not only with the annexation treaty in his pouch but with several letters from Jackson to Houston urging the former president to endorse the treaty. Upon arriving at Washington-on-the-Brazos and while on the way to the executive mansion, Donelson met Elliot and de Saligny headed the other way. The men exchanged pleasantries, but Elliot and de Saligny said nothing about their just-ended interview with Jones. When Donelson arrived at the executive mansion he was puzzled when he found Jones, who was in favor of Texas remaining as an independent nation, cool to the treaty and unwilling to call a special session of Congress to discuss the matter.

Unable to find Houston at Raven Hill, Donelson sent him a copy of the treaty to East Texas, where he had learned Sam was. Houston studied the document thoroughly and upon his return home wrote Donelson a lengthy letter on April 9 stating, "I am in favor of annexation, if it can take place on terms mutually beneficial to both countries."[8] He objected to many things in the treaty as he thought the terms were unfair to Texas. In his opinion, commissioners from both nations should meet and negotiate various aspects of the treaty.

Texas was now in the catbird seat. With the British and French governments guaranteeing to maintain peaceful relations between Texas and other nations, the republic had the choice of remaining an independent nation permanently or being annexed to the United States.

A campaign of villification and slander by politicians and newspapers unfriendly to Houston was begun, charging that he had never been in favor of annexation. The leader of the attacks was the *Telegraph and Texas Register,* edited by the one-armed Dr. Francis Moore. The paper accused Houston of "blood betrayal" and claimed he had tried to annex Texas to Mexico. The paper also charged he had a "villainous" opposition to annexation to the United States and accused him of "accepting British gold." On October 22, 1845, the paper carried an article stating that "the Milliner Queen (Victoria) cannot boast of three more willing servants than Elliot, Houston and Jones." [9] Houston was furious at the attacks, and more so when he found out that his slanderers were courteously received, welcomed, and entertained by President Polk and his cabinet while they were in Washington City. Writing to his friend Donelson to get some of his anger off his chest, he told his friend he was certain that nine-tenths of the solid people of Texas were behind him.

By now the Houston family was on its way to Tennessee and Alabama to visit Jackson and various friends and relatives, but while in Houston City on the afternoon of May 16, the former president addressed the local citizenry at the Houston Methodist Church. He restated his opinion on annexation and took this opportunity to answer some of his critics and, never one to mince his words, referred to editor Moore as a "lying scribbler." That evening the retired president was the guest of honor at a banquet held at the old capitol. Six official toasts were given, followed by thirty-eight volunteer toasts. Houston's own toast was to his old chief, Andrew Jackson.

The Houstons proceeded to Galveston, where they caught a boat for New Orleans. In New Orleans, in late May, Houston, who was always a much sought-after speaker, was asked to speak at the Arcade. Before an overflowing audience, Sam's choice of topic was annexation. In his opinion, he said, the people of Texas favored it, and when the Congress met it would ratify the treaty with the United States. As to whether he was himself opposed to or in favor of annexation, it was true, he said, "that he had coquetted a little with Great Britain and made the United States as jealous of that power as he possibly could." [10] Later on in the same hall, Houston gave a well-attended lecture on temperance.

While in New Orleans, Houston heard that Jackson, who had been critically ill for months, was dying. Immediately he and his family took a steamer to Nashville to see the old general. Unfortunately, the steamer ran aground and the boat was held up for two days while being repaired. The Houstons finally reached Nashville on Sunday, June 8, 1845, immediately secured a coach, and were on their way to the Hermitage when they met the Jackson family physician, Dr. Esselman. It was his sad duty, he told them, to inform them the aged general had passed away just a short time before at about six o'clock. When their coach arrived at the Hermitage and Sam was admitted, with Margaret by his side and Sam, Jr., in his arms, they were shown into the room where Jackson lay. For several moments Houston looked down at the calm face of perhaps the only human being to whose judgment he deferred and to which he postponed his own.[11] He knelt and, sobbing, laid his head upon his friend's breast. Drawing his son to his side, he said: "My son, try to remember that you have looked upon the face of Andrew Jackson." [12] In the Hermitage at midnight, Sam wrote a letter to Polk informing him of the passing of Jackson.

The Houstons stayed in Tennessee for several weeks as guests of Emily Donelson, whose home, Tulip Grove, was across the road from the Hermitage. Emily's husband Andrew was still in Texas trying to get Anson Jones to call Congress into session. While at Tulip Grove, the Houstons visited various friends and relatives and were entertained extensively with barbecues and other social events. In August, while Margaret was indisposed, Houston went by himself to Maryville, his old home town. On the fourteenth of the month he was guest of honor at a barbecue in a beautiful grove near the town.[13] On September 1, the Houstons arrived by stage in Marion, Alabama, for a visit with Margaret's relatives.

In Mexico City, Foreign Minister Luís Cuevas signed the protocol presented to him by Elliot, who rushed back to Texas to present it to President Jones. Jones accepted the document, and in his diary of June 4 wrote:

Issued proclamation of Peace with Mexico. Same day received

297

proposals of peace from the Comanche Chief Santa Anna, the last enemy which Texas had. Accepted them. Now my country for the first time in ten years is actually *at peace with ALL the world.*[14]

News of the Mexican treaty was received with anger by the Texans, and latent anti-British feelings produced all sorts of rumors. Jones became a hated man overnight; there was talk of deposing him or lynching him, and he was burned in effigy. This mounting pressure forced him to forget his promise not to call Congress into session for ninety days, and he called for their meeting on June 16. Next, he called a convention to meet at Austin, the new capital, to consider annexation and other propositions concerning the status of the republic.

The Ninth Congress, rabidly anti-administration, voted down Mexico's offer of independence and on July 4 met in convention at eight o'clock in the morning, with Thomas Rusk as chairman. Sam Houston, delegate from Montgomery County, was absent as he was still on his trip to Tennessee and Alabama. Annexation to the United States was approved and on the following day the convention started writing the state constitution. On the second Monday in October 1845, the people of Texas went to the polls and the new constitution was ratified overwhelmingly.

Houston arrived shortly afterward without Margaret and little Sam. They had remained in Alabama. During her absence he wrote to one of his numerous Tennessee cousins, William Houston Letcher, giving his wife credit for reforming him. "[Margaret] . . . gets all the credit for my good actions, and I have to endure all the censure of my bad ones." [15]

While Houston was in Galveston awaiting the return of his family from Alabama, in December he accepted a gift of fine Durham cattle. To A. B. Allen, editor of *American Agriculturist,* he wrote a letter saying he would raise cattle, as he had originally gone to Texas to do, and that he had plans to cross Texas Longhorns with the Durhams.[16]

On December 29, 1845, Texas was admitted to the United States as the twenty-eighth state when Congress approved the Texas state constitution.

On February 19, 1846, the last president of the Republic of Texas, Anson Jones, and J. Pinckney Henderson, the governor-elect, took their places on a flag-draped platform in front of the old capitol at Austin. They were surrounded by joint committees of the two houses and marshaled by the United States Army. Surrounding them were legislators, other dignitaries, and private citizens. After President Jones gave a brief speech, the Lone Star flag of Texas was lowered into the waiting hands of Sam Houston, and the United States flag, with its stars and stripes gently waving in the breeze, was raised. After ten years as an independent nation, the Republic of Texas was no more.

Two days after the formal ceremonies signifying the entrance of Texas into the United States, the legislature met to elect the state's two new senators. It was a foregone conclusion that Houston would be elected; he received seventy votes. Thomas J. Rusk received sixty-nine votes and became Houston's colleague.

The former president had planned to take Margaret and the younger Sam with him to Washington but Margaret, none too enthusiastic about leaving Raven Hill, was half-heartedly packing when early in March she found she was pregnant. The general departed without her, and vague arrangements were made for Maggie, as he called her, to follow later.

On Saturday, March 28, Sam arrived in the nation's capital, now a thriving city of 40,000 whites, 8,000 free blacks, and 2,000 slaves. The next day he walked up Pennsylvania Avenue to pay a courtesy call on President Polk. The two old friends had a friendly chat, and Polk was gladdened when Sam assured him of his support. Polk needed all the support he could get, as he had come to the presidency with less than 40,000 votes more than his opponent and had little support in either house of Congress. At the moment he was embroiled with Congress in an argument over the status of Oregon, and there were also the questions of California and possible war with Mexico.

The following day the two new senators from Texas took their oaths and had to draw lots to determine the length of their terms of office, since the U.S. Constitution forbade senators from the same state to end their terms on the same day. Houston drew a ballot showing his term to expire on March 3, 1847; Rusk's term was to expire March 3, 1851.

As Houston took his seat in the Senate he presented an appearance that would have been a press agent's dream. Sometimes his tall, husky figure was draped in an Indian blanket while he wore a broad-brimmed white hat and a vest of tiger skin.[17] At other times he wore a military cap and a short military cloak of fine broadcloth with a blood-red lining.[18]

To Oliver Dyer, who had joined a company in New York to go

to Texas to fight Santa Anna but had never gotten there, the new senator was a hero. Now Dyer, a member of the shorthand staff of the United States Senate, was able to see his hero in person and was not disappointed:

> It was easy to believe in his heroism . . . a magnificent barbarian, somewhat tempered by civilization. He was of large frame, of stately carriage and dignified demeanor, and had a lionlike countenance capable of expressing the fiercest passions.[19]

Although it had been seventeen years since Houston last served in the Congress, there were still many familiar faces on the Washington scene. Junius Brutus Booth, who had given Sam so much moral support during the Stanbery trial, was still a frequent caller from his farm in Maryland. Serving with Houston in the Senate were the formidable Martin Van Buren, Thomas Hart Benton, Daniel Webster, and John C. Calhoun; in the House was the aged John Quincy Adams. All these men had well-known names when Houston first went to Congress years previously as a junior congressman from Tennessee, and all had served in high positions in the government. Now Houston was their equal with a national reputation equally as valid as their own. It would be interesting to know what went through the mind of his old antagonist, Calhoun, as he reflected upon the young first lieutenant he had humiliated so many years ago who had become the commanding general of an army victorious over Mexico, twice president of the Republic of Texas and who, when he entered the Senate, brought a nation with him.

And what of Houston himself as he looked around the senatorial chambers at his distinguished colleagues? With the self-confidence he showed throughout his life, did he think that perhaps his Star of Destiny would take him to the White House that had eluded the great Webster and Calhoun? Very likely he did. He was ambitious and considered himself well equipped to guide the destiny of the nation. Ashbel Smith, who certainly knew him about as well as anyone did, once wrote of Sam: "Political power was the only self-gratification the General wanted." [20] To his wife Houston once said of the United States: "Were I its *ruler* I could rule it well. . . . To govern well is a great science." [21]

For some time the Republic of Texas had been known as "Sam Houston's Texas," and when Charles Edwards Lester published his book *Sam Houston and His Republic* in 1846, the description gained greater popularity. Some of Houston's critics jeered at the designation, and none more loudly than Lamar, who was now a colonel in

300

the field opposing the Mexicans. Writing Burnet, he referred to Houston as a "demented monster" and a "bloated mass of iniquity" and continued:

> *His* republic! That is true, for the country literally belongs to him and the people [are] his slaves. I can regard Texas as very little more than *Big Drunk*'s big ranch.[22]

For years Great Britain and the United States by terms of a treaty had jointly occupied the territory west of the Rocky Mountains between the forty-ninth parallel of latitude and 54° 40′ north. During the 1840s organized American immigration to this area — the Oregon Territory — began and the "Oregon question" came to occupy the attention of Congress. By 1843 many voices in the United States were demanding that Great Britain relinquish all of its claims south of 54° 40′ and a popular slogan of the Democrats in the 1844 presidential election became "fifty-four forty or fight." Polk, a staunch advocate of 54° 40′, had asked Congress to grant him authority to notify England that the treaty providing for joint occupation of the Oregon Territory would be abrogated in a year, as was permissible under the treaty.

The president's request to Congress created an uproar as his critics denounced him for "shirking his duty and embarrasing the Congress" by referring the question of abrogation to them. At the same time, many newspapers and politicians, including Calhoun and Governor Henderson of Texas, thought war would result if notice of abrogation of the treaty was given, and they advocated the acceptance of the forty-ninth parallel as the boundary between Canada and the United States. As far as Calhoun was concerned, the threat of war with England was not the only point at issue. The question of slavery loomed large in his mind because he knew if Oregon ever became a member of the Union it would be as a free state and would give the Northern anti-slavery abolitionists two more votes against the South.

Two weeks after Houston had been sworn in as senator, he announced that on April 15 he would speak on the Oregon question. When he took the floor on that day, the galleries were packed as he defended Polk's request for abrogation. He mentioned that repeated overtures to England to negotiate a boundary had failed and that it would be "idle to anticipate an agreeable termination to our negotiations with England upon the subject of Oregon, unless it is brought about by giving this notice." [23] In his opinion,

> If the President had not assumed a claim to the whole of Oregon — if he had not declared that our right to it was unquestionable — that it belonged to us . . . certainly he would have fallen far short of the discharge of his duty. The question had been mooted and canvassed before the American people. . . . The popular voice was conclusive upon this subject.[24]

Houston ended his remarks by stating

> I will vote in favor of the notice, because I believe it necessary to enable the Executive to secure harmony in our foreign relations. If peace is to be preserved, I believe this is the measure to insure it. If war springs from it, it will be because it was inevitable in any event.[25]

When a vote was taken on the issue, the treaty abrogation request was approved 40 to 14. The British were not desirous of war, and before they received official notice of abrogation their foreign minister forwarded a new treaty to Polk suggesting the forty-ninth parallel as the Oregon boundary to the Pacific, with all of Vancouver Island becoming British territory. Polk submitted the treaty to the Senate, where it was passed and then signed on June 15, 1846.

In November 1845, Polk had appointed Congressman John Slidell to negotiate with the Mexican president, José Joaquin Herrera, various issues between the two governments. Among the matters to be discussed were $2 million in claims against Mexico by American citizens who had been injured and their property damaged by the frequent Mexican revolutions; the purchase of California; the recognition of the American annexation of Texas; and the issue of the Texas boundary. If Mexico would pay the American claims, Slidell was authorized to accept the Nueces River as the boundary between Texas and Mexico. However, if Mexico would accept the Rio Grande as the boundary, America would waive the amount claimed against Mexico and in addition the United States would pay $5 million for New Mexico, $5 million for title to northern California, and as much as $25 million for all of California.[26]

Herrera was on his last legs as president, as Mexico was once again in a surge of frenzy because of the question of Texas's admission to the Union. When in December Slidell arrived at Mexico

City, Herrera refused to grant him an audience. Slidell then returned home. On December 29, 1845, the same day Polk signed the act admitting Texas to the Union, Gen. Mariano Paredes y Arillaga entered Mexico City and overthrew Herrera without firing a shot.[27] The new centralist leaders immediately made known their intent to make war on the United States. Polk once more sent Slidell to Mexico City to negotiate with the new *junta*, but Paredes y Arillaga, as had his predecessor, refused to negotiate.

On July 23, 1845, under the American pledge to protect Texas, the short, stocky Brigadier General Zachary Taylor, known as "Old Rough and Ready," had sailed for Corpus Christi with his third regiment. Because the Mexican public was being bombarded with anti-American propaganda and its army was mobilized for action, Polk decided he must take precautions in the face of Mexico's warlike threats and ordered Taylor to take up a position on the northern bank of the Rio Grande. On March 23, 1846, shortly before Houston entered the Senate, Taylor occupied Point Isabel, across from Matamoros, with 4,000 troops and started construction of a post known as Fort Brown.

Gen. Francisco Mexia, a twenty-four-year-old political appointee, was the commander of the Mexican troops at Matamoros opposing Taylor. When Mexia received orders from his general to attack Taylor, Mexia ignored them. The angry Paredes y Arillaga replaced him with Gen. Pedro de Ampudia, who also dragged his feet when it came to starting hostilities but did order Taylor to withdraw northward. Taylor then had U.S. warships off Point Isabel to blockade the mouth of the Rio Grande. On April 23, Paredes y Arillaga declared "defensive" war against the United States and the next day Ampudia was succeeded by Gen. Mariano Arista. A skirmish took place between some Mexican cavalry and a detachment of sixty-three American cavalry under the command of Capt. Seth B. Thornton. In the fighting, Captain Thornton and fifteen other Americans were killed and many others were wounded.

Polk received news from Taylor about the brief skirmish and defeat on Saturday, May 9, and the following Monday presented his war message to Congress. Declaring a state of hostilities existed, he asked for 50,000 volunteers and $10 million and closed his message with "American blood has been shed on American soil." Houston called twice at the White House and, according to Polk, approved administration policy and thought the war should be prosecuted vigorously.[28] A resolution declaring that war existed passed the House of Representatives, although some abolitionist

303

congressmen spoke bitterly against the occupation of "disputed territory" and some even accused Polk of starting the war. When the House resolution reached the Senate, Calhoun was in favor of delay as he did not think there was sufficient evidence that Mexico wanted war; besides, he contended, only Congress could declare war. Houston, a member of the Senate Military Affairs Committee, spoke very briefly on the subject, saying "the state of things requires prompt action — not discussion." On May 12, he spoke again and pointed out that war had existed for ten years between Mexico and Texas; that when the

> question of the annexation of Texas to the United States was agitated, that if that annexation took place the war would not only be continued against Texas, but war would be proclaimed also against the United States. . . . War, therefore . . . unquestionably existed between Mexico and the United States. . . . The United States was therefore placed precisely in the situation in which Texas had been for the last ten years, subject to the aggressions, incursions, inroads, attacks, and outrages of the Mexican forces, acting in obedience to the commands of the constitutional authorities of the Mexican government. . . ." [29]

The next day, with Calhoun abstaining, the Senate passed the war bill by 40 to 2.

Early on in the war Polk had offered Houston a field command with the rank of major general. Houston mulled over the offer and wrote Margaret for her views. From Raven Hill she replied: "Though your personal danger will be far greater than it has been on any previous occasion since our marriage, I will not express one word of opposition." [30] Eventually he rejected the offer, probably after remembering how he had been consistently hampered by the general council and President Burnet and his cabinet during the Texas revolution.

On May 8, on the north side of the Rio Grande at a pond known as Palo Alto, the armies of Taylor and Arista had come to grips. Although vastly outnumbered, the American volunteer infantrymen waited until the Mexicans were within fifty yards of them. Their deadly accurate fire, combined with the highly effective fire of the regular artillery, decimated the Mexicans. The armies encamped for the night, and when the sun rose the next day Taylor found his enemy had departed. A short time later the Americans and Mexicans once more fought at Resaca de la Palma and once more the effective use of artillery and fierce fighting of the infantry gave the battle to the Americans. Arista and his army fled south, abandoning mules, baggage, equipment, and supplies. Taylor's victorious army then marched on and demanded and received the surrender of Matamoros, where the Stars and Stripes were raised on May 18.[31] Taylor was then breveted a major general and named commander of the Army of the Rio Grande.

On May 28, Houston submitted a joint resolution to Congress, suggesting a vote of thanks be given to General Taylor and all the officers and men under his command, both of the army and navy, for their signal gallantry, humanity, and good conduct in achieving the victories on the frontier of Texas. He additionally suggested that President Polk be authorized and requested to have a sword procured, with appropriate devices thereon, to be presented to the general. The resolution passed but was amended to authorize a gold medal for Taylor instead of a sword.

Matamoros was proving an unhealthy place for the Americans due to the blistering heat and the lack of sanitary conditions. Taylor moved his troops upriver to Camargo, a small town whose sanitary conditions were even more primitive than those of Matamoros. The camp's water supply, which was used for drinking, was also used for bathing and the disposal of wastes. Because of the blistering heat, various diseases, and the filthy conditions of Matamoros and Camargo, around 1,500 Americans died. Taylor then decided to march into the interior of Mexico to Monterrey, arriving on September 20. He found the city heavily fortified under the command of General Ampudia, who had stockpiled ammunition and had placed cannon on the nearby hills in anticipation of Taylor's arrival.

The next day Taylor and his forces attacked, and for three days the battle raged until Texas Rangers, infantrymen, and other Americans stormed the hills, captured Ampudia's cannon, and turned it on the city as other Americans entered the town in house-to-house fighting. Late in the afternoon of the twenty-third, Ampudia asked for a truce and an armistice was granted.

When news of the victory reached Washington, the crowds went wild with enthusiasm and the Whigs started talking about running Taylor for the presidency. One who was not so enthusiastic, however, was Polk. Perhaps viewing Taylor as a possible opponent in the next election, he deplored the armistice and said Taylor violated his express orders. Suddenly, four-fifths of Taylor's army were withdrawn and sent to Gen. Winfield Scott. Taylor was left with 6,000 soldiers, mostly volunteers, and ordered to stay in Monterrey.

CHAPTER 30

Peace and Turbulence in a Second Term

The twenty-ninth session of Congress closed on August 10, and while making preparations for going home Houston, who had missed his wife and son terribly, wrote Nathaniel Levin:

> . . . I am most painfully anxious to see my dear Wife and my young Pioneer. I was always fond of home but I now place something like a true estimate upon the source of true happiness — Home.[1]

The two senators from Texas decided to return home together. While on the Mississippi their steamer ran aground, and the vessel *Josephine* stopped to give assistance. On board was Ashbel Smith, who was on his way to New York. The three friends enjoyed a long talk and Houston expressed some dissatisfaction with Polk, whom he had supported. To Smith he also confided that he had not drunk any "spirituous or vinous beverage" since he had left Texas. Rusk confirmed this and said if Houston continued his good behavior he might find himself a candidate for the White House.[2]

Sam arrived at Raven Hill to be greeted affectionately by Margaret, who was awaiting the birth of their second child. On September 6, 1846, Nancy Elizabeth Houston, named after her two grandmothers and always called "Nannie," was born. Within a week Margaret was out of bed. Sam was a proud father, loved children, and took great delight in playing with his young son and daughter and showing them off to the many visitors who called. During the rest of his vacation Sam relaxed, looked over his property, and he and Margaret had some happy times together, with the senator occasionally making a speech someplace. Finally, it was time to return to Washington, and on December 21, three weeks after Congress convened, Houston took his place in the Senate. Once more he was without Margaret or his family.

The war with Mexico was progressing. On the western front Col. Stephen Watts Kearney and his Army of the West swept through New Mexico with little difficulty and then went on to San Diego. John Drake Sloat, commander of the Pacific squadron of the U.S. Navy, occupied Monterrey and Yerba Buena (now San Francisco), California. In August 1846, California was declared a territory of the United States.

In Mexico, Taylor decided to defy Polk's orders to stay where he was and on November 16 captured Saltillo. The latest commander of the Mexican army was Santa Anna, once more president of Mexico after a return from exile in Cuba. He immediately rushed north with 20,000 troops to confront the heavily outnumbered Taylor. On February 22, 1847, at Buena Vista, somewhat southwest of Monterrey, the two armies began a fiercely fought two-day battle. The battle was a close one. On the night of February 23, Taylor's staff wanted him to retreat but the general held firm. That same night Santa Anna ordered a retreat and, displaying fast flight as he had in the Battle of San Jacinto, rushed south so quickly he left his wounded behind, ceding the victory to Taylor. Old Rough and Ready was again voted official thanks from Congress and another gold medal — plus much criticism from Polk. (Later in 1847 he returned to the United States to campaign for the presidency as a Whig.)

In February 1847, Polk asked the House to appropriate $3 million to enable him to negotiate a treaty with Mexico. In a Senate debate on February 19, Houston defended the president and vigorously disagreed with some members that Polk had virtually brought on the war single-handedly. In Houston's opinion the Rio Grande was the southern boundary of Texas, and he said Polk would have been negligent in his duty if he had not sent an army there.[3]

For some time Margaret had been staying at Grand Cane, the

home of her brother Vernal. Developing a series of breast pains that turned out to be caused by a tumor, her condition worsened so much that in late February Dr. Ashbel Smith, the family physician, had to remove the right breast. Adamantly refusing to drink whiskey as an anesthetic, the pious Margaret grimly clenched a silver coin between her teeth as the doctor removed the tumor.[4] Houston promptly wrote Smith complimenting him on his skill and thanking him for the kindness he had shown Margaret. To further express his gratitude, a few weeks later he presented the doctor with a fine stallion named Arabian John.

Congress adjourned on March 4, 1847, and Houston, anxious to see his wife and children, immediately hurried home without waiting for a special session that followed. During his stay at Grand Cane he whittled toys for Sam and Nannie and spent all the time he could with Margaret while she was recovering from her operation.

Margaret had never been very happy at Raven Hill, as she did not like being so far from Huntsville, so in the summer the general traded Raven Hill and some other property to Capt. Frank Hatch for the latter's cabin and 233 acres just outside of Huntsville. On June 12, he wrote Joseph Ellis: "I have traded for another place within two or three miles of Huntsville. It is a bang up place! What you say to a look at it?" [5] Houston had his man Joshua and some of his other servants expand the small cabin he had acquired from Hatch, and when completed the new dwelling, which he named the Wigwam,[6] was a substantial home. The two ground-floor rooms were divided by an open hallway, or dog-trot, and a porch was built across the front. Above the downstairs rooms was a second story with a slanted roof. Behind the house was a fenced yard for Margaret's flower garden, and in the yard on the side of the house were two buildings. One was used as Houston's law office and the other was the kitchen.

Before returning to Washington, on September 15 Houston wrote Sterling C. Robertson that he was willing to sell his horse, Proclamation, if he could get a fair price for him, and made an appointment to show Robertson the horse on the twenty-first.

In March 1847 the army under Gen. Winfield Scott had made an amphibious landing at Vera Cruz on the east coast of Mexico in the gulf. Those troops, joining American troops coming from the landward side, bombarded Vera Cruz for a few days and forced the city to surrender. Leaving a force behind to guard the newly captured city, Scott took 8,500 men and began a 250-mile march inland toward Mexico City. On April 18, 1847, his army defeated Santa Anna at Cerro Gordo; other victories quickly followed and Scott proceeded inland. A shrewd commander who realized it was to his advantage to maintain harmonious relations with the civilians instead of seizing their supplies, the general reaped the good will of the populace by purchasing his necessities and by keeping his troops from looting.

The battle for Mexico City began on August 20. After taking several defensive positions, Scott's troops entered the capital on September 14. The general, known to his troops as "Old Fuss and Feathers," was voted the thanks of Congress and one of its gold medals.

As Houston's senatorial term had expired, it was necessary for the state legislature to elect someone for the position. There was some opposition to Houston this time among various disgruntled politicians, but the pro-Houston forces held firm and on December 18 Sam was elected for a six-year term. He rode to Austin to be sworn in and then returned to Huntsville to spend Christmas with his family. One afternoon in Huntsville he addressed a rally to answer a series of resolutions proposed by Henry Clay, who advocated peace with Mexico without annexation of any territory. Daniel Webster was another bitter opponent of the Mexican-American War as being unjust and unnecessary, and he too opposed the acquisition of new territory. To answer his colleagues at the rally in Huntsville, Houston proposed a series of resolutions. It was his contention the war had been brought on by Mexico and that

> the doctrine of "no territory" is the doctrine of "no indemnity," and if sanctioned, would be a public acknowledgment that our country was wrong, and that the war declared by Congress was unjust and should be abandoned, an admission unfounded in fact and degrading to our national character.[7]

Inasmuch as the issue of slavery was a constant problem between the North and the South and in the halls of Congress, in one resolution Houston gave the views of the South and of himself on that subject:

> . . . on the question of domestic slavery, we abide by the compromise of the federal constitution; that no state has any right to interfere with the domestic institutions of a sister state; and that all interference on this subject by Congress or individuals, is unfor-

tunate for the peace of the Union, and still more unfortunate for the happiness of the slave.[8]

The resolutions were unanimously adopted by his Huntsville audience, and shortly afterward Houston left for Washington. Once more Margaret was left behind — and once more she was pregnant.

When Houston arrived in Washington for the first session of the Thirtieth Congress, among the new faces in the Senate were Stephen Douglas of Illinois and Jefferson Davis of Mississippi, fresh from Taylor's victorious army at Buena Vista. In the House was the young, tall, unbewhiskered Abraham Lincoln, serving his first and only term as a congressman from Illinois.

Fighting in the Mexican-American War was now over, but difficult peace negotiations were under way. Nicholas P. Trisk, chief clerk under Secretary of State Buchanan, was the American negotiator, and on February 2, 1848, at a suburb of Mexico City, the Treaty of Guadalupe Hidalgo was signed. By its terms the Rio Grande was declared to be the southern boundary of Texas and regions north of a line from El Paso in West Texas to the Pacific Ocean, including California, were ceded to the United States. The United States paid Mexico $15 million and agreed to assume all the claims of American citizens against Mexico.

Although the territory ceded by Mexico was more than one-half of its land area, many senators were still not satisfied. Jefferson Davis wanted a boundary farther south than the Rio Grande[9] and Houston, always an imperialist, complained that the treaty did not take in enough territory. Other voices joined in the complaints, but on March 10, 1848, the Senate finally ratified the treaty by a vote of 38 to 14. On July 4, President Polk declared the treaty in effect. At last, the very unpopular war was over and American troops started home.

Houston might have been unhappy with the Treaty of Guadalupe Hidalgo but he was certainly pleased when the news arrived from home that on April 13, 1848, two days after her twenty-ninth birthday, Margaret had given birth to their third child, another daughter. The happy parents named her Margaret Lea, but always called her Maggie.

The year 1848 was a presidential election year and in the spring and early summer Houston — possibly with his eye on the

White House, and in an attempt to give Northerners an opportunity to look him over — was making speeches all over the East. Rusk wrote to his brother David that Sam had been traveling about electioneering for the Democratic nomination:

> He is so anxious for the presidency that he is almost crazy, but I fear won't get it. I have done all I conveniently could for him but I feel he will not succeed. It would be better for Texas if we could elect Houston.[10]

Later he wrote his brother that Houston had been absent two weeks and there was nothing in Washington but confusion and electioneering. Rusk was only one among many Texans supporting Sam for the presidency; in early 1848 Ashbel Smith wrote Houston encouraging him to oppose Taylor in the coming election.[11]

Despite the best efforts of Houston, Rusk, and others, Sam failed to receive the Democratic Party's nomination for president. The party chose Lewis Cass as their candidate, and although Sam campaigned for him vigorously, he was still politician enough to keep a wary eye out for Texas and for patronage. On June 23, he and Andrew B. Gray called on Secretary of State James Buchanan to present Texas's claims to control appointments of the officials to run the boundary line of the territory ceded by Mexico in the Treaty of Guadalupe Hidalgo. In the interview Houston made it plain to Buchanan that Texas wanted the civil appointments, and expected to get them.[12]

The Whigs had chosen wisely at their nominating convention. Zachary Taylor knew nothing about politics — but he was a war hero. When the voting was over in November, Old Rough and Ready was the winner. Taylor's election not only assured the Whig takeover of the administration in March 1849, but intensified sectional animosities pertaining to the slavery issue, the organization of California and New Mexico, and the Texas boundary.

During the first session of the Thirtieth Congress, the Senate was largely engaged during the summer by a series of debates concerning the newly acquired Oregon Territory. As usual, when new territory was acquired the question of slavery was one of the big issues dividing the North and the South. There were even threats of secession from the South. The Missouri Compromise of 1820 prohibited slavery north of 36° 30′ along the southern boundary of Kansas, and when a bill was introduced for the establishment of

311

the territorial government of Oregon and it prohibited slavery, the fiery Calhoun led an attack against it and promptly found himself challenged by Houston. When Sam spoke to the Senate on June 2 he was asked by Calhoun "if the people emigrating to Oregon would be permitted the enjoyment of their property as in the states where they presently resided." [13] Houston replied, "my object is to have protection extended to the people of Oregon." He pointed out that slavery was clearly prohibited north of 36° 30', and

> I would be the last man to wish to do anything to prejudice the interests of the South, but I do not think that on all occasions we are justified in agitating this mooted question.[14]

The debate dragged on and Houston spoke again in August, saying that he was ready to vote for the admission of Oregon as a state, even with the prohibition of slavery attached to it, as it could never affect the southern territories. He deplored the talk of secession and made it plain he wished no separation of the states. He was

> of the South and ready to defend the South, but first he was for the Union. The Union was his guiding star, and he would fix his eyes on that star to direct his course and would advise his friends of the North and of the South to pursue measures of conciliation.[15]

The bill, which included an endorsement of the Missouri Compromise, was voted for by Houston and Thomas Hart Benton and it passed on August 13, admitting Oregon as free soil territory. The next day, Congress adjourned.

The second session of the Thirtieth Congress was to convene December 4. Houston reached Washington two days in advance. The next day, he wrote Margaret that he had arrived after a hard journey. For seven days he had never had his clothes off. "I was exposed to cold, and my head has been aching for two days." [16] Perhaps one of the reasons for his headache, in addition to his cold, was that in Texas Anson Jones was writing letters to various publications claiming that he, not Houston, was the architect of annexation. He was also accusing Houston of conniving with England and France to the prejudice of Texas interests. In addition to these charges, Houston's opponents were lambasting him for his vote on the Oregon bill. The *Charleston Mercury* cried, "The South has been beaten by the South." [17] In Texas, politicians and newspaper editors were calling him a traitor. Shortly after Congress had adjourned the previous August, Calhoun delivered a very inflammatory speech in Charleston justifying his opposition to the Oregon bill and putting a large share of the blame for the bill's passage on the shoulders of Houston and Benton. During his speech he urged the South not to participate in the coming elections but to take the lead in organizing a Southern party to deliver an ultimatum to the North and, if necessary, follow that action by seceding from the Union.[18]

In January 1849, congressmen Joshua Giddings and Abraham Lincoln introduced a resolution in the House to restrict and ultimately abolish slavery in the District of Columbia. Calhoun called for a caucus of Southern legislators, and a committee of fifteen, including Rusk, was appointed to draw up what became known as the "Southern Address." The wording of the document was so hostile and Rusk was so opposed to the language in the address that he was dropped from the committee. The document was also severely criticized by Houston, Polk, and Benton. When the "Southern Address" passed, neither Houston, Rusk, nor Benton signed the document.

For some time Houston had been simmering over the criticism he received for his Oregon vote. To combat this criticism, on Texas Independence Day, March 2, 1849, he released "An Address to My Constituents." The address was a lengthy denunciation of Calhoun, and he accused the South Carolinian of trying to injure him in the good opinion not only of his immediate constituents, but of the people of the South as well. He wondered "upon what authority does Mr. Calhoun assume the character of guardian of the whole South" and then questioned whether Calhoun had ever really represented the South. He claimed Calhoun had "long cherished an ill-concealed design against the Union," and he denounced both the "mad fanaticism" of the North and the "mad ambition" of the South. Near the end he said:

> I would lay down my life to defend any one of the States from aggression, which endangered its peace or threatened its institutions. I could do no more for the Union, but I wish to do more; for the destruction of the Union would be the ruin of all the States.

He closed with the words of Jackson: "The Federal Union — it must be preserved." [19]

At the instigation of Calhoun and some of his supporters, young Senator Isaac P. Walker of Wisconsin had proposed an amendment to an appropriations bill. On the surface the amend-

313

ment was an innocent one providing for the extension of United States laws over all the territory ceded by Mexico after the recent war. The Senate adopted the amendment and Houston voted for it. As it was, Mexican law, which prohibited slavery, still prevailed in the new territory. When the powerful Daniel Webster carefully read the bill with his astute lawyer's eyes, he saw that federal law would override Mexican law and the door would be opened for slavery in the newly acquired territory. Webster was a staunch abolitionist. He swung into action, pointed this feature out to the Senate, and collided bitterly with Calhoun over the measure.

The Senate decided to reconsider the amendment and met in a session lasting from March 3 to early morning the next day. The all-night session was a stormy one with many members getting drunk; curses were exchanged and there was even fistfighting on the floor. When order was finally restored, Houston asked for an opportunity to change his vote. The Senate finally passed the measure, but it was eventually blocked in the House. Congress then adjourned Sunday morning, March 4, and Houston hurriedly packed his bags and left Washington for Margaret, his growing family, and the Wigwam.

CHAPTER 31

Amid the
North-South Chasm

When the Thirty-first Congress convened on December 3, 1849, an old and respected face was on hand. After a retirement of seven years, seventy-three-year-old Henry Clay of Kentucky was back in the Senate. On January 29, 1850, he made his influence felt when, in a two-day speech, the Great Compromiser presented a series of proposals offering solutions to the issues of California statehood, the Texas boundary, the government of the various territories, slave trade in the District of Columbia, and a more effective fugitive slave law. In effect, the proposals were a compromise between the North and the South and became known as the Compromise of 1850.

On February 8, Houston took to the Senate floor and spoke on Clay's proposals, making one of the lengthiest speeches of his career. The galleries were so full and the chamber so packed that women had to sit on stools between the senators' desks. In his oration, Houston covered a wide range of subjects including slavery, the Texas boundary, and the various issues dividing the North and South.

> The North contend that they have a right to interfere with the subject of slavery. . . . The South contend that the North has no such right — no right to interfere with slavery anywhere. . . .

315

He suggested that the Missouri Compromise line be extended to the Pacific coast, with slavery prohibited north of that line and territories south of it having the right to slavery if they desired. He closed by saying that "He who buildeth up and pulleth down nations will, in mercy, preserve and unite us, for a nation divided against itself cannot stand." [1] Eight years later Abraham Lincoln paraphrased this line with his famous "House Divided" speech.

Houston's stand on the Oregon question and his refusal to sign the Southern address had caused him to be the recipient of much bitter vituperation and abuse in Texas and in the South. His latest stand to bring North and South together brought further resentment against him among some of the Southerners, but it found a wide audience of approval in New England and New York.

Shortly after his speech, Houston made a hurried trip home, giving no explanation except to say there was an illness in the family. Besides, he added, nothing of importance was likely to occur in his absence.

Margaret did have a sprained ankle and was pregnant again, but otherwise there was no illness. The truth was that Margaret was engaged in some legal actions pertaining to her ward, Virginia Thorne, the adopted daughter of Margaret's late sister-in-law, Mary Lea. Virginia, who was fourteen, had eloped with the Houstons' hired man Thomas Gott, who was in his mid-twenties, and Margaret was charged with abusing the girl and tolerating suspected sexual behavior between Virginia and Thomas before they were married. There was a grand jury hearing and the charges were dismissed; later, a committee of Baptists looked into the sexual allegations and completely exonerated her. Henderson Yoakum, the Houstons' attorney in the case, made a memorandum in his papers that the whole affair had been instigated by Houston's enemies to discredit him.[2]

The general was on his way back to Washington when, on April 9, 1850, his fourth child and third daughter, Mary Willie, was born. By April 23 Houston had resumed his seat in the Senate and in a letter to his wife several days later mentioned he had had the pleasure of reading several letters from her which had arrived during his absence. He praised Sam's good reports, gave instructions on how to cure Nannie's cough, and expressed his sorrow over the death of his sister Eliza.

On March 4, 1850, Calhoun made his last appearance in the Senate to give his rebuttal to Clay and Houston on the Oregon question. So feeble that he could not stand for any period of time, he managed to sit upright in his seat while Senator James M. Mason read the speech Calhoun had prepared. In the last effort of the dying man he made it clear he was for no compromise at all and his speech further inflamed the differences between the North and South. It was his last hurrah, and on March 31 the South Carolinian was dead.

Three days after Calhoun's speech was read, Daniel Webster addressed the Senate with his famous "Seventh of March" speech in which he appealed to the North for tolerance and deplored the inflammatory attitude of the abolitionists. The speech did much to assure the passage of Clay's compromise proposals, but it ended forever Webster's hopes of attaining the presidency.

On July 9, 1850, Zachary Taylor died of typhoid and was succeeded by Millard Fillmore, who was in favor of the Clay compromises. The debate continued strenuously, but eventually each portion of Clay's compromise was passed by a decisive majority, with Houston voting for each measure. The Texas boundary bill passed by a vote of 30 to 20 and set the boundary at its current location. Texas did not receive as much of the territory as claimed, and when $10 million was received to pay off the state's public debt, it was charged the state was being bribed to give up its territorial claims. In a speech on July 30, Houston denied this accusation: "It is her boundary she asks. Not your millions." [3]

Rusk had also voted for the boundary bill, and in September he and Houston were both home expressing their reasons for their votes to their disappointed constituents. Although Houston had nothing to worry about as he had four more years in office, Rusk was in trouble. He managed to win reelection by the legislature nevertheless.

When the news came via telegraph that both houses of Congress had passed the boundary bill and that Governor Bell had signed it for Texas, Houston confided to Henderson Yoakum: "I may now retire then, for it is the consummation of what I have struggled to attain for eighteen years past." Yoakum knew his man better than that, and in his diary recorded a conversation he had had with Sam concerning the 1852 presidential race:

> He doubtless desires to occupy that high station and believes strongly in his destiny. He is not a man of great reading, but one of the best judges of human nature in the world.[4]

Houston was spending so much time on the speaking circuit that his colleague, Rusk, was complaining that he was having to do

317

all the work for the delegation. On George Washington's birthday celebration in 1851, Houston spoke to the ladies of the Episcopal church at Harrisburg, Pennsylvania, and then went to New York to speak to the Sons of Temperance, but he was soon back at his desk to oppose the creation of the rank of lieutenant general in the army.

For some time Sam had been taking leisurely strolls along the avenues of Washington, and these strolls frequently had led him to the E Street Baptist Church where, while wearing his Mexican serape and whittling toys, he listened to the sermons of the Reverend George Whitfield Samson. This is where he communed with his God. Apparently, the sermons struck a responsive chord because on Saturday, March 5, he wrote Margaret that on the following day he planned "to partake of the sacrament of our Lord's supper . . . I know I am a sinner . . . Pray for me, dearest." [5]

The general was back in Texas during the summer, and on September 4, from the Wigwam, he wrote James Kemp Holland. After expressing his disappointment that a planned visit by Holland had been cancelled due to the latter's illness, the eternal matchmaker in Houston took over. Always urging his bachelor friends to get married, he lost no opportunity to present his views to his friend:

> The young ladies to whom you allude, are all single, and as charming, and beautiful as ever! Had you only made me the visit I would, with the aid of Mrs. Houston, have sent you home married, I have no doubt, and a happier and better man than you now are. To be truly good, you ought to marry, and marry in Texas! [6]

The first session of the Thirty-second Congress convened on December 1, 1851, but Houston wasn't at his desk very long before he hit the road again. By December 29 he was in New York to be initiated into Tammany Hall as member No. 3322, and a few days later was in Hartford, Connecticut, giving a speech on one of his favorite topics — the North American Indians.

The Houston family continued to grow. On January 20, 1852, the fourth daughter, Antoinette Power, was born, and once more Sam and Margaret were apart. By late February he was home to see his newest daughter and to touch bases with some of his political friends, as on January 8 the Democratic state convention had

318

adopted a resolution nominating him as a "favorite son" candidate for the upcoming presidential nomination.

Houston was always writing letters or dropping hints to friends that he was considering retiring from politics and spending the rest of his days at home, but there is little doubt he secretly sought and desired the nomination for the presidency. Rusk, who endorsed him for the nomination, wrote his brother David that Sam was using strong efforts to get the nomination. His own opinion was that Lewis Cass was the most popular of those seeking the honor, but doubted if he would be able to get it.[7] Unlike some of his rivals, Houston was a nationally known figure, and as early as May 1851 Ashbel Smith had written to him,

> Without a shadow of a doubt public opinion at the North as well as the South regards you as decidedly the strongest candidate of the Democratic party; and many Whigs have expressed to me their opinion that you could be elected.[8]

Smith, of course, was a staunch friend of Houston and may be accused of being biased, but his opinion that Sam could win the presidency if he received the nomination was shared by many others. Houston was a proven vote-getter. In the spring of 1852, Congressman Andrew Johnson of Tennessee wrote:

> In respect to Houston, there is but one opinion with friends and foes — all agree that if he could get the nomination . . . he could be elected by a greater majority than any other person now spoken of in connection with the presidency, and that he is the only man in our ranks that can defeat General Scott if he is the candidate of the Whig Party.[9]

"Old Fuss and Feathers" Scott received the Whig nomination, but Sam never got the chance to defeat him. When the Democratic convention met in June, and balloting began after the adoption of the two-thirds rule, he made a poor showing. On the first ballot he received only eight votes to Cass's 116, and in the ensuing balloting the highest number of votes he received was fourteen. Balloting continued, and on the forty-ninth ballot the wholly obscure Senator Franklin Pierce of New Hampshire received the nomination and then went on to defeat Scott in November.

It is very probable Houston could have won the presidency if he had been the candidate opposing Scott. But there was something in the nature of this rebellious, proud man, even with all the confidence he customarily showed, that seemed to prevent him from making a concerted effort to win the nomination by his fellow politicians. Perhaps it was an innate fear of rejection by them, as he seemed to act as if he were a prospective bride waiting to be asked. And the Southern politicians at the convention, angry at him because of his stand on the Oregon issue and his refusal to sign the Southern address, were not asking him.

The old order was changing and the Senate was losing some of its most powerful and respected figures. On June 29, Henry Clay died at the age of seventy-five, and Houston was one of the members of the Senate to accompany the body back to Lexington.[10] Clay was followed in death on October 24 by the great Daniel Webster, and with Webster's passing the Senate had lost three of the mighty titans — Calhoun, Clay, and Webster — who had been influential and powerful in the government for years. All three had aspired to the presidency, and it had eluded all of them.

In a joint session on January 15, 1853, the Texas legislature reelected Houston by a substantial margin to another six years as senator, and on February 3 he was made a Knight Templar in Washington Commandry No. 1, Washington, D.C.

Always open to something new, on April 6 Houston introduced a resolution proposing that the Senate install a new mechanical method of counting votes, if the price did not exceed $1,500.[11]

In the spring he was back in Texas, and at Nacogdoches a group of ministers who knew of his membership in the Sons of Temperance asked him to use his influence in the legislature to enact a law forbidding the sale of liquor on Sunday. Houston told them he agreed with them in principle, but in foreseeing the vicious effects of the Volstead law passed by Congress almost seventy years later, he said,

> When a government like ours undertakes to declare certain acts of individuals unlawful, that a considerable portion thereof honestly believe in, is an abridgement of their inalienable rights, it cannot be enforced, and is calculated to lessen the respect for the laws of their country.[12]

From Huntsville Sam had been writing his former secretary, Washington D. Miller, complaining about a debt he had been unable to collect from a Colonel Ward. Houston had become quickly disenchanted with President Pierce since he highly disapproved of some of the cabinet appointments he had made, and in his letter to

Miller complaining about the unpaid debt, he said that neither he nor Rusk had been able to get any patronage from Pierce.

> Not an auditor, or permanent clerk at Washington, could we get appointed, out of the many hundreds in office! I did too much for Pierce, and he is jealous of me. IF GOD WILLS, I WILL MAKE HIM MORE SO.[13]

On September 13, he again wrote Miller concerning the unpaid debt and told his friend he had bought a house from Mr. Hines in Independence, the property consisting of 200 acres that were enclosed and 165 acres of untimbered land adjoining the town tract — all for $4,000 in short payments. He was planning to move to Independence by November 1. One reason for the move, he explained, was because he thought Independence had the best educational advantages in the state. The Houstons rented their Huntsville home to Professor and Mrs. L. J. Goree.

On October 25, a caravan led by General Houston and Nannie in a black buggy and followed by a coach and accompanying wagon with Margaret, children, nurses, and luggage aboard rolled into Independence, some fifty or sixty miles southwest of Huntsville.

The educational advantages of Independence, to which Houston referred, included Baylor University. The Reverend Dr. Rufus Burleson was president of the Baptist school, and from time to time Burleson and Houston would engage in philosophical discussions as they strolled. Once, Houston infuriated the preacher by insisting that birds brought divine revelations to the future. Houston was never bashful about expressing his opinions, and on one occasion, when Dr. Burleson continued an argument of a previous date in a sermon, Sam became so irritated he stood up, interrupted the sermon, and attempted to correct the clergyman.[14]

The Thirty-third Congress met in December 1853 with huge Democratic majorities in both the House and Senate. Immediately the North and South were at each other's throats.

The previous summer a presidential commission had successfully bargained with various Indian tribes in Kansas for them to cede over 13 million acres of land north and south of the Kansas River, with the understanding that once the treaties had been ratified reservations would be created for the Indians. White settlers, of course, were anxious to move into the region.

321

A bill to organize the Nebraska Territory had been introduced in the House, and an identical bill in the Senate. The Senate bill was referred to Senator Stephen A. Douglas's Committee on Territories, and it made no mention of the Missouri Compromise of 1850. When it was reported to the full Senate, it contained a section allowing the people of Nebraska to decide whether they would admit or refuse slaves. As finally modified, the bill called for a division of the area into two territories — Kansas and Nebraska — and the repeal of the Missouri Compromise.[15] The formal debate on the bill in the Senate opened on January 30, 1854.

All of the South was in favor of the Kansas-Nebraska Bill, and in Texas the measure was extremely popular among newspaper editors, powerful businessmen, and politicians. But not with Houston. He knew he was alone in the wilderness in opposing the views of his party, his state, and the South, and he had made known his intention to vote against the bill. A correspondent for the *Richmond Enquirer* was so upset over Houston's plan to cast a negative vote that he assailed him in his paper on February 6:

> What objects Mr. Houston has in view, and what excuses he may have to gratify them, I know not. Nothing can justify his treachery nor can anything save the traitor from the deep damnation which such treason may merit.[16]

Houston spoke in the Senate on both February 14 and 15, bitterly opposing the Kansas-Nebraska Bill. In his opinion the bill had the seeds of dissension that would eventually bring about disunion, and he predicted "if this bill passes, there will be a tremendous shock: it will convulse the country from Maine to the Rio Grande." He mentioned he had voted for the Missouri Compromise of 1850 and he now denounced the effort to repeal it because, he told his colleagues, "if you tear it up and scatter it to the winds, you will reap the whirlwind; you will lose the benefit of the compacts." [17] Once more he pleaded the cause of the Indians and the failure of the government to live up to its promises to them. He pointed out that Kansas did not have a single white settler and was entirely held and occupied by Indians, and that Nebraska was nearly all Indian territory.

On March 3, he took his case to the Senate again and pleaded against repeal of the Missouri Compromise and against passage of the Kansas-Nebraska Bill, stating that "Congress has no right to legislate upon the subject of slavery in any of our territories of the Union." [18]

322

Houston's words might as well have been uttered in that whirlwind he had mentioned, because when the Senate finally voted on the Kansas-Nebraska Bill it passed by 37 to 14. Sam, of course, held to his word and voted against it while Rusk voted for it. The Texas legislature then passed a resolution commending Rusk for his vote and disapproving the vote of Houston.

The passage of the bill by the Senate caused such a great outcry in the North that 3,050 Protestant preachers presented a petition of protest to that chamber. They were promptly denounced by Douglas, who viciously accused the clergymen of meddling in politics and said the memorial was an attempt to coerce Congress. When Douglas finished his attack on the preachers, Houston took the floor to answer him, claiming they had as much right as anyone else to petition Congress.

Regardless of the furor raised by the bill in the Senate, the dire warnings of Houston, and the petition of the ministers, when the bill reached the House the members followed the Senate and passed it on May 22 by a narrow vote of 113–110.

CHAPTER 32

A Vote Leads
to the End of a Career

Shortly after Houston spoke in defense of the preachers, he hurried home to Independence where Margaret was in her sixth pregnancy and feeling ill. His negative vote on the Kansas-Nebraska Bill and the repeal of the Missouri Compromise had led to vicious attacks by the press, politicians, and his enemies. He was being denounced as pandering to Northern fanaticism in his quest to secure the presidency and was accused of being an alien, a deserter, a traitor to the South, a demagogue — and worse. He could shrug off criticism from those sources, but what hurt most was that some of his longtime friends such as J. Pinckney Henderson would turn their heads and not speak to him when they met.

In explaining his vote to Dr. Burleson, he told the pastor, "While that is the most unpopular vote I ever gave, it was the wisest and the most patriotic." He also told Burleson: "Stephen A. Douglas introduced the repeal of the Missouri Compromise to catch the vote of the South. He is now preparing another bill, called 'squatter sovereignty,' to catch the North, and he hopes that the two will place him in the Presidential chair." Then he predicted a bleak future:

> The result of all this will be, in 1856, the Free Soil Party will run a candidate for president and the whole vote will be astounding.

324

In 1860, the Free Soil Party, uniting with the Abolitionists, will elect the president of the United States. Then will come the tocsin of war and clamor for secession . . . the South will secede. Each section . . . will rush madly into war, each anticipating an easy victory. But, alas! alas! Oh! what fields of blood, what scenes of horror, what mighty cities in smoke and ruins — it is brother murdering brother, it is Greek meeting Greek — rush on over my vision. . . . I see my beloved South go down in the unequal contest in a sea of blood and smoking ruin. I see the proud neck of the South under the slimy heel of the North. I see slavery abolished; military despotism established over the South.[1]

While home, Houston spoke at the Brenham Baptist Church and at the courthouse in Houston, defending his unpopular vote. Although his audience listened to him with courtesy at both places, they were somber and expressed their dissatisfaction by giving him very little applause. One viewer wrote to Rusk giving his shrewd opinion: "The people here are down on Old Sam for his Nebraska vote . . . but you know how they will cry out against him and then turn right around and vote for him." [2]

In spite of the reaction Houston's unpopular vote aroused, he still was supported by some of the press. On April 4, 1854, the *Texas State Gazette* carried an article expressing regret at Houston's vote but said there would be even more regret if he were to leave the Senate at that time, as Texas had vast interests in many questions likely to arise in Congress during the present session and Sam, with his great abilities and experience, would materially aid in securing them.

By late June, Houston returned to Washington, and on the fourth of July was busy making a speech in Reading, Pennsylvania. Back in the nation's capital he took time to defend himself against some of his enemies who were doing everything possible to blacken his reputation. Former Commodore E. W. Moore had placed on the desk of each senator two pamphlets, one of them being a scurrilous attack on Houston. Sam spoke in the Senate on July 12, refuting the charges and giving reasons why he had called Moore a pirate and why he had court-martialed him and dismissed him from the navy; in addition, he accused Moore of getting powers of attorney from widows or families of deceased veterans, receiving compensation due them, and then never turning the funds over to the widows or families.

Gen. Thomas Jefferson Green, of the ill-fated Mier expedition, had written a 484-page book full of vituperation against Houston and accusing him of being the "malicious, vindictive, cold-blooded author of the execution of the Mier prisoners." [3] A copy of the book had ended up on the shelves of the Library of Congress, and Houston was indignant about it — so indignant that he rose in Congress and on August 1 spoke about Green and his record in Texas and Mexico.

On June 21, 1854, Margaret gave birth to Andrew Jackson Houston. At age sixty-one, Sam finally had another son, but due to congressional duties he did not get home to see him until October 17. Only a week earlier, on the eleventh, his name had been placed in nomination for the 1856 presidency by the Democratic general committee of New Hampshire as "The People's Candidate."

During Sam's visit home, Margaret had become determined that he would be baptized. A four-day revival was held in November in Independence, and Margaret worked on her husband virtually night and day, pleading with him to be baptized. Houston went through much soul-searching but finally agreed, and on the bright, sunny morning of November 19, 1854, was immersed by Dr. Burleson into the cold waters of Rocky Creek. Houston later commented that his pocketbook was baptized, too, as he generously engaged to pay half the pastor's salary. Later on, he wrote the Reverend George Baines, forgiving the interest of $140 the preacher owed on a note that was due, stating, "This I am not loth to do as you have the luck to minister to congregations who think that you can afford to preach to them gratis." [4]

Around 1853 a new political party, whose formal name was the American Party, began to rise. It quickly became known as the Know-Nothing Party because its members, when questioned about the aims of the organization, always answered that they didn't know. Basically, the party discriminated against immigrants and Roman Catholics, and in an endeavor to keep foreign-born citizens from holding office, they advocated immigrants should be in the country twenty-one years and pass an intelligence test before gaining their citizenship. It was also part of their credo that the Pope and Roman Catholic priests were wielding far too much political influence among the Catholics. The Know-Nothings gained many adherents: in 1854 they elected 104 of the 234 congressmen in the House of Representatives, and in 1855 they elected governors and legislators in New York and four New England states. The party was generally successful throughout the South and West, but in their presidential convention of 1856, they straddled the slavery issue. By so doing they lost a great majority of their partisans in the North and South to the new Republican Party, which had been formed by disgruntled Whigs and Free Soilers who were opposed to the Kansas-Nebraska Bill. By 1860 the Know-Nothings had just about disappeared from the political scene.

It was probably his disappointment in not securing the Democratic nomination in 1852 that led to Houston's flirting with the Know-Nothings. A prominent characteristic of Houston was that he was the complete independent, the original nonconformist, in bondage to no man and no party, and unwilling to bend to other's wishes if he thought he was in the right. Once he thought he was in the right and set his course, no one on earth could change him, and he knew that when he cast a negative vote against the Kansas-Nebraska Bill he had ruined his chances of ever securing a nomination for the presidency.

By January Houston was in Washington for the first session of the Thirty-fourth Congress, and on January 29, 1855, he spoke to the Senate concerning an increase in the army and the government's Indian policy. He began by saying that when he discussed the Indians he knew he would command little sympathy from the Senate and not much from the country. He wondered why, when people were seeking to civilize and Christianize men on the banks of the Ganges or the Jordan, they didn't exert the same on behalf of the Indians. "Is not the soul of an American Indian, on the prairie, worth as much as the soul of a man on the Ganges, or in Jerusalem?" [5]

Like many of Houston's speeches, this was a lengthy one. When someone interrupted to ask him a question about the Know-Nothing Party, Houston's laughing reply was

> I know nothing and of them I care nothing, but if the principles which I see charged to them in many instances are the principles which they seek to carry out, I can say to gentlemen that I concur in many of them. [6]

When one of the senators accused him of catering for the presidency, he denied the charge by replying, "I would not cater for any office beneath Heaven . . . but I know one thing: if it were to be forced upon me, I should make a great many changes in some small matters." [7]

On February 15, Sam again clashed with Thomas Jefferson

Green, as the latter placed a printed card on the desk of each senator and refuted Houston's speech about him during the previous session and gave what Green considered further proof of Houston's duplicity. Houston answered that the Senate's time was too precious to be wasted on comments about Green's character. Shortly after that, the traveling Texan boarded a train to Boston to debate the issue of slavery with William Lloyd Garrison at Tremont Temple before the Anti-Slavery Society. Houston reminded his audience that at the time of the revolution all the colonies held slaves and regarded slavery as a rightful institution. He pointed out that hastening the end of slavery was not worth the dreadful strife that would result if politicians and agitators continued their clamor, and that time would solve the problem if the South were let alone to regulate its institutions. He closed by saying, "Let us not despair and break up the Union." [8]

On his way to Boston, Houston had stopped at Hartford to call upon the well-known poet Lydia Howard Sigourney and was presented with a book of her poems. Upon his return to Washington he wrote her on March 6, thanking her for the gift and apologizing that the press of business had prevented him from thanking her earlier, as well as his preparations to depart for home to "meet the embraces of my Dear Wife and bairns." [9]

It is unlikely Margaret and the "bairns" got to see much of the general during his visit home, as he was constantly on the move speaking all over the state about the Know-Nothings and the Kansas-Nebraska Bill. In his speeches there was the recurrent theme that antislavery forces had been whipped into agitation by the repeal of the Missouri Compromise, the failure of the Pierce administration, and the abandonment by the Democratic Party of the principles of Jefferson and Jackson.

On April 21, Sam attended the Democratic state convention at Huntsville. Prior to the meeting he spoke in opposition to the state plan for railroad construction. Houston was now sixty-two years old and suffering from recurrences of malaria; in addition, he limped and used a walking cane due to his bothersome wounded leg. Nevertheless, he physically impressed the reporter for the *Texas State Gazette*, who ended his article about the speech with "General Houston is now an old man in years, yet he still wears a fine appearance and promises to live many years yet." [10]

On May 11, Sam was in Nacogdoches and engaged in a friendly debate with Rusk on a variety of subjects. When discussing various railroad proposals, he took notice of the anger his stand on the Kansas-Nebraska Bill had created and drew a laugh from his audience when he commented:

> I do not expect to ride on a railroad in Texas. If I do not get rode on a rail, I shall come off well; and sometimes considering the attacks that are made upon me, and the circumstances by which I am surrounded, I have good reasons to expect the latter.[11]

In his speech, Houston mentioned he had been condemned for sustaining the Indians.

> The Indians have few friends, and I know the reason why. They cannot vote. If they could vote these men would soon make use of them and have them up the top of the pole.

Then once more he answered the attacks upon him of catering to the presidency.

> I have been accused of catering to the Presidency. Why need I want the Presidency? I have twice been President and although not on as large a theater as the [United States], yet the future will show that no President of the United States has ever had the opportunity of doing as much for his country, as I could have done for Texas.[12]

In a letter written from Independence on July 24, Houston gave his opinion concerning the "American Order," as he referred to the Know-Nothings.

> Owing to the heated state of the public mind, the influence of federal patronage and the desperate efforts which are making to smother the American mind, I expect to receive a full share of vituperation and abuse.[13]

He explained he regarded the movement as one growing out of a great crisis in the affairs of the nation, and the purpose of the organization was not to put down Catholics but to prevent Catholics from putting Protestants down. He wrote that from 1850 to 1854 abolitionism appeared to die away as the Missouri Compromise of 1850 had silenced agitation, but that President Pierce, in breaking his pledges to discourage the agitation of the slavery question in and out of Congress, had helped break down the Missouri Compromise, and had helped to build up a Free Soil and Abolition Party, which became the Republican Party. He also charged that an unusual number of convicts and paupers were thrown upon American shores from European prisons and poorhouses as a policy of foreign governments who could never bear the United States any good will.

The state elections were held August 2. On that day, before a large gathering at Washington-on-the Brazos, Houston made a speech reiterating many of the statements he had made in his letter from Independence. According to a reporter who was present, Sam's remarks were frequently applauded until he discussed his vote on the Nebraska Act, which was followed by a *"dead ominous* silence." [14]

When the voting results were in, most of the Know-Nothing candidates went down to defeat. Discussing Houston and his future, the *Clarksville Standard* accused Sam as being a man of expedients who was governed by policy instead of principle. It was the *Standard's* opinion "the General would find his influence in Texas on the wane, for that anti-Nebraska vote was the last feather that broke the camel's back." [15]

Ashbel Smith and Houston had been close friends for almost twenty years, but for the first time the two were on opposite sides politically as Smith, a staunch Democrat, highly disapproved of Sam's position on the Kansas-Nebraska Bill and his connection with the Know-Nothings. Yet, on the floor of the Texas House of Representatives, he rose to defend Houston from the charges of treason and cowardice that were being bandied about. Smith said:

> He bears three wounds in front received in fighting the battles of his country. Let those jest at scars who never felt a wound; the charges of cowardice comes with an ill grace from those who never faced an enemy. And as for treason . . . the charge is an outrage! [16]

When Houston heard of Smith's defense of him, he wrote the doctor on November 20 from Webberville, where he was still stumping the state, and told him "whatever our political differences may be, they will not with me disturb our personal regards," and asked Ashbel to meet with him at Hall's House in Austin when Houston arrived there the following week.[17]

The Know-Nothings were having a parade in Austin on November 23, to be followed by a mass barbecue in Houston's honor. When the former president arrived at the capitol a resolution was introduced to allow him the courtesy of sitting within the bar of the House. In an effort to heckle and insult him another resolution was proposed to allow former Commodore E. W. Moore to also sit within the bar. After much wrangling for three hours, the original resolution passed after Ashbel Smith accused the House of "trying to circumvent the will of the House by gagging it with much speaking." [18]

330

Houston's speech before the Know-Nothing celebrants was held that night in a grove of live oak trees on University Hill.[19] To his large, enthusiastic audience Houston discussed the Kansas-Nebraska Bill and predicted it would endanger the Union, destroy the Democratic Party, and prostrate the administration of Franklin Pierce. He said in all his political life his principles had not changed, and he had only two planks in his platform — the Constitution and the Union.

> I am a Jackson Democrat. I have been a Democrat all my life — I will die a Democrat — I can be nothing else, but as for the Democratic party it has more wings than the beast of Revelations.

He predicted that if the country split into two separate nations, war would be the inevitable result. When he got around to discussing the Know-Nothings, he told his listeners he adopted and admired the principles of the American Party, as it was the only party whose principles would maintain the perpetuity of the nation's free institutions.

The abuse against Houston that he had predicted came to pass. There was an organized campaign to force him to retire from the Senate. The *Clarksville Standard,* the *Austin City Gazette,* and the *Galveston News,* all his bitter opponents, constantly harped on his vote on the Kansas-Nebraska Bill as a reason for the legislature not to return him to the Senate.[20]

On November 26, three days after Houston's speech at the barbecue, the state legislature by a vote of 77 to 3 passed a resolution that stated "the Legislature approved the course of Thomas J. Rusk in voting for the Kansas-Nebraska Act and disapproves the course of Sam Houston, in voting against it." [21] Ashbel Smith was one of those voting for the resolution.

With that vote Houston's senatorial career was at an end, although his term did not expire until March 4, 1859. In an editorial on December 8, 1855, the *Dallas Herald* demanded that he resign at once, complaining that he had forfeited his position by misrepresenting his fellow citizens. Houston ignored the demand.

CHAPTER 33

Defeat in Texas

When Houston was home for the summer, the family vacationed at Cedar Point, on Galveston Bay, where the weather was cooler. His Huntsville property had become vacant as the Gorees moved to nearby Madisonville, and when the Houstons left Cedar Point in the fall they moved back to Huntsville and the Wigwam.

While making preparations to return to Washington for the next Congress, Houston wrote Ashbel Smith on December 8 concerning the widow of Capt. John E. Ross, whose steamboat *Yellow Stone* had enabled Houston and his men to cross the Brazos some days prior to the Battle of San Jacinto. Mrs. Ross had presented a claim against Texas for services the captain rendered but had never been paid. Houston enclosed a copy of an order he had given Captain Ross and requested Smith, who was a member of the Texas legislature in whose district Mrs. Ross lived, to see what he could do about having the widow's claim paid. Signing himself "Thine Truly, Sam Houston," he told Smith he was planning to leave for Washington around December 13.[1]

On his way to the capital, the senator stopped at Crockett and Nacogdoches, where he spoke against the Kansas-Nebraska Bill. His journey east was so delayed by extremely severe winter that by January 11 he had only reached Cincinnati, where he read in a newspaper

332

"the weather on Christmas day was the coldest ever known in Texas and great damage had been done to fruit trees by ice." [2]

The Know-Nothings convened in Philadelphia on February 22, 1856, to select their nominees for president and vice-president, and when the final balloting was over, Millard Fillmore, who had been the party's candidate for governor in 1854 and was in Europe at the time, received 179 votes; Houston received three. Former President Jackson's nephew, Andrew J. Donelson, received the nomination for vice-president. When news of the nominations reached Washington, Rusk wrote his brother David that "Houston is disappointed and I think will refuse to support the ticket." [3]

If Houston was disappointed he showed no evidence of it as he wrote Mrs. Ana S. Stephens of New York on March 22 that he was glad he was not nominated by such an incongruous body and that he had not authorized his name to go before the convention. He told Mrs. Stephens he could not endorse the platform and predicted the Know-Nothings would not carry any state, with the exception of Kentucky. He concluded:

> About the 23rd of April, I have to visit my Dear Wife Maggie & the brats, so you see, by Heaven's blessing I have abundant resources of happiness . . . And just think of the Addendas, no less than six little Houstons to dandle on my knees & kiss them and call them dear Children.[4]

During the first half of 1856, Houston's senatorial activities were largely routine, with most of his important business and speeches concerning the navy — a branch of the service he was interested in as he was a member of the Military Affairs Committee. During March there were many speeches or resolutions by Sam concerning the Naval Retiring Board, which had recommended that various officers be promoted, dropped from the navy, furloughed, or given indefinite leaves of absence. To Judge Peter W. Gray, who had written him requesting he use his influence to save his brother Edward from being dropped as a naval officer, Houston replied that the brother had been promoted and currently stood two hundred eighty-third among the lieutenants.

By May the senator was back in Texas, and the family stayed at Independence, where Houston was ill most of the month with a severe bronchial infection he had first contracted in Washington, and which for some reason was proving very difficult to throw off.

333

The new territory of Kansas was beginning to reap the whirlwind that Houston had predicted. Ever since the repeal of the Missouri Compromise, pro-slavery immigrants from the South and antislavery abolitionists from the North had entered the region, and there had been constant friction between the two factions. Some people contended the first shots of the Civil War were not fired at Fort Sumter but were fired five years earlier at Lawrence, Kansas, when, on May 21, 1856, a pro-slavery mob sacked the town, and two days later a retaliatory massacre of five men at Pottawatomie Creek led by John Brown and his five sons marked the beginning of guerrilla warfare.

When the Democrats met in Cincinnati to nominate their ticket of James C. Buchanan for president and John C. Breckinridge as his running mate, Houston was still in Texas but was soon back at his desk in Washington. The lawyer John Hancock had written a letter to Sam at Huntsville, the letter being mainly about politics, and on July 21 Sam answered him. Houston thanked Hancock for his "kind sentiments," and went on to criticize the present Democratic Party, as it was "a 'compound' of heterogeneous materials . . . dwindled down to mere sectionalism . . . but a faction that had lost the principle of cohesion and no longer boasted a uniform policy." He added that in his opinion the repeal of the Missouri Compromise had led to the insurrections in Kansas, and that it was his intention to support the American Party nominees of Fillmore and Donelson in the coming elections." [5]

The Senate had planned to adjourn on August 18, and on the fifteenth from his desk in the chamber Houston wrote his son Sam that he would be able to embrace his family in three days, and that it was a matter of great satisfaction to him to know that his children would be in circumstances to receive a good education, as his was defective.

The session extended beyond its original adjournment date, and on August 30 Houston addressed the Senate, once more singing the refrain that the American Party, as well as the Republican Party, had grown out of the repeal of the Missouri Compromise. Once home, he stumped for the Know-Nothings and on September 16 he and Rusk debated at Nacogdoches.

Ashbel Smith had written Houston he would like for the two of them to get together for a talk, and from Huntsville on October 20 Houston answered with the hope that the two could meet prior to his departure for Washington, as "there are many things that I wish to hear, such as you can tell me, and many that I will be

334

happy to relate to you." He commented upon the Democratic Party with these words:

> I am satisfied the modern Democracy . . . with the Pierce Dynesty, must go to the wall. I foresaw and foretold it when the Nebraska bill was on its passage. The bill became a law, and the country was thrown into political chaos. This was to be expected when "madness ruled the hour." I hope that Fremont will not be elected, but if unfortunately such should be our doom, I cannot perceive what worse he can do, than Pierce has done.[6]

In November, Buchanan and the Democrats carried Texas overwhelmingly and nationwide had a popular vote of more than 500,000 than the Republican standard bearer, John C. Fremont, with an electoral vote of 174 to 114. The American Party candidate, Fillmore, carried only one state, Maryland, and from then on there was a steady decline for the Know-Nothings.

After the elections, Rusk, who was terribly disheartened by the death of his wife Polly the previous April 23 and who was taking his son Tom and daughter Helen with him back to Washington, invited Sam to return with him for the opening of the second session of Congress. Houston declined the invitation on the grounds that Margaret was feeling ill and that he was suffering so much from his old San Jacinto wound that he was quite lame. "Otherwise," he said, "I am as hardy as a bear and as young as ever." [7]

The lame-duck session of Congress opened on December 1, and on the seventh Houston wrote Sam, Jr., giving his son fatherly advice and advising him to walk erect, be truthful and fearless, be just and fear not, and "seek God while you are young." He then quoted from Matthew 16:26:

> What will it profit a man to gain the whole world and lose his own soul; or what shall a man give in exchange for his soul?

He concluded: "Read the Scriptures!!!" [8]

The news from home was not uplifting, as Margaret had written complaining about not feeling well and reported that their lawyer-author friend Henderson Yoakum had died at his country home. On December 16, Houston answered her, expressing his sorrow at the passing of Yoakum and sympathizing with her for her indisposition. In her letters to Sam, Margaret was a chronic complainer about her health, and Houston was probably taking this into account when he told her, "I fondly hoped as you had more comforts than usual, you would enjoy more health than you had heretofore done." [9]

When Congress recessed for Christmas, Houston spent the holidays relaxing at the Metropolitan Hotel in New York. When Congress reassembled after the Christmas break, he spent most of his time taking care of Texas political affairs by answering his constituents' requests and making several speeches concerning naval desertions. On February 17, 1857, he spoke in favor of a bill increasing the pay of the military and doubling their rations, although, he complained, "I think our military system is all wrong."

The state of Tennessee had offered to give the federal government Jackson's home, the Hermitage, on condition the government use it as a military academy devoted especially to the cavalry. On his birthday and just one day before the adjournment of Congress, Sam spoke in opposition to the government accepting this gift. On the closing day of Congress he made short talks in favor of an appropriation bill for the distribution of seeds and for the enlarging and beautifying of the capitol grounds. Before leaving for home, he stayed in Washington a day or so to sign autographs.

Three days after Congress adjourned, the Supreme Court rendered its far-reaching Dred Scott decision which held that a slave did not become free when taken into free territory, that Congress could not bar slavery from a territory, and that blacks could not be citizens. With that decision the entire West was open to slavery, and the friction between the pro-slavery South and the abolitionist North became greater. The nation was one step closer to the Civil War.

On his way home, Houston honored some of his numerous speaking commitments and expressed his satisfaction with Buchanan's cabinet appointments. He talked about resigning from the Senate and disclaimed any interest in running for state office. That statement amused the anti-Houston watchers, who had heard his previous hints of resigning his senatorial seat, and they were quick to express their skepticism that the old warrior would quit his office before his term ran out.

The state Democratic convention met at Waco on May 4, 1857, and nominated Hardin R. Runnels, an ardent and radical secessionist, for governor. Eight days later Houston, after consulting with Margaret and receiving her encouragement, announced his candidacy for the same office. Perhaps he was still following his dream of becoming president and thought the governorship would give him a platform to achieve that aim — or perhaps he honestly

336

thought he could bring peace between the warring radical and conservative factions of the state Democratic Party. To Rusk he wrote that he had intended to retire from the Senate to private life but decided to run as his opponents were making the issue "Houston and anti-Houston." "So now the whip cracks," he said, "and the longest pole will bring down the persimmon. The people want excitement and I had as well give it as any one." [10]

To Ashbel Smith, whom he had told he would not run, he wrote that what had transpired at the convention had compelled him to run. "I must try, and if spared, I hope to regenerate the politics of the state and save the public money and the land, for public purposes and uses." [11]

Houston conducted a strenuous campaign. From May 27 through July 3, he covered twenty-four cities in East and Central Texas, speaking sixty-three times. It was strictly a one-man campaign as he had no money or organization behind him, and the majority of the state's newspapers opposed him. When the stage refused him transportation, a plow salesman named Ed Sharp came to his rescue and the two of them stumped the state in Sharp's bright crimson buggy with the words "Warwick's Patent Plow" emblazoned in huge gilt letters on either side. To save expenses the two slept at night under the stars.

Old Sam was true to his word and gave his fellow Texans plenty of excitement. The race was exceedingly vicious and bitter, with an abundance of name-calling on both sides. His opponents acknowledged that the current struggle was one for political existence, and when reports came in that Houston was showing great strength and arousing pro-Union sentiment in the eastern part of the state, the Democratic central executive committee denounced him as a "traitorknave" and Louis T. Wigfall, whom Houston contemptuously referred to as "Wiggletail," advocated tar-and-feathering Houston.[12]

Houston was no weakling when it came to defending himself against invective, or using it himself, as he had long ago proved. His former friends Francis R. Lubbock, J. Pinckney Henderson, and Judge William S. Oldham had been following him around the state and speaking in opposition to him. In a July speech at Austin he accused Henderson of forging his, Houston's, name to a deed, and that "Wiggletail," as a lawyer in South Carolina, swindled his clients and had fled to Texas to escape being put in the penitentiary. He accused Oldham of stealing bank books and burying them in an Arkansas River,[13] and he lambasted Lubbock as well.[14]

After listening to Houston speak in Waco, a spectator wrote to a friend,

> Old Sam spoke here on last Monday . . . he spoke nearly three hours. His speech was a compound of abuse and egotism — abusive without the merit of wit or sarcasm and egotistical without the sanction of historical truth, or the relish of his most ultra adherents. . . . It was characterized throughout from beginning to the end, by such epithets as "fellow thieves," "rascals," and "assassins." [15]

The Democrats had been putting tremendous pressure on Rusk to take an active part in the campaign against Houston but he refused, although he did state that he would vote for the Democratic candidates. Privately he had admitted that there was "little or no difference politically" between himself and Houston." [16]

The election was to be held on August 3. Houston closed his campaign in San Antonio on July 28 and returned home immediately to relax with his family and await the verdict of the citizens after they went to the polls. The following day, Rusk committed suicide. Houston was saddened when he heard the news and blamed Rusk's action on the Waco convention. Actually, politics had nothing to do with his friend's decision to take his own life. Rusk had been in a terrible fit of depression ever since his wife Polly died; he had been unable to adjust to life without her and had simply lost the will to live.

When the election results were in, for the first time in his political career the general went down in defeat. Runnels had beaten him by a vote of 32,552 to 28,678. The story of how he first heard the results of the election was later related by Jeff Hamilton, one of his slaves. According to Hamilton, Sam and Margaret were sitting on the porch of the Wigwam when a messenger ran up the walk with the news Runnels had won by a large majority. Sam said nothing, but quietly walked into the bedroom and closed the door behind him. When, after a long absence, he rejoined Margaret on the porch, his first remark was: "Margaret, wait until 1859." [17]

By August 22 Houston had recovered from his defeat sufficiently enough to write Ashbel Smith: "The fuss is over, and the sun yet shines as ever. What next?" [18]

The opposition press took great glee in announcing Houston's political demise once the results of the election were in. On August 22, 1857, the *Texas State Gazette* blared, "He never again will crow on this side of Mason and Dixon's line," while on August 29 the

Dallas Herald claimed Houston would lose influence in Washington since a popular majority of 10,000 voters were against him.

In October, Houston was a delegate to the four-day session of the Baptist Convention, which was held at Huntsville, and served as chairman of the Committee on Indian Missions. When the legislature convened in November, a successor to Rusk had to be elected, and J. Pinckney Henderson, Rusk's former law partner, easily defeated his opponent. In an effort to humiliate Houston and force him to resign his seat, the legislators unanimously elected Judge John Hemphill to succeed him. The lame-duck Senator Houston refused to resign his seat, and before leaving home in November for the opening of the thirty-fifth session of Congress he once more renewed the note of the Reverend Baines without interest. Sam spent another lonely Christmas apart from Margaret and their family, and once more Margaret was pregnant.

CHAPTER 34

Severance From
American Government

When the first session of the Thirty-fifth Congress assembled, Houston was on hand to greet old friends and colleagues. Francis P. Blair, Jr., noticed that Houston was wearing a beautiful waistcoat and, not recognizing the type of skin, asked whether it was a wildcat, a panther, or a tiger coat. Houston replied, "Neither, but a leopard's — which I have chosen to wear next my bosom because the scripture says a leopard cannot change his spots." [1]

On January 19, 1858, Houston announced to the Senate the death of Rusk and explained that his delay in making the announcement was caused by his desire to wait for the newly elected Henderson to arrive in Washington. He decided to wait no longer, he said, as Henderson was ill and his condition was such that he might not even be able to arrive for the first session. In Houston's eulogy he outlined Rusk's career and mentioned his high conservative principles and his fame, which was not sectional but national. Houston said Rusk as a statesman was wise, conservative, and patriotic, and he closed by offering a resolution that the Senate go into mourning by wearing crepe on the left arm for thirty days.

In February, Sam wrote Margaret he was sending her some calico and chintz to make dresses for herself and the girls. He was sending them as far as Galveston by express and hoped to put a set of hoops in the box. The senator told his wife that political matters

340

had come to a stand and there was going to be an investigation in both the House and Senate on the conduct of Kansas officials. "This is the offspring of the repeal of the Missouri Compromise. So, my Dear, facts vindicate the course taken by me!" He followed that letter by writing her again on Valentine's Day, addressing her as "My Dear Love," and said:

> This morning being the Sabbath, the earth is mantled in white, as we have snow on the ground. The Sleigh Bells are tinkling cheerfully in the street, or avenue, and the poor horses are smoking from fatigue. I did not go to Church today for on yesterday I was quite unwell, as you will see from my last letter. . . .
> I look with boundless desire to be with you. . . . Here I am beset by a thousand absurities and foolings. . . . I would rather, My Dear, be thinking about you and home, than to suffer the infliction of nonsense.[2]

For some years conditions in Mexico had been extremely unstable, with wars between the liberal faction of Benito Juárez and the conservative government of Gen. Miguel Miramón devastating the nation. The wrangling was compounded by the notorious bandit, Juan Nepomuceno Cortína, the leader of a large band of robbers that operated on both sides of the Rio Grande, ravaging the lower part of Texas, and then removing their spoils into Mexico to evade capture. Caught in the wars between Juárez and the central government and the machinations of the Cortína bandits, American citizens had been murdered, their property seized or destroyed, and in the process the American flag had been torn down and insulted.

To protect the rights of American citizens, on February 15, 1858, Houston offered a resolution that an efficient protectorate be established by the United States over Mexico, Nicaragua, Costa Rica, Guatemala, Honduras, and San Salvador, and the next day asked that his resolution be forwarded to the Committee on Foreign Relations. On April 20, he offered a substitute amendment to confine the protectorate to Mexico only, characterizing that nation as being little better than a national outlaw. Finding little support in the Senate for his resolution, Houston intimated that other parties might take matters into their own hands if the United States did not act, and when he persisted in asking the Senate to take up his resolution, he was voted down 32 to 16.

Two days later, Sam wrote Margaret that he was disappointed in not receiving any mail from her dated later than the third of the month, and he attributed the slowness of mail being caused by the recent high waters in Texas. He told Margaret he wanted to

> stay with [her] and let the world wag; for I cannot control the destiny of this country. Where I its *ruler*, I could rule it well. The great misfortune is that a nation obtains with those in power, that the world, or the people, require more governing than is necessary. To govern well is a great science, but no country is ever improved by too much governing. Govern wisely and as little as possible! [3]

Houston, who was constantly telling everyone how glad he would be to retire to private life, wrote Nat Young in Delaware to that effect, and stated that due to the recent election in Texas "the grapes are not sour," although many people thought so. He went on to tell his friend that he was delighted with the prospect of retirement, and that

> God had granted us six fine children, two boys and four girls, and there is another in the shuck for June, and for these I wish to be at home and render them all aid in my power.[4]

Later on he wrote his wife,

> I am sick, weary, and I may add disgusted, with all the developments around me. Family, flocks, and honest thrift are all I am now interested in.

On May 25, 1858, the seventh child and third son, William Rogers Houston, greeted the world at Huntsville. It was not until late June that his sixty-five-year-old father gazed upon him for the first time.

Houston's new senatorial colleague, James Pinckney Henderson, had died on June 4, and the next day Houston gave a eulogy for his former friend, briefly sketching Henderson's career in public service and referring to him as a bold, enterprising spirit; a man of indomitable will, of daring enterprise, and firm of purpose.[5] For his efforts, the *Texas State Gazette* lost no time in attacking him, referring to him as a hypocrite, calumniator, and slanderer who had no right to speak in praise of a man whom he had denounced and villified during the campaign of 1857.[6]

When Sam returned to Texas, the family left Huntsville and moved to Independence. Houston had incurred tremendous debts while campaigning for the governorship. Running his strictly one-man show on borrowed money and with no organization or finance

342

committee behind him, he had had to sell the Wigwam and his farm to satisfy his numerous creditors. Like Oliver Cromwell, Houston had his warts, but he always paid his debts.

For a man who was constantly telling his wife and friends that it was his desire to retire and live the life of a country squire and nestle in the bosom of his wife, bairns and brats, he showed little evidence of it. During the month of August he traveled widely and made five speeches. Some of his critics thought he was speaking in the hope the legislature would appoint him to fill the senatorial vacancy created by the death of Henderson, while others thought he was laying the groundwork to run for governor again in 1859. All of his speeches bore the same content and gave a review of his work in the last congressional session. Although in his letters to Margaret he frequently complained about the Buchanan administration, saying it was worse than Pierce's, he did not criticize the president in his talks. On the contrary, he said that he had sustained the leading measures of Buchanan's administration not only because he approved of them, but also because he thought he was obeying the wishes of his constituents, who had so largely contributed to Buchanan's election.

In a speech at Danville on September 11, at a barbecue given in his honor, Houston dwelt on his advocacy of the protectorate over Mexico and attributed the causes of his unpopularity in the South to be due to his unswerving adherence to and support of the Union. He referred to Stephen A. Douglas, the creator of the Kansas-Nebraska Bill, as the "Prince of humbugs," and said that the people were begining to awaken from their delusions upon the bill, now that its objectives were being better understood.

Although Houston strongly believed in the Union, at the same time he was a champion of states rights, and he told his audience each sovereign state should be allowed to pass its own municipal laws and to regulate its own domestic institutions. He denounced both the reopening of the African slave trade and the Southern League, claiming that adherents and defenders of the policy were seeking to achieve their aim by widening the breach between the North and the South. With his lifelong magnetism and charm with the ladies, the old warrior could always count on a large number of enthusiastic women among his audiences, and with his natural courtesy to them the wily old politician always concluded his remarks with glowing tributes to the women present.

The public was remembering some of Houston's predictions about the consequences of the Kansas-Nebraska Bill and beginning to see those predictions come true. His prestige was slowly beginning to rise, and the *Waco Democrat* carried an editorial declaring that if Houston's conduct in the next session of Congress was as satisfactory as in the last, his strength would be greatly augumented. An observer at Houston's Danville speech was so impressed he sent George W. Paschal's *Southern Intelligencer* a synopsis of the speech and closed by stating, "I think there is no doubt about the fact that sober second thought is slightly mollifying the bitterness of his bitterest enemies." [7]

During this time, Sam wrote Dr. B. F. Sharp of San Augustine inquiring about the effect of the Redlands upon asthmatic patients, as Margaret had suffered from asthma for years. He believed Margaret would recover her health if she resided there. He then purchased a new home at Cedar Point on Galveston Bay and wrote Ashbel Smith he was planning on going into the business of raising sheep and offered to buy Dr. Smith's entire flock of sheep at four dollars per head.[8]

If it had been Houston's intention that his summer speaking tour might influence the legislature into appointing him as Henderson's successor, the ploy did not work. The legislature elected Matthias Ward to fill the vacant seat. In late November, Sam, accompanied by John H. Reagan, left for Washington and his last session of Congress. Predictions in Texas were rampant that he would run for governor the next year, and Thomas M. Jack wrote from Galveston to his relative, Congressman Guy M. Bryan, "It seems to be understood that Genl. Houston will fight his battle o'er again next summer — and that he will give the Democracy some trouble." [9]

During the last few months of Houston's lame-duck session, he spoke frequently in the Senate. A personally generous man, he was always quick to take to the floor in favor of any bill proposed concerning a pension for the widow or family of a military man. Such was the case when, on December 23, he spoke eloquently in favor of a pension for Jane Turnbull, widow of a colonel who had died of a disease. Houston cared "not whether he fell by the javelin, the sword, or the cannon ball. When a man gives his life, his all to his country, he can do no more." [10]

Railroads were now slowly becoming a part of the American scene, and on January 12 and 13, 1859, Sam spoke on this subject, advocating a southern route for a railroad running to the Pacific coast. As usual when he spoke, he could not confine himself to just one topic, and he and Senator Alfred Iverson of Georgia engaged in a spirited discussion when he remarked,

> Let gentlemen of the North cease to agitate the subject of Southern institutions. . . . The South has no rights but what belong to the North; nor has the North any rights but what belong to the South.

Houston never stopped talking about how he believed in the Union, and this speech was no exception when he uttered this phrase:

> as a Union man, I have ever maintained my position, and I ever shall. I wish no prouder epitaph to make the board or slab that may lie on my tomb than this: "He loved his country, he was a patriot; he was devoted to the Union." [11]

The senator wrote frequently to Margaret, and on January 20 wrote telling her that frequently he was still immersed in business at midnight, and sometimes as late as 2:00 A.M. "Oh, how I do long to throw off the harness and submit myself to the rule of what is called, in olden phrase, 'petticoat Government.' " [12]

Still plugging for the construction of a railroad to the Pacific, on January 27 Houston told his colleagues that in his view such a railroad was indispensable, and on the last day of the month he spoke in opposition to an appropriation bill that forbid the establishment of an Indian reservation in Texas west of the Pecos River. In spite of his opposition, the amendment passed.

For years various articles and pamphlets had been published which were derogatory to Houston and his conduct during the long march culminating in the Battle of San Jacinto — he himself estimated that there were at least ten to fifteen. All the articles and pamphlets were written by various enemies and were usually of the same tenor, professing Houston to be an opium user, a drunkard, or coward in battle. This was a touchy subject with the general, and in 1857 the first issue of the *Texas Almanac,* published by the *Galveston News,* had raised his hackles when it published a biography of Gen. Thomas Rusk, giving him credit for the victory at San Jacinto and wrote, "It was the mission of Rusk to win laurels on that day, and for other men to wear them." [13]

The 1858 issue of the *Almanac* had carried an article written by Dr. N. D. Labadie so derogatory about the conduct of Houston's commissary general, Col. John Forbes, that Forbes had sued both the *News* and Labadie for slander. Houston was so incensed that he wrote the editor of the *Galveston Civilian* denouncing the article as being completely unfounded and being a "fearfully slanderous and libelous attack" upon the reputation of Forbes. In the same article, Dr. Labadie attacked Houston bitterly, bringing forth the familiar charge of "opium eater" and "coward," and claiming the Battle of San Jacinto was won "almost against the will of the Commander." [14]

On February 28, 1859, Houston addressed the Senate, saying that within a few days his political life would terminate and that, as he had posterity to inherit his good name, he wished to vindicate his character from the attacks that had been made upon him. To his listeners he gave a step-by-step version of his conduct in the Texas war once he had been elected commander-in-chief. His account was documented with letters from Rusk, Joseph L. Bennett, Philip Martin, and Ben McCulloch, all soldiers who had fought with him that sunny day in April so many years previously. "There is not one word of truth contained in all the calumnies of this book, or of others, except one," the old soldier said, "and that is, that the commander-in-chief never communicated his counsel to any one." Houston apologized for not preparing his speech better but explained it had been only within the past few days since he had contemplated addressing the Senate on the subject, and remarked, "This is the last occasion on which I ever expect that my voice will be heard in this Chamber; never again shall I address the President of this body." [15]

The second session of Congress closed on March 4, and the *Washington Evening Star* of March 11, 1859, carried this note:

> This distinguished man left Washington yesterday afternoon for his home in Texas. Up to the hour of his departure, his rooms were crowded by his friends calling to take leave of him. No other public man ever made more, or more sincere, friends here, nor was severance of a gentleman's connection with American public affairs ever more seriously regretted than in his case. [16]

Houston was now sixty-six years of age and had been a dominant figure in the Senate better than thirteen years. Due to the advent of the railroads he would now reach Texas in eight days, and he was a man whose nature was such that he never looked back. When he crossed the Sabine he was in Texas for good; he never again left the state.

CHAPTER 35

Leading Texas Again

If it was truly Houston's desire to retire from public life and devote himself to his family and the raising of sheep, events dictated otherwise. When he returned home politics was on every tongue and there were bitter disputes over states rights, slavery, war, and secession.

While the *Galveston Civilian* reported that Houston was satisfied to retire and had no thought of running for governor, on April 1 Houston's brother-in-law, Charles Power, wrote Ashbel Smith: "I think the Old Dragon will run again, that he can make the race this time; the reaction in his favor is wonderful." [1]

Public sentiment was beginning to turn in Houston's favor and his prestige was slowly on the rise. The *San Antonio Herald* described a "reactionary feeling in behalf of the Old Hero Patriot" and expressed the hope that the people

> are waking up, that the scales are dropping from their eyes, that their great error is coming boldly up to their view and that upon reflection they will remedy the injustice done him and will place him in that position due him for past services. [2]

A man from Waco wrote the *Dallas Herald,* no friend of Houston's, that a "mighty current" was flowing in Houston's favor and that even his enemies were admitting that he had redeemed himself.

347

The writer then urged Texans who respected talent to once more place the Old Chief where he might "continue to stay the tide of disunion, rebuke Sectionalism, war upon Black Republicanism, and, above all, fearlessly expose corruption in his places as long as he lives." [3]

Early in April, the *McKinney Messenger* supported Houston for governor on a platform of "the Constitution and the Union and devotion to these united with integrity and ability, the true test for office." [4]

The Democratic Convention was held May 2, 1859, at Houston, and from the start it was torn by dissension over the secession issue and the reopening of African slave trade. The radicals had their way, and when the fireworks were over the bewhiskered Governor Runnels was renominated by the party.

Houston listened to the entreaties of his friends, talked it over with Margaret, and made his decision. On June 3, from Independence, he wrote George W. Paschal he would run for governor and stated:

> The Constitution and the Union embrace the principles by which I will be governed if elected. They comprehend all the old Jackson National Democracy I ever professed, or officially practiced.[5]

In contrast to the campaign of 1857, the one Houston ran in 1859 was extremely low-key. As once more he had no organized party behind him and no financing, his entire campaign consisted of a couple of letters and one campaign speech. On July 2, he wrote to Ferdinand Flake, editor of the *Galveston Union*, and declared his opposition to all "isms," particularly the isms of nullification, secession, and disunion, and said for free government he would rely upon the Constitution and the Union.[6]

Sam was in Nacogdoches on July 9 purchasing sheep and cattle, and due to the urgings of some of the citizens gave a speech in which he classified himself as a "Democrat of the Old School and an Old Fogy in politics." He said he had wished to retire and had been opposed to allowing his name to go before the people as a candidate, but he had been called forth by the honest yeomenry of the country — men inured to toil — and not kid-gloved politicians. Having done so, however, he planned on doing no canvassing nor making any speeches.

Candidate Houston dryly reminded his audience that two years previously they had given him a "regular drubbing" as he had voted against the Kansas bill, but he reminded his listeners that many prominent congressmen and statesmen had since declared the South was deceived in the bill and it was a delusion, a snare, and a deception from the beginning. As far as national politics were concerned, Houston's talk was a repetition of things he had uttered dozens of times before. When he got around to discussing strictly state matters, he reminded the gathering he had consistently voted for the Pacific railroad to be run through Texas; that his introduction of resolutions to establish a protectorate over Mexico had been occasioned by the inability of the Mexicans to maintain a stable government for the past half century; and that Mexico was powerless to protect the rights of Texans and American citizens within her limits. To Houston, the protectorate would be self-supporting and the infusion of American energy would develop incalculable stores of wealth in the protectorate. On the subject of education, Houston said, he believed it to be the duty of the legislature to provide for the education of the masses:

> Make primitive education as free as possible, then build up your home colleges . . . let them be accessible to the young men of the country.

The general, in his courtly manner, played to the women in his audience when at his close he said: "It is always a gratification to me to behold my fair country women in assemblages like these." He admonished them to instill into their children virtue and patriotism, and to teach them to love their country and to labor for its good. He closed with a tribute:

> Woman is lovely to the sight,
>   As gentle as the dews of even,
> As Bright as mornings earliest light,
>   And spotless as the snows of heaven.[7]

The Houstons spent most of the spring and summer relaxing at their Cedar Point property, which now consisted of 4,000 acres. Margaret in particular loved the sea-air breezes blowing from Galveston Bay, as it seemed to help her asthma, and bathing the sickly Willie Rogers in the salt water seemed to improve his health.

Candidate Houston was back in Independence on July 23, where he answered a letter from the Messrs. McGowen, King, Eliot, and Allen clearing up a question they asked concerning his attitude on railroads. He explained that contrary to charges that he had opposed granting public land to railroad companies to assist road building, he had gone before the legislature in Austin and advocated granting twenty sections to the mile to the railroads.

On August 1, the voters went to the polls and Houston won by a comfortable margin over Runnels, who had beaten him only two years previously. The vote — 36,227 to 27,500 — was almost an exact reversal of the 1857 election, and to many observers Houston's victory was due mostly to his personal popularity.[8]

The heavily pro-slavery Democratic legislature lost no time in expressing its hostility and pettiness to the new governor-elect. There was controversy over whether the carpet of the House should be removed for the inaugural ball, and an appropriation bill for furniture for the executive mansion got stalled when one member questioned the need because "Houston was accustomed only to the wigwam." Houston's reaction was to ignore the slights and make his own inaugural arrangements, which included an inaugural address on the porch in front of the capitol.

On a sunny, windy December 21, 1859, Margaret sat on the pillared piazza of the capitol and watched her husband take the oath of office as governor, becoming the only man in America to be governor of two different states. As the correspondent for the *San Antonio Herald* later reported when Houston rose to make his address:

> The eagle-eyed, lion hearted patriot then arose, like one of the patriarchal family. Then burst forth the mighty heart of the people with a great throb; all former applause was weak with that which now made the old capitol building shake to its center. Long and continued was this spontaneous outburst of feeling, while the hero of San Jacinto — the People's choice for Governor, stood like a mighty Hercules in their midst.[9]

Houston assured his audience he would do everything he could to develop the state's resources, and that the state's situation demanded the construction of railroads on an extended scale. The new governor recommended a system of public education not confined to classes but disseminated throughout the whole community. He mentioned the weakness of the frontier defenses, as the entire Rio Grande boundary was in an exposed condition, and touched upon his resolution while senator to establish a protectorate over Mexico. In his concluding remarks, he reminded his listeners that when Texas united her destiny with that of the United

States she became a member not of the North nor of the South, but of the Union.[10]

The inaugural ball held that evening was a brilliant affair and was attended by citizens from all over the state. A large basket of the finest champagne was given as a prize to the couple judged to be the best-looking and the most graceful dancers, and by unanimous consent the prize was won by Alexander C. Hill and his dancing partner, Miss Roxanna Thompson.[11]

When the Houstons moved into the tall, yellow-brick governor's mansion with the Ionic columns, they settled into a quiet family life. Young Sam, now sixteen, was enrolled in Allen Military Academy at Bastrop, only one day's coach ride east of Austin, while the girls attended the school in Austin and at home were instructed in piano by their mother. Margaret, as usual, paid little attention to the political niceties. Due to the chilly reception the family had encountered on their arrival in Austin — and because she was expecting her eighth child in August — she was withdrawn from the public. Her personal correspondence indicates that she feared for their lives, but the governor's mansion remained unguarded.

While Houston had stood delivering his inaugural address in front of the obelisk that commemorated the Alamo's vanquished, the bandit Cortína and his men had been occupying Brownsville and thumbing their noses at the local authorities. Sam had hardly warmed his chair in the governor's office when, on December 28, he issued a proclamation in both English and Spanish ordering armed bands within the state to disperse, and finally a combined force of Texas Rangers and the United States Army attacked the camp of the outlaws near Rio Grande City. In the resulting battle about sixty of the six hundred robbers were killed. The band was completely routed, with Cortína making his escape to the Mexican state of Tamaulipas. This was only a temporary setback for the outlaw, and from time to time he and his men kept crossing the Rio Grande to make further forays against the Texans.[12]

To compound the state's other frontier troubles, the Indians were committing massacres upon the borders. To protect the frontier against the Indians and the bandits, Houston ordered several companies of Rangers to proceed there. On February 17, he wrote the secretary of the interior urging the department to make treaties with the Indians, with the payment of annuities to be made directly

351

through Texas, and not Arkansas, as was presently being done. In a separate letter to Buchanan he urged the same thing, estimating the treaty would not cost more than $15,000 and that an annuity of $12,000–$15,000 would be the sole cost to the United States.

He followed those letters up to both the secretary of war and to Buchanan, asking for federal troops to be sent to Texas for protection, and indicated that if Texas did not receive some help from the government, the state would take matters into its own hands.

> Texas can and will, if appealed to, in thirty days be able to muster into the field ten thousand men, who are anxious, embarrassed as her finances are, to make reclamation upon Mexico for all her wrongs.[13]

Eventually, the War Department sent Col. Robert E. Lee to take charge of the federal troops which supplemented the Rangers in guarding the Rio Grande against the Indians and the Mexican bandit bands of Cortína.

The governor's advocacy of establishing a protectorate over Mexico had fallen on deaf ears in the United States Senate but had aroused interest elsewhere. Due to the political instability in Mexico and the constant friction between the various factions there, France, Great Britain, and Spain were keeping a watchful eye on developments in that nation. Houston was approached by British agents with a scheme to finance an army of 12,000 for an invasion of Mexico, with himself at its head. The agents offered him "a fabulous sum" [14] and, as a further inducement, guaranteed a lifetime income for Margaret in case Sam should fall in battle. For more than a year the general had been considering an invasion of Mexico and had written Ashbel Smith he might go to take a look at the interior of the "Halls of Montezuma." [15] From Washington, in January 1859, he had written Margaret that he needed her advice on a particular matter, but would make no decision until he saw her: "*In confidence,* I tell you that matter relates to the 'Protectorate.' " [16]

Houston seriously considered the offer and discussed the situation with Margaret. Perhaps she discouraged the venture or it might have been due to his age, but in any event he finally turned the offer down.

Shortly after Houston was inaugurated as governor, the South Carolina legislature passed a resolution asserting the right of any state to secede from the Union, and forwarded the resolution to

Sam with an invitation for him to send delegates to a Southern convention. On January 21, 1860, the governor forwarded the resolution to the Texas legislature with his strong dissent, saying he could not see any advantage that could result to the slaveholding states in seceding from the Union. To bolster his case, he quoted from Washington, Jefferson, and Webster on preserving the Union, saying the Union was intended to be a perpetuity; should the South form a new confederacy, it would only split into smaller fragments eventually.

The year 1860 was a year for presidential nominations. In their convention, starting May 18 in Chicago, the Republicans selected as their candidate the comparatively obscure Abraham Lincoln from Springfield, Illinois. On January 20, a group of Unionists from Galveston had written Governor Houston, asking if he would permit his name to be presented as a presidential candidate at the Democratic convention scheduled to be held in Charleston on April 23. From Austin, after a two-month delay, Houston finally answered them. He pointed out that in the past the Democratic Party had been a national party, but now it was divided by factions. He deplored the convention system as it did not represent the will of the people, and said he would consent to have his name used in connection with the presidency only if the movement originated with the people themselves.

> I will not consent to have my name submitted to any Convention, nor would I accept a nomination, if it were tendered me, and procured by contrivance, trick or management.[17]

April 21 was the twenty-fourth anniversary of the Battle of San Jacinto, and on that date, at the site of the battle, various dignitaries, veterans of the battle, former soldiers of the republic, wives, families, and members of the public gathered. At the meeting, resolutions of loyalty to the Union were adopted, as well as a resolution that Sam Houston be accepted as the people's candidate for presidency "and all conservative men, of all parties, in all sections of the Union, be urged to support him." [18]

Two days later, the Democrats met at Charleston and attempted to have their convention, but from the very beginning there was dissension between the "regulars" and the "radicals" of the party. Eventually the entire Texas delegation, augmented by more than forty other dissatisfied delegates, walked out of the hall. The convention adjourned to reconvene in Baltimore on June 18 and nominated Stephen A. Douglas as their candidate. Those who

353

had bolted decided to have their own convention in Richmond on June 10, and the delegates chose John C. Breckenridge of Kentucky to carry their banner.

Previously, in an unused Presbyterian church in Baltimore, a new political group composed largely of discontented Whigs, Know-Nothings, and independents — calling themselves the Constitutional or National Union Party — had held a convention beginning May 9. Nominations commenced about noon the next day, and Houston's name was placed in nomination for president by Erastus Brooks, editor of the *New York Express*.

Other candidates nominated were the Whig senator John Bell of Tennessee and Edward Everett of Harvard University, known as the greatest public speaker of his era. On the first ballot Bell received sixty-eight and one-half votes to Houston's fifty-seven; on the second ballot Bell closed the Texan out by receiving one hundred twenty-five votes to Sam's sixty-nine. Everett was then selected as the vice-presidential candidate.

When Lincoln heard the results of the three conventions of the Democrats, shrewd man that he was, he must have chuckled with glee as he thought of Ceasar's famous maxim of "divide and conquer." With his opposition divided into three separate parties, he would have no trouble conquering in the coming November election.

In response to a letter from John H. Manley informing him of the San Jacinto Day resolutions, Houston replied on May 17 that the use of his name at the recent Baltimore convention had been unauthorized by him, and on May 24 he wrote Daniel D. Atchison and John W. Harris, editors of *The Standard*, that he would respond to the people of San Jacinto by consenting to let his name go before the country as the people's candidate and, if elected, the Constitution and the Union were the only principles by which he would govern.[19]

Disappointed with everyone nominated for president so far, a splinter group of Union men met in New York at Washington's statue in Union Square on May 29. A large crowd was attracted by the promise of fireworks, Shelton's Brass Band, and well-known speakers, and on a flag-draped platform bearing a portrait of Houston, the Texas governor was chosen as their presidential nominee. Sam made a few speeches around Texas, but on August 14 from Austin he wrote Col. A. Daly, "As to my having any wish to be President, I can say before high *Heaven,* I have not a single wish or desire to be placed in that office." [20]

It is highly possible Houston did not cast his vote in the election, as in the same letter to Daly he said he would not vote for Lincoln under any circumstances, nor could he vote for Bell. Neither could he support Douglas or Breckenridge, unless to save the country, and he could not see that the withdrawal of any two of the three could elect the third. Four days later, he wrote a letter addressed "To Friends in the United States" withdrawing his candidacy and explaining that four opponents of Lincoln would only guarantee the defeat of all, and if he remained in the field he would only prove a stumbling block in the way of those who desired harmony.[21]

On August 12, 1860, the Houstons' eighth child and fourth son, Temple Lea Houston, named after Margaret's Baptist preacher father, was brought kicking and squalling into the world. He was the first child born in the governor's mansion, and it was one of the rare times Houston was with Margaret when one of their children was born.

CHAPTER 36

"Texas is Lost"

On November 6, 1860, Republican Abraham Lincoln was elected the sixteenth president of the United States and garnered 1,866,352 votes. Among his three opponents, Douglas received 1,375,157; Breckenridge 845,763; and Bell finished last with 589,581. In electoral votes, Lincoln totaled 180 to a combined total of 123 for his opponents. In Texas, Breckenridge gathered 47,548 votes; Bell, 15,463; and Douglas, whose Kansas-Nebraska Bill had stirred up so much enthusiasm in the state, ran a poor last with 410. If anyone voted for Lincoln nobody bothered to count the votes.

The next day — even before the Texas results were known — Houston wrote young Sam at Allen Academy: "How the State will go, I can't say, but 'the Union must be preserved.' The fire eaters got their chunk put out." [1]

With the election of Lincoln the secessionist movement in the Southern states became irresistible; South Carolina called for a secession convention and was quickly followed by Georgia. A group of Democratic secessionists, headed by Ashbel Smith, went to Austin to try to persuade Houston to either call the legislature into session immediately or call a convention to take up the matter of secession. Houston stalled, hoping the emotionalism of the moment would pass, and on November 28 issued an invitation to all Southern governors to meet with him in Austin for a conference. Not a single governor accepted his appeal — or even acknowledged it.

On December 3, sixty prominent citizens met in the attorney general's office in Austin and called for a convention to be held on January 28, 1861, to discuss secession. Finally, Houston bowed to the pressure and on December 17 issued a proclamation calling the legislature into special session January 21.

The storm was quickly gathering. On December 20, South Carolina seceded from the Union, to be quickly followed by Mississippi, Florida, Alabama, Louisiana, and Georgia.

Governor Houston spoke to a large gathering on New Year's Day of 1861 in Waco and announced that he would yield to the demand for secession if the people voted for it in a fair election. If Texas did choose to secede, he said, he hoped they would not join the Confederacy but would instead "unfurl again the banner of the Lone Star to the breeze and re-enter upon a national career." [2] He then went on short speaking tours, trying to take the pulse of the public, and was greeted with hostility everywhere. In Austin, a woman drew a pistol on him, and several times his life was threatened. Crowds of unruly men would stand around at night and watch the lighted windows of the governor's mansion, and Margaret became so worried something would happen to Sam Jr., that he was removed from Allen Academy and sent on a geological expedition to Mexico with the state geologist.

When the legislature convened for its special session, the members promptly passed a resolution giving legal status to the forthcoming convention, which met in the chamber of the House of Representatives one week after the legislature. On the second day of the convention a resolution was passed in favor of Texas seceding from the Union, and it was agreed that an ordinance of secession was to be prepared and voted on at noon February 1. Houston assured one of the committees that he would abide by the results if the ordinance was submitted to the people and they voted in favor of it.

Oran M. Roberts, president of the convention, had extended the governor an invitation to attend the February 1 session. As Houston watched the proceedings in silence, he saw the secession ordinance pass by a vote of 167–7. The date of February 23 was set for the public to vote on the measure. If the public voted yes, then Texas would leave the Union on March 2 — Sam Houston's sixty-eighth birthday and the twenty-fifth anniversary of the Texas Declaration of Independence. When the voting in the convention was

357

over, Houston rose impassively from his chair and left the chamber without a word.

On February 23, four days after Jefferson Davis had been sworn in as president of the Confederate States of America at Montgomery, Alabama, the secessionists carried the day when Texas citizens voted to leave the Union by a vote of 46,129 to 14,697. Houston was sitting on the porch of the governor's mansion with his family when he heard the results. Sinking back in his rocking chair, he sighed heavily, turned to Margaret, and said: "Texas is lost." [3]

On March 4, the governor issued a proclamation that Texas had seceded from the Union, but it mentioned nothing about joining the Confederacy. The convention would not be denied and the following day adopted an ordinance uniting Texas with the confederate states. Houston, still fighting a rear-guard action to prevent Texas from joining the Confederacy, protested the legality of the ordinance and wrote a committee of the secession convention that once the convention had performed the functions assigned to it by the legislature, its powers were then exhausted. When the legislature reassembled on March 18, he stated, he proposed to recommend it to call a convention directly from the people, who would have authority to make various changes in the state constitution as may be required.[4]

Abraham Lincoln had been following events in Texas with great interest. George D. Giddings, an emissary of the president, called upon the governor with a secret letter from Lincoln. Houston glanced at the contents and called four of his trusted friends and supporters, all Unionists, into conference at the executive mansion. Included were James W. Throckmorton, who had been a member of the convention and one of the lonely seven who had voted against taking Texas out of the Union; George W. Paschal, head of the Union Party of Texas and editor of the *Southern Intelligencer;* Benjamin H. Epperson; and David B. Culberson. Lincoln's letter offered to make Houston a major general in the United States Army with authority to take over all government property in Texas and, if possible, to recruit up to 100,000 men to keep Texas in the Union. Lincoln also pledged, if his offer was accepted, to give Houston 50,000 federal troops and the full backing of the army, navy, and the government.[5] After reading the long letter, Houston polled his audience, asking for their advice. In military fashion and commencing with the youngest, Epperson spoke first. He was in favor of accepting the offer. Throckmorton spoke next and opposed it, as he thought secession was inevitable. Culberson and Paschal agreed with Throckmorton. The governor pondered a moment and then thanked them. "Gentlemen, I have asked your advice and will take it, but if I were ten years younger I would accept Mr. Lincoln's proposition." He then stepped to the burning fireplace and dropped the letter into it.[6]

The secessionists could not be stopped. By a vote of 109–2 on March 14, they passed a resolution that all state officials must take an oath of allegiance to the confederate states. State officials who were delegates to the convention took the oath the next day. That evening, George W. Chilton, who had been appointed to call upon Houston with the demand he present himself at noon on Saturday, March 16, 1861, to take the required oath, showed up at the executive mansion about eight o'clock. At the time Nannie, the Houstons' eldest daughter, was fifteen. She later described the events of the evening to her son, Temple Morrow Houston: After the evening meal had been cleared away her father read a chapter from the Bible, and the family, including the servants, said prayers. Houston bade his family goodnight and instructed Margaret that under no circumstances was he to be disturbed, or any visitors admitted to the mansion. He then went to his bedroom where he removed his coat, vest and shoes, and paced the night in his socks, wrestling with his conscience as to whether he should take the oath or not. When he finally went downstairs, he had made his decision.

"Margaret," he said, "I will never do it." [7]

When the governor arrived at the capitol at noon on that Saturday, instead of going to the lobby, his office, or the House chamber, he went directly to the basement. When R. P. Brownrigg, the convention's secretary, called roll of those who should take the oath of loyalty to the confederate government, Houston sat silent, whittling while his name was called four times. The only other official to refuse to take the required oath was Secretary of State Eber W. Cave. Presiding officer Roberts quickly called the convention into session, and the delegates unanimously passed an ordinance declaring the offices of governor and secretary of state vacant.

On the same day of his expulsion from office, Houston released a broadside "To the People of Texas!" giving his reasons for refusing to take the required oath. Denying the power of the convention to speak for Texas, he said:

359

I PROTEST IN THE NAME OF THE PEOPLE OF TEXAS AGAINST ALL
THE ACTS AND DOINGS OF THIS CONVENTION, AND I DECLARE
THEM NULL AND VOID! I solemnly protest against the act of its
members who are bound by no oath themselves, in declaring my
office vacant, because I refuse to appear before it and take the
oath prescribed.[8]

Lieutenant Governor Edward Clark, who had taken the oath,
was sworn in as governor on March 18. That same day Houston
submitted his final message to the legislature and blasted the
"high-handed, arbitrary and unconstitutional" acts of the convention, and reiterated that he refused to support annexation to the
Confederacy because it had not been submitted to the people. He
reminded the legislature that he still was the governor elected by
the people. Houston's message to the legislature did no good and he
was notified he must leave the governor's mansion within twenty-
four hours.

Friends came in to help the Houstons with their packing. Finished by the night of the nineteenth, Sam and Margaret were relaxing with their friends in the dim light of a single candle when suddenly there was a knock on the door. Houston opened the door to
find a large group of armed citizens. Their spokesman told him
they were there to prevent his expulsion from office, if he only gave
the word. Houston sighed deeply, declined the offer, and the group
went away. Some thirty years later, one of those present who had
helped the Houstons with their packing revealed what the general
said when he came back to his guests:

> My God, is it possible that all the people are gone mad? Is it pos-
> sible that my friends should be willing to inaugurate a war that
> would be infinitely more horrible than the one inaugurated by
> the secessionists? Do you know, my friends, that the civil war now
> being inaugurated will be as horrible as his Satanic Majesty
> could desire? And after condemning them for their folly and their
> crimes, would you be willing to deluge the capital of Texas with
> the blood of Texans, merely to keep one poor old man in a posi-
> tion for a few days longer . . .?[9]

The Houstons left the executive mansion within thirty-six
hours of their eviction notice, and as they headed for Independence
and retirement the flag of the Confederacy blew in the wind over
the capitol at the head of Congress Avenue. Houston's career as a
public servant was finally over.

For the only time in his life, the unconquerable spirit of the Man of Destiny seemed to have deserted him, as Houston's expulsion from the governorship seems to have broken his drive. He was sixty-eight now, with thinning white hair, and his once-powerful frame was thin. He was stooped and used a cane constantly now as he walked with a limp. The old warrior became reluctant to speak in public because he was averse to arousing the passions of the public, but in Brenham on March 31, 1861, he was persuaded to talk at the courthouse and explain his refusal to take the oath to the Confederacy. As he attempted to speak, the crowd became so vicious and hostile that Hugh McIntyre, an old friend, jumped upon a table, drew a Colt revolver, and vowed to shoot any man who threatened the former governor.

Eventually, the Houstons left Independence for their home at Cedar Point. When Texas entered the Civil War, Dr. Ashbel Smith became captain of Company C, Second Texas Infantry of the Confederate Army, and among his company of volunteers were two sons of Anson Jones, as well as Private Sam Houston, Jr. At dawn on April 7, 1862, during the Battle of Shiloh, young Sam was struck in the groin with a Minié ball and left on the field as dead. Eventually, he was found still alive by a Yankee chaplain who picked up Sam's bible, through which a bullet had passed. Glancing at the flyleaf, he read: "*Sam Houston, Jr., from his mother,* March 6, 1862." The chaplain had been one of those Protestant preachers whose petition to the Senate Houston had defended so many years previously. Noting a spark of life in the barely breathing form, he leaned over to the young man and asked:

"Are you related to General Sam Houston of Texas?"

"My father," young Sam weakly answered.

The stretcher-bearers were called for, and young Sam was given medical treatment and sent to a prisoner-of-war camp. He was later exchanged, although still in poor physical condition, and went home to his parents at Cedar Point. After a lengthy convalescence he rejoined the army, surviving the war as a lieutenant.

After the Battle of Shiloh, Texas was put under martial law by Gen. Louis Hebert, commander of the Department of Texas, and as abuses of power and atrocities took place the citizens began to see some of Houston's predictions come true. Conscription was enforced, and between 50,000 and 65,000 volunteers and conscripts were enlisted in the Confederate army.

In December 1862, the Houstons returned to Huntsville. The Wigwam had changed hands several times and Sam was unable to purchase it on credit; always a poor businessman, he had little ready cash.

Dr. Rufus W. Bailey, president of Austin College in Huntsville, had built a house as a wedding present for his son. Known as the "Steamboat House" due to its resemblance to a sternwheeler, the two-story house had a long, narrow piazza running the entire length of the upper floor, which was reached by a stairway from the outside. The Bailey son and his bride did not like the looks of the house and refused to live in it. As Dr. Bailey had died and the house was for rent, Sam and Margaret rented this picturesque building. It was Sam's last residence.

Federal forces had captured Galveston, and as the horrors of war were brought home to the Texans while reading various casualty lists, they began to squirm more and more under martial law. Sam's popularity began to rise again, and some newspapers even began to mention him as a possibility for governor in 1863. To put a stop to any speculation he might run again, on May 27 Houston wrote the editor of the *Huntsville Item* stating that for months past he had said that he would run under no circumstances. He closed by writing,

> A man of three score years and ten, as I am, ought, at least, be exempt from the charge of ambition, even if he should be charged with having loved his country but too well.[10]

Ambitious or not, perhaps the old general still had thoughts about Texas withdrawing from the war and establishing its own republic once again. In a conference one night with Maj. Eber W. Cave and Alexander W. Terrell, he asked them how they thought the people of Texas would feel about unfurling the Lone Star flag, calling the boys home, and saying "hands off" to both North and South. The reaction of Houston's friends was negative and shocked, and Houston dropped the matter.

The general was aging rapidly now; he was tired, losing weight, coughing unceasingly, and his various war wounds constantly ached. The wound made by the Indian arrow a half-century previously was still abscessed and drained blood.[11]

Weakening rapidly, Houston went to Sour Lake, near Grand Cane, where Margaret thought the mud baths might help him. After he returned home to the Steamboat House, in July he developed chills and a fever which turned into pneumonia, and although

Margaret watched over him constantly his condition did not improve. Ashbel Smith, now a lieutenant colonel and home on furlough from a wound received in the Battle of Shiloh, was called in to attend Sam. He gave him a thorough physical examination but there was nothing he could do. Houston's condition worsened, and at sunset on Sunday, July 26, 1863, as Margaret was reading the Bible to him, the old warrior's lips moved: "Texas . . . Texas . . . Margaret." The Man of Destiny's heart stopped beating. Still on his finger was the ring, with the inscription *Honor*, that his mother Elizabeth had given him a half-century ago when, as a young lad, he had gone to fight with Andrew Jackson.

Epilogue

Sam Houston was buried with a Masonic ceremony in the Oakwood Cemetery in Huntsville. The original plain marker has long since been replaced by one of Texas gray granite bearing a quotation from Andrew Jackson:

> The world will take care of Houston's fame!

Houston had drawn up his last will on April 2, 1863, decreeing that after his just debts were paid the entire remaining estate was bequeathed to his wife and their children, with Margaret to be the executrix. For his eldest son, Sam, Jr., he left the sword he wore in the Battle of San Jacinto, with the request it never be drawn but in defense of the Constitution, the laws, and the liberties of his country. The will specified that his sons should receive solid and useful educations, and that no portion of their time should be devoted to the study of abstract science. Houston desired them to possess a thorough knowledge of the English language, with a good knowledge of Latin, and that they be rendered a thorough knowledge of geography, history, and of the Holy Scriptures. He also wished his sons to be taught an utter contempt for novels and light reading, but particular attention was to be paid to their morals and character.[1]

An inventory and appraisal of the estate showed a value of $89,288, of which $16,748 was in various notes and drafts owed Houston. There were twelve slaves appraised at $10,530, a carriage and buggy, a rifle and brace of pocket pistols, together with five horses and four cows and calves, totaling $1,100. The balance, $60,910, was in various tracts of land.[2]

Ashbel Smith had written that Houston followed dreams all through life, and that money and the making of money bored him when his dreams intervened. It must have been true; there was little ready cash in the estate, the Houstons having lived largely on credit during their married life.

Due to the lack of cash, for some time Margaret was in dire financial circumstances. It was some time before she could purchase even a modest headstone for her husband. The price of land was severely depressed due to the war, but she still had to pay taxes on the many acres she owned. Margaret moved to Independence in November 1863, after the estate was probated and settled, and for a short time she and the children lived with her mother. After the new year she purchased a home of her own. Margaret's mother, the redoubtable Nancy Lea, died on February 17, 1864. In 1866 the Texas legislature finally voted to present Margaret with the balance of Houston's unpaid salary as governor — a little under $2,000.[3]

In September 1867 a yellow fever epidemic struck Texas, killing thousands of people. Eventually, Margaret was stricken with the illness and at age forty-eight, during the afternoon of December 2, 1867, she passed away. She lies buried at Independence, and beside her lies her faithful servant, "Aunt Eliza."

All the children grew to adulthood and married. Sam Jr., returned from the Civil War and became a physician, finally giving up that profession and turning to writing. Andrew Jackson Houston, named after his father's hero, "Old Hickory," was the last of the eight children to die. He was in his eighties, and shortly before his death in 1941 he had been appointed a United States senator by the Texas governor in order to fill a vacancy.

Notes

Due to their frequency of occurrence, the following sources are abbreviated throughout the notes section:

Charles Edwards Lester, *The Life of Sam Houston: The Only Authentic Memoir of Him Ever Published:* cited as *Memoir.*
Amelia W. Williams and Eugene C. Barker, eds., *The Writings of Sam Houston 1813–1863:* cited as *Writings.*

BOOK I

Chapter 1

1. Rev. Sam'l Rutherford Houston, D.D., *Brief Biographical Accounts of Many Members of the Houston Family,* 10.
2. The author in conversation with Charles Thompson, Timber Ridge, Virginia, November 13, 1983, and February 6, 1984.
3. The author in conversation with Dr. Homer T. Cornish, the pastor of Timber Ridge Presbyterian Church, November 13, 1983.
4. Donald Day and Harry Herbert Ullom, eds., *The Autobiography of Sam Houston,* 3.
5. Rev. Sam'l Houston, 24.
6. Day and Ullom, 4.
7. Stanley John Folmsbee, *Tennessee,* 84.
8. Rockbridge County, Virginia, Court Records, Will Book No. 3, 73–76.
9. Inventory of Rockbridge County Court, Virginia. Will Book No. 3, December 1807, 82–84.
10. Folmsbee, 117.
11. The Treaty of Hopewell, finalized on November 28, 1785, was the first treaty between Indian tribes and the new government of the United States. The text of the Hopewell Treaty with the Cherokees is in Charles J. Kappler's *Indian Affairs: Laws and Treaties,* 2:8–11.
12. Rev. Sam'l Houston, 24.
13. Rockbridge County, Virginia, Court Records, Will Book No. 3, 76.

Chapter 2

1. Charles Edwards Lester, *The Life of Sam Houston: The Only Authentic Memoir of Him Ever Published,* 259. Hereinafter cited as *Memoir.*
2. Thomas M. N. Lewis and Madeline Kneberg, *Hiwassee Island,* 18.

3. Grace Steele Woodward, *The Cherokees,* 123.

4. There is considerable discrepancy in the spelling of the American name of Sequoyah. As is true in so many cases of Indians with white blood, doubt exists as to his correct parentage. Some sources say his father was a white man named George Gist. Others state his father was named Nathanial Gist. Sequoyah himself usually used the name "Guess."

5. The *Cherokee Phoenix,* edited by Elias Boudinot, a mixed breed whose Indian name was Buck Oowatie.

6. There is a discrepancy about whether the Cherokee word "Colonneh" means the raven or the rover. Marquis James, in his Pulitzer Prize-winning book *The Raven,* states that it meant raven. Donald Braider, in *Solitary Star,* states the word means rover, and so do some other authors.

Many Cherokees the author has spoken with have never even heard of the word. Dr. Duane H. King, executive director of the Cherokee National Historical Society at Tsa-La-Gi, Tahlequah, Oklahoma, and a noted authority on Cherokee history and culture, emphatically states Colonneh means "raven." A full-blood Cherokee that the author personally knows also makes that assertion. Perhaps some parties associate "the Rover" with Houston because that was the name of the boat he departed on when he went into exile among the Cherokees after he resigned as governor of Tennessee.

7. Stanley John Folmsbee, *Tennessee,* 21.

8. Donald Day and Harry Herbert Ullom, eds., *The Autobiography of Sam Houston,* 5, 6.

9. Minutes of Blount County Court, Maryville, Tennessee, September 29, 1810.

10. Day and Ullom, 6.

11. George Creel, *Sam Houston, Collosus in Buckskin,* 10.

12. Day and Ullom, 8.

13. James, *The Raven,* 29.

Chapter 3

1. Marquis James, *Andrew Jackson, The Border Captain,* 185.

2. Donald Braider, *Solitary Star,* 31.

3. Donald Day and Harry Herbert Ullom, eds., *The Autobiography of Sam Houston,* 9.

4. *Memoir,* 27.

5. Day and Ullom, 9.

6. M. K. Wisehart, *Sam Houston: American Giant,* 651, 652. Taken from Houston's complete U.S. Army record as it appears in the *Historical Register and Dictionary of the United States Army* (1903).

7. *Memoir,* 303.

8. Marquis James, *The Raven,* 33.

9. Day and Ullom, 12.

10. James Mooney, *Historical Sketch of the Cherokees,* 93, 96.

Chapter 4

1. Amelia W. Williams and Eugene C. Barker, eds., *The Writings of Sam Houston,* 1:3. Hereinafter cited as *Writings.*

2. *Ibid.,* 6–7.

3. Official records of Cumberland Lodge No. 8, AF&AM, Nashville, Tennessee.

4. Thurman Wilkins, *Cherokee Tragedy*, 94.

5. *Ibid.*

6. Grant Foreman, *The Five Civilized Tribes*, 355.

7. Jack Gregory and Rennard Strickland, *Sam Houston with the Cherokees*, 19.

8. *Ibid.*, 20.

9. Tahlontusky was a half-brother to Chief John Jolly, and as is usual in these cases of the Indians, there are several versions of how to spell this name. Tahlontusky, Tahlonteskee, Toluntuskee, and Tahlohutusky are among the most prominent.

10. Donald Braider, *Solitary Star*, 451.

11. *Writings*, 1:8.

12. *Ibid.*

Chapter 5

1. Like Sam Houston, Andrew Jackson had little formal education, and his legal training was based on a short period of reading law in the office of a North Carolina lawyer. See page 131 of *Tennessee*, by Stanley John Folmsbee. Even Patrick Henry, one of the greatest of pleaders, knew only his Coke when he started. Trimble put Houston through the classics of the day, Blackstone's *Commentaries*, and *Coke on Littlejohn*.

2. George Creel, *Sam Houston, Colossus in Buckskin*, 26.

3. There is a discrepancy in the spelling of this last name. Both James, in *The Raven*, and Llerena Friend, in *Sam Houston: The Great Designer*, show the spelling as Isaac Galladay. Braider gives the name as Halladay, and Wisehart spells it Golladay. In his book *Wilson County*, Frank Burns spells it Golladay and states Golladay was in partnership with Michael Yerger under the firm name of Yerger & Golladay. Golladay was postmaster for thirty years.

4. The building stood until 1932. Today another building stands on the site, and a bronze plaque marks it as the original Houston law office. See page 25 of *Wilson County*, by Frank Burns.

5. After one becomes a Master Mason, one may continue further work in Masonry by joining either the York Rite or Scottish Rite, or both. The ritualistic work in the two bodies is different, and in the Scottish Rite leads up to and includes the thirty-second degree. The York Rite consists of the Chapter, Council, and Commandery (Knights Templar). The thirty-third degree is honorary, and is conferred on either York Rite or Scottish Rite Masons with distinguished careers in Masonry.

6. *Writings*, 1:19.

7. Donald Day and Harry Herbert Ullom, eds., *The Autobiography of Sam Houston*, 27.

8. James Parton, *Life of Andrew Jackson*, 3:57.

9. In 1876 Samuel J. Tilden, a Democrat, received 4,294,885 votes to the 4,033,850 received by Rutherford B. Hayes, his Republican opponent. The election returns from Florida, Louisiana, Oregon, and South Carolina were disputed, and Congress, in joint session on March 2, 1877, declared Hayes president.

10. *Writings*, 1:25. Letter to A. M. Hughes.

11. Proceedings of the Grand Lodge of Tennessee, October 1825, 155, 156.

12. *Ibid.*, 163, 164.

13. *Writings*, 1:75.

14. Jackson to Houston, February 15, 1826. Day and Ullom, *Autobiography of Sam Houston*, 33.

15. Marquis James, *The Raven*, 65.

16. Mrs. Dorothy Winton Apffel of Nashville, Tennessee, is the great-great-great-niece of General White and one of his many living descendants. In her letter to the author under date of January 8, 1985, she very kindly gave her family's version of the famous duel between Houston and White. According to the White family version, in addition to the Ewing affair, for some time there had been political differences between Houston and White inasmuch as the latter, who had been Andrew Jackson's adjutant general in the Creek and Seminole wars, did not support Jackson in his 1824 bid for the presidency. At the Nashville Inn, Houston continually made various remarks about not only White but others of Jackson's officers who did not support him in his race for the White House. Being the prominent person Houston was, his remarks always made the newspapers, and finally White wrote Houston a letter asking for an apology that could be printed in the paper. Instead of the apology, Houston challenged White to the duel and called for pistols as the weapons.

17. James, *The Raven*, 67.

18. Creel, 32.

19. Proceedings of the Grand Lodge of Tennessee, under date October 10, 1828, 226–227.

Chapter 6

1. There is considerable discrepancy among authors as to the height of Houston. Some authors, most notably Marquis James in *The Raven*, assert he was six feet six. Others state just as emphatically he was only six feet two. Bessie Rowland James in her book *Six Feet Six* states Houston was that height; however, she also remarks "actually Sam Houston was six feet three inches tall." (Page 55, *Six Feet Six*.)

Houston's army records show that he was only six feet two inches. I am inclined to go along with the army version for the following reason: in the more than one hundred years since the death of Houston, men and women have grown taller, heavier and stronger. Even with the better dietary habit and nutrition of today, outside of the basketball court, just how many six-feet-six men does one encounter?

2. A miniature painting of Houston, done while he was in his early thirties, shows him to have been an extraordinarily handsome young man.

3. *Writings*, 7:2.

4. Marquis James, *The Raven*, 70.

5. Eliza was born December 2, 1809.

6. *Writings*, 2:10.

7. Will T. Hale and Dixon L. Merritt, *A History of Tennessee and Tennesseans*, 2:379.

8. Various members of the Allen family do not think Eliza was coerced into marriage with the glamorous governor, as some contend. While doing research on his excellent book *Sam Houston: American Giant*, M. K. Wisehart interviewed Mrs. Eleanor Allen Sullivan of Nashville, a great-niece of Eliza. It was Mrs. Sullivan's opinion Eliza "had gone freely and hopefully into her marriage. No one forced

her." In a personal interview September 14, 1984, I discussed the situation with Elizabeth Allen of Gallatin, Tennessee, Mrs. Sullivan's sister. Miss Allen's opinion was substantially the same as her sister's, based on her knowledge of the Allen family.

9. *Memoir*, 45.

10. *Writings*, 1:130.

11. Hale and Merritt, *A History of Tennessee and Tennesseans*, 2:379.

12. Balie Peyton, also a friend of Sam Houston's, was to become a war hero, a congressman, and minister to Chile. He kept his vow of silence for many years, but while near death in 1878 was questioned by his daughter Emily as to whether he knew anything of the separation. Considering the many years that had elapsed since the death of both Sam and Eliza, he related the story to Emily as Eliza had told it to him. Emily wrote a document of several pages in ink on ruled paper and tucked it away with some family correspondence, where it lay in the attic of the Gallatin home of some nieces. During the very late 1950s or very early 1960s, the nieces, Louise Peyton and her sister Mary Bugg Peyton, sold their home. While going through some old family letters and correspondence, they ran across the long-forgotten account written by Emily. Louise Davis, journalist for the *Nashville Tennessee* magazine, heard about the document from Elizabeth Allen of Gallatin, and in a three-part series running August 5, 12, and 19, 1962, published the story. Elizabeth Allen, in September 1984, also graciously furnished me with some pages of the photocopied story, and the photocopied Emily Peyton document.

Chapter 7

1. *Writings*, 1:149. These vicious attacks and false accusations were still being made several years later. In a letter to Andrew Jackson under date May 18, 1830, Houston answered his critics.

2. *Memoir*, 46.

3. *Writings*, 1:144. In a letter to Judge Overton dated December 28, 1829, Houston, "who never forgot a friend or a favor," expressed his gratitude to the judge for this visit.

4. *Memoir*, 47.

5. Donald Braider, *Solitary Star*, 76.

6. *Memoir*, 47, 48.

7. Although Sam and his parents attended the Timber Ridge Presbyterian Church, apparently he had never been baptized. In a conversation with Dr. Homer T. Cornish, pastor of the church, on November 13, 1983, Dr. Cornish told me that early records of the church were lost in a fire in the nineteenth century, and it is impossible to determine if Sam or his brothers and sisters were baptized there.

8. *Writings*, 1:131.

9. *Nashville Banner*, December 30, 1907.

10. Georgia Burleson, ed., *Life and Writings of Dr. Rufus C. Burleson*, 522.

11. *Ibid.*

BOOK II

Chapter 8

1. There are many stories and much confusion as to who actually invented the famous Bowie knife. Some authorities contend that Jim Bowie, in a fight, cut his hand by striking such a blow with a knife that his fingers slipped down upon the blade, and thereupon he devised a knife with a hilt. Others contend that it was his brother Rezin that had the fight and whose hand was cut, and who then invented the knife. In all likelihood the knife may have been invented years before the Bowies came along. Regardless of who actually invented this weapon, it was the ferocity with which Jim Bowie wielded it in combat that gave it its name. This knife had a length of twelve and one-half inches, with a blade of eight inches, and a width of one and one-half inches. Due to the wide publicity given the exploits of Jim Bowie and his knife, demand for it became so great that in Sheffield, England, a factory was built to manufacture them for the Texas market.

2. Some authorities claim he was born in Burke County, Georgia, and others claim the place of his birth was Tennessee. This sort of confusion is not uncommon when it pertains to many early Americans.

3. Haralson to John Eaton, June 22, 1829. Gilcrease Sam Houston Biographical File, Thomas Gilcrease Institute of American History and Art, Tulsa, Oklahoma. Also, H. Haralson to John Eaton, June 24, 1829, Oklahoma Foreman Typescripts, Oklahoma Indian Archives, Oklahoma Historical Society, Oklahoma City.

4. Charles Fenton Mercer Noland to William Noland, May 11, 1829, Lewis Berkeley Papers. (Photographic copy in Barker Texas History Center, University of Texas, Austin.)

5. M. K. Wisehart, *Sam Houston: American Giant,* 50.

6. Donald Day and Harry Herbert Ullom, eds., *The Autobiography of Sam Houston,* 49.

7. *Ibid.,* 49, 50.

8. *Ibid.*

9. There is some discrepancy as to exactly how Houston left Little Rock. Marquis James, in *The Raven,* states Houston and his servant left Little Rock on horseback, leaving Haralson to bring the luggage, and twenty miles away at Louisburg stayed at the residence of one John Linton. Then he and Linton mounted horses and went to Fort Smith.

M. K. Wisehart, in *Sam Houston: American Giant,* states Houston and Haralson purchased horses and rode thirty miles up the Arkansas to overtake the *Facility,* which Houston boarded, leaving Haralson to ride overland.

Donald Braider, in *Solitary Star,* says Houston, Haralson, and Linton boarded the *Facility* and rode on it until they reached Fort Gibson.

Jack Gregory and Rennard Strickland, in their *Sam Houston with the Cherokees, 1829–1833,* assert virtually the same thing, and in a footnote quote the *Cherokee Phoenix,* June 24, 1829, issue thus: "In an article dated May 20, from Little Rock, Arkansas, the *Phoenix* reported: 'The late governor of Tennessee, Gen. Samuel Houston, arrived at this place a few days since, and after two days stay, took passage in the steamboat *Facility,* ascending the river.' " See also *Arkansas Gazette,* May 20, 1829.

10. From 1817 the army used the term "cantonment" to mean a new military installation. Previous to that time it had referred to temporary military camps. In

1832 the War Department, by General Order 11, directed that all military camps designated "cantonments" hereinafter be designated "forts." That order affected many cantonments besides Gibson. Brad Agnew, *Fort Gibson, Terminal on the Trail of Tears*, 218.

11. *Memoir*, 51.

12. *Ibid.*, 52.

13. Gregory and Strickland, 12.

14. *Ibid.*, 44.

15. George Catlin, *Letters and Notes on the Manners, Customs, and Conditions of North American Indians*, 2:119.

16. *Memoir*, 50, 51.

17. James, *The Raven*, 99.

18. Gregory and Strickland, 29.

19. *Ibid.*

20. Letter from Haralson to Eaton, June 23, 1829. Gilcrease Sam Houston Biographical File, Thomas Gilcrease Institute of American History and Art, Tulsa, Oklahoma.

21. Agnew, 60.

22. Grant Foreman, *Indians and Pioneers*, 223.

23. Charles Francis Adams, ed., *Memoirs of John Quincy Adams, Comprising Portions of His Diary from 1795 to 1848*, 7:499, 502, 503.

24. *Arkansas Gazette*, June 25, 1828, 3; July 2, 1828, 3.

25. *Memoir*, 54.

26. After the Battle of Horseshoe Bend in 1824, when Gen. Andrew Jackson met the leaders of the Creek Nation to impose terms on them, as victor, he showed them no mercy, demanding they give up 23,000,000 acres, or half of the Creek domain. This land comprised huge areas of Tennessee and Alabama. The Creeks had no choice but to accept these harsh terms, and thenceforth referred to Old Hickory as "Sharp Knife." Marquis James, *Andrew Jackson, The Border Captain*, 188, 189.

27. John Jolly, Big Canoe, Black Coat, and eleven others to "My Young Friends," June 8, 1829. Marquis James, *The Raven*, 103.

28. James, *The Raven*, 83. William Carroll to Andrew Jackson, May 25, 1829.

Chapter 9

1. Washington Irving Manuscripts, Notebook No. 6, New York Public Library.

2. Journal of Washington Irving, October 6, 1832, Washington Irving Manuscripts, New York Public Library.

3. Jack Gregory and Rennard Strickland, *Sam Houston with the Cherokees 1829–1833*, 65.

4. Marquis James, *The Raven*, 107.

5. *Ibid.*, 110.

6. Brad Agnew, *Fort Gibson, Terminal on the Trail of Tears*, 31.

7. *Writings*, 2:12.

8. James, *The Raven*, 111. Roly McIntosh and others to Jackson, June 22, 1829.

9. *Ibid.*, 114–115. Houston to Arbuckle, July 8, 1829.

10. *Writings*, 2:139–140.

373

11. M. K. Wisehart, *Sam Houston: American Giant*, 55.

12. *Writings*, 1:140, 143.

13. Gregory and Strickland, 91. Cephas Washburn Report, September 1, 1830, in Thomas Benton Williams, *The Soul of the Red Man*, 85.

14. George Wilson Pierson, ed., *Tocqueville and Beaumont in America*, 388.

15. James, *The Raven*, 122.

Chapter 10

1. *Memoir*, 54.

2. Jack Gregory and Rennard Strickland, *Sam Houston with the Cherokees 1829–1833*, 111.

3. Brad Agnew, *Fort Gibson, Terminal on the Trail of Tears*, 37.

4. *Writings*, 1:143, 144. Original of this letter is in the Sam Houston State University Museum, Huntsville, Texas.

5. Marquis James, *The Raven*, 127–128. Letter from John Jolly to Andrew Jackson, December 3, 1829.

6. Walter Webber, like so many of the leaders among the Cherokees, was of mixed blood. He was one of the Cherokees who had fought with Jackson at the Battle of Horseshoe Bend, and had the rank of colonel. He was enterprising, influential, and a prosperous merchant with a store at Nicksville, where Dwight Mission was located in 1830. He died April 11, 1834.

7. James, *The Raven*, 127–128. John Jolly to Andrew Jackson, December 18, 1829.

8. Agnew, 82. Letters of John Rogers to Secretary of War John Eaton, January 4, 1830.

9. *Writings*, 1:144, 145. John Overton was a lifelong friend of both Sam Houston and Andrew Jackson, and succeeded Jackson as chief justice of the Supreme Court of Tennessee. He was the referee at the duel between Charles Dickson and Jackson, in which Jackson fatally wounded Dickson.

10. *Writings*, 1:147.

11. Agnew, 83.

12. *Memoir*, 57.

13. *Writings*, 1:149.

14. *Ibid.*

15. James, *The Raven*, 133.

16. *Writings*, 1:148.

Chapter 11

1. Marquis James, *The Raven*, 142.

2. *Writings*, 1:151.

3. James, *The Raven*, 141.

4. *Ibid.*, 142, 143, 144.

5. *Writings*, 1:149, 150.

6. *Ibid.*, 188–193.

7. James, *The Raven*, 183. This incident is related in the journal of Frederick Golladay, son of Isaac Golladay, who befriended Houston as a young man.

8. *Ibid.*

9. Jack Gregory and Rennard Strickland, *Sam Houston with the Cherokees 1829–1833*, 4.

10. James, *The Raven*, 277, 278. Letter dated October 6, 1836, from Washington City, addressed to His Excellency, Genl. Sam Houston, from Jno. Campbell.

11. *Ibid.*, 278, 279. Letter from McEwen to Houston, December 13, 1836.

Chapter 12

1. *Writings*, 1:151.

2. *Ibid.*, 154.

3. *Ibid.*, 152, 153.

4. M. K. Wisehart, *Sam Houston: American Giant*, 60.

5. *Writings*, 1:186.

6. Jack Gregory and Rennard Strickland, *Sam Houston with the Cherokees 1829–1833*, 112–113.

7. *Ibid.*, 108.

8. James Mooney, *Historical Sketch of the Cherokees*, 481–482. Also, Gregory and Strickland, 44.

9. On a power of attorney dated June 27, 1833, that Diana gave Houston, her name is signed:

Her

Diana X Gentry

mark

10. In at least three genealogies of Cherokee families to which Diana is related, and the author has seen, she is listed as Tiana Rogers.

11. "Sam Houston's Cherokee Wife Honored by Son," *Muskogee Times Democrat*, September 26, 1919, 1.

12. Morris L. Wardell, *A Political History of the Cherokee Nation*, 7.

13. Emmett Starr, *Early History of the Cherokees*, 217, 218.

14. Sam Houston typescripts, Oklahoma Biographical File, and Oklahoma Reference Library, Oklahoma Historical Society, Oklahoma City, Oklahoma.

15. Gregory and Strickland, 47.

16. *Ibid.*, 56.

17. *Writings*, 1:279.

18. *Ibid.*, 187.

19. *Ibid.*

20. *Ibid.*

21. Gregory and Strickland, 127.

22. Brad Agnew, *Fort Gibson, Terminal on the Trail of Tears*, 85.

23. *Writings*, 5:4.

24. *Ibid.*, 2:12.

25. *Ibid.*, 1:193–195.

Chapter 13

1. *Cherokee Phoenix*, May 28, 1931, 2.

2. M. K. Wisehart, *Sam Houston: American Giant*, 62.

3. Llerena B. Friend, *Sam Houston: The Great Designer*, 29.

4. *Writings*, 1:196.

5. Wisehart, 64.

6. George Vashon to Lewis Cass, January 4, 1832.

Chapter 14

1. Marquis James, *The Raven*, 163.

2. *Memoir*, 57.

3. *Writings*, 1:201.

4. *Ibid.*

5. *Ibid.*, 202.

6. *Ibid.*

7. *Ibid.*, 203.

8. James, *The Raven*, 166.

9. *Ibid.*, 167.

10. *Writings*, 1:204. Throughout his lifetime, Houston always had many different projects going, and he seems to have had a different partner for each in many of them. His partner in his "Gold mine matters" was probably Benjamin Hawkins, an educated half-Creek Indian, who was in Washington during the summer of 1832.

11. *Ibid.*, 1:207–215.

12. *Ibid.*

13. *Ibid.*

14. James, *The Raven*, 170.

15. M. K. Wisehart, *Sam Houston: American Giant*, 78.

16. *Writings*, 1:224, 225.

17. George W. Paschal, "Last Years of Sam Houston," *Harper's New Monthly Magazine*, April 1866, 630–635.

18. *Writings*, 1:228, 229.

19. *Ibid.*, 7:2.

20. *Ibid.*, 1:230, 231.

21. *Ibid.*

22. General Order No. 11 of the War Department, dated February 6, 1832, had directed that "all the Military Posts designated Cantonments be hereafter called Forts." Brad Agnew, *Fort Gibson*, 218, 219.

23. *Writings*, 1:257.

24. William Carey Crane, *Life and Select Literary Remains of Sam Houston of Texas*, 48.

25. *Writings*, 1:263, 264.

26. *Ibid.*, 4:11.

27. *Ibid.*, 1:266.

28. Donald Day and Harry Herbert Ullom, eds., *The Autobiography of Sam Houston*, 76, 77.

29. Around April 1, 1836, Diana married Samuel D. McGrady. Sometime during 1836, when she was in her early forties, she became ill and died of pneumonia.

30. James, *The Raven*, 186.

31. *Writings*, 6:1, 2.

BOOK III

Chapter 15

1. Eugene C. Barker, *Mexico and Texas, 1821–1835*, 33.
2. Henderson Yoakum, *History of Texas,* 1:210.
3. *Ibid.,* 216.
4. *Ibid.,* 217.
5. Eugene C. Barker, *The Life of Stephen F. Austin*, 149.
6. Yoakum, 1:244.
7. Barker, *The Life of Stephen F. Austin*, 195.
8. M. K. Wisehart, *Sam Houston: American Giant*, 118.
9. Eugene C. Barker, *Mexico and Texas, 1821–1835*, 56.
10. Wisehart, 103.
11. Stephen F. Austin to Samuel M. Williams, June 20, 1832. Rosenberg Library, Galveston, Texas.
12. Wisehart, 103.
13. Barker, *Mexico and Texas, 1821–1835,* 41.
14. Barker, *The Life of Stephen F. Austin,* 386.
15. *Ibid.*
16. Yoakum, 1:292, 293.
17. John Austin was a captain in the coastal trade and was second alcalde of San Felipe.
18. Colonel Bradburn returned to Texas in 1836 and was in the Battle of San Jacinto, fighting in the Mexican army. Being in one of the rear divisions, he was not killed or taken prisoner.
19. Barker, *The Life of Stephen F. Austin,* 392.
20. *Ibid.,* 209.

Chapter 16

1. *Memoir,* 64.
2. John Myers Myers, *The Alamo,* 91.
3. *Memoir,* 65.
4. M. K. Wisehart, *Sam Houston: American Giant,* 109.
5. *Writings,* 1:272, 273.
6. *Ibid.*
7. *Ibid.,* 274–276.
8. *Ibid.*
9. *Ibid.*
10. There is a discrepancy as to the three members of the delegation. Yoakum, 1:312, in his *History of Texas,* names Austin, Wharton, and Miller. Barker, in his *Life of Stephen F. Austin,* names the three delegates as Austin, Miller, and Erasmus Seguin.
11. Brad Agnew, *Fort Gibson, Terminal on the Trail of Tears,* 88.
12. *Writings,* 5:34.
13. *Ibid.,* 1:277–279.
14. *Diary of William Barret Travis,* August 20, 1833 — June 26, 1834.
15. *Writings,* 1:283, 284.
16. *Ibid.,* 290.
17. *Ibid.,* 291.

18. *Austin City Gazette,* March 2, 1842.

19. William F. Pope, *Early Days in Arkansas,* 153.

20. Marquis James, *The Raven,* 207, 208.

21. Jim Bowie was on an extended trip east to Natchez, Mississippi, when, between September 5 and 8, 1833, his wife, their two children, and his wife's parents all died from cholera at Monclova, in the Coahuila section, where the Veramendis had a summer home. Bowie was not aware of the catastrophe when he executed his will at Natchez on October 21, 1833. In it he designated as his sole heirs his brother Rezin P. Bowie and their sister Martha Bowie Sterrett and her husband Alexander B. Sterrett. His wife, he explained, had already been provided for. He stipulated that $4,000 be restored to a friend who had advanced him that sum, and $4,000 more to another friend who had secured a loan to him for that amount. The deaths made, in ascending order, Ursula Bowie's grandmother, a Navarro, inheritor of the whole Veramendi estate. She died in 1837, leaving other Navarros to inherit and to make claims against the Bowie estate.

Chapter 17

1. Henderson Yoakum, *History of Texas,* 1:334.

2. *Ibid.,* 335.

3. M. K. Wisehart, *Sam Houston: American Giant,* 121.

4. Yoakum, 1:349.

5. Eugene C. Barker, *The Life of Stephen F. Austin,* 480.

6. *Ibid.,* 481.

7. *Writings,* 1:302, 303.

8. *Ibid.,* 302.

9. *Ibid.,* 209.

10. Houston wrote Anna Raguet telling her the story of Milam. After escaping from the Mexican prison, Milam had ridden night and day to join the Texans. He had stopped in a mesquite thicket to rest when he was discovered by Texans. Sam Houston letter to Anna Raguet, *Ever Thine Truly,* 7.

11. Yoakum, 1:369.

12. Barker, *The Life of Stephen F. Austin,* 486.

13. *Memoir,* 69.

14. Houston to Fannin, November 13, 1835. Archives Division, Texas State Library.

15. Wisehart, 136.

16. James M. Day, et al., *Heroes of Texas,* 122.

Chapter 18

1. Henderson Yoakum, *History of Texas,* 2:43.

2. James M. Day, et al., *Heroes of Texas,* 72.

3. *Writings,* 1:323.

4. *Ibid.,* 330.

5. *Ibid.,* 312.

6. George Creel, *Sam Houston, Colossus in Buckskin,* 114.

7. *Writings,* 7:24, 25.

8. *Ibid.,* 335.

9. *Ibid.,* 1:331.

10. *Ibid.*, 333.
11. Yoakum, 2:55.
12. *Ibid.*, 334.
13. *Writings*, 1:337, 338.
14. Yoakum, 2:58. Order to James Bowie, January 17, 1836.
15. *Writings*, 1:339.
16. *Ibid.*, 342.
17. Andrew Jackson Houston, *Texas Independence*, 100.
18. M. K. Wisehart, *Sam Houston: American Giant*, 156.
19. *Memoir*, 95.
20. *Ibid.*

Chapter 19

1. Peach Tree Village, in Tyler County, Texas, was named because of an enormous peach tree orchard there. It was the principal village of the Alabama-Coushatta tribe, who were in the same Indian confederation as the Cherokees. See: *Sam Houston's Indians,* Prairie View Malone, 21. There is some discrepancy as to where the conference actually took place. According to Mary Whatley Clarke, author of *Thomas J. Rusk, Soldier, Statesman, Jurist,* the conference was held at Chief Bowles's village, about fifty miles north of Nacogdoches. See also Clarke, *Chief Bowles and the Texas Cherokees,* 14, 15.
2. Frank X. Tolbert, *The Day of San Jacinto,* 122.
3. Clarke, *Chief Bowles and the Texas Cherokees,* 14, 15.
4. Henderson Yoakum, *History of Texas,* 2:59.
5. Virgil E. Baugh, *Rendezvous at the Alamo,* 5.
6. *Ibid.*, 6.
7. For those not familiar with the vagaries of Texas weather, this is what is referred to in winter when the temperature can drop twenty to forty degrees in just an hour or two.
8. Baugh, 204, 205.
9. Tolbert, 37.
10. Andrew Jackson Houston, *Texas Independence,* 123, 124.
11. M. K. Wisehart, *Sam Houston: American Giant,* 167.
12. *Memoir,* 90, 91.
13. *Ibid.*
14. Wisehart, 176.
15. James M. Day, et al., *Heroes of Texas,* 80.
16. *Ibid.* The watch was later obtained by Capt. William H. Jack and then by Dr. Tomlinson Fort, a relative of Fannin's wife, Minerva Fort Fannin. It became part of the Summerfield G. Roberts Collection and is now in the Hall of State Building on the grounds of the State Fair of Texas at Dallas, Texas.

Chapter 20

1. Henderson Yoakum, *History of Texas,* 2:81. Account furnished by Mrs. Dickerson, *Telegraph and Texas Register,* March 24, 1836.
2. *Ibid.*
3. Henry Steele Commager, ed., *The West, An Illustrated History,* 42.
4. Frank X. Tolbert, *The Day of San Jacinto,* 46.

5. *Writings*, 1:378.

6. *Ibid.*, 381.

7. Tolbert, 55.

8. *Ibid.*, 48.

9. Mary Whatley Clarke, *Chief Bowles and the Texas Cherokees*, 68.

10. *Writings*, 1:384, 385.

11. *Ibid.*

12. M. K. Wisehart, *Sam Houston: American Giant*, 211.

13. Tolbert, 85.

14. *Telegraph and Texas Register*, June 9, 1841.

15. *Writings*, 1:403.

16. Tolbert, 67.

17. Dudley G. Wooten, ed., *A Comprehensive History of Texas, 1685 to 1899*, 1:272.

18. *Writings*, 1:410, 411.

Chapter 21

1. *Writings*, 1:409.

2. Frank X. Tolbert, *The Day of San Jacinto*, 92.

3. *Ibid.*, 71.

4. Houston's report of the battle to President Burnet, April 25, 1836. Marquis James, *The Raven*, 244.

5. *Memoir*, 111.

6. *Ibid.*

7. *Writings*, 1:413.

8. *Memoir*, 113.

9. Tolbert, 97.

10. *Ibid.*

11. *Ibid.*, 98, 99.

12. Marquis James, *Andrew Jackson, Portrait of a President*, 411, 412.

13. From Houston's report of the Battle of San Jacinto to President David Burnet, April 25, 1836, as carried in the *San Antonio Express*.

14. *Memoir*, 118.

15. George Creel, *Sam Houston, Colossus in Buckskin*, 177, 178.

16. Tolbert, 126.

Chapter 22

1. *Memoir*, 124.

2. Frank X. Tolbert, *The Day of San Jacinto*, 134.

3. *Ibid.*, 28.

4. *Ibid.*

5. *Ibid.*, 124.

6. *Ibid.*, 143.

7. M. K. Wisehart, *Sam Houston: American Giant*, 242, 243.

8. Tolbert, 159.

9. Houston's official report of the Battle of San Jacinto to President David G. Burnet, April 25, 1836.

Chapter 23

1. Houston to Anna Raguet, 1836. *Ever Thine Truly,* 11.
2. Houston's official report of the Battle of San Jacinto to President David G. Burnet, April 25, 1836.
3. *Memoir,* 144.
4. *Writings,* 7:332.
5. *Ibid.*
6. *Ibid.,* 147.
7. Frank X. Tolbert, *The Day of San Jacinto,* 184, 185.
8. *Memoir,* 149.
9. *Ibid.,* 154.
10. *Writings,* 1:425. Houston to Thomas J. Rusk, letter of May 3, 1836.
11. Tolbert, 225.
12. George Creel, *Sam Houston, Colossus in Buckskin,* 195, 196.
13. *Writings,* 1:433.
14. Donald Day and Harry Herbert Ullom, eds., *The Autobiography of Sam Houston,* 128. Letter from Rusk to Houston, July 2, 1836.
15. Thomas J. Rusk Papers, Barker Texas History Center, University of Texas, Austin.
16. *Writings,* 1:436–439.

BOOK IV

Chapter 24

1. Mary Whatley Clark, *Thomas J. Rusk,* 93. Rusk to Houston, August 9, 1836.
2. Henderson Yoakum, *History of Texas,* 2:177.
3. *Writings,* 1:446.
4. Llerena B. Friend, *Sam Houston: The Great Designer,* 78.
5. This saddle is now on exhibit in the Sam Houston Memorial Museum, Huntsville, Texas.
6. *Writings,* 1:448–452.
7. Frank X. Tolbert, *The Day of San Jacinto,* 29.
8. Yoakum, 2:197.
9. Donald Braider, *Solitary Star,* 173.
10. Yoakum, 2:203.
11. Santa Anna promised to repay Colonel Bee the $2,000 with a draft on Vera Cruz, and when the party arrived at Washington he gave Bee the draft, but on his subsequent arrival at Vera Cruz caused the draft to be dishonored. Neither he nor the Mexican government ever repaid the loan. Subsequently, the Congress of Texas appropriated funds to reimburse the colonel.
12. *Writings,* 1:487–488.
13. *Ibid.,* 7:4, 5.
14. *Ibid.,* 1:495, 496.
15. Mary Whatley Clarke, *Chief Bowles and the Texas Cherokees,* 72.
16. *Writings,* 2:28, 29.
17. *Memoir,* 184.
18. Friend, 119.

19. *Ibid.*, 87.

20. *Telegraph and Texas Register,* March 21, 1837.

21. M. K. Wisehart, *Sam Houston: American Giant,* 295.

22. *Writings,* 2:43, 44.

23. *Ibid.,* 4:29, 30.

24. *Ibid.,* 2:82–90.

25. Friend, 88.

26. Yoakum, 2:204, 205.

27. George Creel, *Sam Houston, Colossus in Buckskin,* 220.

28. Friend, 82.

29. *Writings,* 2:29, 30.

30. *Ibid.,* 113, 114.

31. *Ibid.,* 75, 76. Sam Houston to Philip Dimitt, March 26, 1837.

32. *Ibid.,* 114, 115.

33. *Ibid.,* 131, 132.

34. Yoakum, 2:210, 211.

35. *Ibid.,* 212.

Chapter 25

1. George Creel, *Sam Houston, Colossus in Buckskin,* 218.

2. *Writings,* 2:147, 148.

3. *Ibid.,* 149.

4. *Ibid.,* 150.

5. *Ibid.,* 150, 151.

6. *Ibid.,* 152–161.

7. *Ibid.,* 177, 178.

8. *Ibid.,* 189, 190.

9. Llerena B. Friend, *Sam Houston: The Great Designer,* 91.

10. Donald Day and Harry Herbert Ullom, eds., *The Autobiography of Sam Houston,* 39.

11. *Writings,* 2:184, 185.

12. *Ibid.,* 190.

13. *Ibid.,* 226.

14. Masonic records of Sam Houston furnished the author by the Texas Masonic Grand Lodge Library, Waco, Texas.

15. *Writings,* 2:198, 199.

16. *Ibid.,* 244.

17. *Ibid.,* 244, 245.

18. William Carey Crane, *Life and Select Literary Remains of Sam Houston of Texas,* 131.

19. M. K. Wisehart, *Sam Houston: American Giant,* 331.

20. *Ever Thine Truly,* 112, 113, 151, 153.

21. Houston had a sister named Eliza, and it was her children he was speaking of.

22. Hunt to Lamar, May 31, 1839. Ashbel Smith Papers, Barker Texas History Center, University of Texas, Austin.

23. Hunt to Smith, Sept. 5, 1839. Ashbel Smith Papers, Barker Texas History Center, University of Texas, Austin.

24. Letter to L. J. Polk, Columbia, Tennessee, June 13, 1839. Polk Collection, University of North Carolina Archives.

25. Wisehart, 339.

26. William Seale, *Sam Houston's Wife*, 9.

27. Margaret Lea to Sam Houston, Marion, July 17, 1839. Barker Texas History Center, University of Texas, Austin.

28. Crane, 253.

29. Margaret Lea to Sam Houston, Marion, August 1, 1839. Barker Texas History Center, University of Texas, Austin.

Chapter 26

1. Emmett Starr, *History of the Cherokee Indians*, 223. Also, Mary Whatley Clarke, *Chief Bowles and the Texas Cherokees*, 76, 77.

2. In the battle, Chief Bowles was using the sword Houston had given him. After passing through several hands over the years, the sword is now owned by the Tahlequah, Oklahoma, Masonic Lodge.

3. Herbert Gambrell, *Anson Jones: The Last President of Texas*, 181.

4. *Austin City Gazette*, November 27, 1839.

5. *Writings*, 2:322, 323.

6. *Ibid.*, 323–347.

7. Hockley to Houston, February 20, 1840. Houston Unpublished Correspondence. Llerena B. Friend, *Sam Houston: The Great Designer*, 96.

8. James Love to Lamar, March 15, 1840. Mirabeau Buonaparte Lamar, *The Papers of Mirabeau Buonaparte Lamar*, 3:854.

9. Bee to Smith, June 5, 1840.

10. William Seale, *Sam Houston's Wife*, 18.

11. Ashbel Smith to Radcliffe Hudson, Galveston, June 1, 1840. Ashbel Smith Papers, Barker Texas History Center, University of Texas, Austin.

12. Seale, 17.

13. *Ibid.*, 32, 33.

14. Smith to Bee, July 27, 1840. Ashbel Smith Papers.

15. Houston to Margaret Lea Houston, Sept. 23, 1840. Sam Houston State University Library, Huntsville, Texas.

16. James M. Day, et al., *Heroes of Texas*, 99.

17. Henderson Yoakum, *History of Texas*, 2:282.

18. *Ibid.*, 314.

19. Marquis James, *The Raven*, 316.

20. *Writings*, 2:365, 366.

21. Sam Houston to General William G. Harding, July 17, 1841. *Writings*, 3:10.

22. Gambrell, *Anson Jones*, 216.

23. *Writings*, 2:391.

24. *Ibid.*, 399.

25. Gambrell, *Anson Jones*, 224.

26. Yoakum, 2:342.

Chapter 27

1. *Writings*, 4:76.

2. *Executive Record Book*, No. 40, p. 47, Archives Division, Texas State Library, Austin.

3. *Writings,* 2:492.

4. *Ibid.,* 3:27.

5. *Executive Record Book,* No. 40. p. 52, Archives Division, Texas State Library, Austin.

6. *Writings,* 3:24.

7. *Ibid.,* 15.

8. *Ibid.,* 2:528.

9. M. K. Wisehart, *Sam Houston: American Giant,* 410.

10. *Writings,* 3:125.

11. Ashbel Smith on Houston, n.d., Ashbel Smith Papers, Barker Texas History Center, University of Texas, Austin.

12. *Executive Record Book,* No. 40, pp. 141, 142, Archives Division, Texas State Library, Austin.

13. Herbert Gambrell, *Anson Jones,* 263.

14. Henderson Yoakum, *History of Texas,* 2:364, 365.

15. Wisehart, 418.

16. *Ibid.,* 417.

17. William Seale, *Sam Houston's Wife,* 78–80.

18. Yoakum, 2:368.

19. *Ibid.,* 369.

20. *Ibid.,* 373.

21. *Ibid.,* 374.

22. *Writings,* 3:287, 288.

Chapter 28

1. *Writings,* 3:156, 157.

2. Henderson Yoakum, *History of Texas,* 2:381.

3. *Writings,* 3:418, 419.

4. *Ibid.,* 310.

5. Yoakum, 2:385–392.

6. *Writings,* 4:193.

7. *Ibid.,* 434–439.

8. *Ibid.,* 203.

9. *Ibid.,* 211.

10. Yoakum, 2:414, 422.

11. *Writings,* 3:442–455.

12. Gambrell, *Anson Jones,* 297.

13. M. K. Wisehart, *Sam Houston: American Giant,* 357. Anson Jones recorded this in his diary during the 1839–1840 session of Congress.

14. Gambrell, *Anson Jones,* 283.

15. *Writings,* 3:299–302.

16. George Creel, *Sam Houston, Colossus in Buckskin,* 226.

17. *Writings,* 3:322. The "Old Three Hundred" referred to the original three hundred families Austin brought to Texas.

18. Donald Braider, *Solitary Star,* 231.

19. Yoakum, 2:428. Van Zandt to Upshur, January 17, 1844.

20. Marquis James, *The Raven,* 345. Jackson to Houston, January 18, 1844.

21. *Ibid.,* 345, 346. Jackson to Houston, January 23, 1844.

22. *Writings,* 3:261.

23. Llerena B. Friend, *Sam Houston: The Great Designer,* 131.

24. *Writings,* 3:521, 522, 523.

25. Yoakum, 2:428.

26. *Writings,* 3:538–542. Houston explained the letter had been postponed due to the great press of business.

27. Anson Jones, *Memoranda and Official Correspondence . . .,* 329–331.

28. *Writings,* 4:320–325.

29. Wisehart, 467. James Morgan to Samuel Swartwout, September 28, 1844.

30. Gambrell, *Anson Jones,* 369.

31. *Writings,* 4:401–405.

BOOK V

Chapter 29

1. *Writings,* 4:406, 407.

2. *Ibid.,* 408–410.

3. William Carey Crane, *Life and Select Literary Remains of Sam Houston of Texas,* 255.

4. William Seale, *Sam Houston's Wife,* 97.

5. Gambrell, *Anson Jones,* 386.

6. *Ibid.,* 385.

7. "Memorandum of a Conference held at the State Department at Washington-on-the Brazos on the 29th March 1845." Ashbel Smith Papers, Barker Texas History Center, University of Texas, Austin.

8. *Writings,* 4:410–417.

9. *Lamar Papers,* 4(Part I):111–112; 6:9, 10.

10. *Telegraph and Texas Register,* June 4, 1845.

11. Crane, 258.

12. Marquis James, *The Raven,* 357. As told to him by Mrs. Nellie Houston Bringhurst, Sam Houston's daughter.

13. Front page, the *Maryville News,* August 20, 1845.

14. Gambrell, *Anson Jones,* 401.

15. Sam Houston to William Houston Letcher, Galveston, November 25, 1845. See also F. N. Boney, "The Raven Tamed: A Sam Houston Letter," *Southwestern Historical Quarterly,* January 1920, 90–92.

16. *Writings,* 4:430–432.

17. George Creel, *Sam Houston, Colossus in Buckskin,* 302.

18. Oliver Dyer, *Great Senators of the United States Forty Years Ago,* 116.

19. *Ibid.*

20. Seale, 57.

21. *Writings,* 7:99, 100.

22. Lamar to Burnet, March 1847. *Lamar Papers* 4(Part 1):165.

23. *Writings,* 4:452.

24. *Ibid.,* 453.

25. *Ibid.,* 471.

26. Henry Steele Commager, ed., *The West, An Illustrated History,* 69.

27. *Ibid.,* 70.

28. M. K. Wisehart, *Sam Houston: American Giant,* 594.

29. *Writings,* 4:476, 477.

30. Margaret Lea Houston to Sam Houston, Raven Hill, June 20, 1846. New York Public Library.

31. Commager, 75.

Chapter 30

1. Houston to Nathaniel Levin, August 11, 1845. San Jacinto Museum.

2. Elizabeth Silverthorne, *Ashbel Smith of Texas: Pioneer, Patriot, Statesman, 1805–1886,* 107, 108.

3. *Writings,* 4:523–547.

4. William Seale, *Sam Houston's Wife,* 125.

5. *Writings,* 5:13, 14. Also Joseph Lynn Clark, "General Houston's Huntsville Home . . . The Mount Vernon of Texas."

6. Clark, "General Houston's Huntsville Home . . ."

7. *Writings,* 6:18–20.

8. *Ibid.*

9. M. K. Wisehart, *Sam Houston: American Giant,* 517.

10. Mary Whatley Clarke, *Thomas J. Rusk, Soldier, Statesman, Jurist,* 173.

11. Silverthorne, 115.

12. Llerena B. Friend, *Sam Houston: The Great Designer,* 190.

13. *Writings,* 5:54.

14. *Ibid.,* 55.

15. *Ibid.,* 58–60.

16. *Ibid.,* 62.

17. Allan Nevins, *Ordeal of the Union,* 1:25.

18. Friend, 194, 195.

19. *Writings,* 5:78–88.

Chapter 31

1. *Writings,* 5:119–144.

2. Llerena B. Friend, *Sam Houston: The Great Designer,* 201.

3. *Writings,* 5:204, 205.

4. Donald Braider, *Solitary Star,* 266.

5. Marquis James, *The Raven,* 381.

6. *Writings,* 5:307.

7. Mary Whatley Clarke, *Thomas J. Rusk, Soldier, Statesman, Jurist,* 188, 189.

8. James, *The Raven,* 379.

9. Braider, 270.

10. *Writings,* 5:346, 347.

11. Friend, 223. Resolution Proposing Construction of a Voting Machine in the Senate Chambers, April 6, 1853, *Senate Journal,* 32nd Congress, Second Session, 360–362.

12. *Writings,* 6:21–25.

13. *Ibid.,* 450–452.

14. Georgia Burleson, ed., *Life and Writings of Dr. Rufus C. Burleson,* 114.

15. Allan Nevins, *Ordeal of the Union,* 2:93–99.

16. *Ibid.*
17. *Writings,* 5:469.
18. *Ibid.,* 493.

Chapter 32

1. Georgia Burleson, ed., *Life and Writings of Dr. Rufus C. Burleson,* 579.
2. S. P. Hollingsworth to Rusk, April 30, 1854. Thomas J. Rusk Papers, Barker Texas History Center, University of Texas, Austin.
3. *Writings,* 6:76.
4. *Ibid.,* 7:32. Letter from Huntsville, November 23, 1857, to George Washington Baines. This Reverend Baines was maternal grandfather to former president Lyndon Baines Johnson.
5. *Writings,* 6:125.
6. *Ibid.,* 151.
7. *Ibid.,* 152.
8. *Ibid.,* 167–177.
9. *Ibid.,* 179.
10. Llerena B. Friend, *Sam Houston: The Great Designer,* 237.
11. *Writings,* 6:183.
12. *Ibid.,* 203.
13. *Ibid.,* 193.
14. *Ibid.,* 203.
15. Friend, 239. Quoted in the *Texas State Gazette,* September 15, 1855.
16. *Writings,* 6:204–207.
17. *Ibid.,* 207, 208.
18. Elizabeth Silverthorne, *Ashbel Smith of Texas: Pioneer, Patriot, Statesman, 1805–1886,* 135.
19. Friend, 241.
20. M. K. Wisehart, *Sam Houston: American Giant,* 558.
21. Silverthorne, 135, 136.

Chapter 33

1. *Writings,* 6:235, 236.
2. Llerena B. Friend, *Sam Houston: The Great Designer,* 242; William Seale, *Sam Houston's Wife,* 172.
3. Friend, 294. Thomas J. Rusk to David Rusk, February 29, 1856.
4. *Writings,* 6:299, 300.
5. *Ibid.,* 358–362.
6. *Ibid.,* 394.
7. *Ibid.,* 394, 395.
8. *Ibid.,* 7:27, 28.
9. *Ibid.,* 6:395.
10. *Ibid.,* 444.
11. *Ibid.,* 446. Letter to Ashbel Smith, July 6, 1857, from Huntsville; Ashbel Smith Papers, Barker Texas History Center, University of Texas, Austin.
12. M. K. Wisehart, *Sam Houston: American Giant,* 570.
13. *Ibid.,* 571.
14. *Writings,* 7:28–32.

15. Friend, 251.

16. *Ibid.*, 250.

17. Jeff Hamilton, *My Master*, 34.

18. *Writings*, 6:447; Ashbel Smith Papers, Barker Texas History Center, University of Texas, Austin.

Chapter 34

1. Llerena B. Friend, *Sam Houston: The Great Designer*, 256.

2. "A Valentine in a Rough Winter" — a newly discovered letter from Sam Houston to Margaret Lea Houston, February 14, 1858 (booklet).

3. *Writings*, 7:99, 100.

4. Friend, 261.

5. *Writings*, 7:142.

6. Friend, 260.

7. *Writings*, 7:183–187.

8. Letter from Sam Houston, Huntsville, to Dr. Ashbel Smith, October 29, 1858. Ashbel Smith Papers, Barker Texas History Center, University of Texas, Austin.

9. Jack to Bryan, December 23, 1858.

10. *Writings*, 7:191, 192.

11. *Ibid.*, 205.

12. *Ibid.*, 218, 219.

13. Friend, 267.

14. Sam Acheson, *35,000 Days in Texas: A History of the Dallas News and Its Forbears*, 40–43.

15. *Writings*, 7:335.

16. Friend, 268. Quoted in *Southern Intelligencer*, April 6, 1859.

Chapter 35

1. Donald Braider, *Solitary Star*, 292.

2. Llerena B. Friend, *Sam Houston: The Great Designer*, 323.

3. *Ibid.*

4. *Ibid.*, 322.

5. *Writings*, 6:339, 340.

6. *Ibid.*, 341.

7. *Ibid.*, 367.

8. There are several different versions of the number of votes Houston received, but I am using the figures published in the *Texas State Almanac*, published by the *Dallas Morning News*.

9. *San Antonio Herald*, December 27, 1859.

10. *Writings*, 7:379–385.

11. *Ibid.*, 394.

12. *Ibid.*, 393.

13. *Ibid.*, 479.

14. Friend, 308.

15. *Writings*, 7:189.

16. *Ibid.*, 225.

17. *Ibid.*, 545–554.

18. Louis J. Wortham, *A History of Texas*, 4:293.
19. *Writings*, 8:66.
20. *Ibid.*, 119, 120.
21. *Ibid.*, 121, 122.

Chapter 36

1. *Writings*, 8:184, 185.
2. Charles A. Culberson, "General Sam Houston and Secession," *Scribner's Magazine* 39 (January–June 1906), 590.
3. William Seale, *Sam Houston's Wife*, 205.
4. *Writings*, 8:266.
5. Llerena B. Friend, *Sam Houston: The Great Designer*, 345.
6. *Ibid.*
7. *Ibid.*, 338.
8. *Writings*, 8:271–278.
9. *Ibid.*, 293.
10. *Ibid.*, 346, 347.
11. Ashbel Smith, undated. Notes on Sam Houston. Ashbel Smith Papers, Barker Texas History Center, University of Texas, Austin.

Epilogue

1. *Writings*, 8:339, 340.
2. *Ibid.*, 341, 343.
3. William Seale, *Sam Houston's Wife*, 244.

Bibliography

Books

Acheson, Sam. *35,000 Days in Texas: A History of the Dallas News and Its Forbears.* New York: Macmillan Company, 1938.

Adair, Garland, and M. H. Crockett, eds. *Heroes of the Alamo.* New York: Exposition Press, 1957.

Adams, Charles Francis, ed. *Memoirs of John Quincy Adams, Comprising Portions of His Diary from 1795 to 1848.* 12 vols. Philadelphia: J. B. Lippincott and Company, 1874–77.

Agnew, Brad. *Fort Gibson, Terminal on the Trail of Tears.* Norman: University of Oklahoma Press, 1980.

Barker, Eugene C. *The Life of Stephen F. Austin.* Dallas: Cokesbury Press, 1925.

———. *Mexico and Texas, 1821–1835.* Dallas: P. L. Turner Company, 1928.

Baugh, Virgil E. *Rendezvous at the Alamo.* New York: Pageant Press, Inc., 1960.

Bell, George Morrison, Sr. *Genealogy of Old and New Cherokee Families.* Bartlesville: Printed by the author, 1972.

Berlandier, Jean Louis. *The Indians in Texas in 1830.* Reprint. Washington: Smithsonian Institution Press, 1969.

Binkley, William C. *The Texas Revolution.* Baton Rouge: Louisiana State Press, 1952.

Braider, Donald. *Solitary Star.* New York: G. P. Putnam's Sons, 1974.

Bruce, Henry. *Life of General Houston.* New York: Dodd, Mead, and Company, 1891.

Burleson, Georgia J., ed. *Life and Writings of Dr. Rufus C. Burleson.* [Waco? Texas.] Compiled and published by Mrs. Georgina Jenkins Burleson, 1901.

Burns, G. Frank. *Wilson County.* Memphis: Memphis State University Press, 1983.

Callcott, Wilfred Hardy. *Santa Anna, The Story of an Enigma Who Once Was Mexico.* Norman: University of Oklahoma Press, 1936.

Castañeda, Carlos E., trans. *The Mexican Side of the Texas Revolution.* Dallas: P. L. Turner Company, 1928.

Catlin, George. *Letters and Notes on the Manners, Customs, and Conditions of North American Indians.* Vols. I and II. New York: Dover Publications, Inc., 1973.

Clarke, Mary Whatley. *Chief Bowles and the Texas Cherokees.* Norman: University of Oklahoma Press, 1971.

———. *Thomas J. Rusk, Soldier, Statesman, Jurist.* Waco: Pemberton Press, 1977.

Commager, Henry Steele, ed. *The West, An Illustrated History.* London: Orbis Publishing, 1980.

391

Crane, William Carey. *Life and Select Literary Remains of Sam Houston of Texas*. Philadelphia: J. B. Lippincott Company. Dallas: William G. Scarff & Co., 1884.

Crawford, Ann Fears, ed. *The Eagle, The Autobiography of Santa Anna*. Austin: Pemberton Press, 1967.

Creel, George. *Sam Houston, Colossus in Buckskin*. New York: Cosmopolitan Book Corporation, 1928.

Day, Donald, and Harry Herbert Ullom, eds. *The Autobiography of Sam Houston*. Norman: University of Oklahoma Press, 1954.

Day, James M., et al. *Heroes of Texas*. Waco: Texian Press, 1964.

Dixon, Sam Houston, and Louis Wiltz Kemp. *The Heroes of San Jacinto*. Houston: Anson Jones Press, 1932.

Dyer, Oliver. *Great Senators of the United States Forty Years Ago (1848 and 1849)*. New York: Robert Bonner's Sons, 1889.

Ever Thine Truly. Love Letters from Sam Houston to Anna Raguet. Compiled by Shannon, Irion, and Jenkins. Austin: Jenkins Garrett Press, 1975.

Fehrenbach, T. R. *Comanches, The Destruction of a People*. New York: Alfred A. Knopf, 1974.

Folmsbee, Stanley John. *Tennessee*. Knoxville: University of Tennessee Press, 1969.

Foreman, Grant. *The Five Civilized Tribes*. Norman: University of Oklahoma Press, 1934.

———. *Indians and Pioneers*. Norman: University of Oklahoma Press, 1936.

———. *Pioneer Days in the Early Southwest*. Cleveland: The Arthur H. Clark Company, 1926.

Friend, Llerena B. *Sam Houston: The Great Designer*. Austin: University of Texas Press, 1954.

Gambrell, Herbert. *Anson Jones: The Last President of Texas*. Garden City, New York: Doubleday & Company, Inc., 1948.

———. *Mirabeau Buonaparte Lamar, Troubadour and Crusader*. Dallas: Southwest Press, 1934.

———, and Virginia Gambrell. *A Pictorial History of Texas*. New York: E. P. Dutton & Co., Inc. 1960.

Garner, Claude. *Sam Houston, Texas Giant*. Austin: The Naylor Company, 1969.

Gregory, Jack, and Rennard Strickland. *Sam Houston with the Cherokees 1829–1833*. Austin: University of Texas Press, 1967.

Green, General Thomas J. *Journal of the Texian Expedition Against Mier*. New York: Harper & Brothers, 1845.

Grinnell, George Bird. *The Fighting Cheyennes*. Norman: University of Oklahoma Press, 1955. Originally published by Charles Scribner's Sons, 1915.

Guild, Josephus Conn. *Old Times in Tennessee, with Historical, Personal, and Political Scraps and Sketches*. Nashville: Travel, Eastman, and Howell, 1878.

Hale, Will T., and Dixon L. Merritt. *A History of Tennessee and Tennesseans*. 8 vols. Chicago and New York: The Lewis Publishing Company, 1913.

Hamilton, Jeff. *My Master*. As Told to Lenoir Hunt. Dallas: Manfred, Van Nort & Co., 1940.

Hanighen, Frank C. *Santa Anna, the Napoleon of the West*. New York: Coward-McCann, Inc., 1964.

Houston, Andrew Jackson. *Texas Independence*. Houston: Anson Jones Press, 1938.

Houston, Rev. Sam'l Rutherford, D. D. *Brief Biographical Accounts of Many Members of the Houston Family*. Cincinnati: Elm Street Printing Co., 1882.

Huston, Cleburne. *Towering Texan*. Waco: Texian Press, 1971.

James, Bessie (Rowland) and Marquis James. *Six Feet Six, The Heroic Story of Sam Houston.* Indianapolis: Bobbs-Merrill Company, 1931.

James, Marquis. *Andrew Jackson, Portrait of a President.* New York: Grossett & Dunlap, 1937.

———. *Andrew Jackson, The Border Captain.* New York: Grossett & Dunlap, 1933.

———. *The Raven.* Indianapolis: Bobbs-Merrill Company, 1929.

Jenkins, John H., ed. *Houston Displayed, or Who Won The Battle of San Jacinto.* By a Farmer in the Army. Velasco: 1837. Austin: The Brick Row Book Shop, 1964.

Jones, Anson. *Memoranda and Official Correspondence Relating to the Republic of Texas, Its History and Annexation — Including a Brief Autobiography of the Author.* New York: D. Appleton and Company, 1859.

Kennedy, John F. *Profiles In Courage.* New York: Harper & Row, 1955.

Lester, Charles Edwards. *The Life of Sam Houston: The Only Authentic Memoir of Him Ever Published.* New York: J. C. Derby, 1855.

———. *Sam Houston and His Republic.* New York: Burgess, Stringer & Co., 1846.

Lewis, Thomas M. N., and Madeline Kneberg. *Hiwassee Island.* Knoxville: University of Tennessee Press, 1946.

Malone, Henry T. *Cherokees of the Old South.* Athens, Georgia: University of Georgia Press, 1956.

Malone, Prairie View. *Sam Houston's Indians (The Alabama-Coushatta).* San Antonio: The Naylor Company, 1960.

Merk, Frederick. *Slavery and the Annexation of Texas.* New York: Alfred A. Knopf, 1972.

Mooney, James. *Historical Sketch of the Cherokees.* Chicago: Adline Publishing Company, 1975.

Myers, John Myers. *The Alamo.* New York: E. P. Dutton & Company, Inc., 1948.

Nevin, David. *The Texans.* The Old West Series. New York: Time-Life Books, 1975.

Nevins, Allan. *Ordeal of the Union.* 2 vols. New York and London: Charles Scribner's Sons, 1947.

Newcomb, W. W., Jr. *The Indians of Texas, From Prehistoric to Modern Times.* Austin: University of Texas Press, 1961.

Newton, Lewis W., and Herbert P. Gambrell. *Texas Yesterday & Today.* Dallas: Turner Company, 1959.

Oskison, John M. *A Texas Titan.* Garden City: Doubleday, Doran and Company, 1929.

Parton, James. *Life of Andrew Jackson.* 3 vols. New York: Mason Brothers, 1861.

Pierce, Gerald S. *Texas Under Arms, 1836–1846.* Austin: Encino Press, 1969.

Pierson, George Wilson, ed. *Tocqueville and Beaumont in America.* New York: Oxford University Press, 1938.

Place, Marian T. *Comanches and Other Indians of Texas.* New York: Harcourt, Brace & World, Inc., 1970.

Pope, William F. *Early Days in Arkansas.* Little Rock: Gazette Publishing Company, 1895.

Reading, Robert S. *Arrows Over Texas.* San Antonio: The Naylor Company, 1960.

Seale, William. *Sam Houston's Wife.* Norman: University of Oklahoma Press, 1970.

Shirley, Glenn. *Temple Houston, Lawyer With a Gun.* Norman: University of Oklahoma Press, 1980.

Silverthorne, Elizabeth. *Ashbel Smith of Texas: Pioneer, Patriot, Statesman, 1805–1886.* College Station: Texas A&M University Press, 1982.

Smith, Ashbel. *Reminiscences of the Texas Republic*. Galveston: Historical Society of Galveston Series, No. 1, December 15, 1875.

Starkey, Marion L. *The Cherokee Nation*. New York: Alfred A. Knopf, Inc., 1952.

Starr, Emmett. *Cherokees West 1794–1839*. Claremore, Oklahoma: private printing, 1910.

———. *Early History of the Cherokees*. Kansas City: private printing, 1917.

———. *History of the Cherokee Indians*. Oklahoma City: The Warden Company, 1921.

———. *Old Cherokee Families*. Norman: University of Oklahoma Foundation, 1968.

Thorp, Raymond W. *Bowie Knife*. University of New Mexico Press, 1948.

Tinkle, Lon. *13 Days of Glory*. New York: McGraw Hill Company, Inc., 1958.

Tolbert, Frank X. *The Day of San Jacinto*. Austin and New York: Pemberton Press, 1969.

Travis, William Barret. *Diary of William Barret Travis*, edited by Robert E. Davis. Waco: Texas Press, 1966.

Turner, Martha Anne. *Sam Houston and His Twelve Women*. Austin: Pemberton Press, 1966.

———. *William Barret Travis, His Sword and His Pen*. Waco: Texian Press, 1972.

Wallace, Ernest. *Texas In Turmoil*. Austin: Steck-Vaughn Company, 1965.

Wardell, Morris L. *A Political History of the Cherokee Nation*. Norman: University of Oklahoma Press, 1938.

Webb, Walter Prescott and others, eds. *The Handbook of Texas*. 2 vols. Austin: Texas State Historical Association, 1952.

Wellman, Paul L. *The Magnificent Destiny*. New York: Doubleday & Company, Inc., 1962.

White, Owen P. *Texas, An Informal Biography*. New York: G. P. Putnam's Sons, 1945.

Wilkins, Thurman. *Cherokee Tragedy*. New York: The Macmillan Company, 1970.

Williams, Alfred M. *Sam Houston and the War of Independence*. Boston: Houghton Mifflin Company, 1893.

Williams, Amelia W., and Eugene C. Barker, eds. *The Writings of Sam Houston, 1813–1863*. 8 vols. Austin: University of Texas Press, 1938–43.

Williams, Thomas Benton. *The Soul of the Red Man*. Private printing, n.d. (Copies in Grant Foreman Room, Muskogee, Oklahoma, Public Library, and Reference Library, Oklahoma Historical Society, Oklahoma City, Oklahoma.)

Wisehart, M. K. *Sam Houston: American Giant*. Washington: Robert B. Luce, Inc., 1962.

Woodward, Grace Steele. *The Cherokees*. Norman: University of Oklahoma Press, 1963.

Wooten, Dudley G., ed. *A Comprehensive History of Texas, 1685–1899*. 2 vols. Dallas: William G. Scarff, 1898.

Worrell, John. *The Life and Times of Sam Houston*. Temple: F. E. Hutchins, 1906.

Wortham, Louis J. *A History of Texas*. Vol. IV. Fort Worth: Wortham-Molyneaus Company, 1924.

Yoakum, Henderson. *History of Texas, From Its First Settlement in 1685 to Its Annexation to the United States in 1846*. 2 vols. New York: J. S. Redfield, 1855.

Booklets and Pamphlets

Burns, G. Frank, ed. "The Record of a People, an Essay. An Historical Sketch of Wilson County, Tenn. From Its First Settlement to the Present Time." First published in 1879 by James V. Drake.

Clark, Joseph Lynn. "General Houston's Huntsville Home . . . The Mount Vernon of Texas." 13 pp. 1953.

"A Valentine in a Rough Winter." A newly discovered letter from Sam Houston to his wife. Austin: Pemberton Press, 1974.

Articles

Boney, F. N. "The Raven Tamed." *Southwestern Historical Quarterly*, January 1920.

Culberson, Charles A. "General Sam Houston and Secession." *Scribner's Magazine* 39 (January–June 1906), 590.

Davis, Louise. "Sam Houston's Tragic Marriage." *The Nashville Tennessean*, August 5, 12, 19, 1962.

Murchison, A. H. "Intermarried Whites in the Cherokee Nation between the years 1865 and 1887." *The Chronicles of Oklahoma* 6:299–327 (September 1928).

Paschal, George W. "Last Years of Sam Houston." *Harper's New Monthly Magazine* 32:630–635 (April 1866).

Sweat, Joseph. "Nashville's Greatest Love Stories." *Nashville*, February 1984.

Terrell, A. S. "Recollections of General Sam Houston." *Southwestern Historical Quarterly* 16 (1912–13) and 18 (July 1914/April 1915).

Thrall, Homer S. "Sam Houston." *Round Table* 4 (July 1892).

Dissertations

Davidson, William C. "Sam Houston and the Indians: A Rhetorical Study of the Man and the Myth." Ph.D. diss., University of Kansas, 1971.

Interviews

Allen, Elizabeth. Gallatin, Tennessee, September 14, 1984.

Apffel, Dorothy Winton. Nashville, Tennessee. Correspondence dated January 8, 1985.

Cornish, Dr. Homer T. Timber Ridge, Virginia, November 13, 1983.

King, Dr. Duane H. Tahlequah, Oklahoma, May 6, 1984.

Thompson, Charles. Timber Ridge, Virginia, November 13, 1983, and February 6, 1984.

Manuscript Collections

Barker Texas History Center. University of Texas, Austin, Texas: Lewis Berkeley Papers; Thomas J. Rusk Papers; Ashbel Smith Papers.

New York Public Library. Washington Irving Manuscripts.

Oklahoma Historical Society, Oklahoma City, Oklahoma. Foreman Typescripts. Oklahoma Indian Archives.

Thomas Gilcrease Institute of American History and Art, Tulsa, Oklahoma. Sam Houston Biographical File.

University of North Carolina. Archives. Polk Collection.

Masonic Records

Cumberland Lodge No. 8, AF&AM, Nashville, Tennessee. Records.

Grand Lodge of Tennessee. Proceedings. October 1825 and October 1828.

Texas Masonic Grand Lodge Library. Waco Texas.

Newspaper Clippings

Maryville Times. "History Repeats Itself With Lamar Barbecue," by Adele Mc-Kenzie, January 24, 1980.

Nashville Tennessean. "Little Dog Named 'Hero' Foretold Famous Master," by Louise Davis, November 8, 1981.

Wilson County News. Story concerning Eliza Allen Houston, by Adelaide Davis, Lebanon, Tennessee, April 1941.

Other Newspapers

Arkansas Gazette, June 25, 1828, July 2, 1828, and May 20, 1829.

Austin City Gazette, November 27, 1839, and March 2, 1842.

Cherokee Phoenix, May 28, 1931.

Maryville News, August 20, 1845.

Muskogee Times Democrat, September 26, 1919.

Nashville Banner, December 30, 1907.

San Antonio Herald, December 27, 1859.

Southern Intelligencer, April 6, 1859.

Texas State Gazette, September 15, 1855.

Telegraph and Texas Register, March 24, 1836, March 21, 1837, June 9, 1841, and June 4, 1845.

Public Documents

Blount County. Maryville, Tennessee. County Courthouse. Minutes.

Cherokee Nation. *Laws of the Cherokee Nation Adopted by the Council at Various Times.* Tahlequah, Cherokee Nation: Cherokee Advocate Office, 1852.

Historical Register and Dictionary of the United States Army. Washington, D.C.: Government Printing Office, 1903.

Rockbridge County, Virginia. County Court Records. Inventory of Estate of Major Samuel Houston. Will Book No. 3, December 1807, 82–84.

Rockbridge County, Virginia. County Court Records. Will of Major Samuel Houston, dated September 2, 1806. Will Book No. 3, 73–76.

Index

398

399

400

401

402

Louisville Courier Journal, 56
Love, Hugh, 178
  James, 254
Lovely's Purchase, 75, 76, 77
Lubbock, Francis R., 237, 337
Ludlow, Noah M., 39
Lynchburg, Texas, 200, 204
Lynch's Ferry, 190, 202, 204

M

McAnelly, Cornelius, 279
McClellan, William, 88
McClung family, 4
McCorkle family, 4
McCormick, Cyrus, 7
  Peggy, 218
McCormick family, 4
McCulloch, Ben, 211, 346
McEwen, Mrs., 58
  Robert, 53, 106, 228
McGee, Jas. M., 244
McGowen, Mr., 349
McGregor, Colonel, 47
McIntosh, Chief William, 84
  George, 263
  Roly, 84, 85
McIntyre, Hugh, 361
McKenney, Thomas, 98
McKinney, ———, 259
McKinney Messenger, 348
McLemore, John J., 71
McLeod, Hugh, 262
McMinn, Joseph, 33, 35, 41, 43
Macomb, David B., 175
Madero, Francisco, 145–146
Madison, James, 22
Madisonville, Texas, 332
mail service, 232, 261, 267
Manley, John H., 354
Marble City, Sequoyah County, Oklahoma, 75
Marion, Alabama, 248, 251, 255, 297
Marius, Gaius, 121
Martin, Martha, 53, 58
  Philip, 346
  Robert, 53
  Wylie, 193–194, 195, 196, 199
Martínez, Antonio María, 140
Maryville militia, 16
Maryville, Tennessee, 9, 10, 12, 16, 18, 25, 28, 29, 30, 106, 210, 297
Masina (sister of Rosalie Chouteau), 82
Mason, James M., 317
  John T., 220
Matagorda Bay, 261, 278
Matagorda, Texas, 175, 202
Matamoros expedition, 173–174, 176–179, 231, 237
Matamoros, Mexico, 148, 173, 222, 223, 236,

265, 273, 274, 303, 305
Maury, Matthew, 120, 121
Maw, Thomas, 76
Mayes County, Oklahoma, 113
Medine, Francisco, 148
Meigs, Return Jonathan J., 73
Memphis, Tennessee, 69
Menard Bayou, 87, 88
Merritt, Dixon L., 58
Metropolitan Hotel, 336
Mexia, Francisco, 303
Mexican War, 302–305, 307, 308–310
Mexico City, Mexico, 140, 141, 142, 155, 159, 160, 190, 262, 263, 271, 275, 303, 309
Mier expedition, 273–275, 325; prisoners of, 274–275, 280, 282, 289
Mier, Mexico, 273–274
Milam, Ben, 167, 171
Military Affairs Committee, 333
Millard, Henry, 209, 210, 222
Mill Creek, 71, 193
Miller, James B., 155
  Washington D., 260–261, 263, 270, 286, 320, 321
  William P., 187–188
Miramón, Miguel, 341
missions, 13, 90–92, 153
Missouri Compromise of 1820, 311–312, 312, 316, 328, 334, 341
Missouri Compromise of 1850, 315, 322
Missouri Territory, 140
Mobile, Alabama, 249, 277
Molé, Count, 241
Monclova, Mexico, 163
Monroe, James, 31, 35, 36, 37, 49, 139
Monterrey, Mexico, 274, 305, 307
Montgomery, Lemuel P., 28, 39
Montgomery, Alabama, 28, 358
Montgomery County, 298
Montgomery family, 4
Moore, E. W., 277, 278, 325, 330
  Francis, 296
  John H., 166
Moravians, 13, 14
Morehouse, Edwin, 264, 281
Morgan, Daniel, 5
  Emily, 201, 213, 218
  James, 201, 218, 269, 278, 285, 288
Morgan's Point, Texas, 197
Morris, George, 76
  Major, 177, 178
Mottley, Junius William, 212, 214
Murphy, William, 287
Musquiz, Ramón, 149, 150

406

407

Saracen (horse), 203, 211, 212
Saucedo, José Antonio, 143, 144
Saxe Weimar (horse), 294–295
Scott, Dred, 336
  Sir Walter, 255
  Winfield, 305, 308–309, 319
Scurry, Richardson, 186, 270
secession, 311–313, 325, 347, 348, 352–
  353, 356–360
Seguin, Juan, 210
Seminoles, 33
Seminole War, 83
Sequoyah, 13, 27, 76, 111 (see also Guess,
George; Guess, George)
Sertuche, Ignatius, 143
Seventh Infantry, 25, 83
"Seventh of March" speech, 317
Seven Years War, 139
Shackelford, John, 247
Shakespeare, 32
Sharp, B. F., 344
  Ed, 337
Sharp Knife (Andrew Jackson), 79
Shawnees, 23, 78, 85, 148, 178, 182
Shelby, John, 54, 56, 61, 65, 228
Shelton's Brass Band, 354
Sherman, Sidney, 186, 187, 205–206, 209,
  210, 211
Shiloh, Battle of, 361
Sigourney, Lydia Howard, 328
Siloam Baptist Church (Marion, Alabama),
  255
Sinaloa, Mexico, 263
Sinnicton, Dr., 274
Six Bull River Valley, 79
slavery, 294, 301, 309–310, 311–312, 313,
  314, 315–316, 317, 322, 327, 328, 329,
  334, 336, 347, 348, 350
Slidell, John, 302–303
Sloat, John Drake, 307
Smith, Ashbel, 236, 238, 244, 245, 248, 254,
  255, 256, 259, 260, 263, 267, 269, 278,
  282, 288, 294, 295, 300, 306, 308, 311,
  319, 330, 331, 332, 334–335, 337, 338,
  344, 347, 352, 356, 361, 363, 365
  Ben Fort, 244
  Chief John, 87
  Erastus (Deaf), 189, 190, 191, 192, 201,
  202, 208, 211, 215, 217, 239
  Henry, 169, 172, 173, 174, 176, 178, 179,
  180, 181, 182, 227, 228
  John T., 47
  Thomas I., 275
  William P., 174
Smoky Mountains, 10
Solitary Star, 62
Somervell, Alexander, 187, 209, 265, 266,
  271, 273
Sonora, Mexico, 263
Sons of Temperance, 318, 320

Sour Lake, Texas, 362
Southard, Samuel L., 49–50
"Southern Address," 313
Southern Division, 32, 33
Southern Intelligencer, 344, 358
Southern League, 343
Southwestern Army, 273
Spavinaw Creek, 113
Springfield, Illinois, 353
Spring Hill, 248
Springplace, Tennessee, 13
Stanbery, William, 124–131, 132, 133
Standard, The, 354
"Star Spangled Banner, The," 127
states rights, 343, 347
State of the Union, 233, 242
"Steamboat House," 362
steamboat trade, 108
Stephens, Ana S., 333
Sterne, Adolphus, 156, 166–167, 253
  Eva Rosine, 156
Stevenson, Andrew, 126, 128, 130
Stokes Commission, 134, 135
Stuart family, 4
Sublett, Philip, 156, 221, 247
Sumner County, Tennessee, 103–104
sutler, 108
Swartwout, Samuel, 288

T

Tahchee ("Dutch"), 77
Tahlontusky, 73, 75, 92, 111
  Chief, 35, 36, 77
Tallapoosa River, 27
Talleyrand, 269
Tamaulipas, Mexico, 173, 263, 351
Tammany Hall, 318
Tamocuttakes, 182
Tampico Battalion, 212
Taylor, Zachary, 303, 304–305, 311, 317
Tecumseh, Chief, 23
"Tekatoka," 115–116
Telegraph and Texas Register, 197, 200, 258,
  296
Tellico, Tennessee, 13
temperance, 248, 297
Tennessee Antiquarian Society, 40, 63
Tennessee militia, 30
Tennessee River, 13, 50
Tennessee and Tennesseans, 58
Tenorio, Antonio, 164
Tenuta, 182
Terán, Manuel Mier y, 145
Terrell, Alexander W., 362
  George W., 260, 283
Texas: Anglo colonization of, 140–144, 145,
  146–147; annexation to U.S., 151, 154,
  158, 227–228. 229, 230, 231, 233, 235,
  240, 241–242, 250, 257, 282–289, 293–

408

298, 302, 303, 304; archives of, 275–
276; boundaries of, 139–140, 146, 218,
221, 288, 294, 302, 307, 310, 311, 315,
317; as confederate state, 358, 359, 360;
constitution for separate state, 155; constitution of, 298; declaration of independence, 185, 357; division of, 286;
fight for independence, 166–167, 170–
173, 177–179, 182–187, 190–214; first
cabinet, republic of, 228–229; Houston's early interest in, 42, 62, 70, 89,
90, 122, 123, 125, 128, 131–132, 133–
134, 135; martial law in, 361–362; recognition of independence, 231, 233, 234,
257, 260, 267, 279, 283, 284, 288; regular army of, 169–170, 172, 173–175,
178, 209–210, 236–237, 265–266;
secedes from Union, 357–358; Spanish settlement in, 139; treaties with Mexicans, 217–218, 221, 267, 280–281,
282, 297–298; treaty with Great Bri-
tain, 246, 301–302; U.S. involvement
in, 146
Texas Almanac, 345
Texas navy, 277–278
Texas Rangers, 305, 351, 352
Texas Road, 114
Texas State Gazette, 325, 328, 338, 342
"Texas Tories," 204
Thirty-ninth Infantry, 24–25, 26, 28
Thomas, David, 186
Thompson, Algernon, 247
 David, 116
 Mr. and Mrs. Charles, 5
 Roxanna, 351
Thorne, Virginia, 316
Thornton, Seth B., 303
Three Forks, 81, 83, 93, 110, 114, 117
Throckmorton, James W., 358–359
Timberlake, John, 43, 97
Timber Ridge Plantation, 5, 8
Timber Ridge Presbyterian Church, 4, 5, 6
Timber Ridge Valley, 7
Timber Ridge, Virginia, 3, 7, 31
Tocqueville, Alexis de, 91, 123
Tohopeka (River), 27
Tolsa, Eugenio, 192
Tom (Rusk's servant), 163
"To My Husband . . .," 294
Tories, 14, 111
Tower, Dr., 270
Towns, Major, 255
traders, 14, 94, 95, 96–97
Trask, Olwyn J., 205
Travis, William Barret, 147, 157, 164– 165,
175, 182–183, 184, 185, 186, 189, 191,
201
treaties, 10, 23, 33–37, 75–79, 83, 84, 86,
95, 109, 120, 176, 180, 182, 217– 218,
221, 228, 230, 232, 246, 253, 261, 262,

279, 285–286, 301–302, 321, 351
Treaty of 1808, 35, 36–38, 77
Treaty of 1816, 33–34
Treaty of 1819, 139
Treaty of 1828, 77, 93
Treaty of Cordoba, 140
Treaty of Guadalupe Hidalgo, 310, 311
Treaty of Velasco, 262
Tremont Temple, 328
Trimble, James, 39
Trisk, Nicholas P., 310
Tulip Grove, 297
Turnbull, Jane, 344
Turtle Bay, 147
Turtle Bay resolutions, 147–148
Twin Sisters, 197, 204, 205, 211–212
Tyler, John, 283, 284, 286, 287, 294

U

U.S. House of Representatives, 124, 126–
127, 128–131, 234, 243, 303–304, 326
U.S. Navy, 307, 333
Ugartechea, Domingo de, 147, 148, 164, 166
Union Mission, 91–92
United States Telegraph, 99
University Hill, 331
Untanguous, 182
Upshur, Abel P., 283–284
Urizza, Fernando, 190
Urrea, José de, 179, 187–188, 191, 192,
202, 216, 217

V

Van Buren, Martin, 98, 235, 283, 287, 300
Vancouver Island, 302
Van Fossen, John, 99, 100, 116, 123, 133
Van Zandt, Isaac, 283, 284, 285, 286, 287
Vashon, George, 91, 117, 122
Vasquez, Rafael, 264
Velasco, Texas, 145, 147, 148, 172, 220, 222,
239, 278
Vera Cruz, Mexico, 128, 221, 222, 231, 263,
308–309
Veramendi, Juan Martín de, 153, 171
 Ursula, 153
Vicar of Wakefield, The, 32
Victoria, Texas, 187, 188, 217
Vince brothers, 204
Vince's Bayou, 203, 218
Vince's Bridge, 202, 203, 208, 211, 216
Virginia, Upper Valley of, 4
Virginia House, 152, 169–170
Virginia Military Institute, 5
Virginia Militia, 6
Virginia Militia, 8
Volstead law, 320

409

410